D0410618

791.4375 EIS

ST

WIT...

The Cinema of Eisenstein

The Cinema of Eisenstein

David Bordwell

Harvard University Press
Cambridge, Massachusetts
London, England   1993

Copyright © 1993 by the President and Fellows of Harvard College
All rights reserved
Printed in the United States of America

Designed by Annamarie McMahon

This book is printed on acid-free paper, and its binding materials
have been chosen for strength and durability.

Library of Congress Cataloging-in-Publication Data

Bordwell, David.
  The cinema of Eisenstein / David Bordwell.
     p.   cm.
  Filmography: p.
  Includes bibliographical references and index.
  ISBN 0-674-13137-1 (cloth: alk. paper). — ISBN 0-674-13138-X (pbk.: alk. paper)
  1. Eisenstein, Sergei, 1898–1948—Criticism and interpretation.   2. Silent films—Soviet Union—
History and criticism.   I. Title.
  PN1998.3.E34B67   1993
  791.43'0233'092—dc20

      92-45678
          CIP

SOUTHAMPTON INSTITUTE
LIBRARY SERVICES LTD
SUPPLIER SMITUS
ORDER No
DATE 15·12·01

In memory of Jay Leyda
and Michael Glenny

Acknowledgments

A great many people have generously assisted this project. My colleagues at the University of Wisconsin–Madison offered useful comments on portions delivered at our weekly colloquia. Ben Brewster, Noël Carroll, Tom Gunning, and Yuri Tsivian patiently read the manuscript and offered many criticisms and suggestions. Kristin Thompson provided invaluable advice, sharp ideas, and out-of-the-way information; she also printed the photographs for publication.

Several of the ideas in this book were developed in a 1989 seminar on Eisenstein, and I thank all the members of that group, especially John Meany, Doug Riblet, Jillian Steinberger, Gregory Taylor, and Susan Zickmund. John was also indispensable in locating and translating Russian material. Central to this project were the suggestions and criticisms of Vance Kepley, my coteacher of the seminar. This book grew out of plans for a book that he and I were to write together. Many of the ideas presented here were developed in dialogue with him, and the manuscript has benefited from his exacting comments.

A generous grant from the University of Wisconsin–Madison Graduate School helped make this book more comprehensive than I had originally thought possible. The project was finished while I held a John Simon Guggenheim Foundation Fellowship during 1991. I am grateful to the Foundation for its support.

Other people assisted my work: John Belton, Oksana Bulgakowa, Ed Buscombe, Ian Christie, Mary Corliss, Maxine Fleckner-Ducey, Michael Glenny, Edouardo Grossi, Bert Harris, Don Kirihara, Arun Khopkar, Geoffrey Nowell-Smith, Elena Pinto Simon, Alan Upchurch, and Alexander Zholkovsky. I also thank the staffs of the Museum of Modern Art Library, the Nederlands Filmmuseum, the Photography Department of New York University, and the Wisconsin Center for Film and Theater Research. I owe a special debt to the late Jacques Ledoux, curator of the Cinémathèque Royale de Belgique; to his successor, Gabrielle Claes; and to the archive's dedicated staff. As usual, the Memorial Library of the University of Wisconsin–Madison and the Seminary Book Cooperative of Chicago helped locate out-of-the-way research materials.

Portions of Chapter 4 originally appeared in an essay published in *Millennium Film Journal;* I am grateful to the editors for permission to include those passages here.

Any student of Soviet cinema is deeply obligated to the editors and translators who have made texts available to a wider audience. I therefore want to acknowledge Jacques Aumont, Michael Glenny, Naum Kleiman, Jay Leyda, Herbert Marshall, Ivor Montagu, Pietro Montani, Hans-Joachim Schlegel, Richard Taylor, and Alan Upchurch—an "iron ten" who have served Eisenstein well.

Contents

Preface

Sergei Eisenstein stands solidly, even threateningly, within the canon. For seventy years his works have been dissected and explicated, taught and banned, celebrated and condemned. Most of his films achieved renown immediately, and many of his essays became central to film aesthetics. Around the world, when aspiring filmmakers learn their craft, they study Eisenstein.

Like Chaplin, Griffith, and Hitchcock, he is a director about whom everyone has something to say. Why add to the mound of Eisenstein literature? For one thing, students and general readers have lacked a straightforward introduction to his accomplishments. The central purpose of *The Cinema of Eisenstein* is to survey his distinctive contributions to the art and history of film. Furthermore, over the last fifteen years several fresh translations have appeared and many unpublished documents have come to light. New versions of the films have also entered circulation, particularly on video. We in the West are in a better position than ever before to deepen our understanding of his accomplishments, and this aim has guided my efforts.

Eisenstein was a polymath—an innovative theatre director, a gifted graphic artist, a provocative thinker about broad issues of art and culture. In this book, however, he figures primarily as a filmmaker and film theorist. Sharpening the focus in this way allows us to see the familiar Eisenstein in fresh historical contexts. For example, I locate the films in relation to contemporary norms of Soviet cinema and seek antecedents and parallels to his ideas in wider intellectual traditions. In addition, we are now in a position to see Eisenstein's fusion of filmmaking practice with abstract theorizing as offering not so much an aesthetic as a poetics of cinema, an explicit creative and analytical method derived from a reflection on craft techniques.

.

The book's structure flows from its aims. The first chapter provides a sketch of Eisenstein's life and his place in Soviet artistic culture. It also suggests some ways in which his circumstances may have encouraged him to blend theory and practice.

Despite important continuities, Eisenstein's career can usefully be treated as falling into two parts. I take his silent filmmaking as a distinct phase of his work. I then consider his teachings, writing, and films of the 1930s and 1940s. While there is much to be gained by seeing Eisenstein as a unitary thinker, the two-phase division allows us to trace some important changes across his career.

Chapter 2 discusses his four films of the 1920s. After a glance at Soviet film-making norms of the 1920s, I offer analyses of *Strike, Battleship Potemkin, October,* and *Old and New.* The chapter also delineates how Eisenstein's ongoing experimentation expanded the resources of the "heroic realism" of montage cinema. Eisenstein's practical filmmaking raised issues of film form and effect that shaped his thinking for the rest of his career.

The next chapter discusses his writings of the 1920s. At this period Eisenstein explored ideas of viewer response and film style. It is as if each film he made posed certain issues so acutely that he had to expose and elaborate them on paper. This chapter discusses his notions of montage of attractions, expressive movement, and dialectical montage.

Chapter 4 is a pivot. For Eisenstein in the 1920s, practice usually preceded theory, but from the 1930s on, self-conscious theorizing often guided practice. His teaching articulated ideas that he would test in his films. The "practical aesthetics" of his 1930s and 1940s pedagogy vividly displays the fusion of practice and principle characteristic of his work.

Eisenstein's theoretical writings of the period 1932–1948 often seem to be loose, baggy monsters. Chapter 5 tries to show that taken together they present a considerable degree of internal unity, predicated on some significant changes in his conception of spectatorial activity and filmic structure. The chapter traces systematic connections among his ideas of "inner speech," polyphonic and vertical montage, pathos, and ecstasy. More controversially, this chapter also argues that Eisenstein's developing cinepoetics seeks to give a depth and validity to the dogmas of official Socialist Realist aesthetics.

Chapter 6 centers on the two major projects of the last decade of the director's life: *Alexander Nevsky* and the unfinished trilogy *Ivan the Terrible.* Again, my emphasis falls upon "how the work is made": the films as formal wholes, their ties to his theoretical reflections, and the innovations that Eisenstein introduces into current filmmaking practice.

The last chapter scans the major trends that have dominated Eisenstein research since his death and briefly sketches his influence on other filmmakers. The book concludes with remarks on the implications of Eisenstein's poetics of cinema.

Like most introductory works, this keeps to the main pathways and skirts the thickets of the secondary literature. For readers wishing to pursue particular topics, a section on further readings offers a starting point.

I have relied chiefly upon the versions of the films circulating in the West and upon published material available in Western languages. This approach necessarily scants a great deal of material. The Russian edition of Eisenstein's *Selected Works* runs to six plump volumes. At least six more volumes of unpublished material await editing and publication, as do his diaries, his letters, and thousands of pages of stenograms of his lectures. The collection of his papers at the Central Government Archive of Literature and Art (TsGALI) in Moscow includes almost 6,000 files and more than 15,000 documents. Changes in what used to be the U.S.S.R. ought to bring forth much new information about Eisenstein's life, his films, and his institutional context.

As one who neither reads nor speaks Russian, I have not drawn on the material held at TsGALI and other archives. I offer an introduction to the Eisenstein we have known, not to Eisensteins who might be revealed in decades to come. Still, I have examined much material in Russian with the aid of translators, and I have incorporated previously untranslated passages that will clarify or extend my arguments.

This book utilizes the first and second of the transliteration systems outlined in J. Thomas Shaw's *The Transliteration of Modern Russian for English-Language Publications* (Madison: University of Wisconsin Press, 1967). In accordance with Shaw's recommendations, the best-known names remain in their Anglicized forms. So we have the Bolshoi Theatre, Mussorgsky, Meyerhold, Voloshinov, Tretyakov, and the most familiar version of our central figure's name.

It seems that Eisenstein has always been with me. When I was fourteen, I read *Film Form* and *The Film Sense* in the old omnibus Meridian edition. (The copy is dingy now, but its *Nevsky* gatefold still sparks covetous glances from graduate students.) Although I understood almost nothing he said, Eisenstein made me a cinephile. On my bedroom wall I ran an 8mm copy of the Odessa Steps sequence. In my freshman year funds designated for an algebra textbook were diverted to pay for *Lessons with Eisenstein*. That fall I finally saw *October* and *Old and New;* I had to wait until my senior year to see *Strike*. Throughout the decades since, the collections, translations, biographies, newly exhumed material, and updated versions of the films have brought fresh Eisensteiniana to savor.

I return to Eisenstein's films and writings with undiminished curiosity and respect. I have come to enjoy his pedantic digressions, his egotism, his bumbling humor, and his willful obscurities as much as his fierce zest and his daring imagination. He is a frustrating, exhilarating, audacious companion. This book aims to ease the frustration, to transmit some of the exhilaration, and to preserve a little of the audacity.

Abbreviations

The following abbreviations denote collections of Eisenstein's writings cited in the text, notes, recommendations for further reading, and Bibliography.

ADE   *Au-delà des étoiles*, trans. Jacques Aumont et al. (Paris: Union Générale d'Editions, 1974)

CIN   *Cinématisme: Peinture et cinéma*, trans. Anne Zouboff, commentary François Albéra (Brussels: Complexe, 1980)

E2   *Eisenstein 2: A Premature Celebration of Eisenstein's Centenary*, ed. Jay Leyda, trans. Alan Y. Upchurch et al. (Calcutta: Seagull, 1985)

EAW   *Eisenstein at Work*, comp. Jay Leyda and Zina Voynow (New York: Pantheon, 1982)

FE   *Film Essays and a Lecture*, ed. and trans. Jay Leyda (Princeton: Princeton University Press, 1982)

FF   *Film Form: Essays in Film Theory*, ed. and trans. Jay Leyda (New York: Harcourt, Brace, 1949)

FS   *The Film Sense*, ed. and trans. Jay Leyda (New York: Harcourt, Brace, 1942)

IP   *Izbrannie proizvedeniia v chesti tomakh* (Selected works in six volumes) (Moscow: Iskusstvo, 1964–1969)

LF   *Le film: Sa forme/son sens*, adapted from the Russian and French by Armand Panigel (Paris: Bourgois, 1976)

MA   *Le mouvement de l'art*, ed. François Albéra and Naum Kleiman (Paris: Cerf, 1986)

NFD   *Notes of a Film Director*, ed. R. Yurenev, trans. X. Danko (Moscow: Foreign Languages Publishing House, 1958)

NN   *Nonindifferent Nature: Film and the Structure of Things*, trans. Herbert Marshall (Cambridge: Cambridge University Press, 1987)

PC   *The Psychology of Composition*, ed. and trans. Alan Upchurch (Calcutta: Sea-
        gull, 1987)
S1   *Schriften 1: Streik*, ed. and trans. Hans-Joachim Schlegel (Munich: Hanser,
        1974)
TTM   *Towards a Theory of Montage*, ed. Richard Taylor and Michael Glenny, trans.
        Michael Glenny (London: British Film Institute, 1992)
W   *Writings, 1922–34*, ed. and trans. Richard Taylor (Bloomington: Indiana
        University Press, 1988)

Has the hour arrived when each of us who loves art is obliged to withdraw into the solitude of his study, when artists and investigators in the area of aesthetics must resign themselves to being in a position like that of medieval martyrs, suffering for knowledge and creation so as not to be burned at the stake of public disgrace?

Andrei Bely, 1909

1.

A Life in Cinema

Eisenstein led a busy, dramatic life. His achievements and adventures merit far more detailed investigation than can be undertaken here. What is useful for the purposes of this book is an overall orientation to his career, a framework within which we can situate his films and theoretical writings.

From Theatre to Cinema

Sergei Mikhailovich Eisenstein was born in Riga, Latvia, on 22 January 1898 (10 January on the prerevolutionary calendar). His father, Mikhail Osipovich Eisenstein, was an assimilated German Jew and a prominent architect and civil engineer. His mother, Yulia Ivanovna Konetskaya, came from a wealthy merchant family.

Eisenstein had a cosmopolitan childhood, traveling to Paris (where he saw his first film) and learning French, German, and English. From earliest childhood he read avidly, drew caricatures, and displayed keen interest in the theatre. His childhood friend Maxim Shtraukh recalled that he was infatuated with the circus and presented shows in the family's backyard.

Eisenstein would later claim that his sympathy for social protest sprang from his father's despotic rule of the household. In 1909 Yulia Ivanovna left, and three years later the parents divorced. The son stayed with his father but visited his mother and grandmother in St. Petersburg.

At first Eisenstein intended to follow his father's profession. In 1915, after graduating from secondary school, he was admitted to the Institute of Civil Engineering in St. Petersburg. For the next two years, while pursuing his courses, he lived with his mother.

The 1917 revolutions interrupted his studies. In February Eisenstein was called

1.1 Sergei Eisenstein with his parents, Mikhail and Yulia
    Eisenstein, about 1900.

up for military service and sent to the front. After the Bolsheviks seized power in October, Eisenstein returned briefly to the Engineering Institute. In 1918, as the Civil War intensified, he joined the Red Army, serving as a technician in the Engineering Corps. His father joined the White forces.

While in the army Eisenstein continued to draw, making caricatures and decorating the agit-trains that propagandized throughout the countryside. He also became involved in a number of theatrical productions in cities where he was stationed. Eventually he was assigned to organize productions and ensembles on the front.

Eisenstein was demobilized in the fall of 1920 and returned to Moscow. He began studying Japanese in the General Staff Academy, but after serving in the Proletkult Central Workers' Theatre, he left the Academy. At Proletkult he supervised scenic design and the directors' workshops.

Proletkult (the Proletarian Culture movement) had been founded in early 1917 by the philosopher Alexander Bogdanov. Taking up suggestions in the Marxist classics, he advocated the development of a distinctly proletarian art that would replace that of the declining bourgeoisie. Bogdanov asserted that art would play a central role in Communist society by organizing experience into emotional, often utopian "images." Bogdanov also promoted "Tectology," a "science" that would transform the world into a harmonious social system.

At first, Proletkult drama emphasized collective spectacle, plays derived from European Symbolism and Expressionism, and religious and mythological dramas. After the Party had refused to recognize the organization as the official embodiment of Communist culture, Proletkult's Moscow organization moved toward a more experimental stance. Eisenstein entered a wing of the Moscow group whose creative workshops were receptive to the avant-garde.

Eisenstein immersed himself in Moscow's theatre world. At Nikolai Foregger's workshop he studied *commedia dell'arte* techniques. He taught courses in theatre for the Red Army and ran an intensive acting workshop at Proletkult. He worked on more than twenty productions, one of the most notable being *The Mexican,* codirected with Boris Arvatov and V. S. Smishlyaev for Proletkult in 1921. The show included a vigorous boxing match. As the audience onstage cheered the champion, the real audience in the auditorium rooted for the revolutionary underdog. Eisenstein later relished the memory of the "smacking of gloves against taut skin and strained muscles" (1934i:7). By arousing the audience so immediately, the show provided the first step toward the "agit-attraction theatre" that Eisenstein would cultivate over the next three years (1923b:77).

Arvatov, one of the major theorists of Constructivism, was among the earliest influences on the young director. With him Eisenstein built a pedagogical program for the Proletkult directing workshop that envisaged performance as "kinetic construction" of the body and took production as "monumental constructions." At the same time, Eisenstein fell under the sway of the man he later described as his "second father."

Vsevolod Meyerhold was the acknowledged master of Left theatre. His staging of Vladimir Mayakovsky's *Mystère-bouffe* (1918) had recast the story of Noah and the Flood as an allegory of proletarian conquest. In employing cubist designs by Malevich and acting techniques drawn from the circus, the production had been a model of theatrical experimentation turned to propagandist ends. In November 1920 Meyerhold's production of Emile Verhaeren's *The Dawn* transformed a Symbolist drama into a political rally. Actors declaimed oratorically, military searchlights raked the hall, and leaflets were scattered among the audience. In the spring of 1921 Meyerhold and Mayakovsky restaged *Mystère-bouffe* with even more circus elements and allowed the action to spill out into the auditorium.

In the fall of 1921 Meyerhold opened his State Higher Directing Workshop. There Eisenstein studied Meyerhold's performance and production methods, assisted in the training of actors, and contributed set and costume designs to a production of *Heartbreak House* (1922). After a little more than a year, Meyerhold dismissed the younger man, indicating that he had nothing more to learn. He continued to work with Meyerhold as an assistant director.

"All Eisenstein's work has its origins in the laboratory where we once worked together as teacher and pupil" (Meyerhold 1936:311). Meyerhold's claim is exaggerated, but he was certainly a powerful influence. Eisenstein's belief in controlling the spectator through the performer's bodily virtuosity; his emphasis on rhythm and pantomime; his interest in Asian theatre, the circus, and the grotesque; even his 1930s attempt to create a curriculum in which film directors would undergo stringent physical and cultural training—all were initiated or strengthened by the association with Meyerhold. The haughty master cast a spell on Eisenstein. "I never loved, idolized, worshipped anyone as much as I did my teacher" (1964:75). After Meyerhold's arrest in 1939, Eisenstein preserved his papers, carrying them away during the wartime evacuation of Moscow.

Eisenstein was forming other alliances in the early 1920s. The actors Judith Glizer and his childhood friend Maxim Shtraukh worked in Proletkult theatre. So did Grigory Alexandrov, who would become his collaborator. At Meyerhold's workshops he met Sergei Yutkevich, with whom he went to American movies, worked on several productions, and in the summer of 1922 wrote a *commedia dell'arte* parody called *The Colombian Girl's Garter*. In this he and Yutkevich tried out the idea of theatrical "attractions," startling shocks comparable to the roller coaster and sideshow "attractions" of amusement parks. Through Yutkevich Eisenstein met the central members of the Leningrad group FEX (Factory of the Eccentric Actor), Grigory Kozintsev and Leonid Trauberg.

Eisenstein and his associates took for granted that avant-garde artists worked for political ends. Many artists had been converted by the Bolshevik revolution, and the extreme Left atmosphere of "war Communism" had intensified their political fervor. Abstract painting or experimental writing had to be justified as "laboratory experiments" in forms that could have social utility. By 1923 purely experimental art was unacceptable; virtually all artists were obliged to work with recognizable content in the name of agitation, propaganda, or education.

The New Economic Policy (NEP), launched in 1921, introduced a mixed-market economy to aid recovery from the ravages of the Civil War. NEP encouraged various artists' organizations to compete for power and Party recognition. Some groups demanded that literature and the visual arts embrace a traditional realism. Only this approach, they maintained, would be accessible to the masses. Other groups, indirectly derived from Proletkult, called for proletarian art that would articulate new Soviet myths and raise workers' consciousness.

Eisenstein came to be associated with another trend, loosely identified as "Left art." The grouping included such figures as Mayakovsky, Arvatov, Vladimir Tatlin, Alexei Gan, Osip Brik, Alexander Rodchenko, Varvara Stepanova, Lyubov Popova, and Sergei Tretyakov. Most of the Left artists had been associated with some form of Futurism before the Revolution, and they hoped that earlier experiments in pure, dynamized forms could be harnessed to social ends.

The avant-garde of the early 1920s has principally been identified by the general term *Constructivism*. By and large, Constructivism in theatre and the visual arts sought to create out of Futurism and pictorial abstraction a political art based on principles of engineering and properties of the material. Constructivist art was, in a sense, abstract art rethought in terms of machine design and turned to agitational or propagandistic ends. By the mid-1920s most Constructivists had answered the "social command" and had turned to making works of practical utility, such as posters and book illustrations. Many of them thereby moved closer to a kindred trend, Productivism. Productivists sought to bring the results of formal experimentation directly into industrial manufacture, designing textiles, clothes, and furniture. Whereas Constructivists adapted procedures from industrial design to the "fine arts," the Productivists eliminated the distinction between fine arts and applied arts altogether.

Hostile to "bourgeois" tendencies, repudiating the art of the past, and trading on the Futurist desire to startle the viewer, Left artists were vulnerable to charges of what Lenin called "hooligan communism" (Braun 1979:149). Later Eisenstein ruefully recalled his origins: "All around was the insistent demand to destroy art, substitute materials and documents for the chief element of art—the image, do away with its content, put constructivism in the place of organic unity, replace art itself with practical and real reconstruction of life" (1946c:14).

Several Constructivists and Productivists gathered around the literary journal *Lef,* the standard bearer of Lef (the Left Front of the Arts). In a series of manifestos the editors demanded that art agitate the masses and organize social life. Writers were exhorted to practice "language engineering" and to find allies in literary theory (the Formalist critics Viktor Shklovsky and Yury Tynyanov), production design (Rodchenko, Gan), theatre, and film (Dziga Vertov). *Lef* sought to create a broad front of experimenters who amalgamated artistic modernism with radical ideology.

Eisenstein became associated with Lef through Sergei Tretyakov, who was also working with Proletkult. Tretyakov's *Lef* manifestos drew upon Bogdanov's ideas in demanding that the art worker be a scientist, a "psycho-engineer" calculating and organizing the spectator's responses (Tretyakov 1923:216). He claimed as well that these responses would have to be affective ones; even if the artist worked in a coolly rational mode, art required that the perceiver be emotionally engaged. This conception of art and the artist would be reiterated by Eisenstein throughout the 1920s.

In the theatre of the Civil War period, mass spectacles and cosmic pageants had coexisted with experiments in assimilating popular modes, such as vaudeville, circus, and American film comedy. This strain continued in the FEX "electrification" of Gogol's *Marriage* (1922), in Meyerhold's *Magnanimous Cuckold* (1922) and *Tarelkin's Death* (1922), and in works by Sergei Radlov and Alexander Tairov. The productions were considered emblematic of "Eccentrism," a performance style mixing grotesque clownishness with mechanized acrobatic stunts in the manner of American cinema. In a 1922 article Eisenstein and Yutkevich noted that the films of Fairbanks, Chaplin, Arbuckle, and other Hollywood performers yielded "new opportunies for genuine Eccentrism" (31).

In this tumultuous atmosphere Eisenstein became the younger generation's

1.2 *The Wiseman,* staged in 1923 by Eisenstein.

most noteworthy stage director. A series of Proletkult productions with Tretyakov made his name.

Most notorious was their 1923 production of Alexander Ostrovsky's classic play *Enough Simplicity in Every Wise Man,* known in their version simply as *The Wiseman.* For the hundredth anniversary of the playwright's birth, Commissar of Education Anatoly Lunacharsky requested that radical artists pay obeisance to the classics, summoning them "Back to Ostrovsky!" Eisenstein and Tretyakov did not exactly enter into the spirit of things. They splintered Ostrovsky's three-act play into several episodes while inserting topical commentary and low comedy. On a stage resembling a circus arena, the characters cavorted as clowns and acrobats. Emotions were expressed through flamboyant physical stunts. In one scene, Shtraukh expressed his anger at a caricature by hurling himself through the portrait and rolling into a somersault. The shifts in action were so abrupt, and the representations of situation so oblique, that every performance began with Tretyakov reading out a summary of the plot. As the hero Glumov, Grigory Alexandrov walked a tightrope stretched over the audience; at the finale, firecrackers exploded under the spectators' seats.

Tretyakov promoted the play by publishing in *Lef* Eisenstein's manifesto "Montage of Attractions," in which the director explained that the theatre could engage its audience through a calculated assembly of "strong moments" of shock or surprise. Tretyakov praised the theory of attractions as offering a way to shape the spectator's psyche for social tasks. In the summer of 1923 Eisenstein and Tretyakov collaborated on a pamphlet aiming to recast Proletkult's regimen for training actors. "Expressive Movement" enunciated doctrines that went beyond Meyerhold's biomechanical theories, which Eisenstein found too mechanistic and unsystematic. The authors advocated a "dialectical" integration of mechanical movements with organic ones. Expressive movement, a keystone of Eisenstein's thinking thereafter, would constitute a middle ground between Eccentrism and more naturalistic performance.

Quite different from *The Wiseman* was Tretyakov's "agit-guignol," *Do You Hear, Moscow?* staged by Eisenstein in November 1923. Here the Communist rebellions in Germany and Hungary were treated with a schematic mixture of melodrama and Grand Guignol. In its grandiose abstractions and caricatural figures (Pound the financier, the artists Grubbe and Grabbe) the play resembled the protest dramas of German Expressionism. Tretyakov and Eisenstein reduced the number of attractions and gave each scene simpler action and a greater unity. According to anecdotal accounts, the audience was stirred: spectators called out to the performers and responded with a mighty roar when the play's title was yelled out at the climax.

Eisenstein's last Proletkult production was Tretyakov's *Gas Masks* in the spring of 1924. It too bore the traces of German Expressionism, but now the performance space was a real locale, the Moscow Gasworks. Meyerhold had already introduced motorcycles and machine guns into his production of *The Earth in Turmoil* a year earlier, but now the audience, seated on benches, surrounded by machinery, engulfed in the sights, sounds, and smells of a factory, watched actors scramble across turbines and race down catwalks. The "agit-melodrama" centers on a bourgeois factory manager who squanders the factory's safety funds; as a result, there are no gas masks when a leak is discovered. The workers manage to patch the leak. At the conclusion of each performance, the gas workers came on duty and turned on the jets, filling the factory with light.

Just as each of Eisenstein's silent films would experiment with new materials and methods, his three Proletkult productions were fairly diverse. *The Wiseman* maximizes fragmentation and Eccentrism; *Do You Hear, Moscow?* recalls the inflated caricatures of *Mystère-bouffe*; *Gas Masks* offers a more sober, tightly knit plot in a setting that eliminates theatrical artifice.

In the spring of 1924 Eisenstein proposed that the Moscow Proletkult undertake a seven-part series of agitational films, *Toward Dictatorship* (referring to that "dictatorship of the proletariat" prophesied by Marx). The cycle of films would portray Russian revolutionary movements before 1917, culminating in the October revolution. At this point Eisenstein had no professional filmmaking experience. In the winter of 1922–23 he had briefly attended Lev Kuleshov's film workshop. For *The Wiseman* he had made a short film, *Glumov's Diary* (1.3). In the spring of 1923 he assisted Esfir Shub in editing Fritz Lang's *Dr. Mabuse der Spieler* for Soviet consumption. Despite his limited experience, he undertook the fifth film in the cycle, *Strike*. With this he left behind a promising career in the theatre. "The cart dropped to pieces," he wrote, "and its driver dropped into cinema" (1934f:8).

1.3 *Glumov's Diary,* Eisenstein's first film,
    included in the production *The Wiseman.*

The Silent Films

The cinema in which Eisenstein landed offered him distinct opportunities. Under
the NEP, the Soviet film industry worked largely within market conditions. Its
recovery after the Revolution and the Civil War was funded in large part through
the importation of foreign films. The government created a centralized trust,
Goskino (later Sovkino), which licensed private companies to produce and dis-
tribute films for a share of income. Soviet films had to compete with foreign
imports and to turn profits. The government intervened chiefly by investing in
Goskino's stock and by encouraging projects with short-range goals—celebrating
an anniversary in revolutionary history, popularizing a new policy. Such projects
created important opportunities for Eisenstein and other Left directors.

Once Goskino agreed to support *Strike,* Eisenstein prepared the script with
Alexandrov and other collaborators. He took as his cameraman Edward Tissé, a
Latvian newsreel photographer who was to work on all his films. *Strike* was shot
and edited very quickly, from June to December 1924. Set in tsarist Russia, it
sought to portray the conditions that triggered the October revolution and the
methods by which the Bolsheviks solidified working-class resistance. Although no
other films in the *Toward Dictatorship* cycle were made, *Strike* established Eisenstein as a significant young director.

The film owes a great deal to the Proletkult productions. Its acrobatic fights
and clownish spies recall *The Wiseman,* while its factory flywheels and mazes of
catwalks hark back to *Gas Masks.* Like *Do You Hear, Moscow?* the film turns the
characters into abstractions (capitalists, police, workers), presenting the villains
in comically grotesque terms and the workers in more realistic shades. The film
also utilizes the direct address of the plays in a final image of eyes staring at the
camera and a hortatory title: "Proletarians, remember!"

Strike displeased Proletkult's leaders, who attacked the film for its "superfluous,
self-directed formalism and gimmickry" as well as "dubious incidents of Freudian
purport" (Pletynov 1925:4). Eisenstein broke with the organization. The film was
better received by the critics; *Pravda* praised it as "the first revolutionary creation

of our screen" (Koltsov 1925). Eisenstein accompanied the film's release with an abrasive, immodest article, "The Problem of the Materialist Approach to Form," which attacked the documentarist Dziga Vertov and called for a "Kino-Fist" to pummel audiences.

Eisenstein entered Soviet filmmaking at a propitious moment. After years of privation during the Civil War, the industry was expanding. Film culture revived, and more foreign films were imported. Whereas around 120 features were produced between 1921 and 1924, the years 1925–1929 yielded more than four times as many. Furthermore, films based on distinctively Soviet themes were starting to appear. In 1923 *Little Red Devils* offered a Civil War adventure story, while *Aelita* presented a fantasy of interplanetary revolution. Vertov's *Kino-Pravda* newsreels developed into feature-length documentaries, the first being *Kino-Eye* (1924).

There was also a cadre of new talent ready to make fictional, or "played," films. Lev Kuleshov's filmmaking workshop attracted talented young people, notably Vsevolod Pudovkin, Boris Barnet, and the elongated actress Alexandra Khokhlova. The FEX directors Kozintsev and Trauberg turned to cinema as well. The Ukrainian Alexander Dovzhenko was to emerge shortly. These people were astonishingly young: in 1924, Kuleshov turned twenty-five, Pudovkin twenty-seven, Trauberg twenty-two, and Kozintsev nineteen. Eisenstein, comparatively senior at twenty-six, was known to all as "the Old Man."

In only a few years, these and other young people would define Soviet filmmaking as one of the most audacious and powerful forces in world cinema. The canonical corpus includes Kuleshov's *The Extraordinary Adventures of Mr. West in the Land of the Bolsheviks* (1924) and *By the Law* (1926); Pudovkin's *Mother* (1926), *The End of St. Petersburg* (1927), and *The Heir to Genghis Khan* (also known as *Storm over Asia*, 1928); Barnet's *Moscow in October* (1927) and *House on Trubnoy Square* (1928); the FEX productions *Devil's Wheel* (1926), *The Cloak* (1926), *SVD* (1927), and *The New Babylon* (1929); Abram Room's *Third Meshchanskaia Street* (also known as *Bed and Sofa;* 1927); Ilya Trauberg's *Blue Express* (1929); Frederick Ermler's *Fragment of an Empire* (1929); and Dovzhenko's *Zvenigora* (1928), *Arsenal* (1929), and *Earth* (1930).

Although NEP culture proved comparatively pluralistic, filmmakers bore the burden of major investments and were responsible for producing works that could compete with foreign imports. Some of these films, such as *Mr. West* and Barnet's *Miss Mend* (1926), frankly modeled themselves on American adventure films. Others, such as *Fragment of an Empire* and *Third Meshchanskaia Street,* presented domestic dramas of political import. Yet Kuleshov warned against "chamber cinema" and called for large-scale works, "a simple, intelligible, and heroic cinema" (1922). This appeal coincided with a move toward monumentalism in other media. Associations of proletarian writers and painters demanded that artists affirm the heroic role of the masses in the revolutionary tradition.

The effort to create an epic Soviet cinema propelled Eisenstein, Pudovkin, and Dovzhenko to world fame. Although most of their films were not widely popular, they created a monumental cinema that vividly embodied the Bolshevik interpre-

1.4 Eisenstein in 1924.

tation of history and society. Pudovkin concentrated upon typical individuals caught up in the mass movements of history. Dovzhenko lyricized Soviet ideology by treating it with motifs drawn from Ukrainian folklore. Eisenstein invigorated the Soviet cinema's "monumental heroics" through a wide-ranging exploration of film form and style. Other directors' films prodded him to surpass them and to differentiate himself. At the same time, he pressed his colleagues toward further experimentation—most dramatically in his next work, *The Battleship Potemkin*.

After *Strike* Eisenstein began planning an adaptation of Isaak Babel's *Red Cavalry*, but, as would often happen in his career, "social command" took priority. He was assigned to produce an anniversary film celebrating the 1905 revolution. He proposed an epic-scale project, *The Year 1905*. In the spring of 1925 he began shooting the film with Alexandrov, Shtraukh, Alexander Antonov, Alexander Levshin, and Mikhail Gomorov—his "Iron Five."

The original scenario allotted only a single sequence to the Black Sea mutiny aboard the armored cruiser *Prince Potemkin*. Upon arriving at Odessa, however, Eisenstein expanded the original episode into an entire film. He took as his central event the tsarist troops' massacre of Odessa's citizens, which he decided to stage upon the steps that run down to the waterfront. Eisenstein wrote the script during each day's filming. Maritime scenes were filmed on a drydocked ship, *The Twelve Apostles*.

Potemkin was, by all judgments, a more unified and intelligible work than *Strike*. Eisenstein put emotion firmly at the center. Revolutionary fervor spreads from the sailors to the people of Odessa to a navy fleet, which lets the mutineers' ship pass in a cheer of "Brothers!" Eisenstein portrayed the ship's officers as ferociously oppressive, the tsarist troops as mechanically brutal, and the sailors and the people of Odessa as ordinary people caught up in an event of epochal importance. Scene after scene used shocking "attractions" to arouse strong feelings—the worm-infested meat fed to the sailors, the near-execution of the sailors covered by a tarpaulin, the vigil over the slain Vakulinchuk, and above all the slaughter on the Odessa Steps. This set piece displayed a horrific violence that was unprecedented in silent filmmaking, and it quickly became the single most famous sequence in world cinema.

The finished film was premiered in December at an anniversary ceremony at the Bolshoi Theatre. It was released in January 1926, to generally favorable response. Some press reviews declared it the finest Soviet film yet made. One writer found it a success in the monumental mode: "He knows that the revolution *is not a personality but the masses,* and he seeks a language to express emotions of the masses" (Volkov 1926:94). Although Kuleshov and others criticized the editing technique, *Potemkin* became the most influential "montage" film.

Abroad *Potemkin* yielded unprecedented profits for the industry and blazed the trail for Soviet exports. It had its most spectacular success in Germany, where it bid fair to be the hit of the 1925–26 season. In the United States, although it was restricted to art theatres, the film opened the market to Soviet films. In most countries, *Potemkin* suffered cuts through censorship, but even then it attracted audiences and won praise from the intelligentsia. The film also became a rallying point for left-wing political activity through screenings in workers' clubs and political meetings.

Eisenstein always treated *Potemkin* as the benchmark of his career. His detractors had to grant the power of this film, which would remain the most famous Soviet contribution to world cinema. *Potemkin* also yielded ideas that would guide Eisenstein in solving future problems in theory and direction.

The twenty-seven-year-old director became the central figure of Soviet film culture. His emphasis on "left guignol" and mass spectacle brought Meyerhold's "theatrical October" into cinema. His "montage of attractions" was presented as flowing from his theatrical experiments. He was also credited with inventing "typage," the representation of character through external traits of class or role. In *Potemkin,* the crookedly smiling Senior Officer Gilyarovsky is something of a dandy, while the sailors are shown as forthright, serious, and muscular (1.5, 1.6). Typage, Eisenstein and others pointed out, was a long-established practice running from the *commedia dell'arte* to Daumier and Soviet political posters; more than most directors, he exploited it as a resolutely nonpsychological means of characterization.

His working methods also became famous. Although he assigned key roles to professional actors such as Alexandrov, Glizer, and Shtraukh, most parts were

1.5 *Battleship Potemkin* (1925): Typage for the oppressors.

1.6 *Battleship Potemkin:* Typage for the workers.

played by ordinary people. Contrary to his earlier emphasis on training performers precisely, he selected nonactors who could execute simple actions; it was the editing that would create a dynamic expressive movement. To enhance such editing potential, on *Potemkin* he began to film retakes from different angles, so that even the simplest action could later be chopped into several shots.

More controversial was his insistence that the film scenario should be a "literary" one. In the 1920s film professionals began to advocate using the "cast-iron" or "steel" scenario, a strict shooting script that would guide efficient planning and budgeting. To the end of his life Eisenstein resisted this regimen, arguing that the scenario should convey only the overall artistic "image"—the action or mood—to be rendered. This "emotional" scenario would serve its purpose if it stimulated the director's imagination. The filmmaker's intuition would then guide the shooting. Eisenstein's refusal to be pinned down to a detailed shooting script would embroil him in many conflicts in the sound era.

Along with Eisenstein's technical innovations went an insistence that the artist must fulfill a political task. He demanded that the government encourage the production of films that embodied the U.S.S.R.'s world view. The job facing the filmmaker was that of "cinefying (i.e., giving cinematic form to) the theses of the Party and state leadership which are a strategic resolution of a particular stage in the struggle for socialism" (1928g).

In 1926 Eisenstein and Alexandrov set about "cinefying" the Fourteenth Party Congress' "general line" on collectivization of the countryside. Once the scenario for *The General Line* was approved, Eisenstein and Alexandrov shot for several months in the summer and fall. But this project had to be postponed because they were commissioned to make a film commemorating the 1917 Bolshevik revolution.

The deadline was the anniversary itself, 7 November 1927 (the date as revised on the postrevolutionary calendar). As a consequence, *October* was hurried from the start. Eisenstein's script was approved in February 1927, and shooting began in April. The crew filmed day and night, sleeping on statues and cannons and the steps of the Winter Palace. According to Eisenstein, his crew photographed more

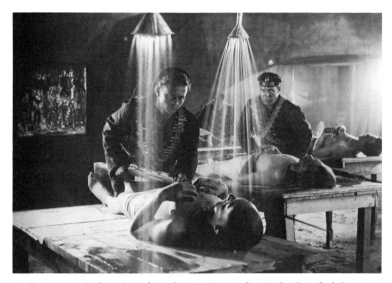

1.7 From an excised portion of *October* (1928): Invading Red sailors find the
   bodies of their comrades in the Winter Palace.

than 100,000 people. In September Alexandrov and Tissé were still filming in
Leningrad while Eisenstein began editing in Moscow. Shooting was finished in
early October. Portions of the film were shown on 6 November, but the finished
version was not released until March 1928.

October (also known in the West as *Ten Days That Shook the World*) underwent
many alterations. The original script had included a second part devoted to the
Civil War, but this had to be eliminated. More significantly, the film was caught
in the middle of conflicts among the Soviet leadership. During the October
revolution, Trotsky had been president of the Petrograd Soviet, and Lenin credited
him with organizing and leading the insurrection. But within a few years of Lenin's
death in 1924, Stalin had outmaneuvered Trotsky and the opposition. In October
1927 Trotsky was expelled from the Central Committee, and later that year he
was expelled from the Party. Now Eisenstein could not include him in the anniversary film, and he recut it accordingly.

October aroused much more criticism than *Potemkin*. Eisenstein had pushed
many of his previous experiments to new extremes, particularly in the use of
"intellectual montage." He saw this as an attempt to create a "film language"
consisting of visual figures of speech and abstract discursive arguments. But a
major national meeting on the cinema had recently declared that films had to be
made in a "form that is intelligible to the millions" (Party Cinema Conference
1929:212). *October*'s intellectual montage was thus attacked as formalistic and
incomprehensible to ordinary viewers.

Eisenstein also risked criticism by having a performer play Lenin. Stalin had
encouraged a cult around the deceased leader, and his image adorned busts and
paintings in public places throughout the Soviet Union, but many viewers were
not prepared to see him portrayed in a film. This was a sore point for many of

Eisenstein's Lef associates. After the collapse of *Lef*, Mayakovsky and Brik had founded *New Lef* on "factography," an aesthetic of documentary reportage that championed the "unplayed" film of Vertov and Shub. *New Lef* decried *October* as a compromised project, neither authentic newsreel nor straightforward fiction. Eisenstein defended *October* as exploring a third way between the "played" and the "unplayed," but he later recalled that the Lef group considered him a "deserter" (1989:429). He broke with them.

Undeterred, he became fascinated with the prospect of a discursive cinema that could lay out arguments and present entire systems of thought. He envisioned using montage to generate not only emotions but also abstract concepts: "From image to emotion, from emotion to thesis" (1930a:199). He began to plan a film of Marx's *Capital,* basing it on the "God and Country" sequence of *October,* which had sought to criticize the idea of God solely through the juxtaposition of images. The film would create "intellectual attractions" that would "teach the worker to think dialectically" (1927b:12, 10). At the same time, Eisenstein read Joyce's *Ulysses* and saw there a "de-anecdotalization" and sharp, vivid details that "physiologically" triggered general conclusions (1928b:96). *Capital* would be dedicated to the Second International, but "the formal side is dedicated to Joyce" (1927b:21). The *Capital* film was never made; Stalin quashed the idea during Eisenstein's 1929 meeting with him. Still, Joyce's novel remained a pervasive influence on the director's work.

The year 1928 saw Eisenstein appointed instructor in a course in direction at the State Technical School for Cinema (then abbreviated GTK; later GIK and VGIK). He devoted his main effort, however, to *The General Line,* which he and Alexandrov resumed filming in the spring of 1928. But once more an Eisenstein project was caught by changing policy winds. A grain shortage in the winter of 1927–28 drew the Party's attention to the developing power of the kulaks, or prosperous peasants. Within the Party, radicals pressed for elimination of the kulaks, while more moderate forces argued that by taxing them the government could finance industrialization. Stalin advocated speeding up industrialization through forced collectivization of the peasantry.

By November, when Eisenstein and Alexandrov had completed a version of the film, the Bolshevik "general line" was that peasants should be encouraged to form voluntary cooperatives. The film was initially approved, but in early 1929, when the Party moderates had lost their case, Stalin requested changes in the film, including added footage of the mammoth collective farm near Rostov-on-the-Don.

The film was finished by midsummer and scheduled for an October release, to coincide with "Collectivization Day." Since its title had become anachronistic, the film was renamed *Old and New.* It presented the story of a peasant woman's efforts to induce her peers to form a cooperative and to adopt tractors and mechanical cream separators. Tissé's complex photographic effects—arguably the richest he had yet produced—allowed Eisenstein to create densely packed shots. This led to a new stylistic strategy that the director called "overtonal" montage,

1.8 Filming a tractor for *Old and New* (1929). Tissé uses a mirror to reflect a dazzling light into the shot.

the organization of subsidiary aspects of the compositional elements into patterns that might reinforce or undercut the main line of imagery.

Old and New bore little relation to contemporary life in the countryside. Almost no farms could get a tractor, and the party had already begun collecting grain through coercion. Soon after the film's release, Stalin declared virtual war on the peasantry. Party officials expropriated and exiled thousands of families, imprisoning and killing resisters. Stalin's rural policies and the resultant famine would cost between 8 and 10 million lives. But the "liquidation of the kulaks as a class" was yet to come when Eisenstein left the Soviet Union on a three-year journey.

Europe, Hollywood, and Mexico

Eisenstein had gone abroad in early 1926, when he and Tissé had traveled to Berlin to oversee the release of *Potemkin* and to study German production methods. They had worked on the score with Edmund Meisel and had visited UFA Studios, where they met F. W. Murnau, Karl Freund, Fritz Lang, and Thea von Harbou. Now, in the summer of 1929, Eisenstein, Tissé, and Alexandrov were sent abroad to study film technique in a more thoroughgoing way. In addition Eisenstein hoped to persuade Meisel, who had scored *October,* to help with a sound version of *Old and New.*

Their first explorations took them to Europe. They attended a congress of independent filmmakers at La Sarraz, Switzerland, and they visited Germany, France, England, Belgium, and the Netherlands. *Potemkin*'s renown made them celebrities. Eisenstein met Köllwitz, Richter, Döblin, Grosz, Piscator, Pirandello, Shaw, Cocteau, Gance, Léger, Tzara, Le Corbusier, Cendrars, Aragon, and Ein-

1.9 At the 1929 La Sarraz conference on independent film.
     From left to right: Tissé, Jean-Georges Auriol, Eisenstein,
     Jean Lenauer, Alexandrov.

stein. He spent an afternoon in Paris with the nearly blind Joyce, who expressed a wish to see *Potemkin*.

Legend has it that upon leaving the Soviet Union each of the travelers was given twenty-five dollars for expenses. They were therefore obliged to earn money however they could. Eisenstein lectured and wrote articles for the foreign press. In Paris the group was involved in making a short subject with sound, *Romance sentimentale* (1930). Eisenstein attributed the film wholly to Alexandrov. In Zurich Tissé directed *Frauennot—Frauenglück* (Woman's Misery—Woman's Hope, 1930), a film advocating legalized abortion. On both productions Eisenstein's name was included to add luster to the project, although neither production is particularly distinguished. *Romance sentimentale* uses the worst clichés of French Impressionist filmmaking (1.10) and for the most part repudiates Eisenstein's conception of audiovisual "counterpoint." *Frauennot—Frauenglück* presents a cautionary fable about back-alley abortions, followed by documentary material on safe clinics.

1.10 *Romance sentimentale* (1930).

In April 1930, just as the Paris police were preparing to expel the trio as subversives, Paramount invited them to Los Angeles. Eisenstein had been interested for some years in going to America. When Douglas Fairbanks and Mary Pickford visited the Soviet Union in 1926, they marveled at *Potemkin* and promised the young director that United Artists would contact him. Upton Sinclair, the socialist novelist, had also visited Russia and had suggested that Eisenstein make a film in America. Now, with a Paramount contract signed and visas to allow a stay in the United States, the three Soviet filmmakers sailed for New York.

After a lecture tour on the East Coast, Eisenstein and his entourage, which now included the Englishman Ivor Montagu and his wife, Hell, settled in Hollywood. The Soviet filmmakers were lionized, visiting Disney, Dreiser, and other notables and becoming fast friends with Chaplin. Eisenstein lectured at universities and at the Academy of Motion Picture Arts and Sciences. As in Paris, however, he was also perceived as a Bolshevik agent: anticommunist forces headed by Major Frank Pease demanded that the government expel him.

From June to October 1930 Eisenstein and his collaborators prepared several projects for Paramount. Most important for Eisenstein was a film he had already planned, *The Glass House. The Glass House* was to be a satire of American life, portraying bootlegging and religious mania through a series of clichés drawn from Hollywood films. It was to take place in a towering skyscraper with glass walls and ceilings. Developing the deep-focus imagery of *Old and New,* Eisenstein envisaged shots showing one character in the foreground and another figure, in another room or on another floor, in the background. A love scene, for instance, was to be filmed from a toilet on the floor above. Although Chaplin was enthusiastic about the project, Paramount executives were not, and it was set aside.

In Paris Eisenstein had received Blaise Cendrars's permission to adapt his novel *L'or.* This developed into *Sutter's Gold,* a project whose historical sweep recalls the monumentality of the director's Soviet projects. Eisenstein, Alexandrov, and Montagu created a script portraying the Gold Rush of 1849. Like most of the films Eisenstein considered for Hollywood, this was to have been what Naum Kleiman calls a "tragedy of individualism" (Eisenstein 1979:106). Sutter's discovery of gold destroys his life and despoils California. The scenario also sketches

1.11 Eisenstein in Hollywood, 1930.

out several elaborate sonic ideas. For example, the prospectors' picks and shovels are organized rhythmically and swell into a loud "tearing sound" that metaphorically expresses the ruin of the land (Montagu 1967:181). Despite Eisenstein's detailed planning, he could not convince the Paramount executives that the film would not be too expensive, and so it was abandoned.

The next project proposed by the team was an adaptation of Dreiser's novel *An American Tragedy*. "Main point in my treatment—conditions of education, bringing up, work, surroundings, and social conditions *drive* characterless boy to crime" (Leyda and Voynow 1982:59). Eisenstein again experimented with sonic effects, most notably the inner monologue leading up to the death of Roberta, the factory girl whom Clyde has made pregnant. The train wheels hammer out "Kill—kill—" while the visual track presents a flurry of associative imagery aiming to convey Clyde's panic. Comparable to the subjective sound employed by Hitchcock (*Blackmail*, 1929) and Lang (*M*, 1931), Eisenstein's usage owed most to Joyce's *Ulysses*, which he now conceived as a literary model of stream of consciousness.

1.12 Eisenstein in Mexico, with Frida Kahlo (second from left) and Diego Rivera (center).

The visitors submitted *An American Tragedy* in early October, attaching the insouciant envoi *Honi soit qui mal y pense*. The studio was initially enthusiastic, but the ardor quickly cooled. The picture, David O. Selznick asserted, "cannot possibly offer anything but a most miserable two hours to millions of happy-minded young Americans" (Selznick 1972:27). Paramount terminated its contract with the Eisenstein group, and shortly thereafter the U.S. government asked them to leave.

Eisenstein considered pursuing filmmaking possibilities in Japan, but Upton Sinclair, his wife, and some friends offered to finance a film about Mexico. In December 1930 the Russian troika entered the country, leaving the state that Eisenstein would later call "Californica" (Seton 1952:165).

Qué viva México! was to be a panoramic survey of the nation's history and culture. Like many leftists, Eisenstein was impressed that Mexico had created a socialist revolution in 1910. He had met Diego Rivera in Moscow and was stirred by the monumental art of the muralists, who combined modernist techniques with indigenous popular traditions. He referred to his films as "my moving frescoes (for we also work on walls!)" (1935b:229). Anita Brenner's book *Idols behind Altars* (1929) also became a source for the film.

Eisenstein and Alexandrov planned *Qué viva México!* as a series of "novellas," each featuring a different region and historical period. Although the order of the novellas seems to have changed fairly often, each was to show life at a single period in a different region of the country. Every episode was to be dedicated to a different Mexican artist, from Posada to Orozco.

Eisenstein fell in love with Mexico. He poured his energies into filming a "poem

1.13 In Mexico: Filming for *Qué viva México!* (1930–31).

of love, death, and immortality" (quoted in Karetnikova and Steinmetz 1991:28). After almost a decade, he began to draw again. Influenced by pre-Columbian art and the "pure linear structure" of the Mexican landscape and costumes, his drawings adopted a "pictographic" style. Bereft of shading, supple "protoplasmic" masses are indicated by a single, flowing contour, with results somewhere between Matisse and Cocteau (1.15). His extravagantly sensual crucifixions, bullfight scenes, and Mexican youths suggest a libido unleashed. Many of the sketches would be seized by customs authorities upon his return to the United States.

The filming of *Qué viva México!* consumed all of 1931 and January of 1932. The project, budgeted at the absurdly low sum of $25,000, was constantly running short of funds, and Sinclair began to feel traduced. As tens of thousands of feet of rushes were shipped to Hollywood, he watched with growing horror. A November 1931 telegram from Stalin informed Sinclair that Eisenstein was believed to be a "deserter" who would not return to the Soviet Union (Geduld and Gottesman 1970:212). Sinclair defended the filmmaker as a loyal Soviet citizen. Nevertheless, he and the agent for Amkino, the Soviet film distribution office in

1.14 The finished shot.

New York, halted the project shortly afterward. The Soldadera segment had not yet been filmed.

Sinclair wired Eisenstein his intention to ship the footage to Moscow. Eisenstein, Alexandrov, and Tissé left Mexico expecting to salvage a film from the enterprise. In New York Eisenstein viewed some rushes for the first time. He then sailed for home. In the meantime, Sinclair decided to retain the footage. In order to recoup some of Sinclair's investment, Sol Lesser turned the Maguey story into a short feature, released in 1934 as *Thunder over Mexico*. Sinclair and Lesser also assembled a short film, *Death Day*, before selling off the footage for stock shots and compilation films. Sinclair's abandonment of the project embroiled him in a bitter conflict with the American Left from which his reputation never recovered. The loss of his Mexican film plunged Eisenstein into a period of acute depression, and for the rest of his life he kept Sinclair's telegram pinned above his desk.

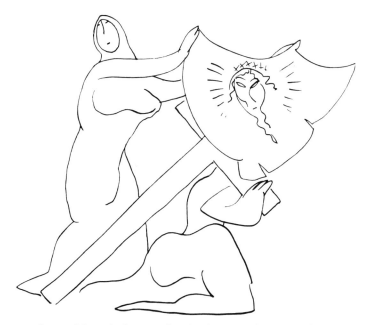

1.15 "Extasy," from the "Veronica" cycle of Eisenstein's Mexican drawings.

Projects and Problems

Eisenstein returned to a changed Soviet Union. The First Five-Year Plan (1929–1933) had achieved enormous industrial output, but there were still food shortages, largely as a result of the forced collectivization of the countryside. A cult of Stalin had begun to emerge. New legislation punished "anti-Soviet behavior" with death, and the internal passport, one of the most hated features of tsarist rule, reappeared. A class system was emerging, and the Party elite began to acquire bourgeois comforts.

In the cultural sphere, the comparatively relaxed and pluralistic atmosphere of the New Economic Policy had waned. During the NEP, the ideology of workers' centrality had supported the proletarian artistic organizations, and these in turn had sought to dominate every field. Encouraged by the Party, such groups as RAPP (the Russian Association of Proletarian Writers) had assailed and dislodged "bourgeois" elements in the intelligentsia.

Eisenstein had taken a strong stand against RAPP trends before he left the U.S.S.R. He had signed the manifesto of the "October" group, an assembly of artists hoping to merge Left art's "rational and constructive approach" to form with the proletarian imperatives of the Cultural Revolution. His essay "Perspectives" (1929) criticized several trends of the moment, including RAPPist ones. During his trip abroad, Left cinema had been attacked by proletarian spokesmen, and Eisenstein had been singled out. *October* and *Old and New* were charged with "formalistic" experimentation that made them incomprehensible to the U.S.S.R.'s 120 million peasants and workers.

In 1932, after many intellectuals had been cowed by the proletarian groups' assault, the Party's Central Committee abolished all such organizations and oversaw a centralization of artistic power. In each medium, creators formed a union. Now intellectuals would receive graduated pay and perquisites in exchange for policing their ranks and supporting the emerging social hierarchy. This development coincided with a general strengthening of professional cliques throughout industry and the bureaucracy. The Department of Culture and Propaganda (Kultprop) was given control over all academic and cultural activities.

In the late 1920s the film industry became more structured and bureaucratic than it had been under the NEP, and the government played a central role in planning output and censoring projects. In 1930 the film trust Sovkino was reorganized as Soyuzkino and placed under the leadership of Boris Shumyatsky, an opponent of Eisenstein and the Left cinema he stood for. Vladimir Sutyrin, a RAPP official who denounced "formalist cinema," served as his production director. Shumyatsky promoted a "cinema for the millions" and pressed for vigorous storytelling, realistic acting, and emotional appeal. Typage and montage were forbidden. During Eisenstein's absence, Shumyatsky and the proletarian forces managed to bring Kuleshov, Pudovkin, Room, and others to heel.

Upon Eisenstein's return, he turned down Shumyatsky's invitation to make

1.16 Eisenstein upon his return to Moscow, early 1930s.

Happy Guys (also known as *Jazz Comedy*). Alexandrov accepted the project and launched his career as a director of musical comedies. The two collaborators separated.

Eisenstein proposed a light work of his own, *MMM (Maksim Maksimovich Maksimov)*. In its final form, the scenario was a satire set in the Soviet Intourist agency. Here a slick official (reminiscent of the NEPman of 1920s comedies) encounters feudal boyar clans who have returned to Russia as tourists. In its fantastic juxtaposition of past and present and its mockery of the Soviet bureacracy and privileged elite, *MMM* recalls the satirical comedies of Mayakovsky, *The Bedbug* (1928) and *The Bathhouse* (1929), as well as the dreamlike grotesquerie of Shostakovich's opera *The Nose* (1928). The script was initially accepted, with Maxim Shtraukh and Judith Glizer assigned the main roles, but then production was abandoned.

Eisenstein contemplated other projects: an epic history of Moscow, an adaptation of Malraux's *La condition humaine,* and *Black Majesty,* an account of the Haitian revolt of 1802. None came to fruition, and Eisenstein became severely depressed. In the meantime he became chair of the film direction division of the Soviet film school VGIK and taught the division's course. He also continued work on *Direction,* "my still (and I am afraid for ever!) 'forthcoming' book" (Seton 1952:218).

During the hiatus in Eisenstein's filmmaking, Soviet artistic activity was consolidating around the policy of "Socialist Realism." Socialist Realism was posited as a new stage in world art. Balzac and Tolstoy had ushered in a "critical realism," but with Gorky's *Mother* (1906) and works such as Fyodor Gladkov's *Cement*

(1925), the Communist era had discovered an artistic form that captured "reality in its revolutionary development." Sensitive to the class struggle, loyal to the Party and the nation, Socialist Realism was to have an enthusiastic, idealizing thrust. It would present the typical character (the heroic and selfless worker, the wise Party representative) and the political essence of a situation (the latter guaranteed by a "dialectical" analysis according to Marxism-Leninism).

The program was familiar, vague, and apparently flexible. Most explicitly, Socialist Realism fused 1920s trends toward proletarian realism and "revolutionary romanticism." It also adhered to Engels' strictures that realistic works should portray typical characters in typical situations. In addition, the doctrine had affinities with 1920s Left theses, as when one apologist echoed Tretyakov in asserting that the new Soviet art "aims at the organization of the psychology of the masses" (Selvinsky 1934:113). Unlike most "isms" of the 1920s and the RAPP era, Socialist Realism did not seem to be cutting itself off from history; part of its public rationale was that the artist should "critically assimilate" the art of the past.

At the 1934 All-Union Congress of Soviet Writers, Socialist Realism was accepted as guiding policy for the Writers' Union. In contrast to RAPP's dogmatism it seemed to offer a framework loose enough to accommodate most writers' interests. Socialist Realism quickly became the official norm in all arts. Shumyatsky endorsed it in cinema, and a canon emerged: *Counterplan* (1932), *Petersburg Nights* (1934), *The Youth of Maxim* (1935), and above all *Chapayev* (1934).

By January 1935 Eisenstein had been back two and a half years and still did not have a film in production. His inactivity became a central theme of the All-Union Conference on Soviet Cinematography, held in January. The setting was calculated to demonstrate the regime's control of intellectuals and to prod directors into stepping up production. The major Soviet filmmakers indulged in several days of flattery, abasement, affirmations of Socialist Realism, and attacks on the most famous figure in their midst. After his rather abstruse opening lecture, the Old Man was pilloried.

> *Pudovkin:* [Eisenstein's speech] was complex, like a galaxy I would say. Galaxy—it is the system which is star-like, fascinating, greater than our solar system [Laughter].
>
> *Yutkevich:* Your mattress is stuffed with gold and yet you want to live off nothing but beautiful phrases and deftly chosen words. But you, fool, why don't you dig into your mattress and eat your gold?
>
> *Dovzhenko:* If I knew as much as he does I would literally die [Laughter and applause] . . . I'm convinced that in more ways than one his erudition is literally killing him . . . Sergei Mikhailovich, if you do not produce a film at least within a year, then please do not produce one at all. It won't be needed by us and it won't be needed by you.
>
> *Sergei Vasiliev:* The theoretical and scientific matters in which you are immersed in your study where you sit wrapped in your remarkable robe covered with Chinese hieroglyphs, and surrounded by a great many books, wonderful

statuettes and many other beautiful things, is not everything, because it keeps you from participating . . . You have created *Potemkin*. You possess an unusual revolutionary passion and a burning feeling, but something has happened to you. I do not care to enter into the causes, but I do want you to discard your Chinese robe and participate in our Soviet reality of today.   (Seton 1952:337–339)

Eisenstein's humiliation was capped by his receiving a minor award, Honored Worker of the Arts, while his former students Georgi and Sergei Vasiliev won the highest accolades for *Chapayev*. Eisenstein closed the conference with a self-criticism that won a standing ovation. "I am not broken-hearted because the heart which beats for the fulfilment of a Bolshevik aim cannot be broken" (Seton 1952:349). Though continuing to defend the importance of theoretical research, he promised to enter production.

Since his return Eisenstein had remained a significant figure. Regional studios sought his advice; he was a guest at the epochal 1934 Writers' Congress; he served on the jury of the first Moscow Film Festival. Even after the public admonitions at the Film Congress, he received handsome incentives. Since the early 1920s he had lived in a single room in Shtraukh's "collective apartment," but in 1935 he was assigned to a new four-room apartment, and a year later he received a two-story dacha in a Moscow suburb.

Shortly after the congress Eisenstein took leave from VGIK and with A. G. Rzheshevsky began to prepare a new film about the contemporary countryside. Directors had run into problems with such a subject—both Dovzhenko's *Earth* (1930) and Pudovkin's *A Simple Incident* (1932) had been attacked—but *Bezhin Meadow* seemed to be the sort of project that could reestablish Eisenstein's pre-eminence in film culture. Celebrated in songs and children's literature, Pavlik quickly became a model for Soviet youth. The story was drawn from Turgenev but reshaped around the contemporary hero Pavlik Morosov, a Komsomol boy who had been killed by his father for denouncing the old man's counterrevolutionary activities. *Bezhin Meadow* was also to exploit many new techniques. It would make novel use of the wide-angle lens, rear projection, inner monologue, and audiovisual polyphony, the knitting of picture and sound patterns into a single expressive "image."

Scripting and shooting occupied much of 1935. After Shumyatsky declared the first results unsatisfactory, Eisenstein brought his friend Isaak Babel onto the project and they worked out a second script. Filming was delayed when Eisenstein was stricken with smallpox in late autumn, and then influenza in early 1936. After yet another revision of the script, the filming of *Bezhin Meadow* resumed in August 1936 and continued through the fall. In early 1937 the work-in-progress was screened, criticized, and banned.[1] Film professionals convened in a three-day conference to discuss Eisenstein's errors.

---

1. The negative and workprint of the film were destroyed in a fire during the war. The only portions known to survive are individual frames kept by Eisenstein.

1.17 *Bezhin Meadow* (1935–1937): Eisenstein directing Vitia Kartachov as Stepok.

Shumyatsky accused Eisenstein of ignoring the criticisms of 1935. He had been seduced by Eccentrism and myth. He had ignored the class struggle, posing the father-son conflict in archetypal and religious terms. In addition, the Party Central Committee found the work anti-artistic and "politically quite unsound" (Shumyatsky 1937:380). A pamphlet, *Against Formalism in Film Art,* formulated the chief criticisms and included Eisenstein's self-criticism, "The Mistakes of *Bezhin Meadow.*" He agreed that he had gone too far toward the "untypical," seeking exaggerated dramatic gestures and hyperbolic settings. In a phrase that recalls the *Qué viva México!* novellas, he acknowledged that the primal figures of Father and Son presented "mythologically stylized figures and associations." Having been absorbed in his research and teaching, he had lost touch with the people (1937b:373–377).

It was a hazardous moment to be in the spotlight. In 1934, after the assassination of Sergei Kirov, a wave of political terror began. It would carry old Bolsheviks and prominent leaders to torture, confessions of sabotage and conspiracy, public trial, and death. At first the pressures upon artists were comparatively mild, but in early 1936 the leaders of cultural policy adopted more threatening tactics. Composers, architects, and painters found themselves under siege. At the moment Shumyatsky first halted *Bezhin Meadow,* the cultural administrators were assaulting Shostakovich, Meyerhold, and other "formalists." The new canon was to consist of more accessible contemporary artists and the "realistic" Russian tradition of Pushkin, Mikhail Glinka, Mussorgsky, Ilya Repin, and Vasily Surikov.

Soon the Terror spread into the artistic world. Many of Eisenstein's contemporaries were swept away. Tretyakov and Pilnyak were arrested in 1937, Osep Mandelstam in 1938, Babel in 1939. All died in prison. Authorities seized Meyerhold's theatre in 1938; a year later the secret police arrested him, tortured him, and stabbed his wife to death; he was executed in 1940.

Most of the prominent figures in film escaped the writers' fate, perhaps because Stalin valued cinema highly, perhaps also because the industry already had few trained personnel. Nevertheless, Vladimir Nilsen, a cinematographer who had been one of Eisenstein's most admiring students, was arrested and never reappeared. Nilsen's fate was widely interpreted as a warning to the film community. Moreover, according to Kleiman (1992), Eisenstein composed "The Mistakes of *Bezhin Meadow*" under fear of arrest. At Babel's suggestion, he wrote to Stalin to ask for another chance. Shumyatsky then offered Eisenstein two projects; he chose the one that treated the Russian warrior prince Alexander Nevsky. Soon the purge claimed another victim. Shumyatsky was dismissed in January 1938 and executed six months later.

Triumph and Decline

Under Stalin's reprieve, Eisenstein plunged back into work. With Pyotr Pavlenko, a politically safe leader of the Writers' Union, he completed the script of *Alexander Nevsky*. Here, he announced, "patriotism is my theme." Making a sanctified Russian warrior the protagonist was in accord with the new nationalism and hero worship of Stalinist culture. The scenario, originally called *Rus* (Russia), drew parallels between the thirteenth-century Teutonic Knights and contemporary German aggression. Yet Eisenstein also seized the opportunity to experiment with a stylized version of history. According to Romm, Eisenstein picked Nevsky as a subject because "nobody knows much about him, and so nobody can possibly find fault with me" (Swallow 1977:123).

The production went as rapidly as that of *Strike* and *Potemkin*. Shooting began in June 1938, and the editing was finished by November, five months ahead of schedule. Eisenstein saved time by having his assistant director, Dmitri Vasiliev, film several scenes. Eisenstein and Tissé shot the famous Battle on the Ice first, during an intense summer on an open field covered with sodium silicate. During the editing, when Eisenstein was napping, Stalin requested to see the film. An assistant packed up the film, minus the reel Eisenstein was working on. Stalin approved the film as he saw it. The missing reel (depicting a brawl among the people of Novgorod and introducing one of the romantic subplots) was consequently omitted from the finished print.

Starring the popular actor Nikolay Cherkasov (a powerful figure in the Party) and embellished with Prokofiev's score, *Nevsky* became one of the most prestigious productions of the era. The film was released in December and won a huge success. Legend has it that Stalin slapped the director on the back, declaring: "Sergei Mikhailovich, you are a good Bolshevik after all!" (Seton 1952:386). In the summer of 1939, however, Germany and the Soviet Union signed a nonaggression pact, the first of many accords that allowed the two powers to annex territory. As a result, *Nevsky* was withdrawn from Soviet distribution. It would

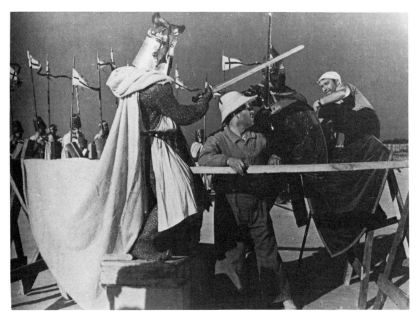

1.18 Eisenstein filming the Battle on the Ice for *Alexander Nevsky* (1938).

be reissued in 1941, when the German invasion of the U.S.S.R. made it timely propaganda again.

For several years Eisenstein basked in renewed glory. Vsevolod Vishnevsky, an influential dramatist within the Party and an Eisenstein supporter even during the *Bezhin Meadow* incident, wrote a pamphlet praising Eisenstein's work and blaming his problems on saboteurs (Vishnevsky 1939:19). Although some of Eisenstein's projects came to naught—notably *Perekop, The Great Ferghana Canal,* and the Pushkin biography *Loves of a Poet*—he enjoyed great respect. For *Nevsky* he won the Order of Lenin (1939) and the Stalin Prize (1941). He was made doctor of arts, artistic director of Mosfilm, a member of the Artistic Council of the Committee for Cinema Affairs, and a member of the *Iskusstvo kino* editorial board. He was picked to direct the Bolshoi Theatre's production of Wagner's *Die Walküre,* a gesture of German-Soviet amity. His first book, a collection of four major essays translated by Jay Leyda, was published in New York in 1942 as *The Film Sense.*

In 1941 Andrey Zhdanov assigned Eisenstein to make *Ivan the Terrible.* Stalin perceived parallels between himself and this tsar, and he was convinced by revisionist historians that Ivan had been a progressive leader. Eisenstein was expected to make a grandiose historical pageant about a ruler who had striven to unify Russia and protected it from foreign influence. Contrary to normal Soviet procedure, Eisenstein was permitted to write his own script.

When the Germans advanced on Moscow in late 1941, he and other major directors were evacuated to Alma-Ata in Kazakhstan. The shooting at Alma-Ata ran from April 1943 to June 1944, with Tissé photographing the exterior scenes

1.19 An official portrait from 1939.

1.20 Eisenstein rehearsing Wagner's *Valkyrie* at the Bolshoi Theater, 1940.

and Andrei Moskvin, the cameraman for the FEX group, handling the interiors. Prokofiev again supplied a score.

The first part of *Ivan the Terrible* was approved late in 1944 and premiered in January of the following year. Beginning with Ivan's coronation, the film traces his growing military success and his intensifying struggle with the feudal boyars, who resist the unification of the nation. Ivan's wife is poisoned by the boyars, and his loss plunges him into despair. The film ends with Ivan in self-imposed exile, called back to serve his country by a procession of the people.

Eisenstein had originally planned a two-part film like Ivan Petrov's acclaimed *Peter the First* (1937–1939), and *Ivan*'s literary scenario published in 1943 contained such a division. But early in production Eisenstein expanded the portions involving the boyars' court intrigues, thereby creating a trilogy. The central section would form a kind of Jacobean chamber drama to be set against the third part, a return to the expansive martial mode as Ivan defeats the Livonians and finally reaches the sea.

In June 1944 Eisenstein and his staff resumed production in Moscow. The first part of *Ivan* was submitted for examination in the fall and was released in January 1945. While continuing to write and teach, Eisenstein worked on filming and cutting *Ivan* Part II through early 1946.

His position seemed secure. In January 1946 *Ivan* Part I won a Stalin Prize, First Class, and Part II was tentatively approved. After finishing cutting Part II on 2 February, he went to a celebration in his honor. In the course of the festivities he collapsed with a cardial infarction.

Hospitalized and then resting in a sanatorium, Eisenstein whiled away his time drawing, receiving guests, writing his memoirs, and watching films ("I'm terribly fond of Judy Garland!" [1946e:1–2]). But more blows were to come in the summer. His mother died. Part II of *Ivan the Terrible*, examined and moderately criticized by his colleagues, became one of four films denounced by the Party Central Committee in August as "unsuccessful and faulty": "Eisenstein in the second part of *Ivan the Terrible* displayed his ignorance of historical facts by portraying the progressive army of the *oprichniki* [Ivan's bodyguards] as a band of degenerates similar to the American Ku Klux Klan, and Ivan the Terrible, a man of strong will and character, as a man of no will and little character, something like Hamlet" (Babitsky and Rimberg 1955:301–302). The censure of Eisenstein, Pudovkin, and other directors formed part of the committee's general attack on the Ministry of Cinema, which was accused of complacency, financial carelessness, and insufficient vigilance in rooting out apolitical films.

This critique was in turn part of a broader postwar assault on cultural life led by Zhdanov. The comparative creative openness of wartime conditions vanished in a new round of threats, punishments, and accusations of "formalism." Zhdanov's onslaught struck literature, theatre, and music as well as cinema. The works of Zoshchenko and Akhmatova were banned, while Pasternak, Prokofiev, Shostakovich, and many other artists were obliged to submit recantations. The Party's censure of Part II was part of an effort to regain control of the senior film

1.21 Filming Cherkasov in *Ivan the Terrible* (1941), with Andrei Moskvin at
      the camera.

community, who had been felt to be too charitable toward one another's works
(Yurenev 1985 2:280).

In October 1946 Eisenstein wrote his self-criticism. Some nonformulaic points
crept in: he suggested that his childhood reading had biased his treatment, and
he asked with mock innocence whether it was possible that Ivan never doubted
his historical mission. On the whole, however, he followed the strategy of his
Bezhin Meadow recantation, criticizing his conduct in terms virtually identical
with those used in the accusations. He confessed to misrepresenting history,
neglecting "Ivan the builder," and ignoring the progressive role of the *oprichniki*
(Eisenstein 1946j:462).

Since his return to the Soviet Union in 1932, Eisenstein had suffered influenza,
bouts of depression and exhaustion, ptomaine poisoning, and smallpox. After the
Ivan the Terrible crisis his strength waned. He gave some public lectures and saw
students in his apartment. He continued to be honored, being made director of

1.22 Eisenstein with his American visitor Lee Bland in the woods near his dacha,
     July 1946.

the Cinema Section of the Institute of Art History of the U.S.S.R. Academy of
Sciences. He planned to teach a course on the psychology of art with Alexander
Luria. He also continued to write, and he approved another collection of essays,
Film Form, for Leyda to translate and publish in America. He began to contem-
plate new projects, including an updating of *The Glass House,* an anniversary film
to celebrate the founding of Moscow, and a version of *The Brothers Karamazov.*

Above all, Eisenstein sought to complete the *Ivan* project. Virtually all the
material shot for Part III had been destroyed, but he believed that the second
part could be corrected and new scenes could be filmed. In February 1947 he and
Cherkasov had a late-night session with Stalin, Molotov, and Zhdanov. The leaders
offered criticisms and corrections, sometimes in grimly hilarious detail. (Zhdanov
objected to the length of Ivan's beard.) Stalin opined that Eisenstein had failed to
show "why *it is necessary to be cruel*" (Eisenstein 1947d:8; translation corrected).
This Ivan was too paralyzed by remorse to fulfill his mission of destroying the
boyar families. Nevertheless, Stalin gave permission to create a new second part.
Eisenstein asked if he must hurry, and Stalin replied that he could take three years
if necessary. "May there be fewer films, but of high quality." In March Eisenstein
cabled Leyda: "Everything okay continue working Ivan" (1947b).

Probably few people believed that Eisenstein had the stamina to finish *Ivan,*
and he confessed to a friend that he probably could not stand the rigors of filming.
He had long feared that he would not live past the age of fifty. In the night of
10–11 February 1948, soon after his fiftieth birthday, he suffered a fatal heart
attack while writing a letter to Kuleshov.

The Particularities of Method

This sketch of Eisenstein's life has confined itself to the barest outlines. Many gaps remain. His diaries are currently inaccessible, so certain aspects of his personality remain obscure. His Jewish lineage was exploited for international propaganda during the war but may have posed difficulties for him. Leonid Trauberg conjectured that had Eisenstein lived longer he would have been an obvious target for the regime's campaign against "rootless cosmopolitans" (Van Houten 1989:166).

Eisenstein's sexual identity is also somewhat ambiguous. He married his assistant Pera Attasheva in 1934, but the couple lived apart for most of their marriage. (Her apartment became the site of his reconstructed quarters.) Hints in Marie Seton's biography have led most Western scholars to assume that he was homosexual or bisexual. Since homosexuality was long a major crime in the Soviet Union, this side of his life has not been publicly documented.

In place of detailed personal knowledge we have had a biographical image of him. More than most filmmakers, Eisenstein built up a public conception of his identity and artistic project. As early as the mid-1920s he was presenting himself as a coldly rationalistic creator for whom making a work of art was a problem in practical engineering, no more complicated in principle than designing a chicken coop. By the early 1930s he had taken as his model Leonardo da Vinci, whom he would synthesize with Marx, Freud, and Pavlov. He would become the twentieth-century equivalent of the Renaissance artist-savant. In the era of Socialist Realism he described himself as a failed Constructivist. Out to murder art, he had been obliged to master its secrets; and once he had done so, he drew away from the extreme Left position and toward a wholehearted Bolshevik creativity. Throughout the 1930s he presented himself as an academic researcher. His triumphant return to filmmaking with *Alexander Nevsky* cast him as a patriot working for the new russophilia of Stalin's regime, and the first part of *Ivan* confirmed him as a supreme "national" artist.

Alongside this "biographical legend" we could also set a few political facts. Although Eisenstein never joined the Party, available evidence gives little reason to doubt his commitment to its mission. Nineteen years old at the time of the Bolshevik coup, he was of a generation who sought to build the new society. His silent films of the 1920s are predicated upon myths reinforcing the Bolshevik hold on power. Film, he wrote, had the task of "irrevocably inculcating communist ideology into the millions" (1929h:160). *Bezhin Meadow* promoted reporting family members' "counterrevolutionary" activity, while *The Great Ferghana Canal* was to celebrate a massive building project executed by forced labor.

Most intellectuals outside the academy were unfamiliar with the Marxist-Leninist classics, and apparently Eisenstein did not read them seriously until the late 1920s. Yet shortcomings in his political education did not restrain him from polemical infighting. His theoretical pronouncements of the period have a strident dogmatism that echoes the harsh polemical tone of Lenin and Trotsky. Unlike Shostakovich and Prokofiev, who shrank from publicity, Eisenstein indulged in noisy exchanges. He argued with Vertov, Proletkult, and the Proletarian groups. Upon his return to the U.S.S.R. from Mexico, he presented himself as a militant defender of the Soviet line.

His aggressiveness seems to have subsided in the years after his chastisement at the 1935 cinematography conference. The *Bezhin Meadow* humiliation, coinciding with the full unleashing of Stalin's Terror, may have encouraged him to withdraw from the polemical battlefield. Nevertheless he remained a loyal spokesman. He praised *Lenin in 1918* (1939) for its portrayal of Felix Dzerzhinsky (head of the secret police) and its attack on "enemies" such as the recently executed Bukharin (1939b). He declared that *Ferghana Canal* would celebrate the Party's victories in Mongolia and the rapprochement with Hitler (1940c:108–109).

We still know too little about the effects of the Great Terror on Eisenstein. As the files of the secret police become available, new information should come to light.[2] It may be significant that near the end of his life he reflected on the scene in *Ivan* in which the stricken tsar must beg the boyars to support his family line. Eisenstein wrote:

> In my own personal, too-personal history I myself too often perpetrated this heroic deed of self-abasement. And in my personal, too-personal, innermost life, perhaps somewhat too often, too hurriedly, even almost too willingly and also . . . unsuccessfully.
>
> However, I have also, like Ivan, managed to cut off heads sticking out of fur coats; the Terrible Tsar and I have pressed the proud gold hems together, accepting humiliation in the name of our most passionate aspirations.
>
> And often, after lifting up the sword over another's head, I have brought it down not so much on his as on my own.   (1964:226)

Whatever the biographical revelations to come, we can arrive at some understanding of Eisenstein's accomplishments in cinema. The chapters that follow survey his 1920s films and theoretical writings, his teaching, and his later writings and films.

This career was marked by a tight intertwining of theory and practice. Sometimes Eisenstein saw the two as quite distinct: "Now analysis would 'examine' creation, now creation would serve to test certain theoretical premises" (1946c:17). At other moments he claimed to forget theory in the heat of filmmaking, only later to be gripped by the need for "ever-increasing, precise knowledge about what we do" (1940f:2).

2. We should expect that the picture will be complicated. Recent evidence shows that in 1939, almost certainly under torture, Isaak Babel asserted that he and Eisenstein had had "anti-Soviet conversations"— a crime punishable by death. Shortly before his execution Babel repudiated this claim, but such "confessions" probably enabled the secret police to amass a file on Eisenstein for future use (Shentalinsky 1991:33, 35).

The unity of theory and practice was a tenet not only of Marxist political philosophy but also of the 1920s avant-garde. Meyerhold, Mayakovsky, and the Constructivists in the graphic arts all explored and exposed the principles underlying their work. More broadly, within Soviet culture as a whole there were strong tendencies toward what we might call *technē*-centered thought. *Technē* is Aristotle's term for the unity of theory and practice within skilled activity. Any craft, artistic or not, includes not only practices but also a systematic knowledge underlying them.

The view that art is a goal-directed, material craft *(masterstvo)* was widespread in early Soviet culture. The artist, no longer seen as an inspired creator, became an artisan placing expertise at the service of the new society. But how was one to discover the principles of artistic craft? Artists drew ideas from social theory, engineering, and industrial practices.

Immediately after the Bolshevik revolution, tendencies toward "systems thinking" came to the fore. A central theme was that scientific knowledge of abstract structural principles could enable one to organize any body of human activity. One of the most vocal proponents of such an idea was Bogdanov, founder of Proletkult. His "Tectology" was to be an empirical science that would lay bare the laws underlying physical work, art, and social behavior in general. Proletkult attracted thinkers who sought to restructure work processes along the lines of Frederick Winslow Taylor, the American time-and-motion expert. Alexey Gastev, who directed the Central Institute of Work, typified this approach. Gastev insisted that the human is simply a perfectible machine and that "engineering is the apex of wisdom in science and art" (Kozulin 1984:16). It was to such a concept that Tretyakov appealed in calling the artist a "psycho-engineer."

Constructivist painters began to treat art-making in terms of the engineer's distinctions among material, form, texture *(faktura,* the working of surfaces), and purpose. "A construction," wrote Rodchenko in 1921, "is an objective or a task performed according to a particular system, for which purpose particular materials have been organized and worked in a manner corresponding to their inherent characteristics." On the whole the Constructivists emphasized the demands of the material, whereas Bogdanov concentrated on the constraints of organizational structure. Nonetheless, all the thinkers of this tendency held that cultural artifacts and processes could be systematically understood and rationally mastered.

The *technē*-centered trend also included non-Left literary figures, most notably Andrei Bely. Although he propounded some of the most mystical doctrines in Symbolism, Bely took an utterly practical attitude to his craft. In his prerevolutionary writings, he insisted that the poet should study literary technique just as a composer studies counterpoint. Up to his death in 1934 Bely scrutinized prosodic patterns in minute detail, generating tables and graphs through which he hoped to discover poetic laws and to found an empirical science of literary form.

Like Bely and the Constructivists, the Russian Formalist literary critics also maintained a concrete approach to their subject. They recast the form/content duality as a distinction between form and materials, with both to be understood as fulfilling determinable functions. Shklovsky notoriously declared a literary work to consist of "devices" assembled into an aggregate by the artist's technique (1917:24). Yury Tynyanov proposed a "systemic-functional" model of the literary text, viewing it as a sustained dynamic of material and formal organization, a struggle between dominant factors and subordinated ones (1924:31–35). The Formalists were to influence theories of painting, music, and cinema.

In all, the avant-garde's interest in *technē* corresponded less to post-Kantian aesthetics than to what has been known since Aristotle as "poetics." The term (from *poiēsis,* or "making") puts the stress on understanding the work of art as produced by craft, with an eye to some use or effect. Indeed, "making" *(delat'),* with its connotations of the systematic transformation of materials, became something of a slogan in the systems-conscious avant-garde. Shklovsky explained "how *Don Quixote* is made" (1921), and Mayakovsky composed a book titled *How Are Verses Made?* (1926).

This backdrop throws Eisenstein's endeavors into relief. More than almost any other artist emerging from the Left avant-garde, he combined artistic work with a sophisticated poetics of his medium, a unity of theory and practice that he sustained well beyond the avant-garde years.

The 1920s films were made to fulfill immediate political purposes, but, as the next chapter suggests, they also attempted to mark out new paths for Soviet cinema. They represent experiments in stretching the medium, in exposing thematic and filmic material and devising new techniques. Eisenstein considered *Strike* a "menu of methods" (Vishnevsky 1939:5). *Potemkin* attempted to maximize emotional intensity. *October,* by contrast, explored "intellectual" attractions and film language. *Old and New* was an effort to synthesize previous work and make the experiments of that work accessible to a larger audience. In most cases, Eisenstein stressed that the film's implications for cinema craft emerged out of the concrete case, out of intensive struggles to shape the material in accord with a specific purpose.

Theory would arise from tangible creative work. After discussing how to handle one scene, Eisenstein rejected a colleague's proposal. "To challenge his point of view I worked out a concrete solution—and out of that came some basic solutions. (N.B.: It's always this way, not something thought up from thin air or something outside concrete emotional and visual impact.)" (Leyda and Voynow 1982:91). He had little interest in examining other directors' films or theories. Knowing the creative decisions behind his own work best, he drew upon them for instances of cinematic form and effect.

Eisenstein's theoretical writing sought to disclose a "method" of filmic construction. "Constructing cinema from the 'idea of cinema' and abstract principles is barbarous and absurd . . . We expect, through particular concrete work on particular material, to arrive at the methods of cinematic creation for the director" (1932a:220–221).

Unlike most of his Left colleagues, he brought to bear upon these problems the weight of the world's culture. Unlike many Constructivists, he did not consider art a bourgeois category, to be replaced by production engineering. He defended *Strike* against Vertov's attacks by suggesting that Vertov unconsciously practiced art (Impressionism, no less), and that a fresh approach to art could reveal its "materialist" basis (1925d). He believed that new social tasks would transform art—widen its boundaries, regenerate its methods—but not eliminate it as a distinct activity.

Nor did he urge the destruction of the great achievements of the past. He sided with Bukharin, Bogdanov, Trotsky, and Lunacharsky in considering bourgeois culture worth preserving and assimilating. His research, like the Formalist critics' analyses, projected the contemporary emphasis on *masterstvo* back into the past. He scouted the great traditions, both Eastern and Western, for material, devices, and compositional principles that could exemplify solutions to problems of craft. This strategy might be called "Leninist formalism," an adaptation to the artistic sphere of Lenin's belief that the most advanced techniques of capitalism should be appropriated for progressive purposes. Doctrinally, Eisenstein was far from a "pure" Constructivist, but in his urge to see every cultural artifact as bristling with instructive problems of "mastery" he was true to the broader *technē*-centered trends of the time.

Eisenstein's absorption in artistic tradition proceeded at least in part from his commitment to moving the spectator. Whereas most Constructivists embraced a severe "objectivism," emphasizing the artwork as a material thing, he aimed at understanding how the audience could be excited perceptually, emotionally, and intellectually. This emphasis puts him in a tradition that includes thinkers as diverse as Tolstoy, Bogdanov, and Tretyakov. As Chapter 3 indicates, Eisenstein's interest in effect obliged him to oppose Futurism's doctrinaire rejection of the cultural heritage. The artist-researcher who wanted to grasp the principles of artistic impact would have to look to the most successful, emotionally arousing art of the past.

His 1920s films, functioning partly as attempts to discover principles intuitively, brought him to reflect upon what works on the screen. His writings tried to systematize those reflections. And his teaching, as Chapter 4 will suggest, sought to establish a similar approach in training young directors. Speaking in his defense at the 1935 cinematography conference he maintained: "I feel that it is important to produce films, and I will produce films; but I feel that the work of making films must go parallel with intensive theoretical work and research . . . When I am in my study I do not look at my statuettes and contemplate abstractly. When I am in my study I am working on problems which will help the growth of the coming generations of cinematographers" (Seton 1952:348). Here *masterstvo* became the *masterskaia,* the "workshop" that would explain general principles in the light of concrete craft.

Eisenstein's refusal to consider art a bourgeois illusion, his interest in the history of the arts, and his pluralistic, even eclectic, search for a "method" synthesizing theory and practice all may have made him better equipped for the transition to Socialist Realism than many of his colleagues. At the 1934 Writers' Conference, Bukharin proposed that the Socialist Realist work would be a dialectical integration of new and old, in which traditions would continue "in suspended form" (Bukharin 1935:208). Advocates of Socialist Realism presented it as a new "method," the term implying both an all-encompassing world view and concrete guidelines for artistic practice. Thereafter Eisenstein's own work on "method" (the planned title for his book on artistic creation) presented itself as a synthesis of the most fruitful aspects of older artistic traditions. At the 1935 cinematography conference he announced his intention to search "for a general method and mode for the problem of form, equally essential and fit for any genre of construction within our embracing style of *socialist realism*" (1935a:147).

During the 1920s Eisenstein's practice had largely preceded theory, and his theoretical writing worked to defend, amplify, or systematize the workings of the films. In the 1930s and 1940s, theory prepared for practice. Eisenstein became absorbed in general problems of artistic method, seeking ever more detailed knowledge of material, form, and effect. In these years, I shall suggest in Chapters 5 and 6, he recast his poetics of cinema in order to bring even the dogmas and clichés of Socialist Realism within its sweeping view of artistic creation.

His three last films, *Alexander Nevsky* and the *Ivan* series, tested the principles of form and effect that he had formulated on paper and in the lecture hall. They are experiments in *mise en scène* and "polyphonic" montage, in "vertical" image/sound relations, and in "pathos" and "ecstasy." The late films push in other new directions as well: toward new ways of representing history, toward new conceptions of spectatorial response, and toward the possibility of cinematic epic and tragedy.

The unity of theory and practice continued to occupy Eisenstein's last years. The *Ivan* films furnished specimen sequences for his analytical essays. He appended to *The Film Sense* a quotation in which Delacroix, castigating critics who ignored technique, defended the right of artists to seek the principles governing their craft (*FS:* v). And Eisenstein continued to assert that the search for principles had to be guided by an eye for the concrete. Both theory and practice had to converge upon "the awareness of the particularities of artistic method" (1989:178).

This minuteness of focus had the result of excluding certain issues from his writing and teaching. His poetics does not offer much in the way of an account of plot or narrative structure in cinema. He is far more illuminating on stylistics, both at the level of shot-to-shot relations (the primary concern of the 1920s writings) and at the level of a film's overall stylistic texture (which receives more emphasis in the later writings). Yet the films themselves raise issues of narrative construction that are no less intriguing than the issues he articulated in his writings. Trained by Eisenstein, we can discern in the films illuminating "particularities of method."

From a historical perspective, we can see that Eisenstein sustained the *technē-*centered impulse of the avant-garde far longer than virtually any other Left artist. During the 1930s and 1940s, when many capitulated to ideological conformity and intellectual stagnation, Eisenstein kept alive the idea of the artist as both experimenter and poetician.

2.

Monumental Heroics:

The Silent Films

Eisenstein's silent films were, like those of his Left contemporaries, didactic works. Yet he saw no contradiction between creating propaganda and achieving powerful aesthetic effects. Indeed, central to his thinking was the belief that only if propaganda was artistically effective—structurally unified, perceptually arousing, emotionally vivid—would it be politically efficacious. This urge to plumb the artistic capacities of film made Eisenstein the most ambitious and innovative director of Soviet cinema.

His experiments drew on diverse sources. Certainly Constructivism, particularly its theatrical manifestations, strongly influenced his films. Yet Constructivism's moment had passed when Eisenstein began filmmaking. Moreover, the movement's reliance upon abstract design was not suited for a medium that would, in the Soviet state, have to utilize representational imagery. Kasimir Malevich quickly recognized this, criticizing film directors for plagiarizing academic realist art and refusing to use pictorial abstraction to expose the materials of "cinema as such" (Malevich 1925:228–229).

Eisenstein's films can usefully be understood as part of a broad tendency toward "heroic realism" in 1920s Soviet art. This trend had its immediate sources in the Civil War period, which generated lyrical, episodic portrayals of collective action. In agit-dramas and novels the hero became the mass, and appeal to the spectator was posterlike in its directness. By the mid-1920s, when the avant-garde had declined, most painters, writers, and theatre workers accepted the obligation of celebrating the Revolution or portraying Soviet society through some version of "realism" (although the exact meaning of this concept was hotly debated).

Several trends emerged, notably Gorky's "revolutionary romanticism," which aimed to idealize the individual, and the easel painting of the Association of Artists of Revolutionary Russia, which demanded accessible content and comprehensible form. Other artists sought to meld the imperatives of heroic realism with avant-garde experimentation. Collage and photomontage could convey a pulsating modernity; Mayakovsky's machine-gun prosody could pay homage to Lenin; posters and typography could use Futurist design to galvanize the spectator's eye.

Like other Left artists, Eisenstein enthusiastically acceded to demands for a Soviet mythology that would stir proletarian consciousness. All his silent features start with quotations from Lenin, and the leader's image is central to the last two of them. In *Toward Dictatorship* and *The Year 1905* and the two-part *October* he conceived multi-part sagas tracing the victories of Bolshevism. These mammoth works went unmade, but the finished films did present a history of the Party's ascendency, from the turn of the century *(Strike)* and 1905 *(Potemkin)* to 1917 *(October)* and the contemporary era *(Old and New)*.

In constructing a cinematic mythology of the new regime, Eisenstein drew upon cultural formulas and iconography from his youth. For example, propaganda and popular legend already defined the key events of the *Potemkin* mutiny—the spoiled meat, the death of Vakulinchuk, the display of the body. (See Gerould 1989.) Public celebrations also furnished filmmakers a wealth of tales and storytelling strategies. From soon after the October revolution through the 1920s, the government sponsored mass spectacles to celebrate public holidays and commemorate historical turning points. On May Day in 1920, for instance, 4,000 participants performed in the "Mystery of Liberated Labor" for an audience of 35,000. Such spectacles, and the festivals and processions associated with them, were echoed in Eisenstein's films. The ritual of parading zoo animals dressed as class enemies finds its equivalent in *Strike,* while the mass spectacle "Storming of the Winter Palace" in October 1920 forms a plot outline for *October.*

Eisenstein was prepared to romanticize revolutionary action. In his films men (and occasionally women) fight, women and children endure, and all may die at the hands of the oppressor. The enemy slaughters innocents: the Odessa Steps are populated by mothers, infants, old men and women, a male student, and amputees. Yet these films never show a slain enemy. *October*'s Bolsheviks are murdered, but the government's side appears to suffer no casualties. In *Potemkin,* Vakulinchuk is shot, but the officers are merely tossed overboard. Sometimes the film flatly ignores the question of revolutionary justice; *Potemkin*'s priest, feigning death in the hold, is never seen again; in *Old and New,* the kulaks who poison the bull go unpunished. Eisenstein concentrates on the spectacular moments of upheaval, suffering, and victory and avoids confronting the ethical problems of insurrectionary violence.

Eisenstein's diverse aesthetic impulses find a place within heroic realism. Like

means of avant-garde techniques that would not mock them. In Eisenstein's case, perhaps *Potemkin* handles the matter most successfully, presenting the enemies in less caricatural terms than does *Strike* and using its montage experiments to elevate class allies. *Old and New* uses mildly modernist techniques to create moments of affirmative comedy. *October* is far more schizophrenic; as Eisenstein himself remarked at the time, intellectual montage was as yet appropriate only for satirizing the enemy (1928c:104).

In showing the masses making history, 1920s Left cinema builds its plots around social crises that trigger changes in the characters. Often an individual's dawning awareness of revolutionary doctrine furnishes major stages of the plot. In Pudov-kin's *Mother* (1926), *The End of St. Petersburg* (1927), and *The Heir to Genghis Khan* (1928), the drama often hinges on the transformation of the individual's consciousness.

No such psychological conversion interests Eisenstein. His oppressed multi-tudes are quivering on the brink of revolt, needing only agitation, direction, and discipline. A historical crisis provides the clear-cut outlines of a momentous process, a strike or a mutiny, mounting an insurrection or building a cooperative. Even in *Old and New*, the peasant protagonist needs no convincing of the right path; she simply lacks allies.

Once one has abandoned the psychologically motivated plot, the problem is how to unify the film. We have already touched on one means of achieving unity, the conceiving of a larger process within which actions form stages. A second unifying strategy, touched on by Petrovsky, is stylistic: the film achieves a single effect partly through a dynamic organization of material and technique.

Thus, for instance, the narration will typically rely upon parallelisms to display the broad sweep of the historical process. These parallels are typically *diegetic*—that is, they liken or contrast characters, settings, or actions that are located in the fictional world of the story. In Pudovkin's *Mother*, for instance, the climactic march of the militants is compared with the thawing and cracking ice on the nearby river.

Again, however, Eisenstein goes further. First, he also utilizes *nondiegetic* ma-terial. In *Old and New*, the slaughter of pigs is intercut with spinning pig statuettes; these statuettes are evidently not in the same "world" as the pigs (2.2, 2.3). As this example indicates, Eisenstein's typical cues for nondiegetic inserts are shots of objects framed in close-up and filmed against black backgrounds. Such inserts serve as a kind of abstract commentary on the action, making the viewer aware of an intervening narration that can interrupt the action and point up thematic or pictorial associations. Sometimes, however, Eisenstein's narration relativizes the distinction between diegetic and nondiegetic imagery. We find images that fall between the poles—concretely located in the story world, but treated with a freedom that "emancipates" the action from time and space (1929c:177).

Eisenstein's parallels differ from those of his peers in another way. His com-parisons often emit a radiating network of graphic or thematic implications. Piotrovsky follows contemporary usage in calling this "associative montage" (105).

2.2 *Old and New.*

2.3 *Old and New.*

2.4 *October.*

2.5 *October.*

One of the most famous of Eisenstein's visual analogies occurs in *October*. There he intercuts Prime Minister Kerensky of the Provisional Government with shots of a mechanical peacock (2.4, 2.5). The most obvious connection is the association of peacocks with preening. Eisenstein pictorializes a figure of speech: Kerensky is as vain as a peacock. But the sequence triggers other implications as well. The peacock is mechanical, and it enables Eisenstein to reiterate the artificial pose and gesture of the man. Like motifs elsewhere in the film, the peacock's sparkling highlights and suggestion of precious metals associate Kerensky with a static opulence due to be overturned by revolutionary energy. The whirling of the bird and the spreading of its tail coincide with Kerensky's standing at a door that will not open, suggesting that the mechanical toy works better than the government. Moreover, the bird's spinning is edited so that it seems to control the door's swinging open; a toy becomes the mainspring of the palace. The peacock's mechanized dance also suggests an empty ritual, like Kerensky's grand march up the stairs and the flunkies' insincere greetings. In ways such as these, Eisenstein takes fairly dead and clichéd metaphors and enlivens them through contextual associations. His filmic figures go beyond one-for-one comparisons and acquire the penumbra of connotation that distinguishes a rich poetic metaphor.

Eisenstein's exploration of associative montage exemplifies his fascination with the concrete properties of the film material. In his theorizing, he was driven to account for all the pictorial qualities and conceptual implications of each shot.

This line of inquiry gave birth to ideas of "intellectual cinema," "overtonal montage," and other concepts that we shall examine in the next chapter. His decision to make "plotless" films committed him to a corresponding dependence upon the specific features of film technique.

Whereas most Soviet directors became identified with a severe, even laconic shot design, Eisenstein pursued sensuous lighting and intricate compositions. His cinematographer, Edward Tissé, agreed with Eisenstein's ideas about making images perceptually arresting. Tissé used large mirrors to focus sunlight, marking out hard-edged blocks of space (as in 2.1) or endowing objects and faces with sculptural gleams. His expertise with the short focal-length lens (typically 28mm) enabled Eisenstein to create dynamically deep images.

It was with the technique of editing that Eisenstein was to be most closely identified. Pudovkin, along with Kuleshov, Barnet, and others more partial to Hollywood-style drama and comedy, came to be considered the proponents of a "montage" approach to filmmaking. This style emphasized abrupt, fragmented cutting. Soviet directors broke a scene into many shots, building up a dramatic action out of many short, close-up pieces.

Although Eisenstein influenced other directors, they tended not to carry montage techniques as far as he did. Whereas most directors' films use crosscutting to convey simultaneity and parallelism, Eisenstein uses it as well to create graphic similarities and to suggest abstract meanings. He also presses the Soviet standard of rapid editing to extremes by cutting "excessively." Calculated at twenty-four frames per second, the average shot length of *Old and New* is 2.6 seconds, of *Strike* 2.5 seconds, of *October* and *Potemkin* about 2 seconds—these latter figures being lower than those for almost any other Soviet director.[1]

A montage tactic he particularly cultivates is overlapping editing. This consists of cutting so that the action on screen is prolonged beyond its presumed duration. The technique has its source in the American cinema, but Kuleshov, Eisenstein's teacher and a subtle observer of Hollywood practice, took the device further. In *The Extraordinary Adventures of Mr. West in the Land of the Bolsheviks* (1924), a brawl is rendered in four markedly overlapping shots. A year later, in *Strike*, Eisenstein refines the procedure. While overlapping the movement of a wheel striking a foreman, he shows the action from sharply different angles. The editing makes the vectors of movement clash (2.6–2.11). Later in this and other films Eisenstein experiments with lengthy prolongations, oscillations, even complete replays of events. Overlapping editing creates a nervous, vibrating rhythm and allows him to rearrange elements from shot to shot.

Such montage techniques fulfill a more general purpose. All Left directors sought to dynamize each scene, but Eisenstein often abolishes the sense that an independent, coherent fictional event is rendered by a series of shots. This strategy

---

1. At twenty-four frames per second, Pudovkin's silent films consistently average about 2.5 seconds per shot, while Dovzhenko's range between about 3.5 and 4.5 seconds. Only Ilya Trauberg, much influenced by Eisenstein, approaches his rapid pace in *Goluboi Express* (1929), with an average shot rate of 1.7 seconds. At the same period in Hollywood, a silent film's average shot length was 5 to 6 seconds.

2.6 *Strike.*

2.7 *Strike.*

2.8 *Strike.*

2.9 *Strike.*

2.10 *Strike.*

2.11 *Strike.*

exemplifies that elimination of "real time" to which Piotrovsky refers. The tractor driver in *Old and New* is "matched" in the same position in two different places; the priest aboard the *Potemkin* strikes the cross into his right hand, then abruptly into his left (2.12, 2.13); the massacre on the Odessa Steps yields incompatible spatial arrangements from shot to shot; one sequence in *October* refuses to specify whether action is occurring on a single bridge or on several. In all these instances, the very idea of a consistent story event falls into question. Once again the action becomes "quasi-diegetic," hovering between the story world and a realm of abstract, emblematic significance.

In using such rapid and disjunctive editing, Eisenstein creates a narration that

2.12 *Battleship Potemkin.*   2.13 *Battleship Potemkin.*

sacrifices strict realism to perceptual and emotional impact. As in the metaphorical ramifications of certain passages, the result, however apparently didactic, goes beyond rhetoric and becomes aesthetically complex. Eisenstein pushes dynamized style to the limits of deformation, creating a mannerist version of Soviet cinematic norms.

The emphasis upon the moment-by-moment stylistic texture calls forth one more strategy in Eisenstein's "plotless" approach to heroic realism. It goes unmentioned in Piotrovsky's discussion, but it is a significant innovation in silent film history. It involves using recurrent objects and graphic patterns as motifs to unify the film.

We are very familiar with this organizational principle today, but motivic construction of Eisenstein's sort, and on his scale, was not yet a commonplace of prestigious cinema. In dramatic cinema, both in Hollywood and Europe, the motif was typically a prop that was invested with some narrative or thematic significance. In William deMille's *Miss Lulu Bett* (1921), for instance, the title character's bedroom slipper takes on a charged dramatic significance in the course of a scene. In the course of Abel Gance's *La roue* (1923) flowers and the locomotive acquire symbolic implications by virtue of their association with the characters' feelings and experience. In such mainstream usage, the motif either enhances characterization, plays a specific causal role in the plot, or intensifies the thematic point of the scene. Moreover, the spectator is expected to notice and recall the motif upon its reappearance. Soviet filmmakers used motifs in comparable ways.

As a self-consciously modernist artist, Eisenstein took a somewhat different perspective. He was aware that imagistic motifs played a central organizing role in poetry and drama. His studies of Zola, Bely, Joyce, and other artists convinced him that a rich, truly unified art work coordinates cross-referring systems of repeated images, verbal tags, and compositional devices. He could have found in Shklovsky's essay on Bely the remark that contemporary Russian prose was largely "ornamental" in that large-scale patterns of imagery prevailed over plot structure (1925:180). Later, in a lecture to aspiring directors, Eisenstein described a motif in *La bête humaine* as "delineated in order to be remembered," like the cradle in Griffith's *Intolerance* (1928h:102). The idea of motivic construction led Eisenstein

2.14 *Old and New.*

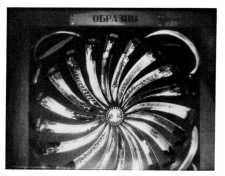

2.15 *Old and New.*

2.16 *Old and New.*

to make the pictorial or thematic implications of an image stretch across the entire film.

Sometimes he treats his motif as a simple geometric figure. In *Old and New* the bureaucrats are linked to the kulaks by the fancy circles seen on the kulak's gate (2.14) and in the agency office (2.15). Eisenstein often dynamizes such a static motif in the course of a film, as when in *Old and New* the fleet of tractors plows in concentric circles (2.16). Less abstract motifs, such as objects and gestures, will also bind the film together, but in a way that broadens to include remotely associated items. In *Potemkin* eyes, worms, and hanging objects form a thematic cluster. The Eisensteinian motif does not simply repeat; it develops, expands its implications, and intertwines with others to create a network of visual and thematic associations.

Some films, such as *October* and *Old and New,* display a strictly binary motivic organization: a basic thematic opposition (such as "God and Country") is mapped onto a welter of constantly varied visual and dramatic items. In *Strike* motifs associated with one group of characters abruptly "change sides" at turning points in the action. *Potemkin* relies more on a "nodal" principle, in which a single event, such as the inspection of a piece of rotten meat or the gathering of a crowd at the quai, knots together several motifs.

Although the principle of large-scale motivic organization gets almost no attention in Eisenstein's theoretical writings of the 1920s, he would articulate it in later years. For instance, in 1933 he noted: "A motif of the content may be played not only in the story but also in the law of construction or the structure of the thing" (1933c:308). As in most aspects of his 1920s work, practice preceded theory.

The innovations of Eisenstein's "plotless cinema"—the construction of the action around stages of a historical process, the radiating network of motifs binding the film together, the foregrounding of style in image and montage— were not simply onetime accomplishments. Every project pushed further. This effort is particularly apparent in his last two films, which react against what he perceived as a hardening of Soviet montage conventions. After seeing *October*, Shklovsky noted that the "logical" montage of psychological analysis practiced by Kuleshov and Pudovkin had "ceased to be felt." Eisenstein's intellectual montage responded to a need for even more "perceptible" methods (1930:111). *Old and New* sought to go still further, exploring "overtonal montage" as a way of integrating intellectual stimuli with other aspects of the shots.

The urge to experiment drove him to surpass the norms of his own works. As Eisenstein repeatedly insisted, each of his silent films was an answer, a "dialectical" antithesis, to its predecessor. Each offers fresh stylistic experiments and new methods of plot construction, motivic organization, mise-en-scène, and montage. But each film can also be seen as pointing out one path for Soviet film. *Strike* borrows methods of Civil War art, using Eccentrism and mass spectacle to create an openly agitational appeal to the audience. *Potemkin* works within an epic mode, using carefully developed emotional progressions to carry away the spectator. *October*, more episodic than its predecessors, suggests that Left cinema could exploit a pluralistic "montage" of different types of filmic discourse. Finally, *Old and New* seeks not only to make the innovations of the earlier films "intelligible to the millions" but also to imbue Soviet myth with a spiritual fervor. Each film tries something strikingly new, and each offers a different model for heroic realism in Soviet cinema.

Strike (1925)

Strike sets the pattern for Eisenstein's silent features in several ways. It launches his chronicle-myth of revolutionary history; it establishes his mixture of naturalism and stylization; it initiates his research into "film language" and methods of montage. But *Strike* is unique in his oeuvre for its eclectic experimentation, its exuberant leaps of tones and style, its posterlike extremes of clownishness and romanticism. Rediscovered by Western cinéphiles in the mid-1960s, it looked far more vibrant and playful than the master's canonized classics. Its unremitting Eccentrism gives every reel a pursuit, fistfight, or gymnastic exhibition; each scene is enlivened by unexpected pictorial effects or performance flourishes. *Strike* constitutes what Eisenstein and Tretyakov called *Do You Hear, Moscow?*—an "agit-guignol."

The vibrant experiments, however, are held together by a fairly rigorous structure. *Strike* seems loose only in contrast with the extraordinary unity of *Potemkin*.

As in Eisenstein's next two films, the decision to create a mass historical drama impels him to devise a coherent structure and vivid motifs that will carry the propagandistic lesson.

Strike's theme is laid out in the opening quotation from Lenin: "The strength of the working class lies in its organization . . . Organization means unity of action, unity of practical operations." The film's plot traces how Bolshevik factory workers, after laying the groundwork through agitation, turn a spontaneous protest into a strike. At the moment when the strike is born, the factory workers reassert Lenin's lesson: they have power, they say in their meeting, "when we are united in the struggle against capital."

But solidarity loosens. The prolonged strike intensifies workers' family problems. A strike leader, acting in a moment of undisciplined violence, allows a spy to identify him. After police torture, he accepts a bribe to betray his comrades. At the same time, provocateurs from the lumpenproletariat provide the authorities with an occasion to attack the workers. The principal Bolshevik is captured, and the police launch a massacre that sweeps through the workers' quarters. *Strike* both pays homage to the struggles that preceded the October revolution and warns that class solidarity and Party unity must be maintained against enemies, both within and without.

The film insists on the generality of the lesson by presenting a composite of several historical strikes. The action is based upon the 1903 strikes at Rostov-on-the-Don, which spread to more than five hundred factories and involved almost a quarter of a million workers. But the film, shot in and around Moscow, makes no explicit reference to these events; indeed, Alexandrov claims that spectators did not recognize the historical source (1976:43). The film further generalizes the action with a concluding title that lists other strikes that were harshly repressed, ranging from a 1903 massacre of workers in the Urals to a 1915 strike in spinning factories. As the film's title suggests, *Strike* becomes an anatomy of the forces at work throughout several critical moments of Russian labor's struggle for socialism.

Eisenstein's habitual strategy of making every reel constitute a distinct "chapter" or "act" contributes to this generalizing quality.[2] Each part is presented as a phase through which a typical strike will pass. The first reel, starting with the title "All is quiet at the factory / BUT—" covers the agitational phase of activity. Reel two, labeled "The immediate cause of the strike," dramatizes the theft of a worker's micrometer, the harsh response of the management, and the worker's suicide. The death triggers an uprising that bursts into a full-blown strike. The third reel opens with the title "The factory stands idle" and portrays the effects of inactivity on both the capitalist owners and the workers. Reel four, "The strike is prolonged," traces the debilitating effect of the strike on the workers. Here the turning point comes with the strike leader's betrayal of his comrades. "Engineering a massacre,"

2. Most Soviet theatres and workers' clubs had only a single projector, so filmmakers began to construct their films in reel-length episodes. In *Strike* and *Potemkin* particularly, Eisenstein used this material constraint to demarcate stages of plot action.

the title of the next reel, becomes a parallel to the Bolsheviks' agitation in the factory: a police spy hires some provocateurs. They set fire to a vodka shop, and although the provocation fails, the firemen turn their hoses on the workers, enabling the police to seize the main leader.

Although a spy, the police chief, and the captured Bolshevik appear in the last reel, "Liquidation," the segment functions principally to expand the implications of the dramatic action. First comes a savage cossack assault on workers' tenements. Previously, the factory workers have been shown living in suburban cottages; this new locale becomes a more generalized representation of workers' homes. The tenement massacre is followed by the most abstract sequence of all, the intercutting of cossacks' firing upon an anonymous horde of fleeing workers with butchers' slaughter of a bull. The latter line of action is wholly nondiegetic, pushing the sequence into a realm of pure "attraction." The last reel is virtually a detachable short film, a showcase of Eisenstein's "free montage of attractions" that, operating independently of narrative, stimulate strong emotions and wide-ranging concepts.

Strike, then, presents an anatomy of a political process. It displays the techniques of the revolutionary underground, creating a film that, as Eisenstein somewhat obscurely suggested, paralleled the "production" of a strike with the process of industrial production itself (1925d:59–61). The plot also schematizes the typical stages, tests, and crises through which a strike must pass. In addition, the film diagnoses those forces with which the working class must contend. Seeking to dramatize the class struggle, Eisenstein builds up an enormous range of oppositions between the workers and their class enemies. And many of these call forth the sort of stylization that Eisenstein associated with "theatrical October," the stage pageants during and immediately after the Civil War.

On one side are the forces of capital, personified at the outset by the obese, top-hatted factory director, who leers out at the camera (2.17). He oversees scurrying clerks, disdainful typists, a straw-hatted factory manager, and an old foreman. The director in turn answers to the factory's owners. Aligned with the capitalist and their flunkies are the police, with their herd of spies, and the lumpenproletariat, recruited by the spies. All these forces are presented as a spectrum of stylized types, ranging from the most realistic (the police) through caricature (the capitalists and their staff) and theatrical grotesquerie (the animalistic spies) to circus eccentrism (the hobo king and his retinue). Eisenstein introduces a bizarre touch into even more naturalistic moments: the bribery of the captured Bolshevik by the police administrator is accompanied by a pair of midgets tangoing on the table, their seductive dance mocking the traitor's acquiescence (2.18).

The workers, by contrast, are idealized in a manner typical of "heroic realism," with none of the bourgeois forces' exaggeration of costume or demeanor. Moreover, they are far less individualized. The film's opening depersonalizes the agitators: after the director's frontal close-up, they are presented obliquely, as silhouettes and reflections (2.19). Later, the workers are characteristically shown en masse. Individuals are momentarily picked out, but none is portrayed in depth.

2.17 *Strike.*   2.18

2.19

Indeed, any worker developed as a distinct character is likely to die soon (the suicide) or to join the bourgeoisie (the traitor). And individualization itself is used to point up thematic oppositions. The capitalist's mistress, who frenziedly urges the police agents to beat the captured worker, contrasts with the more anonymous female Bolshevik leader who battles the police to get to the fire alarm.

The contrast between the caricature of class enemies and the romanticization of class allies will become central to Eisenstein's later films, but its sources lie in Civil War art. *Strike* is indebted to the *agitki,* propaganda vehicles that emerged in the wake of the October revolution, particularly the "epic" version seen in poster art and mass festivals, with their satirically individualized rulers pitted against a mass of workers. Mayakovsky's *Mystère-bouffe* and his emblematic designs for store windows had already shown that Left art could utilize such schematic material. The boss's sadistic mistress in Eisenstein's film has a parallel in Tretyakov's *Roar, China!* in which the merchant's daughter eagerly watches two men being strangled.

Strike finds vivid motifs to sharpen its conventional opposition. From the start the workers are associated with machines; when they go on strike, so does the equipment, so that the factory director's typewriter snaps itself away from his touch. The capitalists are associated with an intricate bureaucracy, in the factory and in the police force. One sequence uses reporting and phone calls to trace the chain of command running from foreman through managers to police officers.

This contrasts with the machine-centered production process in the agitators' printing shop, where a handwritten text becomes—without human intervention—a leaflet, copies of which shower down on a locomotive in the factory. Through the opposition of machines and bureaucracy, Eisenstein again moves to the abstract level, portraying the Marxist distinction between the forces and relations of production. He further shows, by the radicalization of the workers, that a revolutionary situation has come to pass. The progressive factors in the base have outstripped the institutions that they originally supported.

Such clusters of imagery are reversed in the course of the film. Initially the workers occupy the factory catwalks (2.20); but the brutal cossacks eventually take over the catwalks of the tenements (2.21). Whereas the workers are established as in the heights, the lumpenproletariat are introduced as living in huge underground barrels (2.22); soon the Bolshevik leader will be captured by being hosed into a hole and surrounded by barrels (2.23). The children associated with the strikers come to prominence in the last reel, when toddlers become victims of the cossacks' rampage (2.24).

Again and again, Eisenstein's motifs reflect the drama's progression. Three of these—animals, water, and circles—undergo particularly rich development. In each case, a motif initially associated with one side of the political struggle becomes transferred to the other.

In the early scenes the capitalist forces are likened to animals. As the factory sits idle, the factory director is intercut with a crow and a cat. More explicitly, each police spy is given an animal identity: Bulldog, Fox, Owl, and Monkey are visually linked with their counterparts and move in a roughly appropriate fashion. In the same portions of the film, the proletariat are established as being in control of animals: geese and other domestic animals are part of their milieu, and children run a goat in a wheelbarrow as their elders had turned out the factory manager. But at the film's end, it is the workers who are equated with an animal—the bull, slaughtered by a casually proficient butcher likened to the soldiers.

The motif of water develops in the same way. At the film's start, agitating workers are glimpsed in a reflecting puddle; later they plot their conspiracy while swimming. During the battle for the steam whistle during the factory uprising, workers spray water to knock the guard off balance, and a dripping worker joyously pulls the whistle cord. But as the workers' cause wanes, water turns against them. The first leader is captured in a soaking downpour. As the hobo king spruces himself up, he sprays water from his mouth onto his mirror.

Perhaps the richest development of motifs involves a geometrical shape, the circle. Introduced in an intertitle ("HO," that is, "BUT—"), the O takes on a life of its own by becoming a circle and then a rotating wheel in the factory. It is firmly associated with the workers: they run the wheel of a turbine; a wheel turns their printing press. The agitators meet in a scrap heap of wheels (2.25). A crane operator slams the foreman to earth with a suspended wheel, which at another point aggressively hurtles at the camera (2.26). During the strike uprising, wheelbarrows roll the manager and foreman into the runoff pit, while the stopping of

2.20

2.21

2.22

2.23

2.24

the factory is conveyed by a symbolic image showing workers folding their arms and a wheel ceasing to rotate (2.27). As the strike continues, Bolsheviks meet in huge pipes (2.28), another circular contrast with the barrels in which the lumpenproletariat live.

The motifs of water and circularity culminate in the sequence of the firemen's assault. One of the most sensuously arousing passages in Eisenstein's cinema, the hosing sequence uses rhythmic editing and diagonal compositions to create a pulsating movement. The water motif reaches its apogee as spray slashes across the frame in vectors that evoke El Lissitzky's Constructivist compositions (2.29). The firemen turn their hoses' punishing force on the workers. Now the wheel is

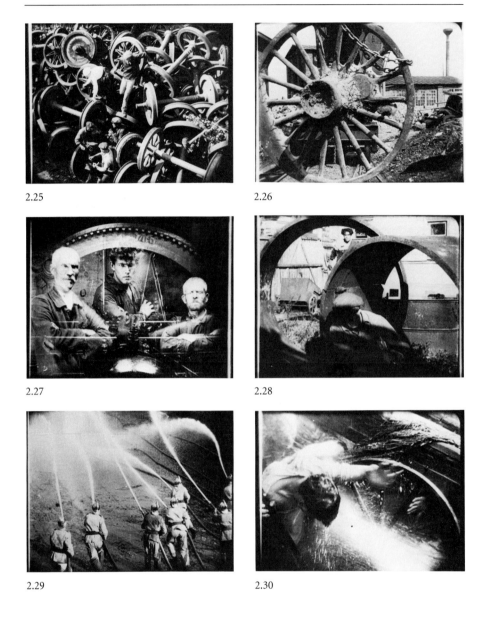

2.25

2.26

2.27

2.28

2.29

2.30

on a fire truck, working against the strikers; the spume pins a worker helplessly
to a cartwheel (2.30). In terms that Eisenstein would elaborate in his later theory,
water and circles constitute image-based "lines" that weave through the film and
"knot" in this climactic massacre.

Such opposed and transformed motifs function as associations reinforcing the
film's agitational purpose. Eisenstein uses other means to drive home the lesson.
To a greater degree than his contemporaries, he overtly acknowledges the audience. Most obviously, this direct address occurs in expository intertitles. Eisenstein
has already perfected the ironically echoic intertitle: "Preparation" denotes the
activities of the workers and the police agents; "Beat him!" recurs in scenes in

2.31   2.32

which the captured worker is thrashed. More daringly, Eisenstein creates "collective" intertitles. At the workers' meeting in the factory, for instance, dialogue titles alternate with crowd shots, as if the words issue from the entire mass. Still other titles blur the distinction between diegetic and nondiegetic sources. We must often ask if a line, such as "Thief!" when the worker is accused, comes from a character or the overarching narration itself. Meyerhold approved of Eisenstein's use of such direct address: the intertitle acts directly on the viewer, he suggested, and "the director assumes the role of agitator" (Meyerhold 1925:160).

Images also assault the audience. Sometimes characters face the camera, either in shot/reverse-shot confrontations with other characters or simply in direct address to the spectator. The film concludes with a pair of staring eyes in extreme close-up and the title, "Proletarians, remember!" This final appeal to the audience was a convention of Civil War drama; at the close of *Do You Hear, Moscow?* the protagonist shouted the title line at the audience.

The engagement of the spectator arises more indirectly from Eisenstein's use of symbols and tropes. Like other art deriving from the Civil War tradition, *Strike* invokes religious iconography. The scene of the worker's suicide becomes a proletarian Descent from the Cross (2.31), and the writhing figures of demonstrators under the firemen's fusillade of hoses echo the postures of martyrs (2.32). *Strike* also shows a firm commitment to metaphorical filmmaking. Sometimes the intertitles create the linkage, as when, after the factory director petulantly kicks his wicker chair off his patio, a title remarks: "Their thrones rest on the labor of the workers." Some titles are integrated with the visual motifs more dynamically. The title "Spreading ripple," coming after the shot of workers reflected in a puddle, ties the agitational process to the water motif and suggests the expansion of the workers' discontent. At the end of the firehose sequence, an abstract burst of spray introduces the final reel, punningly titled "Liquidation": the literal "liquidation" has been a prelude to the massacre.

Eisenstein explores an assortment of purely visual metaphors as well. Most are firmly located within the story world and are brought to our attention by means of close-ups and editing. Through crosscutting, the capitalists' squeezing juice out of a lemon becomes analogous to the harassment of strikers by the mounted

2.33   2.34

2.35

police. Intercutting the machine belts with the worker's belt (2.33, 2.34) makes his suicide an ironic contrast to the machines' activity. The animal motifs we have already considered are largely metaphorical, rendering the police spies bestial through symbolic superimpositions (2.35).

In this connection, the last sequence is especially revelatory. Eisenstein has often been criticized for intercutting the final massacre with nondiegetic footage of the butchering of a bull. Kuleshov, for instance, objected that the slaughter-house footage is "not prepared by a second, parallel line of action" (Kuleshov 1967:32). A more narratively motivated treatment would situate the slaughter-house in the time and space of the story, as the pet shop contextualizes the animal imagery that characterizes the spies. But it is clear that after using so many diegetically motivated metaphors—beasts, belts, lemon-squeezer, and so on— Eisenstein experimented with a more conceptual possibility.

Eisenstein prepares for the leap into nondiegetic metaphor by a rapid series of more motivated ones. Confronted by the defiant Bolshevik leader, the raging police chief pounds his desk, knocking bottles of ink across the map of the workers' district. The shot literalizes the metaphor of "the streets running with blood" (2.36). The chief slaps his hand in the pool of ink, giving himself the gory hand of the executioner. Now comes the leap. Eisenstein cuts to connect the chief's pounding gesture (2.37) to that of the butcher coming down to stab the bull (2.38), and the nondiegetic metaphor emerges—a literal slaughter in an

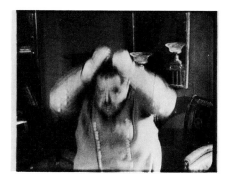

2.36   2.37

2.38

abstract time and space, a figurative slaughter in the story world. In context, the slaughter sequence climaxes the film's experimentation with metaphor by catapulting the event into a realm outside the time and space of the story. In *October* we will find that the nondiegetic metaphors dominate the first half of the film and become "narrativized" in the course of the action.

The wide-ranging exploration of cinema's metaphorical possibilities is typical of *Strike*'s pluralistic approach. The performances, especially in the capitalist faction, constitute an anthology of contemporary theatrical styles. A similar breadth of experimentation characterizes the film's editing. At many points Eisenstein demonstrates his command of orthodox editing strategies: the breathless crosscutting between tumultuous strikers and the steam whistle, for instance, or the crisp shot/reverse shot when Monkey negotiates with the king. On the whole, however, the film moves a critical distance away from American-style editing and from Kuleshov's earliest work.

We have seen that Eisenstein's overlapping presentation of the wheel's assault on the foreman revises Kuleshov's reworking of American-style expansion of movement. This is only the extreme edge of a practice that pushes visual fragmentation to unprecedented limits. When Owl struggles into his pants, Eisenstein breaks the action into six shots, with slight overlaps and ellipses. As the strikers burst into the factory courtyard, seven shots of the swinging gates present graphically smooth but spatially inconsistent movement. Eisenstein often treats his

2.39

2.40

2.41

sensational attractions less as discrete elements within the shot than as kinesthetic impulses to be connected by cutting. As the strikers dump the foreman and the manager into the muck, an old woman's fiercely pounding forearms continue the gesture of descent. The pulsating crowd in the hosing sequence becomes, thanks to editing, pure patterns of flowing or clashing movement.

Despite his eclecticism, Eisenstein is at pains to organize many of his editing techniques. He systematizes Kuleshov's manipulation of dissolves, superimpositions, and similar optical devices. He associates the police agents with irises and mirrors, as if to present visual analogues of their spying (2.39). He pushes such camera tricks further when he introduces the spies as a set of animated photos (2.40), a motif that finds its parallel when the clandestine photo of the strike leader comes furtively to life. Later, the agitators meet in a cemetery (itself a token of the strike's decline), and Eisenstein superimposes the fist of the police chief hovering over a pen (2.41), not only indicating his power over them but also foreshadowing the hand that will hammer the ink-bloodied map in the last sequence.

That sequence also exhibits the most elaborate of Eisenstein's "montage of attractions." The editing certainly has some linguistic and conceptual basis. The workers are figuratively "slaughtered," and the metaphor endows the soldiers' act with the connotations of impersonal, efficient butchery. The cutting works out the conceptual parallels: as the soldiers fire, blood pours out of the bull. But

Eisenstein's primary goal of provoking the spectators' emotions poses problems for the cinema. Whereas Grand Guignol theatre shocks its audience by portraying decapitations or electrocutions, the cinema, being a mediated presentation, must stir its audience to political consciousness through pictorial associations. The massacre scene can gain maximal intensity only if the filmmaker arouses the proper associations. Thus the documentary shots dwelling on the bull's torrential bloodletting and thrashing legs aim less to tease the mind than to arouse a revulsion that will take the massacre as its object. Eisenstein told a visitor that the bull's death should "stir the spectator to a state of pity and terror which would be unconsciously and automatically transferred to the shooting of the strikers" (Freeman 1930:222).

Looking back from 1934, Eisenstein reflected that *Strike* "floundered about in the flotsam of a rank theatricality" (1934i:16), perhaps tacitly acknowledging its mixture of Eccentric and epic tendencies. It seeks to create a heroic Soviet cinema by leavening the "monumental" aesthetic of the Civil War years with elements of theatrical grotesquerie. Nevertheless, *Strike* establishes Eisenstein's creative method as one of balancing set pieces and ornamental flourishes against a pervasive unity of theme, technique, and motif.

The Battleship Potemkin (1925)

The Battleship Potemkin was long considered the masterwork of the silent cinema. In 1958 an international critics' poll voted it the greatest film of all time. In later years, however, the film slipped into the shadows, an object of casual acceptance or debunking dismissal. Even for Eisensteinians the rediscovery of *Strike* and the reevaluation of *October* made *Potemkin* seem a tame official classic.

For our purposes, *Potemkin*'s importance is manifold. Within Eisenstein's career, its stringent unity represents an attempt to turn the experimentation of *Strike* to fresh purposes. With respect to film form, Eisenstein's subtleties run deeper than is generally supposed. The careful organization of the film's chapters and episodes is matched by rich development of visual motifs. Eisenstein also explores certain staging and editing options with an unprecedented rigor, a tendency that reaches its culmination in the Odessa Steps sequence. More generally, *Potemkin* can be seen as a synthesis and transcendence of contemporary tendencies in literature and theatre. Owing less to Constructivism than to NEP "heroic realism," *Potemkin* lays down one path for a distinctively Soviet cinema.

At the time, Eisenstein insisted that *Potemkin* was not simply the successor to *Strike* but a contemporary answer to it. As the NEP assimilated market economics, he claimed, so *Potemkin* deliberately adopts the "pathos" of "right art": sentiment, lyricism, psychological portrayal, and passionate fervor. And as NEP policy aimed to achieve socialism through a deliberate swerve in the *opposite* direction—that is, through capitalism—so *Potemkin* seeks to arouse emotion and partisanship by more traditional cinematic means. Putting aside the possibly disingenuous comparison with the NEP, we can see that Eisenstein considers *all* stimuli potentially of equal value in creating the desired effect on the spectator. The mists of Odessa Harbor become no less powerful than a slaughtered bull (1926b:68).

Another source of emotional engagement in the film is Eisenstein's decision to restrict our knowledge. *Strike, October,* and *Old and New* utilize omniscient narration that shuttles freely between protagonist and antagonist, always supplying the spectator with the maximum amount of information. In *Potemkin,* with the exception of a few moments showing the plotting of the ship's officers, Eisenstein confines us wholly to what the affirmative characters know and feel. The attack on the Odessa Steps startles the viewer because there has been no indication of what the cossacks have been planning. Similarly, suspense is aroused at the climax by Eisenstein's refusal to take us aboard the tsarist fleet and divulge the officers' reaction to the *Potemkin*'s passage. In general, by restricting our range of knowledge to the progressive forces in the struggle, the narration solicits a stronger emotional tie with them.

Potemkin, then, aims at revolutionary pathos. "*Strike* is a treatise; *Potemkin* is a hymn" (1926b:69). It is no less an attack on the audience, but by more unified and "motivated" means: not an agit-guignol but a Communist epic. Eccentrism survives only in subdued form, as the somersaults of officers hurled overboard or the mild caricature of the priest. Whereas *Strike* uses the Civil War aesthetic of agitation to pay homage to aborted insurrections, *Potemkin* is Eisenstein's first saga of revolutionary triumph. The Lenin epigraph in *Strike* serves as a warning, but the epigraph for *Potemkin* launches a national *epos:*

> Revolution is the only lawful, equal, effectual war. It was in Russia that this war was declared and begun.
>
> —Lenin

The generalized composite of events offered by *Strike* is replaced by a precise delineation of three days in 1905 when mutinous sailors were caught up in the spirit of revolution. In *Potemkin,* the Bolshevik appropriation of revolutionary impulses finds concrete and heroic manifestation.

That manifestation, as we might expect, owes more to mythmaking than to historical fidelity. Although Eisenstein was proud of his research into records and the mutineers' memoirs, and although he used the student agitator Konstantin Feldman as a performer and a historical consultant, the film takes great liberties. (See Amengual 1980:155–159; and Wenden 1981.) Eisenstein synthesizes 1905 events: the mourning over Vakulinchuk in Odessa refers to an interlude during the Moscow uprisings, and the Steps sequence fuses the Odessa massacre with one in Baku. Through the use of typage, the sneering anti-Semite at Vakulinchuk's tent becomes a premonition of the reactionary Black Hundreds society that emerged as a response to the 1905 uprising. Most notably, the triumphant ending cuts the historical episode short, omitting reference to the eventual exile and imprisonment of the mutineers. "We stop the event at this point where it had become an 'asset' to the revolution," Eisenstein admitted (1926b:67). Twenty years later he explained that the ending shows 1905 to be "an objectively victorious episode, the harbinger of the triumph of the October Revolution" (1945b:29).

As in *Strike,* history is made collectively: the sailors are driven to rebellion, the Odessa citizens are stirred by Vakulinchuk's sacrifice, the fleet refuses to fire on the *Potemkin.*[3] But *Potemkin's* referential dimension, as well as its urge to arouse emotion, allows for a new relation between the individual and the mass. In *Strike* the bourgeois forces, though typed, are far more individuated than the Bolsheviks. By contrast, accounts of the *Potemkin* mutiny had already created a gallery of heroes: the agitator Matyushenko, the martyr Vakulinchuk, the student Feldman, and others. Though broadly portrayed in Eisenstein's film, these individuals have more distinctive identities than do the agitators and workers of *Strike.* Even the anonymous townspeople slaughtered on the Steps are more vividly characterized than the massacre victims in the previous film. Tretyakov commented that playwrights had trouble "in shifting from the depiction of human *types* to the construction of the *standards* (exemplary models)" (Stephan 1981:184). *Strike* failed to make this shift; *Potemkin* succeeds. Its creation of "exemplary models" marks a new phase in heroic realism in Soviet cinema.

The film breaks into five distinct parts, each corresponding to a reel and bearing a "chapter title." Most reels contain two or more segments, yielding a total of ten distinct sequences. This "plot-carcass," as Eisenstein called it (1926c:75), presents an ever-expanding revolutionary impulse. Like the waves that crash on shore in the opening shots, rebellion steadily gathers force, spreading from agitators to a faction of the crew, to the entire crew, to all sectors of the populace of Odessa, and finally to the tsarist navy.

Structure of *The Battleship Potemkin*

I. Men and Worms
   1. Vakulinchuk and Matyushenko meet on the bridge.
   2. Crew's quarters: The first mate whips a sleeping sailor; Vakulinchuk agitates.
   3. Morning: The crew objects to the rotten meat.
   4. Lunch: The crew refuses the soup.

II. Drama in Tendre Harbor
   5. The captain prepares to execute the dissenters; the crew mutinies. Vakulinchuk is killed.
   6. A launch takes Vakulinchuk's body to shore in Odessa.

III. An Appeal from the Dead
   7. Morning: Odessa's citizens discover Vakulinchuk's body lying in state. Agitators arouse the populace.

3. According to Hill 1978, the film's original epigraph was from Trotsky: "The spirit of insurrection hovered over the Russian land . . . The individual was dissolving in the mass, and the mass was dissolving in the outburst" (74–86).

IV. The Odessa Steps
    8. Citizens bring supplies to the *Potemkin*. Onlookers on the Steps are massacred.

V. Meeting the Squadron
    9. The sailors meet and resolve to confront the navy.
    10. After a night of tense waiting, the *Potemkin* meets the squadron and is allowed to pass through.

Within each part the curve of dramatic intensity rises. In "Men and Worms,"[4] for instance, the discontent of the crew grows: a sleeping sailor takes a casual whipping; the men object to the worm-ridden meat; they refuse to eat the soup; at the end of the reel, the abused sailor disgustedly smashes a plate. Similarly, reel two's insurrection builds up gradually, from the men's calm breaking of ranks, through the intensification of suspense during the execution, to the long-suppressed outburst ("Brothers!") and Vakulinchuk's rallying cry: "Kill the dragons!" *Strike* takes it for granted that the workers have long suffered exploitation, but *Potemkin*'s mutiny is the culmination of a series of vividly particular indignities.

After Eisenstein left Proletkult, a colleague recalled, he transformed his initial experiments "into an orderly aesthetic system" (Levshin 1966:64). The rigorous architecture of *Potemkin* shows just how highly organized this new approach was. Each reel, for instance, concludes on a dramatic note: the sailor smashing the plate, Vakulinchuk's body lying on the jetty, the red flag (hand-colored) snapping atop the mast, the *Potemkin*'s bombardment of the generals' headquarters, and the low-angle shot of the battleship's prow slashing upward across the screen.

Similar parallels inform the sequences as units. In a 1939 essay Eisenstein points out that most of the reels split into contrasting parts. Thus the tension on the quarterdeck erupts into the mutiny; the calm mourning for Vakulinchuk leads to the angry meeting. In each reel, a pause marks the transition from one phase to another. Eisenstein also suggests that the same structure is found in the film as a whole, with the misty opening of "An Appeal from the Dead" serving as a large-scale caesura (1939f:14–15).

One could also see the five parts as forming a headpiece and two pairs of structurally comparable segments. Part I is expository and relatively elliptical in its presentation of several episodes spread out over a night and a morning. But then we have symmetry. Part II (Drama in Tendre Harbor) and Part IV (The Odessa Steps) both concentrate on a single day's events, and both explode into violence. Parts III (An Appeal from the Dead) and V (Meeting the Squadron) have a somewhat different structure: each part moves from night to dawn, then traces a rising tension that culminates in the assertion of group unity.

In another sense, of course, Part V neatly answers Part I in that the rebellion

---

4. Throughout this chapter I provide a literal translation of the Russian titles rather than standard translations. As we shall see, "Men and Worms" has a significance not captured by the "Men and Maggots" of the standard English-language version.

2.46

2.47

2.48

2.49

2.50

2.51

2.52

2.53   2.54

2.55   2.56

2.57   2.58

crowd and others thrust their caps up (2.53). The sorrowful hands knot into fists
(2.54). Another agitator, this time a woman, raises her fist (2.55). Now the weeping
woman of an earlier shot recapitulates the movement from sorrow to rage:
clutching her handkerchief, she makes a sweeping fist (2.56, 2.57). As if launched
by her gesture, other arms burst into the air, and soon the entire crowd is shaking
its fists in anger (2.58). *Strike* has nothing like these minute modulations from
one expressive gesture to another.

The same fine-grained process governs the use of intertitles. "All for one" cuts
to a group of four workers; "And one—" is followed by a shot of the dead
Vakulinchuk; "—for all" cuts to an extreme long-shot of the people gathered by

the pier. This intertitle becomes a motif in itself. In Part V the *Potemkin* confronts the squadron, and the title "One against all" precedes a shot of the cannon swiveling to the camera; "All against one" follows soon after—the titles emphasizing the separation that is soon to dissolve into the joyous cry of "Brothers!"

Eisenstein often coordinates intertitles with images to create metaphorical motifs. A shot of boiling soup is followed by shots of sailors angry about the rotten meat, and a title tells us that the men's rage "overflowed" all bounds. A similar tactic gives a poetic cast to titles in the opening of segment 6. "With the night, a mist spread . . . ," and shots of mist lead to "From the pier a rumor spread . . ." Then come shots of the city awakening, accompanied by the title, "Along with the sun, the news made its way into the city . . ." The news of the rebellion is compared to the natural processes of mist and daylight seeping from the sea into the port. Such verbal-visual associations form part of Eisenstein's conception of "film language" at the time and anticipate notions of "intellectual" montage. In his theoretical writings, as we will see, Eisenstein considers both verbal and visual metaphors to be extensions of basic kinesthetic ones.

Across the entire film we find the same detailed reworking of motifs. Meat hangs, mess tables hang, and eventually men and eyeglasses hang. The hammocks of sequence 1 anticipate the tarpaulin tossed over the condemned seamen in sequence 5, which is soon used to wrap officers before they are chucked over the side. Similar stretches of canvas become Vakulinchuk's tent (Part III) and the sails of the boats that bring supplies to the ship (Part IV). In the final reel, the tarpaulin finds its authentic function when men use it to cradle shells lugged to the cannons.

A more central motif is that of the single eye. It is introduced in sequence 3 when Dr. Smirnov examines the meat (2.59) and declares that the worms are only maggots. The single eye is initially linked to a power that simply denies visible truth. During the mutiny (sequence 5) the motif becomes a sign of duplicity when the priest feigns unconsciousness but checks his surroundings by opening one eye. Soon after this, as Gilyarovsky fires at Vakulinchuk, Eisenstein gives us an extreme close-up of his eye widening (2.60). But in segment 8, a title tells us that "Alert and sharp-sighted, the shore watched over the battleship," transferring the power of vision to the townspeople. At the end of the scene, however, the old schoolmistress on the Odessa Steps suffers a hideous wound to the eye (2.61). Like the animal motif in *Strike*, the single-eye motif now evokes not the strength or cunning of the oppressors but the suffering of their victims.

So tightly intertwined are *Potemkin*'s motivic "lines," though, that the eye motif cannot be fully understood apart from a larger imagistic cluster. Another way into the network is provided by the motif of eyeglasses. Smirnov is characterized by his pince-nez, which he uses to scrutinize the rotten meat (2.62). This prop carries stereotyped associations with the petty bourgeoisie and the bourgeoisie.[5]

5. The association would not be unique to Eisenstein's film. In Bely's novel *Petersburg*, for example, spectacles, pince-nez, and lorgnettes are associated with upper-class life.

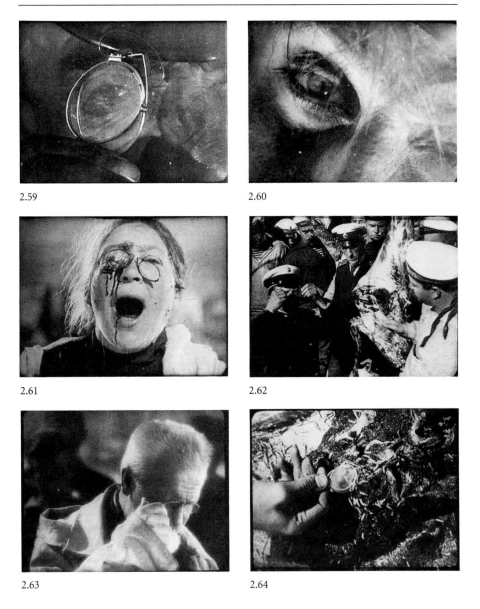

2.59

2.60

2.61

2.62

2.63

2.64

But since Eisenstein's aim is to show Russia uniting against tsarist rule, he presents many of Odessa's middle-class citizens as aligned with the rebellion. Well-dressed women with parasols join workers at the tent sheltering Vakulinchuk's body. An old man, typed as a pensioner or a shopkeeper, takes off his pince-nez to weep (2.63). A student with spectacles, a rich woman with a lorgnette, and a school-mistress with a pince-nez cheer the *Potemkin* at anchor. On the Odessa Steps, however, the troops indiscriminately open fire. Thus the image of the schoolmistress' wounded eye and smashed pince-nez (2.61) bears witness to a brutal widening of the struggle. All classes fall victim to tsarist oppression.

The motivic linkage of the eye and the pince-nez nicely exemplifies the principle

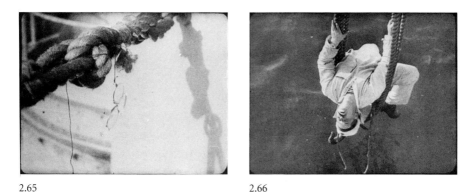

2.65   2.66

of the "double blow" that Eisenstein would articulate in his pedagogy of the 1930s. The wounding of the woman's eye is repeated and intensified in the cracking of the lens of her pince-nez, just as the effect of the worms wriggling on the meat is amplified by Smirnov's folded-over pince-nez, which he uses as a magnifying glass (2.64).

These elements are suspended within a still broader web of metaphorical motifs. One nodal point involves the rotten meat. The first reel's "chapter title," "Men and Worms," initiates a complicated series of analogies. When the crew complains of the rotten meat, Smirnov's point-of-view shot shows wriggling worms. "These are not worms," he announces, "only dead maggots." Apart from portraying his denial of the truth, the episode clinches the metaphor: the navy's oppression reduces the men to parasites, with rotten meat their natural food. But when Smirnov is thrown overboard, an intertitle compares him with the meat ("He has gone to the bottom to feed the worms") and a brief image shows the infested meat. In this new parallel, the old order is rotten. By contrast, the opening of sequence 8, in which Odessa's boats bring fresh bread and meat to the battleship, shows the Russian people nourishing the uprising.

Smirnov is another motivic knot. After he confronts Vakulinchuk over the meat, the two are made parallel. Smirnov is thrown overboard; Vakulinchuk tumbles over. Smirnov clutches at ropes in resisting the mutineers; Vakulinchuk's body is snagged by ropes from the winch. And when Smirnov is flung overboard, his pince-nez is shown dangling from the rigging (2.65). Apart from strengthening the eyeglass motif, the shot is quickly paralleled with the image of the slain Vakulinchuk, hanging above the sea (2.66). Interestingly, it is not the elimination of Captain Golikov that marks the crew's victory but rather the dunking of Smirnov, the real embodiment of tsarist oppression; at almost the same moment the leader of the rebellion becomes its first martyr.

Integral to *Potemkin*'s conception of "heroic realism," then, is a core of realistically motivated elements—eyes, eyeglasses, meat, worms, dangling objects, and so on—that can radiate into a network of emotional and thematic implications. Instead of creating isolated, posterlike "attractions," Eisenstein assumes that ever-expanding metaphorical fields will stimulate complex emotional associations in

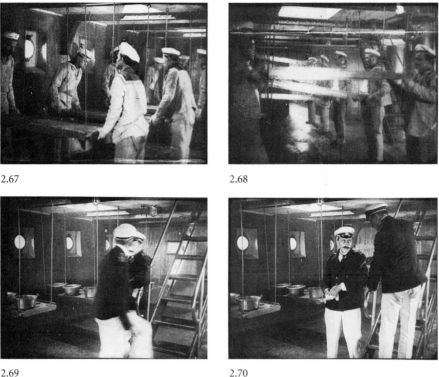

2.67   2.68

2.69   2.70

the spectator. Writing in 1929 about shot-to-shot organization, he notes that in cinema, an action is effective only when presented "in montage pieces, each of which provokes a certain association, the sum of which amounts to a composite complex of emotional feeling" (1929c:178). Although he does not make the point, longer-range motif-based associations also govern his filmmaking.

A comparable rigor and concentration inform *Potemkin*'s staging and editing. Certain cutaways, especially during the mutiny, comment on adjacent action in straightforward ways. For example, after an officer is flung overboard, Eisenstein cuts to the still-mounted life preserver that will not help him. Eisenstein's new emphasis on extensively developed scenes also allows him to push his rapid cutting further. Alexander Levshin recalls that he usually filmed retakes from different angles so that during cutting he "could literally swim in editing pieces" (Levshin 1966:67). Many passages have a jittery quality, rendering a single actor or action in a flurry of shots that jump to and fro between two angles. Sometimes an action notably overlaps from shot to shot, as when the mess attendants lower the hanging tables (2.67, 2.68). Eisenstein also relies on a device explored occasionally in *Strike*: accentuating an action by repeating it almost *in toto* in succeeding shots (2.69–2.71). But such overlapping cuts typically alternate with smoother or more elliptical ones, so Eisenstein gains many possibilities for rhythmic emphasis.

Above all, Eisenstein's cutting on movement generates oscillating conflicts. In a hail of overlapping shots, a sailor knocks an officer off a cannon; at each moment

2.71

2.72

2.73

his swing slices in opposite directions. When the tarpaulin is tossed, a cut to the opposite side contrasts the guards' gesture of flinging it with the protesting arms of the victims (2.72, 2.73). The priest taps his cross into his palm, but the two shots render the action contradictory by making the cross switch hands over the cut (2.12, 2.13).

The film's dramaturgical and stylistic concentration reaches its apogee in the sequence on the Odessa Steps (Part IV). As already suggested, its didactic function is to show the punishment exacted on all classes for the spread of the revolutionary impulse. Narratively, the episode develops out of sequence 7, which shows Vakulinchuk's body lying in the tent. This presents the people uniting with the sailors' cause while introducing some of the "cast" of the Steps scene. In addition, the earlier part of 7 identifies Odessa with several flights of steps. People pour down them to the pier, which serves as a middle ground joining sea and city, sailors and citizens. At the end of the sequence, Odessa is bound more tightly to the ship when Eisenstein shows various classes of people on flights of steps waving to the sailors.

In the first half of the Steps scene, citizens bring supplies to the ship while the people on shore watch over them. Again, braided motifs bind the shots together. Eisenstein discusses some graphic elements in one passage, as we shall see in Chapter 5; for now we can notice a particularly careful knitting of elements during the crowd's waving to the ship. The modulating motifs are italicized:

1. (ms):   Old *woman* with *pince-nez* and younger girl, the latter *waving* with her *left* hand (2.74). This shot introduces the schoolmistress, who will furnish one of the "counter-movements" of the sequence; the shot also picks up the pince-nez motif.

2. (mcu):   *Well-to-do woman* with *lorgnette*; she starts to *twirl* it in her *right* hand (2.75). Her gesture is continued by:

3. (ms):   *Well-to-do woman* with *parasol*; she *twirls* it in her *right* hand as she *waves* her *left* hand (2.76).

4. (mls):   Another *parasol* is opened (2.77); a legless *man* comes into the shot and *waves* his *right* hand (2.78).

5. (mcu) as 2: *Well-to-do woman* with *lorgnette twirls* it with her *right* hand (2.79). Her gesture matches that of the man in 4.

6. (mls) as 4: The legless *man* grabs his *cap* and *waves* it in his *right* hand (2.80).

By intertwining various items in the image—woman/man, rich/poor, right/left, waving/twirling, pince-nez/lorgnette/cap—Eisenstein presents the cross-class solidarity aroused by the *Potemkin*'s rebellion. The caps and fists shaken in anger in Part III have become caps, hands, and eyeglasses waved in fraternal greeting.

"Suddenly": one of the most famous titles in world cinema introduces four percussive shots of a woman's body jerking spasmodically (2.81). Barely comprehensible in projection, the jump-cut series of shots functions, Eisenstein remarks, as the detonator in an explosion (1964:85–86). But it also breaks apart the unified diegetic space of the scene. Where is this woman located? (The blank white background gives no information.) What exactly has happened to her? Are we seeing her staggered again and again by a fusillade, or is this a single convulsion presented repeatedly (as scenes aboard the *Potemkin* repeat events like the laying of the mess tables)? This four-shot series begins to loosen up the space of the Steps, presenting "quasi-diegetic" images: never completely outside the story world (as are the butcher and bull in *Strike*), yet not firmly located in it, they function as immediate perceptual and emotional stimuli.

As soldiers stalk down the staircase and begin firing, the action breaks into several lines. The overall momentum is provided by the crowd, which descends en masse. (As Shklovsky notes, the use of two amputees emphasizes the steps as such [1926a:7].) Within the crowd's flight two parallel lines of action are crosscut. One centers on the schoolmistress with the pince-nez, who huddles with a group. The other line of action involves a mother whose little boy is shot. The two lines of action create an upward thrust that opposes the descending troops. But the expressive qualities of the two lines differ sharply. The schoolmistress leads her group upward in an imploring attitude, trying to appeal to the soldiers. The mother, half-demented, carries her son up the steps to confront the riflemen and demand help. Cutting between the shots contrasts expressive gestures of beseeching and defiance (2.82, 2.83).

The mother is shot down mercilessly, and the old woman's companions fall to

2.74

2.75

2.76

2.77

2.78

2.79

2.80

2.81

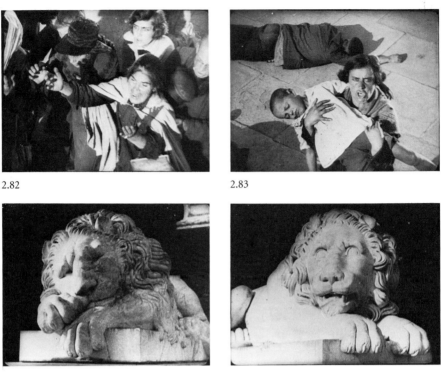

2.82   2.83

2.84   2.85

another volley. There emerges a third line of action, one involving another mother and her baby. She is shot, and her crumpling fall sends her baby carriage jouncing down the steps. As the cossacks cut off the crowd at the foot of the stairs, the carriage intensifies the descending movement of the crowd. And now another series of close-ups frees the imagery from the dramatic space. The schoolmistress' face is intercut with the baby carriage, but we cannot be sure that she is watching it. The carriage upends, its destiny suspended. A cossack fiercely slashes with his saber, but nothing firmly establishes him as attacking the infant. After four shots of him slashing (twice) we are shown the old woman's smashed eye (2.61); is this a saber gouge or a bullet wound? The scene thus climaxes in a string of galvanizing attractions. Their force comes partly from their sharing a concrete diegetic realm, and partly from their being pushed toward a purer, more direct arousal.

The move into a realm that is only loosely diegetic is repeated and intensified when the *Potemkin*'s guns target the military headquarters. The attack reiterates, at a higher level, the unity between sea and city forged by the citizens' trips out to the ship. As the cannons swivel, three shots of bronze Cupids adorning the theatre are edited to suggest their panicky flight from the onslaught. After the bombardment, three shots of sculpted lions combine to create the image of a single lion leaping to his feet (2.84–2.86). Since the lions were prominent Crimean landmarks (2.87), Eisenstein probably assumed that they would not be taken as existing in the abstract realm of *Strike*'s slaughtered bull. Like the jerking woman at the beginning of the sequence, they are quasi-diegetic. But what is their function in the climax of the sequence?

In general, the shots imply an upheaval that shakes even statues to life. Like many of Eisenstein's cinematic tropes, however, the passage is polysemous. Perhaps the leaping lions represent the generals stirred to rage by the bombardment. But the lion is usually associated with courage, a quality unlikely to be ascribed to the forces that ordered the Steps massacre. The lions may also be taken to symbolize the Russian people, aroused by the massacre and reasserting themselves in the ship's counterattack. This reading would be consistent with Eisenstein's

2.86

2.87 The Lions' Terrace of the Palace Museum in Alupka, a city in the Crimea.

somewhat oblique formulation: "The marble lion leaps up, surrounded by the thunder of *Potemkin*'s guns firing in protest against the bloodbath on the Odessa Steps" (1929c:174).

But "symbolic pictorial expression" (1929c:172) is only part of Eisenstein's purpose. His writing gives far more attention to the emotional and perceptual side of the passage. The rampant lion, he says, exemplifies the "artificially pro-

timent are sharply expressed. Yet the film's version of events is selective and exaggerated in many ways. Eisenstein never details the behind-the-scenes wrangling within the Bolshevik ranks, nor does he articulate the positions of the Mensheviks and the Social Revolutionaries. In accordance with Bolshevik historiography, he also presents the 25 October coup as far more carefully planned than it was. The small detachment that invaded the Winter Palace becomes—for all time—a crowd of thousands. A *New Lef* critic objected to Eisenstein's portrayal of Red sailors virtuously destroying the wine in the tsar's cellar, recalling that the sailors in fact drank it: "The result is not a symbol, not a poster, but a lie" (Pertsov 1928:319).

Other key events are altered for ideological effect. The 10 October Central Committee meeting, which did not set a date for the insurrection, becomes in Eisenstein's hands a vote for an exact date (based in turn on a mythical story about what Lenin said on another occasion). Moreover, the two dissenting votes on the committee are not presented. (In order to preserve Lenin's persona, the film also neglects to show that he came to this meeting clean-shaven.) Similarly, Lenin's address to the Soviet Congress, which in the film seems to follow the capture of the Palace immediately, actually occurred in the evening of the following day.

As indicated in Chapter 1, one of the key distortions involves the role of Trotsky. For several years after the Revolution Trotsky was praised, even by Stalin, as the leader of the uprising; but by the end of 1927 he was being vilified as a traitor and saboteur. He appears in the film only in the scene showing the 10 October meeting, where he is shown arguing with Lenin before grudgingly voting for insurrection with the rest of the group.

Trotsky nonetheless remains present in ghostly ways. A ringing phrase from one of his speeches—"The time for words is past!"—is put into another Bolshevik's mouth during the congress debates. More visibly, Trotsky is replaced by V. A. Antonov-Ovseenko, the secretary of the Military Revolutionary Committee. It is he who coordinates the attack on the Winter Palace, issues the ultimatum to the Provisional Government, and charges into the palace to arrest the ministers. A contemporary audience would have recognized Antonov as a Trotskyite who had only recently been reconciled to Stalin's supremacy.

The film abounds in such oblique references to the events of 1917. Why does Eisenstein show machine-gunners disarmed and arrested after the "July Days" massacre? Because the demonstrations had their origins in the Bolshevik-dominated First Machine Gun Regiment. Why are Kerensky and Kornilov represented as twin Napoleon statues? Not only because both were accused of tyrannical ambitions; according to the Bolsheviks, Kornilov planned the coup in collusion with Kerensky. A shot of a newspaper sinking into the river refers to the Provisional Government's closing down of *Pravda*. A rifle assembling itself after the aborted coup becomes a poetic image for the clandestine arming of the Bolshevik forces. When Kerensky is fleeing the palace, his vehicle flies an American flag because the U.S. embassy loaned him a car.

2.89 *The Fall of the Romanov Dynasty* (Esfir Shub, 1927).

2.90 *The Great Way* (Esfir Shub, 1927).

From such citations it is a short step to more symbolic allusions. For example, the film's opening represents the downfall of the aristocrats in almost allegorical fashion. Although it is Nicholas II who is deposed, the film begins with shots of a gigantic statue of his father, Alexander III. By starting with a symbol of a tsar particularly hated by the Bolsheviks, Eisenstein portrays the tsarist regime as a whole. A female worker mounts the statue and summons workers to throw ropes around it. This gesture alludes to the fact that the February revolution was triggered by strikes of female textile workers on International Women's Day. As the ropes tighten, Eisenstein suddenly shows the statue unencumbered and tumbling down of its own accord. The statue's self-propelled downfall indicates the Marxist dialectic at the center of the Russian Revolution: spontaneous class action brought it about, but the regime collapsed from internal weakness as well.

In reworking historical events, *October* also elaborates on already-circulating conceptions of those events. Eisenstein's film synthesizes versions of the Revolution drawn from many sources. One is John Reed's eyewitness account, *Ten Days That Shook the World* (1919). Reed portrays the Military Revolutionary Committee bending over a map in their Smolny office, a burly sailor halting the Committee to Save the City, the Provisional Government cadets trying to loot the palace, and a small boy clambering atop an armored car and peering down a machine gun's barrel. Eisenstein's film also owes something to Mayakovsky's propagandistic poem *Vladimir Ilych Lenin* (1924), which sketches the plot of *October* and caricatures Kerensky in effeminate terms close to Eisenstein's: "The Premier / wields power / with feathery splendor: / none of your commissar's snarling. / Sings in a tenor / maidenly tender, / even kicks up hysterics, / the darling" (Mayakovsky 1986:177).

Eisenstein creatively reworks newsreel material too. For example, the statue that is hauled down at the outset was in Moscow, not St. Petersburg, and it was pulled down in 1921. Fragments of the actual statue had a prominent role in Esfir Shub's compilation films *The Fall of the Romanov Dynasty* and *The Great Way* (both 1927), in which images of the tsar's orb and a boy sitting on a fragment of the statue look forward to specific shots in *October* (2.89, 2.90). Newsreel footage

2.91 *The Great Way.*

of fraternizing soldiers exchanging caps at the front (2.91) is restaged in *October's* early sequences. The metaphorical elaboration of actuality footage becomes part of Eisenstein's strategy to take his film "beyond the played and the nonplayed" (1928c).

Such correlations reveal more than the sharing of imagery among artists. By the early 1920s, Soviet culture had made the October revolution into a fairly stable story, complete with emblematic incidents and clichéd portrayals of the protagonists. Posters and cartoons presented the heroic sailor and Red Army soldier, the Napoleonic Kerensky, the fighting and uncompromising Lenin surrounded by banners. Parades and floats in the anniversary celebrations of 1927 and 1928 revived the stereotypes of Mensheviks, Social Revolutionaries, and Provisional Government ministers.

Mass anniversary spectacles also promulgated schematic narratives of the Revolution. The 1920 *Storming of the Winter Palace* is particularly apposite for *October.* In November 30,000 spectators gathered to watch the pageant in the square before the Winter Palace. On one platform Kerensky, his ministers, the women's battalion, and the cadets enacted the buffoonery of coalition government. On another platform the Red Guards assembled and grew in strength. Battles between the two forces were fought on a connecting bridge. Armored cars approached, searchlights raked the streets, and salvos from the *Aurora* mingled with rifle and artillery fire. As the government was routed, the palace's windows came alight, revealing silhouettes struggling inside. At the conclusion, sirens, banners, and fireworks celebrated victory. An estimated 10,000 people participated in the production. Such huge reenactments vanished after the Civil War, but their stories and iconography became standardized. *October* can be seen as a synthesis of ten years' development of a revolutionary myth, fixing its images permanently on film.

Accordingly, the film draws upon familiar elements, organizing the dramatic and thematic forces around two poles:

Enemies	The People
Tsarism, Provisional Government, Mensheviks, and Social Revolutionaries	Bolshevik Party
Clowns	Heroes
Winter Palace	Smolny
Languid inertia	Purposeful activity
Grotesque satire	Revolutionary romanticism
Ornate decadence	Streamlined functionality

As we might expect, many motifs are organized around differences between the groups' leaders. Both are rendered in stereotypical ways—Kerensky in his khaki uniform, Lenin in his sanctified gesture of orating while gesturing with his cap. Lenin's arrival at the Finland Station associates him with traditional Soviet iconography such as light, height, and banners. The stasis/dynamism opposition enables Eisenstein to present Kerensky strutting through the palace or sitting on his throne whereas Lenin hurls himself to the top of an armored car. In a luxurious apartment Kerensky toys with a crystal decanter, whereas beside a twig hut Lenin's teakettle steams over the fire.

The basic opposition of forces is manifested through other images. On the enemies' side loom statues, introduced first as an emblem of tsarism and then identified with the Provisional Government. Kerensky's posturing is linked with sculptures of Napoleon, and a statue figuratively crowns him with a laurel wreath. The women's Shock Battalion is juxtaposed with sentimental sculptures of kissing lovers and doting mothers. On another scale, Kerensky's petty ambitions are expressed by cuts to ranks of toy soldiers. By contrast, the Bolsheviks are associated with mechanized weaponry. Kerensky's toy soldiers are compared with rows of pistols at Smolny, and an entire sequence is devoted to the animated assembly of a rifle: "Proletarians, learn to use arms!"

Almost every detail in the film lines up on one side or the other. Kerensky's leather boot lying carelessly on a pillow contrasts with the stiff, rough boots of the peasant delegate to the Soviet Congress. Earlier, the leaping boots in the cossack dance cut directly to Kerensky flopped on a divan, his booted legs floundering. At Smolny, Lenin's shoes, scraping impatiently as he waits for the attack, are contrasted with the pointy shoes of the liberal woman who refuses to stamp her feet during the debates. A central motif, given by the film's title, involves time and timing. Tsarism and the Provisional Government dwell in a world of artificial time. The swirling peacock to which Kerensky is likened forms part of an ornate clock that (as later shots reveal) measures the hours by means of a rotating owl. Upon Lenin's arrival at the Finland Station, however, the Bolsheviks are identified with the clock behind him (2.92), indicating "real," historically dynamic time. The spontaneous uprising of the July days was, in Bolshevik doctrine, an authentic expression of popular will, but, as one orator puts it in the film, "Not until the

2.92 *October.*

2.93

2.94

time is ripe will we give the call to arms." Party leaders quarreled over the schedule for the insurrection, which Trotsky hoped would coincide with the Second Soviet Congress. But in the film as in Soviet historiography, Lenin has the prescience to name the date, and a meticulously planned uprising follows. The last half of the film, set on 25 October, emphasizes the passage of hours and minutes, with Lenin looking at his watch as the twenty-minute ultimatum runs out. In a violation of historical verisimilitude, the storming of the Winter Palace coincides with the stroke of midnight (2.93). At the moment of success, a flurry of clocks showing the time around the world emphasizes the event's historical significance (2.94). *October*'s insistence that the Bolsheviks mastered history by mastering time exemplifies a broader tendency in 1920s Soviet culture, also manifested in the "Time League," which rooted out inefficient work processes.

Such motifs are imbued with force by Eisenstein's characteristic methods of staging, shooting, and editing. As in the two previous films, overlapping editing accentuates gestures—the swivel of a parasol, the opening of doors. But Eisenstein has widened his range of poetic editing devices. He pushes rhythmic editing to new limits, as when the cossacks' dance presents shots only one frame long. *October* also goes beyond the earlier films in its synesthesia. A rapidly edited machine gun evokes a hammering rattle; the Bolsheviks' bombardment sets palace chandeliers jingling. Eisenstein also displays a new mastery of the false eyeline-match, as when the soldiers huddling in the trenches (2.95) seem to be shrinking

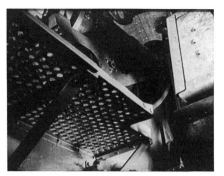

2.95   2.96

from a cannon lowered off the assembly line (2.96). A similar effect is created by sound: through editing, the sailors smashing wine casks in the Winter Palace cellar startle the government ministers upstairs, as if they hear the revolution knocking at their door.

Eisenstein shifts diegetic "registers" across the film as he did during the Odessa Steps sequence. Some elements, such as the descending cannon that seems to flatten the troops, acquire symbolic force without being removed from the story world. In the July Days sequence, many elements, while concretely in the story world, float somewhat free of spatial determination. The links become even more tenuous with the frequent cutaways from Kerensky in the Winter Palace. The toys, cutlery, plates, glassware, and other luxury goods are evidently in the palace, but they are filmed in such intense close-ups or framed against such neutral backgrounds that they seem to hover in a purely symbolic space.[6]

Still more uncertainly placed is the famous mechanical peacock, which spreads its tail and whirls when Kerensky waits for a door to open (2.5). Filmed against a black background, it seems a good candidate for a purely nondiegetic metaphor. Yet the bird is actually part of a clock kept in the palace (2.97).[7] Eisenstein complicates matters by cutting from the peacock to an enormous padlock on the claws of a carved bird; although the padlock links to the following shots of Bolsheviks in prison, it suggests a poetic contrast with the ornate peacock.

Among the most clearly nondiegetic shots are those of harpists and balalaika players, which are intercut with the liberals' pleas for peace during the congress (2.98). Yet even these "conceptual" images develop out of diegetic motifs. Earlier we have seen a languid minister in the palace idly strum an etched glass harp

6. These experiments may have been born of necessity. According to Alexandrov, Eisenstein was annoyed that the objects in the Winter Palace had been filmed in an abstract, unsituated way (Alexandrov 1976: 107). Along similar lines, Tsivian (forthcoming) has suggested that the need to compress an enormous amount of footage led to the breakdown of a concrete space and time: "'Intellectual montage' was born from the attempt to cover the action at a very rapid pace . . . In order to do this, Eisenstein had to strip the diegetic space of many of the orientation marks required for the continuity editing."

7. The peacock clock seems to be a private joke: it was given to Catherine the Great by Admiral Potemkin (Alexandrov 1976: 107–108).

2.97

(2.99). The motif is then picked up by a statue (2.100). Soon the Menshevik orator is compared to the heavenly harpists (2.101, 2.102), who appear to disturb the dozing peasant at the congress (2.103). The motif shifts to statues of angels with lyres before coming to rest with shots of the angel on the pillar outside the Winter Palace. *Strike* carries its animal metaphor from a pet shop into the non-diegetic slaughter of the bull; the harp motif shifts saccharine sanctimony across degrees of diegetic "presence" and across different sensory modes (sight, touch, and sound).

In film history textbooks the July Days episode, particularly the passage involving the rising bridge, ranks second only to the Odessa Steps as evidence of the emotional power of Soviet montage. In its detail it is not as carefully modulated as many scenes in *Potemkin*, but it remains a powerful demonstration of how Eisenstein's editing interweaves motifs and generates dramatic tension.

"July Days" operates under the aegis of the banner, a motif initiated in the previous scene of Lenin's return to St. Petersburg. The sequence opens with a segment showing thousands of workers massing in the streets and gathering at Bolshevik headquarters. Although a Bolshevik orator (another Trotsky surrogate) warns the crowds against insurrection, he is swallowed up in banners (2.104), a

2.98

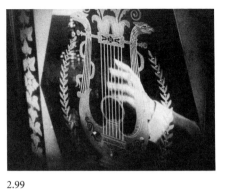

2.99

2.100

2.101

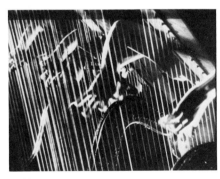

2.102

2.103

2.104

neat way of indicating how the people's undisciplined urgency momentarily overcomes their loyalty to the Party.

The demonstrations reach a corner where, a title tells us, the right-wing press offices stand. Through rapid montage, Eisenstein associates the anti-Bolshevik newspapers with a machine-gun attack on the crowds. At this point, as in the Odessa Steps sequence, several lines of action emerge. The first involves a marcher who tries to save his banner by running to the riverside. There he disrupts an officer cuddling with his doxy. The officer grabs the marcher. Bourgeois women converge and begin thrashing him. Eisenstein claimed to have derived the idea from an episode during the Paris Commune, but it is also an elaboration of *Strike*'s scene of the agitator's capture in the rain. Rapid cross-cutting contrasts the fallen banners with the furled parasols wielded by the ferocious women.

As workers flee across the bridge, a burst of machine-gun fire cuts down a horse pulling a carriage. This assault initiates two parallel lines of action on the bridge. A dead woman lies amid fallen banners; the dead horse lies across the join of the bridge. In the meantime, the attacking women tear the marcher's banner, rip open his shirt, and begin stabbing him with their parasols (2.105).

A minister orders that the bridges be raised, cutting off the workers' districts from the city center. Now begins Eisenstein's most famous experiment in expanding time through editing. Cutaways to other actions, overlapping match cuts of the same movement, and abrupt skips back to earlier instants all make the raising of the Nevsky bridge an epically extended moment. First the bridge lifts the woman's hair, strand by strand (2.106). When the bridge has risen considerably, Eisenstein starts over, now showing the horse lifted slowly (2.107). Next back to the woman, with the bridge retracing the path it took during the horse shots. Then back to the horse, lifted through several shots until it is dangling high above the river.

The spatial relations are puzzling. Are we seeing one bridge or several? Is the woman's body on the same bridge, or on the same side of it, as the horse and carriage? At one point, in extreme long-shot, something seems to slide down a half-bridge: is it the woman's body? As in the Steps sequence, the concreteness of space is subordinated to a series of perceptual and conceptual "attractions." There is the kinetic fascination of an enormous machine suddenly tilting up weightlessly; the dangling horse, presenting a literal "suspense"; and editing that makes man, woman, and animal all victims of the government. The swiveling thrust of the bridge also inverts the crushing descent of the cannon in the trench scene earlier. Compositionally, the slowly rising bridge becomes a peak or pyramid, a monument to the workers' defeat (2.108). The entire episode is overseen by statues of the Sphinx and Minerva, perhaps reminders of the ancient lineage of political oppression.

Now imagery of water conveys the failure of the demonstration. The river laves the agitator's corpse; the bourgeoisie scatter banners and Bolshevik leaflets onto the water. Through editing, the cascading banners are matched to the plummet and splash of the horse's body. The scene culminates in close-ups of *Pravda*

2.105

2.106

2.107

2.108

2.109

sinking into the river (paralleling the reference to the right-wing newspapers earlier) and a punning title: "Drowning the Bolshevik Truth [*Pravda*]" (2.109). After a scene showing the machine-gunners taken captive, the sequence ends with shots of the destroyed Bolshevik offices and a final shot of a balcony from which droops a tattered banner.

In such segments as the "July Days," *October* fuses its mythologizing purpose with bold stylistic experiment. But in other respects the film is troubled by thematic tensions that are better managed in *Strike* and *Potemkin*. Here Eisenstein's usual interplay of satiric Eccentrism and revolutionary affirmation reaches a point of strain. In a critical but sympathetic review, Tretyakov pointed out that

2.110

2.111

buffoonish satire was well suited for Civil War agitation, but heroic art of the new society demanded a purer pathos (Tretyakov 1928:105–106). The difficulty of what he identified as an "unstable equilibrium" is manifested in at least two realms.

The more outrageous problem involves the representation of sexuality. The enemies are given sharply-defined sexual identities. The rightist officer and his jaded woman in the July Days form the only heterosexual couple in the film. More commonly, the reactionaries display an equivocal, even "abnormal" sexuality. The women in the Provisional Government's Shock Troops are satirized through their grotesquely "masculine" demeanor (2.110) and their lesbianism. Correspondingly, the Menshevik men become feminized when their office in Smolny, a former girls' academy, is shown bearing the plate "Schoolmistress." Eisenstein installs Kerensky in the apartment of the tsarina, suggesting a scurrilous pun: Kerensky's name (Alexander Fyodorovich) is the masculine form of the empress' name (Alexandra Fyodorovna).

By contrast, the Bolsheviks and the proletariat are characterized throughout as "normal," that is, asexual. From this perspective, the Bolshevik attack on the Winter Palace becomes a reassertion of aggressively masculine sexuality. Whereas the February revolution starts on Women's Day, October belongs to men, as one juxtaposition of a machine gun and a male statue makes hyperbolically explicit (2.111). A later scene in which a sailor bursts into the tsarina's bedroom is staged and filmed as a symbolic rape: when the sailor thrusts his bayonet into the mattress, women soldiers in hiding stiffen as if sexually assaulted. A close-up presents the sailor wiping his bayonet.

The parodic masculinity of such passages anticipates the vulgar bull-cow nuptials in *Old and New*, suggesting that Eisenstein sought to exaggerate "normal" eroticism no less than he had caricatured "perversion." What seems less deliberately controlled is the status of the Bolshevik women. A woman leads the attack on the statue in February, but thereafter women become less prominent. In the film's second half, with the exception of a single female orator, women are shown making lists and stacking pamphlets while men bear weapons and charge the palace. By the end of the film, a bevy of secretaries at the congress plunges

2.112

frantically into transcribing Lenin's words. It is as if the excessive representations of "masculinity," both of the Shock Troops and of the besieging Bolsheviks, have pushed the film into an assault on "feminist" tendencies of the moment. A *New Lef* reviewer encapsulated the dilemma: "Carried away by his satirical portrayal of the woman soldier, [Eisenstein] creates . . . a general satire on women who take up arms for any cause at all" (Pertsov 1928:317).

A second area of tension involves politics. The film must present the October revolution as both impelled by popular sentiment and directed by the Bolshevik Party. The asexuality of the heroic forces stems from their accepting the primacy of political struggle. Unlike Kerensky, Lenin is never seen in private; his identity is defined as Party leader. Eisenstein uses typage to represent the link between the Party and the people. Soldiers, sailors, agitators, and tacticians such as Antonov-Ovseenko emerge as somewhat distinct individuals but also as prototypes of the disciplined Bolshevik. Moreover, "typical" members of the audience at the congress are shown as embracing the Red cause. Peasants, workers, and soldiers all respond to the Party orators and mock their opponents. Lenin embodies the people's trust in the Party, an attitude rendered in standard fashion through their awestruck reception of his arrival at the Finland Station, as well as through their celebration when he takes the rostrum at the film's close.

Most crucially, during the attack on the Winter Palace the film's narration reasserts the primacy of political forces. The rape of the tsarina's bedchamber is followed by the sailors' discovery of chests of medals, which brings back the topic of war with which the film began. The attack on the palace concludes with a lesson in revolutionary discipline: the cadets are captured by force of will, the cabinet surrenders without a struggle, and the troops systematically restrain looting. Sailors prevent the crowd from stealing wine by smashing the bottles, a properly disciplined political equivalent of the assault on the bedchamber. The little boy who winds up asleep on the throne (2.112) can be interpreted as a sly development of the erotic motif: he is the issue of a decadent regime ravished by revolutionary élan, the male heir of the Bolshevik cause. But more explicitly the boy constitutes a conventional, desexualized symbol of a new political era, the replacement of the statue in the film's opening. Just as the film's erotic implications are forcibly tamed by overblown images of masculinity and political discipline, the political difficulties of merging the people and the Party are swept away in a surge of correctly focused revolutionary energy and a return to canonized symbols—the child, the rally, Lenin.

Eisenstein's experimentation, then, becomes a baroque elaboration of a revolutionary *mythos*. Drawing icons and situations from many sources, he pushes them to hyperbolic extremes. This tactic can in turn be seen as part of a larger experimental impulse: that of making his narration a rhetorically and poetically forceful discourse on history.

The marks of overt address are evident. The editing breaks up characters' speeches into sloganistic bits. Commentative intertitles mock, inflate, or challenge adjacent images. Even when the cues are purely visual, Eisenstein often uses a verbal cue as the narration's commentary. The "drowning of the truth" is given as the sinking of a copy of *Pravda*. Kerensky's desire to rise in power is conveyed through showing him trudging up endless staircases, a pun on the word *lesnitsa,* which connotes mounting "the ladder of success." The soldiers huddling in the trench "under" the cannon are literally "oppressed" by the Provisional Government's war. Such language-based abstractions were not alien to Soviet propaganda art: posters and parades offered images of scissors cutting up speculators, or White soldiers squirming in frying pans. The *Capital* project, Eisenstein promised, would use such puns as springboards for didactic generalization.

The most salient examples of the narration's intervention are those commentaries on the action that Eisenstein and generations of critics have identified with "intellectual montage." Recognizing that such passages as the Kerensky/peacock analogy and the Menshevik/harp sequence have a forbidding air about them, Eisenstein argued that *October*'s conflict between pathos and intellection was the dialectical answer to *Potemkin*'s balance and unity (1928c:105). Just as the film pushes both Eccentrism and heroic realism to new limits, so it insists on exploring uncompromisingly conceptual regions while also intensifying emotional and kinesthetic appeal.

In many respects, the "intellectual" sequences fulfill an obvious propagandistic function. Kornilov becomes Napoleon, the Mensheviks try to lull the people to sleep, Kerensky is as vain as a peacock. The most famous sequence, "For God and Country," also discredits the enemy, but in a more abstract way. Taking Kornilov's slogan as a basis, Eisenstein juxtaposes statues of gods from different cultures (2.113, 2.114), followed by shots showing military medals (2.115). Eisenstein explains that the earlier portion attempts to demystify the idea of God by ranging idols along "a descending intellectual scale," suggesting the primitive origins of the concept (1929e:194).[8]

In a broader perspective, the sequence forms part of a process of motivic development akin to that at work in *Potemkin*. "God" and "country" are present from the very start in the orb and scepter gripped by the statue of Alexander III,

---

8. Carroll 1973 has suggested that the sequence displays the logical form of a *reductio ad absurdum.*

2.113

2.114

2.115

2.116

and the motifs weave through the ensuing action. Moreover, these images serve as the occasion for a still more abstract reflection on the conventional aspects of representation—on, as semioticians would say, the "arbitrariness of the sign."

Postrevolutionary culture showed a keen awareness of the practical semiotics of power. As the Soviets tore down statues, renamed locales, and destroyed imperial regalia, thinkers debated the proper signs of the revolutionary regime. In the late 1920s Eisenstein was interested in the highly "conventional" art forms of China and Japan. In this context, *October* becomes a "theoretical" film, exploring different conceptions of the sign and identifying those conceptions with particular historical forces.

The opening presents a frozen image of the tsar, leader of both church and state. But the next sequence, showing soldiers fraternizing on the battlefield, puts forth a different conception of the sign. Russian and German soldiers exchange helmets, an act indicating that merely conventional differences divide them. A Bolshevik agitator shows that the two signs are equivalent (2.116).

The Provisional Government becomes bewitched by signs: statues promise power, Kerensky commands toy troops, female soldiers fall into tears at the sight of a sculpted mother and child. The Bolsheviks, however, put their faith in instruments and action. Revolution is kinesis. If Russian soldiers' fraternization with the Germans indicates an emotional unity, the lesson is intensified when Kornilov's Savage Division is won over. A frenzied dance triggers a montage that

2.117   2.118

2.119   2.120

creates a corporeal unity, intercutting the legs of a cossack with the torso of a Bolshevik. Static signs get swept into the revolutionary impulse: banners ignite the July Days; a royal insignia affords a foothold in scaling a palace gate; statues shelter troops (2.117).

God and Country thus become the prime instances of static, arbitrary, duplicitous signs. The Provisional Government is blessed by priests and celebrated by generals. Kerensky, dreaming of power, caps his decanter with a crown bearing a cross. As he flees the Winter Palace, he is made the tsar's petty descendent by juxtaposition with the angel's orb and scepter (2.118). Most crucially, when the Bolsheviks invade the tsarina's bedroom, they find a host of sentimental icons portraying the allegiance of religion and the state, including Christ blessing the imperial family (2.119). At the same time, the invaders discover crates of medals ("Is that what we fought for?"), which they overturn in disgust (2.120).

In this respect, *October* reverses *Strike*'s narrational organization: instead of presenting a nondiegetic conclusion, Eisenstein maps out the central motifs in an early nondiegetic episode. The abstract images of God and Country, debunked through intellectual montage early in the film, get demystified through plot action at the climax. The conceptual demonstration of a thesis is recast as an emotional, historically concrete process of dramatic revelation: the sailors discover in action what the filmic discourse has already demonstrated.

2.121

The progress from ideation to enactment is characteristic of the film's general movement. Originally conceived in five reel-length acts like *Potemkin*, *October* bursts beyond the confines of the earlier films. Its initial four reels trace events over eight months, ending with the defeat of Kornilov. Fairly self-contained scenes, interrupted by experiments in intellectual montage satirizing the authorities, dominate this first half. Once the film fastens on 25 October, however, a less episodic construction emerges. The last five reels by and large constitute one long sequence that crosscuts the debates at Smolny, scenes involving troops stationed around St. Petersburg, and incidents inside the Winter Palace. During the assault, Eisenstein breaks the action into still more distinct lines before drawing all together in the arrest of the ministers.

The second half, as Eisenstein and his critics acknowledged, is also dominated by a more traditional "pathos." Apart from the interludes of the harps and the bicycle corps, intellectual montage is all but absent. Farcical touches, such as the shots of ministers' clothes empty on their chairs, are rare. Instead we have heroic vignettes. A charging soldier topples into the mud, strains to lift his head, and urges his comrades forward. Speakers at the congress seem to launch the shells that assault the palace. Sailors jubilantly smash the wine racks; old wine floods the cellars as crowds pour into corridors; and Antonov, in string tie and floppy hat, uses his pistol to sweep the conference table clean. The little boy, whooping and whipping his cap, joins the assault (2.121) and ends up asleep on the throne. Depicting the revolution as an explosion of exuberant energy accords with the "revolutionary romanticism" that, tied to highly individuated protagonists, would found Socialist Realism.

Eisenstein seems to have agreed with his critics that *October* failed to integrate its official purpose with its experimental aspirations. He admitted that the film contained "awkward, vulgar, even shameful symbolism," but at the same time a passage such as "God and Country," "like the battleship's lions, serves as a ladder to a completely different idea of cinema" (Moussinac 1964:28–29). This idea would, he remarked elsewhere, be popularized in *Old and New* and then taken to its limit in *Capital*. Ironically, however, within Soviet cinema the film's strongest influence came from its more "realistic" side. In consolidating a historical image of the Bolshevik insurrection, *October*'s revolutionary romanticism influenced later portrayals of the October events.[9] Indeed, countless documentaries have treated shots from the July Days and the storming of the palace as newsreel footage.

In a sense, though, Eisenstein's most significant experiment was the very decision to juxtapose, even more starkly than he had in *Strike*, strategies of representation: historical myth and cinematic innovation, Eccentrism and revolutionary romanticism, abstract dissertation and kinesthetic montage, rhetoric and poetic, narrative and argument. A heroic Soviet cinema, the film suggests, might be based as much on this impure amalgam as upon the "classical" unity of *Potemkin* or *Mother*. The experiment yields excesses and obscurities but also moments of unsurpassed power.

Old and New (1929)

A peasant family is asleep in a cramped, smoky *izba*, the traditional farmhouse. An old woman rouses them. Two men stand outside, flexing a crosscut saw. Intertitles explain: "If one brother leaves the other / they divide the farm." As women and children watch, the brothers saw the *izba* in two. Rapid shots of the blade are intercut with images of fences crisscrossing the fields. "The land is split." A family stands by the bisected *izba*, staring at the fences. "Thus are the farms ruined." Close-ups portray the miserable children and the old woman.

This parablelike beginning, much more explicit than the oblique opening of *October*, encapsulates many of the qualities of Eisenstein's last silent film. *Old and New*, begun as *The General Line*, responds to the imperative of the Fourteenth Party Congress, which had urged peasants to form cooperatives. Accordingly, the film's first scene portrays circumstances that cry out for improvement. Splitting a house emblematizes the state of ignorance and fragmentation into which the peasantry has fallen. The film will go on to trace a peasant woman's efforts to unify and elevate her peers.

A second social command shaped *Old and New*. The 1928 Party Conference on Cinema had resolved that Soviet films should be "intelligible to the millions." Eisenstein and Alexandrov announced that their film, while promulgating the agricultural policy, would also break new ground cinematically: "May this experiment, however contradictory it may sound, be an *experiment intelligible to the millions!*" (1929d:257).

Consequently, many of Eisenstein's earlier stylistic innovations become less arcane here. For example, the film's nondiegetic inserts are usually more easily understood than those in *October*. Cuts to flames blazing across a plain convey the strenuous demands of Marfa's worker ally; the smooth porcelain pigs inter-

9. See, for instance, M. Sokolov's painting *Arrest of the Provisional Government*, reproduced in Nilsen 1936: 172.

rupting the slaughter sequences assure that we perceive the sequence as mildly comic. Similarly, the rhythmic montage of the religious procession and the scythe race builds excitement and conveys the peasants' passionate energy. The opening scene's sliding optical wipes are similarly readable as imitating the saw's movement. In general, Eisenstein claimed, *Old and New* would popularize the recondite film language of *October* (1928c:105).

Yet *Old and New* also goes beyond Eisenstein's earlier accomplishments. He seeks to avoid what he perceived as ossifying conventions of Soviet montage. In 1928 he complained that an academic classicism was creeping into Soviet cinema. "It will again be necessary to revolutionize to the roots what has become sterile stylization instead of palpitating life and true passion" (Moussinac 1964:152). Eisenstein believed *Old and New*'s principal editing innovation to be "overtonal" or "harmonic" montage, which based the cutting on secondary pictorial or sensuous qualities in each shot. The religious procession, for instance, highlights a number of secondary stimuli. Along with the plot action, the increasing passion of the peasants' supplication, Eisenstein presents inter-shot "overtones" of heat, thirst, delirium, and other qualities. A shot of dripping candles evokes heat and liquidity, properties that are also combined in a shot of a drooling goat.

Other novelties give *Old and New* an experimental flavor. As usual, the reel-acts are quite distinct, but the breaks between scenes may be signaled only retroactively. As Marfa leaves the kulak and walks down the road, the season changes imperceptibly from spring to summer. A similarly ambiguous shift starts a later scene, in which a shot of a glowering peasant may indicate either his rejection of the priests' prayers for rain or his skepticism about the cream separator.

The weakening of sequence divisions motivates some more extreme editing experiments. Marfa's raging in the field is intercut with her giving a speech at a later period. A more sustained creation of "impossible time" involves the letter sent by the agency to Marfa. The clerks' preparation of the letter is crosscut with her reading of it. The montage suggests the bureaucrats' mechanically routine refusal of credit and, by intercutting the office activity with storms that scatter the grain ricks, implies that not all dangers to collectivization come from natural forces. Such parallel time frames suggest Eisenstein's desire to go beyond the narrational conventions that Soviet montage had developed in a mere three years.

Another new stylistic option would fascinate Eisenstein for the next several years. The *izba*-cutting scene introduces the film's use of a 28mm lens, which yields great depth of field and exaggerated foregrounds (2.122). Throughout the film Eisenstein composes his shots to create a "montage within the frame" of the sort discussed in the 1929 essay "The Dramaturgy of Film Form." The human/animal linkages that *Strike* creates through editing can now be presented within the shot, as when Marfa enters the kulak's farm and her skinny frame contrasts with the well-fed animals munching in the foreground (2.123). Shots such as 2.124, which create "floating detail" compositions akin to those in Carl Dreyer's *La Passion de Jeanne d'Arc* (1928; 2.125), suggest that the wide-angle lens can cut signs loose from their exact locales, making the frame a more abstract, tension-

2.122 *Old and New.*

2.123 *Old and New.*

2.124 *Old and New.*

2.125 *La Passion de Jeanne d'Arc* (Carl Dreyer, 1928).

2.126 *Old and New.*

2.127

ridden unity. The distortion of scale and shape also offers what Eisenstein would later call "Gogolian hyperbole" (2.126).

By comparison with *October,* however, this film's innovations are more subdued. In toning them down, Eisenstein makes them serve two major demands: a comic tone, and a protagonist-centered plot.

Viewers used to the dramatic tenor of *Potemkin* and *October* are often surprised to find *Old and New* such an amusing movie. As usual, Eisenstein's satire is broad, and it relies upon symbolic objects. For example, the obesity and torpor of the kulaks are expressed not only in the performance (2.127) but also in deep-focus

2.128

2.129

2.130

2.131

2.132

imagery that contrasts them to Marfa (2.128) and in cutaways to a spherical jar of kvass in which a ladle sinks lethargically (2.129). In his stolid indifference, the kulak becomes equated with his bull (a refinement of the spy/animal analogies in *Strike*).

Similar tactics are used to denigrate the indolent bureaucrats. The wide-angle lens bloats them and magnifies their typewriter (2.130, 2.131). One clerk wipes his pen on a bust of Lenin, literally besmirching the leader's memory (2.132), while another licks a stamp and leaves Lenin hanging on his tongue. An official's outlandishly flourishing signature becomes a rich symbol of self-absorption, decadence, and wasted energy. The satire of the new Soviet managerial class (the

2.133   2.134

2.135   2.136

vydvizhentsy, or "promoted people") is more concrete and detailed than the gibes at the Mensheviks and the Women's Battalion in *October.*

As we have seen, Soviet filmmakers had difficulty using Eccentric or grotesque techniques to represent progressive forces. *Old and New* draws upon mildly modernist stylization to create a simple, good-natured humor. A tractor, assembled piecemeal by animation, rolls on its own accord into a barn. Disjunctive cutting that splits the tractor driver's body in "impossible" ways presents him as frantically mating with his vehicle (2.133, 2.134). In another scene, a peasant declares that he needs no tractor because he is already a machine. The declaration itself brings a Constructivist slogan down to earth, but the shot's wide-angle distortion of the man's fist (2.135) at once mocks his bragging, celebrates his earthy strength, and makes a verbal-visual pun (the Russian word for fist is *kulak*).

The comic lightening of experimental tendencies reaches its apogee in the bawdy wedding of a cow and the bull Fomka. The general tone is set by a series of simple gags which suggest that a human wedding will take place, only to reveal a garlanded heifer as the bride. In jump-cut shots, Fomka grows from a calf into a lowering bull. As if in eyeline-matches, the cow moos longingly for him, and there are even some fantasy inserts suggesting her point of view. Contradictory shots place him sometimes in the barn, sometimes in a daisy field. Editing for temporal expansion postpones the consummation hilariously: let out of the barn, Fomka gallops in fast motion toward his bride, but he is filmed in a barrage of comically opposed trajectories. Throughout, Eisenstein provides glimpses of the heifer's hindquarters seen from Fomka's eager point of view. At the moment of copulation, shots of dynamite exploding are followed by images of foaming milk and swirling cream from the earlier sequence, some black frames, and finally ranks of calves in a barn. Fomka's nuptials vulgarize (in two senses) editing innovations that Eisenstein had introduced in earlier films.

Kuleshov and his circle had been taken to task for their "Americanitis," but *Old and New* incorporates a few Hollywood touches in its overall attempt to make its experimentation accessible. The final big scene, in which peasants leap onto their horses and pursue the tractor, is an affectionate burlesque of a Western chase, complete with men shading their eyes like Indians scanning the horizon. The comic epilogue creates a pastiche of *A Woman of Paris* (1923). Chaplin's film ends with former lovers, one in a car and one in a wagon, passing on a country road, each lover ignorant of the other's presence. In *Old and New,* the city-bred tractor driver, now happily lounging in a hay wagon, passes Marfa, the peasant woman become a tractor driver. The Soviet couple recognize each other and clinch in a coy finale out of Hollywood romantic comedy.

Although it seems a throwaway gesture, the epilogue is not completely arbitrary. Dramatically, it is prepared during Fomka's wedding, when Eisenstein cuts away from the cow and a title announcing "The Bride" to Marfa holding flowers. Later, during the test of the tractor, the interdependence of city and country is indicated when the driver must tear pieces off a blushing Marfa's skirt in order to make the machine run. Moreover, as we shall see shortly, the driver is the last of a string of male partners who help Marfa achieve her goals.

Apart from comedy, the presence of a protagonist motivates the film's stylistic innovations. Although the sawing of the *izba* does not introduce the film's central character, it does (unlike the opening of *Strike* or *October*) begin the film by delineating the plight of individuals. Thereafter the drama will center on distinctive figures who also represent the larger problem. In the second sequence Marfa Lapkina is introduced as "one of many"; at once individuated and typical, she will be the heroine.

Instead of offering the epic breadth of *Potemkin* and *October,* then, the film's version of "heroic realism" celebrates the accomplishments of the ordinary person. Not only does this fulfill the mandate of the Fourteenth Party Congress, which urged each peasant to take up collectivization voluntarily; it also accords with a major trend in art of the First Five-Year Plan. Maxim Gorky exhorted novelists and playwrights to take as their hero the "little man"—a lowly factory worker or peasant—who accomplishes great things. Although there were debates about how much psychological depth was appropriate to the "little hero," the strategy sought to balance the emphasis on collective activity in Civil War literature and drama against a need for sympathetic characters with whom the spectator could identify.

By centering on Marfa, Eisenstein alters his characteristic plot structure. Like *Potemkin,* the film consists of distinctly developed scenes, each part of a larger reel-length unit; but now the film is structured around Marfa's struggle to collectivize her region. She fights to form and preserve a cooperative. She works to acquire a cream separator, a breeding bull, and finally a tractor. At each stage she encounters resistance from the kulaks, suspicious peasants, and bureaucrats. Her triumphs take place against a background of regressive habits: the *izba*-cutting, the religious procession, the kulaks' indifference and hostility, the peasants' suspicion of technology and new forms of social organization.

Many of the contrasts of old and new are played out in parallel sequences portraying Marfa's situation. At the beginning she kneels in her yard with her cow; after the death of Fomka the bull, she sits weeping in despair . . . until a calf wanders in to console her. The difference between past and present is sharpened by an epilogue that contrasts the smiling, goggled tractor driver Marfa with shots showing her at earlier points in the film. Other contrasts of old and new grow out of the background conditions of her story. The scene of cutting the *izba* is balanced not only by the ending, in which fences are smashed down, but also by the scene in which factory workers build a stable for Marfa's *kolkhoz*, or collective farm. (The very shots echo each other; compare 2.122 and 2.137.) To the early scenes of Marfa's fruitless plowing is counterposed the climax, in which a platoon of tractors cuts whorls in the land.

Marfa becomes a balancing point for diverging tendencies within Eisenstein's earlier films. She stands between the caricatured enemies and the comparatively undifferentiated mass, neither a grotesque nor a cipher. As hero, she is more down-to-earth than Lenin in *October,* more fully characterized than Vakulinchuk or *Strike*'s anonymous agitators. Marfa also constitutes a link between emotional appeals and intellectual ones. She is a figure of *pafos* (pathos)—drive, enthusiasm, and revolutionary ardor. She not only propels the plot but also stirs the audience. Her rage at having to plow without a horse, her exhortation to the peasants to form a cooperative, her passionate defense of the money box, and her dreams of a collective farm create the emotional basis for experimental passages, even intellectual montage.

A striking example occurs early in the film. The kulak will not lend Marfa a horse, so she must use her cow to plow. Eisenstein generalizes her plight by intercutting her efforts with those of a peasant plowing with an emaciated horse and those of an old couple who must pull their harrow. As the peasants' efforts become more hopeless, the montage creates analogies among them (such as a cut from Marfa's thrashing cow to the old man, his strength ebbing). Finally Marfa bursts out: "Impossible!" She violently flings down the plow and hammers its handle with her fist (2.138). The gesture recalls the old woman cheering on the dunking of the factory bureaucrats in *Strike* and the old woman grieving at Vakulinchuk's tent in *Potemkin* (2.57). Eisenstein cuts on Marfa's gesture to a medium shot of her, elsewhere, pounding her fist (2.139), and then cuts back to her in the field, still railing (2.140). After more shots juxtaposing present and future, the narration settles into a new scene of Marfa at a meeting, urging peasants to unite: "We cannot live this way!" (2.141). Her outburst, fueled by concrete circumstances we have witnessed, initiates an experiment in montage. It

2.137

2.138

2.139

2.140

2.141

is as if the sailor who smashes the plate in *Potemkin* had become the emotional center of the entire film.

October's passages involving Kerensky and the peacock, the Mensheviks and the harps, and the God and Country icons start with conceptual comparisons and then graft on emotional effects, usually attitudes of mockery. *Old and New*, like *Potemkin*, begins by arousing emotion and builds toward a tendentious judgment. Thus the "intellectual montage" of the first scene arises from the pathos of the displaced family whose home is foolishly sawed in two; only after the family's misery is established does Eisenstein point out the custom's social consequences. Similarly, Marfa's emotional involvement helps develop conceptual implications.

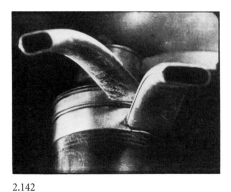

2.142

2.143

2.144

This is evident in a sequence that has become an Eisensteinian set piece in the tradition of the slaughter in *Strike,* the Odessa Steps, and *October*'s bridge-raising.

The cooperative has acquired a mechanical cream separator. While the peasants look on suspiciously, Marfa pours milk into it. The agronomist and the youth Vasya crank it steadily, and Eisenstein cuts rapidly between skeptical faces and the machine's spinning parts. For a few moments, when no one is shown turning the crank, the machine takes on a life of its own. Sparkling light plays over it, its spouts swivel (2.142), and cream dribbles out. As the cream thickens, the peasants break into smiles. Suddenly Eisenstein begins to alternate diegetic images with nondiegetic ones. Against a black background, jets of cream spurt up (2.143). These are intercut with the peasants' delighted faces, dappled as if by reflections of the foaming cream. Marfa kneels by the separator, bathed in spray (2.144); then torrents of cream fill the shots. The dramatic climax is capped by a conceptual one: whirlpools and fountains of cream are very rapidly intercut with numerals (4, 17, 20, up to 50) that convey the growth of the cooperative.

As is usual in Eisenstein, the sequence fulfills broad thematic purposes. The burst of liquid from the machine figuratively lifts the drought that the peasants' religious procession has failed to relieve, and the scene's connotations of orgasm and insemination point toward Fomka's marriage. In addition, the scene builds an emotional high point through the accelerated cranking and spinning, the rise in the quantity of cream, the arc of the fountains of cream, the increase in the

2.145   2.146

number of members of the cooperative, and even the enlarging size of the numerals. If the scene's "dominant" is the practical value of the separator, its principal "overtone" is fecundity. Once more, the intensification of affect through the
protagonist's response has furthered a conceptual point.

Although the film concentrates on Marfa, other figures play important roles.
Throughout, she is paired with a series of urbanized men who guide and aid her.
The film offers a string of variants—some serious, one lighthearted—upon the
Soviet slogan of the alliance between the peasantry and the proletariat.

At the rally Marfa declares that the peasants must unite, but it is the local Party
leader who proposes organizing a *kolkhoz* and the government agronomist who
takes the vote. As is the norm in Soviet narrative, the toiler embraces socialism
but requires the Party to formulate and lead decisive action. Over the next several
scenes, Marfa is assisted by the agronomist, who unveils the cream separator and
who protects her when the other peasants want to divide the treasury of the
kolkhoz. The Party agronomist is associated with Lenin, through a rough facial
resemblance (2.145) and through his practical commitment. After the cream
separator helps expand the cooperative, he tells the camera: "Congratulations!"
In all, he helps Marfa fulfill Lenin's dictum in the film's epigraph: "It is sometimes
the case than an exemplary production by local labor, even though accomplished
on a small scale, has greater state significance than many branches of centralized
state labor."

Later, when Marfa goes to the city to appeal for a tractor, a male foundry
worker helps her defeat the bureaucracy. In the sequence titled "Lenin's legacy,"
the leader is again invoked. The bureaucrat who sullies Lenin's image is shown
to resemble the dead leader, and Eisenstein distinguishes this false image from
the authentic Leninist spirit by several remarkable shots. Marfa and the worker
are aligned with a colossal bust of the leader (2.146). A portrait of Lenin reading
Pravda is blasphemously replicated in the clerk at his desk below, and Eisenstein
emphasizes the bureaucrat's petty egotism by inserting his face into the painting.

The last of Marfa's male partners is the tractor driver, a figure who transposes
the theme of urbanizing the countryside into a more comic key. The reversals
that put a peasant woman on a tractor and an engineer in a hay wagon—and

each in the other's arms—are summed up by a title: "This is how we erase boundaries between city and country!" The film's protagonist has found a mate without searching for one, and the plot concludes on a note of conventional gaiety that tones down the preceding cinematic experiments.

Old and New's interrupted production and the Party debates surrounding collectivization made the film quite divorced from contemporary circumstances. By the fall of 1929, the time of the film's release, the brutal expropriations from better-off peasants had begun in earnest. Middle and poor peasants, promised tractors and credit, were being coerced into joining collective farms; some resisted with violence or by slaughtering their livestock. The rapid changes in Party policy explain not only the air of stylization hovering over the film's comedy, but also certain strategic omissions and ambiguities.

For one thing, Eisenstein's kulaks get off easily. They are not stripped of their lands, and their murder of the collective's breeding bull goes not only unpunished but undiscovered. Moreover, the film is vague about exactly how Marfa's *kolkhoz* works. The organization follows common practice in that each member seems to keep a cottage and a small private plot. But the sequence showing the members milking cows suggests that the organization is at first predominantly a distribution cooperative (a form that both Lenin and Stalin maintained would have to precede collectivized production). The later scene of building a stable and the climax showing collective plowing and the smashing of fences suggest that production is becoming fully communal. But how the transition to production is made, how the organization functions, who determines workloads and outputs, and what role is played by the Party all remain quite obscure.

To some degree these uncertainties can be attributed to political factors. At the time of the film's release, many Party members, including Lenin's widow Krupskaya, declared that Lenin would not have approved of the general line of accelerated collectivization. From this perspective, the film's citations of Lenin take on new significance. François Albéra has argued that *Old and New* in effect criticizes forced collectivization by recalling Lenin's emphasis on persuasion and long-term education of the peasantry (1977).

Much in the film supports this reading. Marfa is a *bednyak*, or poor peasant (usually defined as one possessing a small farm but no horse). It is doctrinally proper that her ally be Vasya, a *betrak*, that "rural proletarian" who has no land and must work for others. Marfa's principal conflict is not with the kulak but with the middle peasants *(serednyaki)*, as Lenin anticipated. Furthermore, the reconciliation of old and new centers on what Lenin called the problem of "two cultures in one." Any historical epoch, he argued, constitutes a battle between progressive and reactionary forces. The film portrays this in showing a backsliding peasantry. For example, the scene in which *kolkhoz* members try to seize the treasury is prefaced by a title that quotes from Lenin: "The past is turned back but is not dead."

Yet the film has another side. In public statements of the mid-1920s, Stalin followed Lenin in insisting that the middle peasants must not be alienated from

Communism and in stressing persuasion and voluntary collectivization. How-ever far such public rationales diverged from practice during 1929, *Old and New,* itself a public rationale, seems compatible with them. In addition, the depiction of the huge dairy farm accords with the radicals' policy of creating centralized and specialized state farms far larger than the *kolkhoz.* The film's homages to Lenin are also consistent with Stalin's willingness to foster a cult around a leader whose inevitable heir he would become. "Way of October," the name of Marfa's *kolkhoz,* may be seen as a tribute both to Lenin and to Stalin, the leader of "rural October" (Tucker 1990:129). Finally, the film's move into utopian fantasy prefig-ures conventions of mainstream Stalinist art of the 1930s, particularly *kolkhoz* musicals such as *The Rich Bride* (1938) and *Tractor Drivers* (1939).

The ideology of *Old and New* emerges as calculatedly vague. The treatment of Lenin is readable simply as a broad affirmation of the collective ideal. The nature of Marfa's cooperative and its relation to the Party remain uncertain because to specify more would require predicting what was in fact a fluctuating general line. The film leaves the punishment of the kulaks suspended because the problem of how to deal with them had not yet been solved, or because it had been solved in too many divergent ways, or because the emerging solutions were too drastic to be faced. Instead, the film's comedy and its dynamic protagonist not only motivate its experiments but also permit the narrative to treat current issues obliquely.

Eisenstein activates a range of broader subjects and themes that sidetrack the contentious political issues of the moment. One theme, given in the film's last intertitle, is that of "erasing boundaries" between rural tradition and technical progress. At first the modern city is separated from the backward countryside. But factory workers leave the Palace of Labor to help build the collective farm, Marfa finds help from an urban worker, and eventually the sporty tractor driver settles down in the village. *Old and New*'s ending provides strongly emblematic resolutions of the thematic gap. The fences that spring up at the beginning are smashed down by the fleet of tractors, and images of industrial and agricultural productivity are intercut. In the embrace of Marfa and the tractor driver, rural life has become modern, and the city has become countrified.

In accordance with Lenin's "two cultures" doctrine, city life is not portrayed as flawless. The driver preens (until his tractor malfunctions), and Eisenstein delightedly sees to it that his dandified outfit gets smeared with tractor grease and country soil. Yet the progress represented by the city remains the key to rooting out the superstition of the conservative peasantry. In 1928 Soviet authorities were alarmed to discover that peasants' religious attachments had increased in the previous five years (Schapiro 1971:343). The frenzy of faith is evoked in the priests' procession to relieve the drought, which triggers an orgy of prayer but no miracle. To spiritual religion *Old and New* counterposes technology, but the film intro-duces it in ways that aim to be compatible with folk tradition.

The case for collectivization is made through elemental imagery. Before the peasants unite, spring is barren: a pregnant woman stands in despair under a dead tree, rains churn up mud, emaciated cows shiver in the damp. Summer's drought also makes the land infertile, but the arrival of the cream separator brings a symbolic fecundity. Later, after Marfa has defended the cash box from the peasants, she falls asleep. She dreams of a gigantic bull washing the parched landscape in a creamy shower (2.136). This image is followed by footage showing oceans of milk, herds of cattle, and a flotilla of pigs, all under the auspices of an immense state farm. Suddenly an intertitle asks: "You think that this is a dream?" Marfa is now shown entering a barn and selecting a calf. The sequence utilizes the technique of the ambiguous transition in order to glide imperceptibly between folkloric fantasy and an abundance provided by Communist technology and organization.

The connection between sexuality and traditional religion is integrated into the film in a more covert way as well. In 1929 Eisenstein remarked that *Old and New* had revealed to him that "eroticism is far too strong a force not to be utilized," so in the cream separator scene, eroticism gets "delocalized" (1929f:70), shifted from the body to the machine. Several years later he explains further. In portraying the transport created by the cream separator, the scene manifests a movement from pathos to "ecstasy." After the unproductive debauch of the religious procession, deliverance appears in technology, the Bolshevik Holy Grail (1947g:38–59).

As we shall see in Chapter 5, Eisenstein came to believe that ecstasy, spiritual or sexual, closes the gap between perceiver and perceived, between subject and object. In *Old and New* revolutionary pathos moves toward the erasure of all boundaries. Instead of sawing houses in two, workers unite to build. At the highest reaches of commitment to socialist development, even the tools—a cream separator, a tractor—come to incarnate the task's ideals; and the participants share in a passion that is no less exalted than that enjoyed by the celebrants of a Mass. Communism approaches Communion. Eisenstein seeks to arouse something like this exaltation in the spectator as well. His last silent film offers a conception of heroic realism that at certain moments, in its very method, acknowledges Bolshevism as secular religion.

Dmitri Shostakovich is said to have learned from Meyerhold to strive for something different in each composition, "so that each new work stuns" (Volkov 1979:82). This strategy underlay Eisenstein's 1920s filmmaking. Within the ambit of the NEP and heroic realism, he sought to assimilate diverse artistic traditions and to recast contemporary innovations. In the process, he devised fresh ways of making films. He explored new techniques of telling stories, unifying a narrative, staging movement, joining shot to shot, and arousing audiences to sympathy, indignation, and partisanship. His "plotless cinema" renders cinematic texture an object of vivid perceptual, emotional, and cognitive engagement.

The innovations were not born of a process of simple trial and error. At each step along the way, he reflected on the intuitive discoveries made in filming or at the cutting bench. From making a film, to writing about the questions raised by the film, to making a new film that would sharpen or answer those questions and raise new ones—this shuttling to and fro between practice and theory is the characteristic movement of Eisenstein's activities during the 1920s.

A Note on Versions of Eisenstein's Silent Films

Eisenstein's silent films survive in differing versions of varying quality. Some of these are available in North America, Europe, and the United Kingdom.

My analysis of *Strike* is based primarily on the Soviet version of the film released in the West in the late 1960s. This print has been "stretch-printed": that is, every second frame is printed twice. The effect is to slow the action to 24 frames per second (fps) so that a soundtrack can be added. Unfortunately, the film should be shown at about 20 fps, so the print drags out the movements distractingly. There is also a 1960s version of the film that contains British titles and is not stretch-printed. It includes some footage not in the Soviet rerelease print but lacks material found in the stretch-printed version.

Many versions of *Potemkin* circulate in the West. By 1929, the original negative was said to have been so heavily copied and so extensively recut to meet different countries' censorship demands that good and complete positives were difficult to obtain (Anonymous 1929:130). In 1937, when Jay Leyda left the Soviet Union to return to the United States, Eisenstein gave him "one of the original copies" to take back to the Museum of Modern Art (Leyda 1960:338). This is the basis of the print (containing only English-language titles) now distributed by the Museum. A careful, largely accurate découpage of this version has been published (Mayer 1972). A stretch-printed Soviet version, very close to the Museum of Modern Art version but containing more accurate intertitles, was released in 1976 by Mosfilm Studios. (See Hill 1978:74–75.) It is available in the United States on Corinth Video. Of all video versions presently in circulation, this has the finest pictorial quality. Among the other versions of *Potemkin* in distribution, perhaps the most notoriously unreliable is the 1950 Soviet reissue (unfortunately, recently released on U.S. laser videodisk), which is stretch-printed and recut. I have relied chiefly upon the Museum of Modern Art print but have used the 1976 reconstruction for information about original intertitles.

Soon after the completion of *October* in early 1928, a short version, known as *Ten Days That Shook the World*, was prepared for German and U.S. release. Apparently the first reasonably complete version of *October* (9,774 feet, or about 130 minutes at 20 fps) to be shown in the West premiered in 1934 at the London Film Society. This print, which has only English-language intertitles, is the source of the Museum of Modern Art print, the one commonly seen in North America today. My analysis is based upon this print. A slightly shorter Soviet print circulates in Europe; it is the basis for most French analyses. In 1967, for the fiftieth anniversary of the Revolution, Alexandrov prepared a sonorized version. Despite its current availability in video formats, this print cannot be recommended. Some portions have been stretch-printed, some shots have been dropped, and sequences have been rearranged and optically altered.

The London Film Society is also the source of the only version of *Old and New* currently available on film in the United States. This print offers only English-language titles and lacks several key portions of Marfa's dream (such as the pigs in 2.2 and 2.3), a sequence of workers helping build the *kolkhoz*, several shots of the scything competition, and shots of the clerks' degrading of Lenin's memory (such as 2.132). According to the Film Society's program notes, Eisenstein approved the removal of these passages because he had been obliged to add some of them to his original version completed in early 1929 (Anonymous 1930:158). In the Film Society print, the transition between Marfa plowing and Marfa addressing the peasants has also been reedited for smoother continuity. My discussion of *Old and New* is based on a Soviet version, apparently close to the one originally released, that is held in European and American archives. In the United Kingdom this version is available on Connoisseur Video.

3.

Seizing the Spectator: Film Theory in the Silent Era

Eisenstein was a prolific writer. Articles, lectures, and book chapters poured from his pen for twenty-five years. Many of these works are occasional pieces—polemical attacks and rejoinders, tributes and commemorative essays—but his most influential writings are devoted to the theory of cinema. This chapter, along with the two that follow, lays out and organizes his principal ideas about film's nature and functions. While the writing cannot be fully understood apart from the films, it is of great interest in its own right.

Eisenstein's theoretical work can usefully be treated as falling into two fairly distinct stages. While many concerns span his entire career, his 1920s work concentrated on certain key ideas and developed them with considerable consistency. Over the 1930s and 1940s he revised several of them significantly. In addition, the relation of his writing to his filmmaking changed. Whereas the writing of the silent era tends to reflect on experiments conducted in the films, the writing of the later phase is somewhat more proleptic, advancing ideas to be tried out in future projects.

For such reasons, this chapter focuses on Eisenstein's essays from 1923 to 1929. On the whole, these writings offer provocative conceptions of cinematic form, style, and effect.

Between Theory and Practice

Most generally, "film theory" refers to any reflection on the nature and functions of cinema. In the period 1920–1960 the most significant European and American film theorists concentrated on defining cinema as a specific art or medium. What features of film set it off from literature, theatre, painting, and other arts? What is the nature of cinematic representation, and what relation does it have to the physical and perceptual world it portrays? Such questions were answered in various ways by Hugo Münsterberg, Rudolf Arnheim, André Bazin, and other theorists. Classical film theory also had a prescriptive bent: once one had isolated the differentiating feature of cinema, one could judge films according to how fully they realized the unique possibilities of the medium. Arnheim, for instance, argued that a good film imposed a significant form on its material, thereby making the subject matter more vivid or bringing out its expressive qualities.

Soviet film theory in the early 1920s shared the concerns of this Western paradigm. In a series of essays the young Lev Kuleshov asked what distinguished film from theatre and painting, and he settled upon "montage," or editing, as the differentiating factor. Shortly thereafter, Dziga Vertov suggested that cinematic representation had a unique relation to visible reality; the camera's ability to record movement yielded a mechanized vision, the world seen through a "kino-eye." Both theorists also assumed that theorizing would be prescriptive: inquiry into principles would yield criteria for judging good cinema.

Throughout his career Eisenstein was no less prescriptive in his aims than his contemporaries. The young man who wrote in red ink "out of principle" (1940b:143) proclaimed that cinema must be politically progressive and must steer the audience in a useful direction. In supporting his claims, however, he seldom tried to locate the essence of cinematic representation or to determine its unique relation to physical or perceptual reality. He did not try to demarcate film sharply from other arts. His main effort was to unite his practice with a theory that would provide a wide-ranging, detailed reflection on film form, material, and effect.

This tendency is not surprising. Movements with which Eisenstein had affinities, such as Proletkult and Lef, sought to link concrete problems of artistic practice to broader principles, often derived from scientific research. In the course of the 1920s Eisenstein drew increasingly upon current debates around "materialist" psychology and philosophical dialectics. Throughout his life he would seek to make cinema a part of a scientific knowledge of the mind and human action.

At the same time, his concern with practice had parallels in the work of his peers. Unlike most Western theorists of cinema, Kuleshov and Vertov treated problems of film theory within the *technē*-centered context of 1920s Soviet art. From this perspective, cinematic specificity was not taken as an aesthetic essence. (Vertov in fact denounced aesthetics as a bourgeois discipline.) Instead, the search for specificity fell into line with the Constructivists' and Formalists' concern with defining the basic materials of the artisan's craft. Furthermore, both Kuleshov and Vertov were practicing filmmakers. They sought to unite theoretical principle with practical decisions about how a film should be shot and cut. From the start, both thinkers approached film theory not as a purely speculative endeavor but as a practical "cinepoetics": a systematization of the principles of *making* effective works.

The most ambitious Soviet writing that followed Kuleshov and Vertov's pioneering forays tended to treat theoretical problems along craft-centered lines. Pudovkin's 1926 pamphlets on film direction and scriptwriting were largely practice-based, as were books such as Semyon Timoshenko's *The Art of the Cinema and the Montage of Films* (1926) and *What a Film Director Must Know* (1929) and Sergei Vasiliev's *Film Montage* (1929). The Formalist critics, many involved in scriptwriting, also furnished important essays, such as Shklovsky's pamphlet *Literature and Cinema* (1923) and Tynyanov's essay "Cinema—Word—Music" (1924). The most notable Formalist contribution was the 1927 anthology *The Poetics of Cinema*. This volume ventured toward general aesthetic conclusions, but these remained, as the title indicates, grounded in particular technical possibilities. As Boris Eikhenbaum noted about the Formalist method as a whole, it avoided abstract speculation ("problems of beauty, the aims of art") in favor of inquiry into concrete problems of artistic form and its development (1926:104).

In these circumstances, Eisenstein was in an ideal position to mount a unified poetics of cinema. For one thing, he cared more deeply than his peers about creating one. The essays of most directors offer primarily practical suggestions for the novice. Eisenstein was more intellectually restless, never satisfied that he had followed an innovation or an idea to its end. He was concerned to show how the craftsman's propositions about individual technical matters contributed to a larger whole. In his essays there is a pressure to build an architectonic framework within which each aspect of filmmaking will find its place. Late in life he described his impulse through a quotation from Blake: "I must create a System or be enslaved by another Man's" (1989:64). The Formalists might also have pursued such ends, but, concentrating on literature, they were content merely to suggest directions for future work on cinepoetics. Eisenstein the director had a stronger stake in undertaking a systematic inquiry into the fine points of his medium—in forging what he would call throughout his life a "method" that bound theory to practice.

More learned than other directors, more practiced in film craft than the Formalist poeticians, he is able to extend his thought in two complementary directions. On the one hand, he is drawn toward broad and basic speculations. "I'm interested in everything besides . . . the cinema. Cinema is absorbing only in so far as it is 'a miniature experimental universe' by which one can study the laws of phenomena much more interesting than fleeting little pictures" (*E2*:47). Unlike most of his contemporaries, Eisenstein links cinema to widely varied intellectual disciplines and doctrines. He finds insights in the history of the arts (Western and Eastern), psychology, historical materialism, anthropology, and linguistics. A single aspect of cinema becomes the occasion for an excursus—sometimes dazzling, sometimes exasperating—on the nature of thought, the conventions of language, the physiology of sight, or the essence of the dialectic.

At another extreme, Eisenstein's theoretical writings launch forays into the fine points of film form and style. He wants to know how to stage an action or move the body, how to account for every bit of data within the frame, how to catalogue the possible ways in which sound can interact with the image. More than any other theorist of his time, Eisenstein probes the details of his "fleeting little pictures."

Characteristically Eisenstein's early poetics of cinema oscillates between these two tendencies. Sometimes he exposes a detailed technical problem and then borrows ideas from adjacent disciplines in order to resolve it. Sometimes the connection between problem and solution is looser, and the ransacking of other realms yields tangential observations that have intrinsic interest but postpone confrontation with the cinematic issue. At their best, the writings lay bare the intricacies of some directorial problem in cinema while connecting it with broader issues of film practice and of artistic creation in general.

By virtue of his eclectic interests and divagative reasoning strategies, we ought not to expect Eisenstein's writing to exhibit a strictly rational structure. Soviet directors had to promote their projects in an atmosphere of competition, and polemic was common. Rhetorically, Eisenstein's essays are indebted to the manifesto styles flourishing in the wake of the Revolution; his telegraphic syntax echoes that of Tretyakov, Shklovsky, and Mayakovsky. His tone is peremptory, and his labored wordplays, scattered exclamation points, and sarcastic asides to opponents are at once exuberant and aggressive.

Typically, the arguments do not develop straightforwardly. Eisenstein is apt to begin with a pun, an anecdote, or an arcane etymology. His thesis may slip out sidewise, being elaborated intermittently before finally appearing, many pages later, as a taken-for-granted premise. Digressions abound, and argument by analogy is much in evidence. Often Eisenstein proposes a taxonomy, but the undergirding logic of the distinctions remains obscure, or the boundaries between categories become fuzzy. The most salient examples are passages from his own films. The essay characteristically ends by hailing the new expressive possibilities brought to light and looking forward to their exploitation in his future films.

Among these often diverse and obscure formulations, I concentrate on the most cogent and coherent arguments. First I consider how, under the impetus of his theatrical work, Eisenstein developed an account of cinematic effect based on a materialist theory of "expressive movement." Next I examine his distinctive contributions to the emerging debates about cinematic montage. I then study his effort to construct an "intellectual cinema" derived from semiotics and Bolshevist dialectical materialism. All these developments show that the interplay between specific problems and broad doctrines is central to his reasoning. After discussing his two major essays of 1929, perhaps the most influential formulations of his thinking during this era, I consider how Eisenstein's very eclectic sources fed into his emerging poetics of cinema.

Despite the originality of Eisenstein's theoretical essays, they cannot easily be disentangled from the tissue of assumptions and debates within the *technē*-centered tendencies of his time. Often the work of others prodded him to consider a particular problem. For example, in the Civil War era several directors' attempts to codify actors' performances led him to postulate a system of expressive movement, while in the mid-1920s other writers' efforts to classify types of montage pressed him toward his own solutions. Although he seldom acknowledged his debts, current disputes shaped his theoretical agenda.

Agitation as Excitation

Eisenstein's earliest theoretical writings, from 1923 to 1925, mark his transition from theatre directing to filmmaking. In these years he is occupied chiefly with the problem of how theatrical spectacle moves audiences.

All his thinking presupposes that art in the new Soviet state had to inform, educate, and above all persuade citizens. It was to celebrate the victory of the working class and attack enemies of socialism. Like most contemporary artists, Eisenstein shared Lunacharsky's belief that if art was to fulfill social purposes, it could not be coldly didactic. It had to arouse emotion, inspiring the masses with a dedication to the new society that was being built.

Conceiving film and theatre in relation to such effects was already on the agenda when Eisenstein launched his career. He had seen mass spectacles mobilize thousands; he had watched Meyerhold's productions provoke frenzied cheers. In 1922 Kuleshov pointed out that "to meet this or that demand an art must have the power to impress" (1987:54–55). At the same time, the FEX group called for a "nerve-wracking, openly utilitarian" theatre (Kozintsev 1978:12). Eisenstein's contribution was to propose a physical, even physiological, conception of the spectator's response.

He starts, in Constructivist/Formalist fashion, by seeking to define the material upon which the theatre director works. Surprisingly, he takes the material of theatre to be neither the real world of human action; nor the stuff of the spectacle itself, the flats and costumes and bodies; nor even the language the actors speak. "Theatre's basic material," he writes in his 1923 manifesto "The Montage of Attractions," "derives from the audience: the moulding of the audience in a desired direction (or mood) is the task of every utilitarian theatre" (1923b:34). The stage apparatus, including the actors, becomes a set of tools for "processing" the spectator.

This conception of the spectator-as-material may be hyperbolic, since Eisenstein's filmmaking will treat both the event in front of the camera and the strip of photographed film as materials of filmmaking. Nevertheless, his chief point in "The Montage of Attractions" will retain its salience throughout his career: every artistic decision is to be guided by how the film will affect the spectator. More drastically, Eisenstein views the spectator as putting up a material resistance that must be overcome by violence. The audience must be attacked; the work of art is a tractor plowing the spectator's psyche; the artist administers a series of "shocks" (1923b:34); Soviet cinema must crack skulls. Denigrating Vertov, Eisenstein asserts: "It is not a Cine-Eye that we need but a Cine-Fist" (1925d:64). The spectator-as-material is worked, worked up, worked out, and worked over.

In order to affect spectators emotionally and intellectually, Eisenstein argues, the production must manipulate their physical states. The spectacle "subjects the audience to emotional or psychological influence, verified by experience and mathematically calculated to produce specific emotional shocks in the spectator" (1923b:34). By reflexively repeating the performer's action the spectator becomes "infected" with emotion (1923a:38). Although Eisenstein will assert that this process includes both "motor imitation" and something else he calls "psychological empathy" (1924:40), the former gets far more emphasis.

Broadly, this view echoes ideas of other Russian thinkers, such as Tolstoy and Bukharin, who emphasized art's power to "infect" the spectator with feeling. More proximate is Theodore Lipps's doctrine of empathy, a term for the emotional absorption of the spectator in the spectacle. Many thinkers recast Lipps's account in physiological terms, and Eisenstein follows them in treating emotional arousal as arising from bodily changes. William James, whom Eisenstein would later mention as an influence, had stated the case this way: "We feel sorry because we cry, angry because we strike, afraid because we tremble . . . Without the bodily states following on the perception, the latter would be purely cognitive in form, pale, colorless, destitute of emotional warmth" (James 1892:376). James, however, rejected strict materialism. By contrast, Eisenstein assumes that emotional states are simply physiological processes operating at some higher level of activity. In support of this he invokes the language of reflex responses. The artist must create "a new chain of conditioned reflexes by associating selected phenomena with the unconditioned reflexes they produce" (1924:45). Throughout the 1920s Eisenstein will speak of spectatorial effect as "reflexological."

Such ideas do not commit Eisenstein to a single doctrinal position. He draws his physiological notions from various sources: Meyerhold's biomechanics (but now applied to the spectator), Tretyakov's insistence that art must organize the human psyche through the emotions, and purified Taylorist ideas promulgated by Alexey Gastev of the Central Institute of Labor. Likewise, it would probably be profitless to assign Eisenstein to a distinct "reflexological" tradition. His essays and interviews mention two researchers in physiology, Vladimir Bekhterev and Ivan Pavlov. Both men held that the reflex was the basis of animal behavior, and both distinguished between innate and acquired reflexes. Bekhterev, less cautious than Pavlov, extended reflex theory to all human action and social processes; his work may have encouraged Eisenstein to treat reflexes as central to aesthetic response. In later years, however, Eisenstein would attribute his "theory of artistic stimulants" solely to Pavlov, who came to enjoy great authority in Soviet science.[1]

1. Throughout the 1920s Eisenstein also read Freud, and he told interviewers that he sought to integrate Freud's and Pavlov's doctrines. His major theoretical writings of the period, however, do not invoke psychoanalytical accounts of the spectator. After 1930, when Freud was considered politically regressive

From the standpoint of avant-garde art, one advantage of Eisenstein's physiological model of effect is that it is frankly nonmimetic. The spectacle can stimulate the viewer even if it does not resemble the real world. No matter how stylized the spectacle may be, it stamps its effects on the spectator's body. These effects will, Eisenstein is confident, lead the perceiver to absorb the political theme. Eisenstein maintains that, just as primitive tribes' dances with animal skins were not imitations but rather practice exercises for hunting, so agitational theatre arouses emotion in order to train the Soviet citizen in the attitudes of the new society (1924:49).

If spectatorial impact is the end, formal organization becomes the means. Eisenstein describes form as a matter of "stimulants and their montage for a particular purpose" (1925d:66). In the 1923–1925 essays Eisenstein considers the basic unit of stimulation to be the "attraction."

Early in his career Eisenstein and Yutkevich formulated this idea in relation to fairground "attractions"—the sideshow, the roller coaster, the acrobatic turn. In 1923 Eisenstein offers a core definition: the attraction is "any aggressive moment in theatre" (1923b:34). The attraction is thereby defined functionally, not substantively. Anything that jolts the spectator's sensory apparatus counts as an attraction, regardless of source or artistic status: Romeo's soliloquy, the color of an actress's tights, a drumroll. Traditional theatre buries its attractions within a plot structure, but the theatre of agitation can isolate and organize them for political ends.

Attractions can be manifested in setting, lighting, or any other aspect of theatre (including firecrackers under the seats of the audience, as in *The Wiseman*). Eisenstein spends most time seeking to define how the actor's performance can become an attraction. This leads him to formulate one of the most pervasive and perduring concepts in his theoretical writings: expressive movement.

During the 1921–22 theatre season Eisenstein studied at Meyerhold's workshop, where he learned biomechanics. Meyerhold publicly announced the technique in the spring of 1922, emphasizing the training of the actor's reflexes through techniques borrowed from the eurhythmic gymnastics of Emile Jaques-Dalcroze. Eisenstein also worked with Nikolay Foregger, who undertook an actor-training regimen based upon a dancelike organization of movement. Foregger's *tyefe-trenage* system eventually became a grid of three hundred poses depicting stylized gestures. When in the summer of 1923 Eisenstein and Tretyakov recast the training regimen of the Moscow Proletkult's acting troupe, they proposed a "left" revision of such proposals.

Rejecting Jaques-Dalcroze and ignoring choreographic models, Eisenstein and Tretyakov argue for adapting the gymnastic theories of the German Rudolf Böde. In his *Expression-Gymnastics* (1922), Böde treated the human body as characterized both by physical constraints (wholeness, submission to gravity, and so on)

---

within the Soviet Union, Eisenstein seldom refers to him. Still, some psychoanalytic beliefs did influence his theories and films; he was particularly aware of his representations of male authority (1964: 20–33).

and by voluntary impulses, such as the desire to act. Eisenstein and Tretyakov take Böde's ideas as a point of departure for a theory of performance. By coordinating pure reflex-bound activity with conscious control, the actor creates the conditions for genuine expression.

The actor, therefore, does not pretend. The actor produces a movement that empathically registers in the spectator. This idea had circulated among theatre people well before World War I (Yampolsky 1991:32), but Eisenstein and Tretyakov stress the need for exaggerated delivery. Suppose the actor must deliver the line, "But there are two." The actor could simply utter the line and hold up two fingers. But this would not infect the audience with emotion. Eisenstein and Tretyakov recommend a more vigorous, stylized gesture: "How much the persuasiveness of the phrase itself would be strengthened, the expressiveness of the intonation, if on the first words, you made a recoil movement with the body while raising the elbow, and then with an energetic movement you threw the torso and the hand with the extended fingers forward. Furthermore, the braking of the wrist would vibrate (like a metronome)" (1923a:38). The spectator feels within his or her own body the actor's tension between impetus and muscular restraint. The muscular response triggers emotion.

A conventional gesture, such as making the sign of the cross, can also be considered expressive. It requires that the performer brake reflex by volition, and it calls forth emotional responses in the audience. For Eisenstein and Tretyakov even theatrical language is a type of expressive movement. Speech displays the pervasive tension between reflex and will, the pressure in the diaphragm versus intonational and articulatory control. In treating language as gesture, the writers subsume referential and denotative phenomena to the all-powerful expressive impulse. It is as if theatrical signs can yield conceptual meanings only after they have been given emotional thrust.

For many later theorists, a theory of artistic meaning starts with reference (to things) or denotation (of concepts). Affective qualities somehow arise from or are grafted onto these more basic "informational" properties. By contrast, Eisenstein will take artistic effect to be initially perceptual and emotional. Referential meanings and more abstract implications build upon "the emotional seizure of the audience" (1925d:61).

Eisenstein's move from theatre direction to filmmaking affected his thinking in ways that set him significantly apart from his contemporaries. Most Western and Soviet film theory sought to draw a sharp line between theatre and cinema. If cinema were likened to theatre, many worried, the purely reproductive role of the camera would be unduly emphasized and cinematic specificity would be ignored. Even theorists who emphasized photographic reproduction, such as Vertov, often denounced theatre as artificial and urged the director to take the camera out into raw reality.

In this context Eisenstein is anomalous. Although he does suggest important differences between theatre and film, he adapts many of his theatre-based ideas to his new medium. In cinema as in theatre, the goal of the spectacle is to shape the audience's response. Expressive movement will therefore have a place as a cinematic attraction.

Kuleshov had proposed the idea that the film actor ought to become a "model" or "mannequin" *(naturshchik)*. "We need unusual, striking people, we need 'monsters' . . . The 'monsters' are people who could train their bodies and achieve complete mastery of its [*sic*] material construction" (Kuleshov 1987:56). Kuleshov recommended adapting the pantomime techniques of François Delsarte. In 1924 Eisenstein rejects such a static, codified approach to film acting because it turns the actors into "mechanical dolls" (1924:58). He continues to insist that only organic movement can create truly expressive gesture. He repeats that movements expressing a character's psychology will stress the conflict between reflex and volition.

Throughout the 1920s, expressive movement is central to Eisenstein's film practice. In the flurry of fists that explodes during the mourning for Vakulinchuk, the clash between political restraint and instinctive rebellion yields a disciplined collective outrage. When Marfa Lapkina cries "No more can we live thus!" her spontaneous revulsion in hurling down her plow is transformed into a conscious gesture of exhortation to her comrades. Eisenstein's pedagogy will return to the concept of expressive movement in its consideration of *mise en jeu* and *mise en geste*.

Still, he is obliged to admit a major difference between theatre and cinema. Theatre's attractions trip off immediate effects. The presence of the performer creates the "physiological perception of actually occurring fact . . . a direct animal audience action through a motor imitative act towards a live character like oneself" (1924:41). Film, however, operates indirectly. It shows not facts but "conventional (photographic) representations." A piece of stage guignol, with agonizing screams and spurting blood, can never be matched in intensity on film.

How, then, is the film spectator to be moved? Eisenstein, perhaps building on suggestions by Pavlov, Bekhterev, and Freud, concludes that only by creating *associations* in the viewer's mind can an attraction achieve perceptual and emotional power. A shot of a hand with a knife evokes a range of associations that can be coordinated with associations attending a shot of a screaming face. Later in the 1920s he will contrast his work with that of the Surrealists; they try, he says, simply to *expose* "subconscious emotions," whereas he seeks "to use them and play with them to *provoke* emotion" (1930a:202; italics added).

Eisenstein's emphasis on cinematic association has several implications. Most explicitly, it fits neatly with his reflexology. Associations allow the filmmaker to "condition" the audience's response by training preexisting reflexes through the proper combination of stimuli.

Moreover, processes of association can replace the romances and intrigues of traditional cinema. Eisenstein envisions the "plotless" agit-film as one dominated by chains of association triggering perceptual and emotional "shocks." This conception in turn hints at a rationale for his strategy of building a film through intertwining motifs. The dangling pince-nez in *Potemkin* can represent the overthrow of a decaying class because the spectacles, already associated with petit-bourgeois mores, have been introduced and developed in a controlled context that includes Smirnov's haughtiness and the worm-infested meat. The conflict in *Strike* is intensified by associating the capitalists with animals and the workers with machinery. Within a scene and across the whole film, the director can create emotional and expressive effects by weaving associative networks.

From his belief that cinematic effect requires association Eisenstein draws the conclusion that to compensate for the mediated quality of cinema, a film must dwell upon its attractions for a longer time than a theatrical production needs to. The associations must be firmly in place before they can be recast and combined. In his films the emphasis on prolonging the process produces gradual modulations of action and imagery, as in *Strike*'s slaughter or the extended massacre on the Odessa Steps. In his later teaching and writing he will insist that a lengthy crescendo produces a powerful emotional climax.

The concept of association also encourages Eisenstein to probe the very texture of the cinematic material. Once one has decided to guide the audience's process of association, then one must scrutinize every scrap of material in the frame and any possible join of shot to shot. The result is not only a practice that experiments with the minute particulars of the medium but a film poetics that attempts to systematize the principles governing form and style.

Montage in Theatre and Film

Eisenstein is commonly thought of as a "formalist" theorist. But this does not mean that he emphasizes "form" over "content." This distinction does not have much force for him, since he sees both factors as part of a broader process. Like most of those working in the Soviet *technē*-centered trend, he refuses the standard concept of form as a vessel holding "contents." Instead, he conceives form as a transformation of material in accordance with the art work's social tasks. Form also represents the perceptible dimension of the work and thus serves as the basis for the spectator's engagement. Form, as a dynamic process of construction, will therefore trigger the work's effects.

Early on, Eisenstein conceives of the spectator as his material, with the techniques of theatre furnishing the tools for working on it. The particular theatrical production will be built out of attractions—theatrical techniques selected for their power to stimulate strong perceptual and emotional reactions. The attractions will in turn be arranged in a certain pattern. The idea of *montage* represents Eisenstein's most basic and persistent conception of the ways in which formal units may be combined.

The Russian *montazh*, taken from the French *montage*, retains many of its original meanings. One is "machine assembly," in the sense of "mounting" a motor. This sense came to be metaphorically applied to artistic work in the Constructivist era. Photomontage, *litmontazh* ("literature-montage"), and other terms described the construction that resulted from the labors of the artist-engineer. "One does not create a work," writes Eisenstein in his diary in 1919; "one constructs it with finished parts, like a machine. *Montage* is a beautiful word: it describes the process of constructing with prepared fragments" (Aumont 1987:150).

To the machine-based sense of montage the Constructivist ethos linked a second one: assembling materials in a way that generates a degree of friction among them. In this way, the concept of montage constituted the Constructivists' recasting of the Cubists' practice of collage. The notion of montage as a tension-based assembly is also central to Eisenstein's earliest usage. His productions of Tretyakov's plays became famous for their "montage" of attractions—a dissonant juxtaposition of fragments.

In the theatre, montage was thus a macrostructural principle, a way of governing the overall form of the production. Tretyakov pointed out that theatrical montage could be conceived in two ways, depending on its relation to the plot of the piece. In *The Wiseman*, Ostrovsky's plot provided a minimal continuity for a string of circus and variety attractions. Eisenstein celebrates this aspect in his 1923 manifesto: *The Wiseman* offers "a free montage with arbitrarily chosen independent . . . effects (attractions)" (1923b:35). In contrast, in *Do You Hear, Moscow?* Tretyakov indicated that the montage of attractions entered into a dynamic interplay with the plot; the attractions, both naturalistic and stylized, intensified or commented upon the action. The tension-based side of montage remained, less in the friction among separate attractions than in the clash between a relatively coherent plot and moments of amplified, emotionally arousing spectacle. It is this form of construction, the accentuation of a large-scale plot through diverting attractions, that Eisenstein uses in his silent films.

Upon coming to cinema, however, Eisenstein was confronted with a more microstructural conception of montage. In both French and Russian, *montage* also denotes film editing. Although the concept has implications for macrostructure, most writers restrict it to matters involving what we might call the stylistic texture of the film: the ways in which shots A and B could be joined to create a particular impression.

Again it was Kuleshov who gave the concept particular significance. As early as 1917 he argued that cinema is distinguished from other arts by virtue of the fact that montage organizes "separately filmed fragments, disordered and disjointed, into a more advantageous, integral and rhythmical sequence" (Kuleshov 1917:41). For Kuleshov, montage was the essential factor differentiating cinema from the other arts and forming the basis of the specific impact that film can make. In a series of informal experiments, he showed that editing could create emotions and ideas not present in either of the single shots. A man and woman look offscreen; cut to a building. We will assume that they are looking at the building, even if the first shot was made in Moscow and the second in New York. A man with a neutral expression looks off; cut to a shot of a banquet table; cut back to him, and now he will look hungry. Kuleshov's doctrine treated montage as the director's principal tool in shaping the exact response desired.

Kuleshov's account was almost wholly craft-bound; he offered no explanation for these phenomena. His student Pudovkin went only a little further, suggesting that certain editing devices are transpositions of ordinary perceptual acts, such as the focusing of attention on a detail or the shifting of attention across a scene (1926:67–73). On the whole, however, he too simply recommended certain editing options as most effective in achieving the preferred results. Along similar lines, in 1926 Timoshenko published a detailed typology of montage devices ("concentration" cuts, "expansion" cuts, rhythmic editing, point-of-view editing, and so on). His comprehensive inventory of editing techniques indicates the extent to which Soviet filmmakers sought to put film craft on a systematic basis.

Kuleshov and his followers drew only oblique comparisons between film editing and the Constructivist conception of montage. Dziga Vertov was more forthright. Like Kuleshov, he celebrated the power of editing to create a whole out of details— to assemble a man "more perfect than Adam" (1984:17). But he took the machine analogy much further. For him, the very analysis of movement was an act of montage. So, indeed, was the entire filmmaking process. Selecting and researching a subject, filming it, and assembling the results were to be understood as montage in the broadest sense (72). Film production became like factory production, the assembly of a whole out of pieces trimmed to fit. This analogy between filmmaking and manufacturing forms a major theme of Vertov's *Man with a Movie Camera* (1929).

Immersed in filmmaking, neither Vertov nor the Kuleshovians had the inclination or the leisure to elaborate a broad theory of cinematic montage. The most systematic attempt was made by the Formalist literary theorists, who sketched a poetics of cinema parallel to the one they proposed for literature. Approaching a film as a system of interrelated components, the Formalists studied how formal devices transformed material and accomplished particular functions.

Two important accounts of montage were offered in the 1927 Formalist collection, *The Poetics of Cinema*. Boris Eikhenbaum suggested thinking of montage as purely a stylistic system, distinct from plot construction. He proposed that it was analogous to syntax in language, and he traced levels of articulation: the frame, the "cine-phrase" (a string of shots grouped around an accentual nucleus such as a close-up), and the "cine-period" (a larger unit based on spatiotemporal unity) (1927b:21–25).

By contrast, Yury Tynyanov compared montage to prosody. He argued that editing does not so much group shots as force them into a system of rhythmic equivalences. When shot B replaces shot A, there is a jump like that occurring between lines in verse. The result, according to Tynyanov, is a shift in semantic energy: the break-up into shots or verse lines, by creating equivalent rhythmic units, invites the reader to compare meanings across units. Citing *The Battleship Potemkin* as an example, Tynyanov declared that a plot cannot be easily divorced from its stylistic patterning, and concluded that "the study of plot in cinema in the future will depend on the study of its style and, in particular, of its material" (1927:52).

In the second half of the 1920s Eisenstein draws on all these ideas. Like Kuleshov, he considers that the relation of shot to shot forms "the essence of cinema" (1926a:79), and he uses a pun to stress that a new quality emerges out of the conjuncture. "The conditions of cinema create an 'image' [*obraz*] from the juxtaposition of these 'cuts' [*obrez*]" (80). Like Vertov, he suggests that the montage principle goes beyond the technique of editing. And like the Formalists, he will examine in detail the concrete effects of montage juxtaposition.

He therefore highlights certain features of montage. Editing, coordinated with sharp changes in camera angle, can intensify a sequence's "accuracy and force of impact" (1924:46). Montage can provoke and prolong those associations that distinguish cinematic response from theatrical response. Montage enables the director to dwell on salient material long enough to enable "the thorough inculcation of the associations" (41). Whereas Kuleshov considered montage to be a storytelling technique, Eisenstein sees no reason for it to be bound by plot requirements. As cinema's chief tool for creating perceptual and affective impact, montage can freely deviate from the story's demands, just as the assembly of attractions did in his theatrical productions.

In such ways, Eisenstein follows the Constructivist tradition of treating montage as a strategy for forming material in any medium. One consequence of this decision is an idea that will dominate his career: cinema is not opposed to theatre by virtue of some specific essence, but rather represents the stage beyond theatre in the evolution of art. Eisenstein will soon apply the concept of montage far more broadly than any Constructivist would, finding it in Kabuki, Zola, and *Ulysses*. Denoting both a powerful film technique and a pervasive principle of *poiēsis*, the concept of montage becomes obsessively interrogated and reworked throughout his career.

Film Language and Intellectual Cinema

From 1923 through 1927 Eisenstein concentrates largely upon the ways in which expressive movement and shot juxtaposition can arouse the viewer's senses and emotions. In the late 1920s he expands his theoretical purview. Perceptual and emotional effect on the viewer remains central, but he also speculates on how cinema can provoke ideas. He starts to examine film's resemblance to language and other convention-based systems of signification. At the same time he begins to explore finer-grained questions of film style: the factors that go into the composition of a shot, the multiplicity of options opened by montage. And in his most celebrated theoretical sally of the period, he seeks to integrate his evolving notions of film form with current Soviet reflections on dialectical materialism.

His thinking continues to be driven by the prescriptive concerns of agitprop filmmaking. How can one impell the audience to entertain certain doctrines? The task of cinematography is "the deep and slow drilling in of conceptions" (1929g:34). The artwork's "message" will then be furnished a priori—a slogan, a Party policy, a general thesis. But if form is to remain a process, it cannot be simply the statement of a message. Form must engage the audience in an activity that yields the concept as a product. And Eisenstein insists that this process must still constitute a *total* engagement of the spectator: not only thought but also perception and affect. He aims for a synthesis of right thinking and emotional transport: "It must restore to science its sensuality. To the intellectual process its fire and passion" (1929h:158).[2]

As so often in his career, the theoretical problem issued from a filmmaking project. In editing *October* (1928) he had experimented with moments of "intellectual cinema." By intercutting between the battlefield and the home front, he had materialized metaphors: the tsarist eagle swooping down on the troops, a flunky's document triggering a bombardment, a tank lowered off an assembly line "oppressing" soldiers in the trench. He had shown Kerensky as at once walking to his quarters and ascending through the ranks of official titles. Most memorably, the "God and Country" sequence had turned a group of statues into emblems of incompatible ideas of deity. Cutting *October* left Eisenstein burning to make a film of *Capital* and to explain theoretically how one could use cinema to generate concepts.

As a category, "plotless cinema" included films without an individual-centered romantic plot, but Eisenstein now speculates that cinema can dispense with plot entirely. "Plot is only one of the means without which we still do not know how to communicate something to the spectator" (1929c:179). The *Capital* film was to be an essay in which the development of ideas would hold central place. This cinema of intellectual discourse would, Eisenstein believed, transcend the distinction between newsreel and fiction. Showing nonfictional events and dealing with history, it would also present a poetically charged argument about the abstract laws of social change.

The urge to explore an intellectual cinema leads Eisenstein to extend reflexological assumptions to the realm of ideas. Like emotion, thought becomes a physical activity, involving the brain and the nervous system. Eisenstein does not try to demonstrate this; he simply assumes that thought cannot be radically different from, say, vision or digestion. "The 'psychic' in perception is merely the physiological process of a *higher nervous activity*" (1929e:183). Such a reductive materialism had become widespread in the Soviet academy. Bekhterev had advocated a sweeping and reductive reflexology, and Pavlov's research was popularly understood along the same lines. The educational psychology of A. P. Pinkevich took unconditioned reflexes as the basis for creating new reactions and associations that would mold correct intellectual behavior. Many scholars and scientists, often identified as "Mechanists," held that a properly Bolshevik science of the mind would eventually reduce all "mental" phenomena to physical factors.

As usual, currently circulating views stirred Eisenstein's speculations. In "The

---

2. The essay from which this is taken, "Perspectives," may have been aimed at the literary "fellow travelers" sympathetic to the doctrines of Alexander Voronsky. Voronsky wrote in the same year: "Art and science have one and the same subject—life, reality. But science analyzes, art synthesizes; science is abstract, art concrete; science is directed to man's reason, art to his sensuous nature" (Mathewson 1975: 181).

Montage of Attractions" he had claimed that in theatre "the path to knowledge" runs through "the living play of the passions" (1923b:34). Now he asserts that "intellectual attraction by no means excludes 'emotionality.' After all, a reflex action is perceived as the so-called presence of an affect" (1927b:25). His writings of the late 1920s sketch out a three-stage process, passing from perception through emotion to cognition. Perception of an event triggers some motor activity, which in turn yields an emotion; the emotion then launches a process of thought. This three-stage model will become central to Eisenstein's theoretical work, shaping several taxonomies of formal options.

He further exploits monistic materialism in order to link cognition to expressive movement. Watching spectators rock to and fro during the mowing sequence of *Old and New,* he is confirmed in his conviction that a primitive motor activity is the basis of more refined responses, and that these can be harnessed to produce intellectual effects. "Who has not drummed rhythmically with his fist, memorizing 'Surplus value is . . .' In other words who has not given visual stimulation a helping hand by including some sort of motor rhythm in order to memorize abstract truths?" (1929h:157) In its fullest manifestation, cognition becomes kin-esthetic.

The reductivist thesis also enables Eisenstein to revive the possibility of finding that "common denominator" of response first broached in "The Montage of Attractions." In the Japanese theatre he discovers a "monistic ensemble." Here stage setting or music is not subordinated to action or dialogue. Instead, Kabuki grants various sensory channels an equal status in triggering spectatorial response. Eisenstein's example is a scene from *The Loyal Forty-Seven Ronin* in which the protagonist is leaving the castle. The idea of separation is conveyed via a series of staging devices: the actor walks farther away, then the setting is changed to a more distant view of the castle, then a curtain drops in front of the castle, and finally, as the actor moves out onto the stage ramp, a *samisen* is heard. For Eisenstein, since the realm of physiological response is uniform, all stimuli are equivalent. Thus one stimulus may do duty for another or reinforce another by repetition. When two or more channels act simultaneously, the effect is even greater, yielding "a brilliantly calculated blow of the billiard cue at the audience's cerebral hemisphere" (1928f:119). The artist remains a calculator of stimulants, choosing and arranging them for maximum physiological impact.

Not satisfied with conceiving film form as a matter of choosing and arranging stimulants, Eisenstein starts to consider the possibility that cinema constitutes a system of signs. It is likely that he was encouraged in this line of inquiry by the 1927 *Poetics of Cinema* collection, wherein several authors suggested treating the shot semiotically. In addition, *October*'s motivic opposition between static signs and dynamic ones probably helped crystallize Eisenstein's interest in semiotic problems.

Eisenstein never wholly abandons the concept of attractions, but his essays of 1928–29 propose that the shot can also be considered a depictive sign. Central to his argument is the suggestion that like language, visual systems of representation rely on convention. His conception of convention seems to be that of a widespread agreement among members of a social group.

Eisenstein distinguishes "pure" conventionalism (what semiologists today would call "arbitrary" signs) from the "logical" (or "motivated") signs of theatre. Sometimes, he says, the logical sign resembles what it represents, as when concentric circles painted on the Chinese actor's face identify him as the "Oyster Ghost." Sometimes an object with a specific function has withered into a conventional sign; the general's epaulettes once served to ward off blows. But no matter how a sign is motivated, Eisenstein suggests, it remains tied to a social whole by convention. "Positivist realism is by no means the correct form of perception. It is simply a function of a particular form of social structure, following on from an autocratic state that has propagated a state uniformity of thought" (1929b:142).

If cinema manipulates conventional signs, what are the features of this semiotic system? Some theorists of the era were tempted to draw analogies to verbal language. It was commonplace to talk of a "film language," as in Eikhenbaum's conception of "cine-phrases" and "cine-periods." Eisenstein is closer to Tynyanov in conceiving film "language" as more like poetic language; he speaks of borrowing techniques from literature to achieve a "figurative" use of cinema (1928b:96). He focuses this figurativeness by means of analogies drawn from his knowledge of Asian culture.

Eisenstein first compares cinema to the Japanese writing system. Individual shots are like the simpler graphic characters or "ideograms." For example, one character denotes "dog" and one denotes "mouth." Eisenstein points out that each character is pictorial, retaining a degree of resemblance to the physical referent. In order to convey certain concepts, the writing system combines signs: the character for "dog" plus that for "mouth" yields a third one, which signifies a new idea, "to bark." Eisenstein sees this process as analogous to film editing, which creates a meaning that cannot be represented in either shot.[3]

The process is figurative because the meaning is not denoted in either sign; it emerges through juxtaposition. The metaphorical quality of the process is made plain by another example supplied by Eisenstein: the character for "sorrow" consists of the combination of the characters denoting "knife" and "heart."

Here is a starting point for the formal process of intellectual cinema. Still, the ideogram yields only a "dry" concept. It lacks emotion. Eisenstein turns his attention to Japanese lyric poetry, where the method of combination creates a

---

3. By contemporary standards of linguistic inquiry, Eisenstein's account is problematic. Linguists reject the term *ideogram* for describing Chinese and Japanese writing systems, since it tends to suggest that these systems somehow represent ideas or things pictorially, without appeal to the spoken language. Eisenstein seems to succumb to this error when he talks of a new concept's being born through the conjunction of two characters. In fact, Chinese and Japanese writing are "glottographic": they represent units of speech, so that "dog," "mouth," and "bark" are already imbued with semantic content by virtue of their place in the overall conceptual space of the spoken language. In contemporary terminology, Eisenstein is interested in the "motivated" aspects of the Japanese writing system, but these consist of relatively few "depictive" characters. See Sampson 1985: 148–150.

more evocative result. A verse of three or five lines juxtaposes concrete referential images in order to create an emotionally charged idea. This suggestion seems close to Tynyanov's proposal that the jump from line to line in verse resembles that from shot to shot in cinema. Yet Eisenstein sees less of an equivalence or exchange between unfolding elements than a holistic assembly out of distinct pieces.

From poetry Eisenstein moves to other realms. He points out that the woodblock artist Sharaku represents the separate features of a face accurately but creates an expressive portrayal by combining the features disproportionately. Ever alert for the "monistic ensemble," Eisenstein also implies that the principle of juxtaposition is present in the Japanese puppet theatre, in which the combination of the silent puppet onstage and the verbal commentary of the *joruri* chanter yields a new meaning for the spectator.

Eisenstein's argument here is not a paradigm of linear reasoning. The analogies shift treacherously. At first the shot is said to resemble a single graphic character in Japanese writing; then the shot becomes equivalent to the several characters composing a line of verse. Moreover, neither the character nor the line offers a strict parallel to the shot, since Eisenstein really uses both analogies to get at different ways in which a shot may behave. A shot may be neutral and univocal, like an isolated character; or it may be rich in suggestion, like a line of verse.

Eisenstein pursues this idea further, claiming (on obscure grounds) that the lone ideogram conveys a concept unemotionally, whereas the poem is suffused with feeling. Yet Eisenstein does not say what *concepts* are conveyed by the lyric. On the face of it, *haikai* or *tanka* verse would seem unlikely vehicles for "drilling in" political doctrine. By the time Eisenstein puts forward his claims about Sharaku's distortions, he has narrowed his case to a single instance that may not be typical of Japanese art as a whole, let alone cinema.

As Eisenstein's ideas stand, they remain unrefined. He seems torn between a need to make the perception-emotion-cognition chain serve a strictly sloganizing purpose and a fascination with the more intractable, fine-grained aspects of the cinematic material. These receive increasing attention in the last essays of the decade.

Film Form as Dialectics

After his brief exploration of the linguistic analogy, Eisenstein tries to conceive the formal process of montage in yet another way. In several essays of 1929, he explores the possibility that montage makes shots "collide."

Eisenstein's views again echo broader debates of the era. In 1922 Lenin had advocated "the systematic study of Hegelian dialectics from a materialist standpoint" (1922:233). The year 1925 saw the publication of Engels' *Dialectics of Nature* and Lenin's notes "On the Question of Dialectics." Engels declared that modern science was not only materialist but dialectical, while Lenin observed that dialectics was at once a scientific method, a law of the world, and "a law of cognition" (Lenin 1925:359). These rediscovered writings threw the Soviet intelligentsia into a turmoil, challenging the supremacy of the Mechanistic materialists and giving comfort to the emerging faction known as the Dialecticians. In philosophy, Dialecticians gathered under the banner of Avram Deborin and began an unremitting campaign against reductivist doctrines. The Dialecticians, following Engels, argued that any material system was in ceaseless movement. Necessary contradictions within the system yielded not only quantitative changes but also qualitative transformations.

In psychological circles, the reflexologists found themselves facing formidable Dialecticians, notably K. N. Kornilov, who had launched a "Marxist psychology" as early as 1923. For Kornilov and his followers, there was necessarily a qualitative leap from physiological processes to subjective activity. Consciousness became defined as a "property" of the most highly organized matter known to science, the human brain. Kornilov believed that the scientific explanation of behavior would eventually conform to Engels' three laws of dialectics: the transformation of quantity into quality, the interpenetration and struggle of opposites, and the negation of the negation. As head of the Moscow Institute of Psychology, Kornilov attracted brilliant young researchers such as Lev Vygotsky and A. R. Luria.

Artists joined the controversy. Critics of painting began to invoke the leap from quantity to quality, while even the Symbolist Andrei Bely sought (in his 1929 monograph *Rhythm as Dialectics*) to link his poetics to the new trend. Eisenstein was drawn into the debates. During the late 1920s, he met frequently with Vygotsky and Luria (Ivanov 1976:66), and he undoubtedly knew of Vygotsky's view that the artwork is predicated upon conflicts between form and content. "By making opposite impulses collide, [the artwork] destroys the affect of content and form, and initiates an explosive discharge of nervous energy" (Vygotsky 1925:215).

In 1929 Eisenstein begins to frame questions of film form and effect in dialectical terms. The key text, and perhaps his most influential essay of the silent era, is "The Dramaturgy of Film Form."

He starts from the Engels-Lenin view that every phenomenon, natural or social, constitutes a tense field of opposed forces pressing toward a synthesis at a higher level. He declares that art is a dialectical interaction of organic and rational form, and that it seeks to "reveal the contradictions of being" (1929c:161). The individual artwork is also a dialectical whole, holding in precarious balance rigid formula and expressive distortion (as instantiated in the tension between meter and rhythm in verse).

He also posits a dialectical epistemology, whereby the very process of coming to know reflects the actual course of the world. That is, correct thinking is dialectical in form. For Eisenstein, who always treats form as process, the agitational artwork must not only reflect the dynamic of the world but also provoke the spectator into patterns of thought. Intellectual cinema has a new task: it will teach the worker to think dialectically.

Eisenstein proceeds to recast his conception of film form in terms of dialectical

conflict. He starts from the Constructivist belief that factors composing the individual image can be considered as dynamic elements flung together in tense
juxtaposition. Drawing examples from his films, he goes on to itemize all the
conflicts that may be found in the frame. There are conflicts of line, of plane, of
volume, of lighting, of tempo of movement. There are also conflicts between the
object and the framing (yielding the camera angle), between the object in space
and the properties of the lens (yielding optical distortion, as in wide-angle shots),
between the event and its temporal representation on film (yielding slow- or fast-
motion effects).

Eisenstein sees conflict within the shot as only "potential" montage. Dialectical
montage operates fully when one image is put into interaction with another.
Kuleshov and Pudovkin conceived editing as a linkage of shots, an assemblage
built "brick by brick." But Eisenstein asserts that linkage is only a weak version
of the more basic process of conflict.

Both Engels and Lenin took the biological "cell" as the model of dialectical
change, since its splitting produces a new unity. Eisenstein therefore speaks of the
shot as a "montage cell" (1929c:166). The analogy is somewhat obscure, but it
appears to rest on two points of resemblance. First, as the shot accumulates
quantitative tensions, such as that of figure and background or light and dark, it
cannot resolve them internally and thus "divides" into another shot. Second, this
process of division goes beyond mere proliferation: as in biology, the assembly of
cells produces a complex entity of a higher order. In this respect, the juxtaposition
of conflicting shots is a "leap into a new quality" in Engels' sense: an impression
or concept not present in the individual images.

A dialectical concept is also at the basis of the "tentative film syntax" proposed
in "The Dramaturgy of Film Form," one of the two hierarchical taxonomies
Eisenstein will build in 1929. At the lowest level he finds conflict governing the
perception of motion in cinema. He claims that when the visual system registers
the quantitative disparity between two frames, there occurs a leap to a new
quality—movement. This phenomenon takes place at the level of the shot, but
the noncoincidence of the two frames forms the determining technical basis for
later types of montage.

We arrive at montage proper when we move to a second level. Here the
filmmaker can create an illusion of movement by juxtaposing two shots. Eisenstein's example of a "logical" use of this technique is a passage in *October* wherein
he creates a machine gun's rattling burst by intercutting very brief shots of parts
of the gun. An "alogical" instance is the stone lion that appears to leap up after
the Odessa Steps massacre. In both the first and the second domains, the montage
affects principally the spectator's perception.

A third possibility is to move to the level of emotion. Here conflicts between
shots yield those associations that Eisenstein believes to be central to cinema's
impact. His principal example is that of the slaughter of the bull intercut with
the massacre of the workers at the conclusion of *Strike.* Interestingly, Eisenstein
does not treat this as a metaphor or a piece of intellectual cinema; the two

conflicting shot series aim for "a powerful emotional intensification of the scene" (1929c:176).

Eisenstein's final category of montage moves sharply toward concept and metaphor. Here montage frees the action from "its conditioning by time and space" (1929c:177). This category is fairly roomy. It includes cutting between two diegetic events, as when in *October* shots of soldiers huddling in a trench are intercut with shots of a cannon lowered off an assembly line. This category of montage also includes instances that depart from the story world altogether, as in *October*'s little dissertation on God and country. In both types, spatial and temporal relations remain undefined. Eisenstein insists that such montage remains "dialectical" in producing emotion-laden concepts as a synthesis out of conflict.

This taxonomy can be read as Eisenstein's effort to bring a systematic order to the rather helter-skelter typology of montage offered by Timoshenko in his 1926 monograph. Overall, Eisenstein's scheme corresponds to the three-stage model of perception-affect-cognition and thus has the virtue of subsuming an empirical list of formal possibilities in a unified conception of the viewer's activity.

At the philosophical level, Eisenstein's use of dialectical concepts is highly questionable. The concept of conflict is simply applied too broadly to be of much explanatory value. The term seems to denote any incongruity, comparison, or juxtaposition; it dwindles to difference. When Eisenstein insists on recasting all differences as conflicts, he extends the idea to questionable cases. In what meaningful sense does a camera angle represent a conflict between the profilmic object and the framing? Similarly, two long shots of a prairie, with the horizon in approximately the same zone, are hardly in conflict unless one postulates in advance that all shot changes instantiate conflict—in which case no counterexample will ever test the explanatory hypothesis.

Furthermore, the idea that every conflict between shots produces a "third something" in the Hegelian manner presumes that the spectator is building ever-ascending dialectical unities. Not only does a synthesis arise from the conflict of shots A and B, B and C, and so forth; if the dialectical model applies, the unity derived from the A-B conflict itself ought to enter into conflict with the unity derived from the B-C one. This conflict gets resolved in a unity that in turn conflicts with one arising from the interaction of shots C and D and shots D and E; and so on indefinitely. As an account of how spectators make sense of movies, this is wildly implausible.

Although the "dialectical" side of Eisenstein's story is conceptually weak, it bears fruit at the level of a practical poetics. In the 1927 Formalist anthology, Boris Kazansky proposed that montage constitutes "the 'dramaturgy' of film form . . . Cinema has still not worked out the formal methods for its own 'word,' it still does not have its own 'language' which would allow the cinematic craftsman to 'think in frames' in the same way that a poet thinks in verbal images" (1927:77–78).

Eisenstein replies with a poetics of cinematic construction that suggests how the filmmaker might "think in frames." For example, Eisenstein's principled inventory of compositional options remains a useful advance in the consideration of shot design in cinema. Treating the film image as a dynamic ensemble of elements sensitizes the analyst to stylistic properties that can be systematically explored. Likewise, the great influence of the "Dramaturgy" essay in the West may be partly a result of the tendency of filmmakers to find visual conflicts an ad hoc guide for imagining possible compositions and editing patterns.

Eisenstein marks out another area of inquiry in his speculations about how abstract meanings are generated. Kuleshov had pointed out that viewers tend intuitively to construe disparate shots as spatially and temporally continuous. Eisenstein asks how spectators, confronted with shots that they take as spatially and temporally *discontinuous,* create a more abstract meaning or idea. Does the viewer take continuity as a default value, dropping it only when presented with some specific cues, or with the absence of others? Does the filmmaker who wants shots to be perceived as signs have to stage them a certain way—say, film an object against a neutral background, like many of the nondiegetic shots in *October*? In raising such questions, Eisenstein's close attention to editing options and levels of spectatorial response stands alone in Soviet film theory of the period and remains an important heuristic probe into central issues of film form.

Another major essay of 1929, "The Fourth Dimension in Cinema," retains the dialectical emphasis of the "Dramaturgy" piece but offers a richer taxonomy of formal options. Instead of postulating a conflict between equal forces within the shot, Eisenstein proposes that every cut juxtaposes two shots on the basis of some salient feature, the *dominant.* In cinematic montage, Eisenstein claims, the dominant is not absolute or stable. Shots A and B might be joined according to similarity of length, whereas shots B and C might take as the dominant factor the movement within the frame.

Cutting on the dominant does not exhaust the editing possibilities. Every image bristles with "a whole complex of secondary stimulants" (1929e:182). Joining shots A and B by similarity of length will demote all other factors, such as shot content and pictorial composition. Eisenstein names these secondary factors *over-tones.* In acoustics, overtones are resonances produced by the dominant tone. Juxtaposing shots according to some dominant automatically creates elusive but rich relations among succeeding shots' overtones. Scriabin and Debussy organized harmonic overtones into new musical structures; the filmmaker who is sensitive to visual overtones can discover more powerful sources of filmic structure and affect.

The concept of the dominant retains ties to Eisenstein's physiological interests; Bekhterev and others had used the term to refer to brain centers that "dominate" a given behavior. More proximately, the term had also emerged in Russian Formalist literary theory. Yury Tynyanov had described the dominant as "the preeminence of one group of elements and the resulting deformation of other elements" (Erlich 1981:199). Yet Eisenstein does not simply apply the concept of the poetic dominant to cinema. He tries to refine the concept itself. By positing a fluctuating dominant and by seeking to describe the interplay among subsidiary factors, "The

Fourth Dimension in Cinema" pushes further Tynyanov's concept of the artwork as a dynamic system (1924:33–34).

Armed with a dominant/overtone model of editing construction, Eisenstein lays out a new set of montage options.

1. The simplest sort of montage is that which takes as its dominant the absolute length of each shot. Eisenstein calls this *metric* montage. Although this option takes no notice of the content of the shot, it offers some formal possibilities, chiefly involving the establishment of a consistent beat from shot to shot. Eisenstein gives as an example the accelerating dance of the Wild Division in *October*.

2. *Rhythmic* montage is that which determines shot length by content. A simple example would be the customary practice of allowing long shots more screen time than close-ups. Eisenstein appears to conceive of rhythm as working with both *tempo* and *accent*. As in music, filmic rhythm will emerge in interaction with the norm established by the meter. Thus the Odessa Steps sequence utilizes rhythmic montage in that the lengths of the shots of the descending soldiers never fall into a stable beat-pattern.

3. A less clear-cut category is that of *tonal* montage. Eisenstein seems to conceive 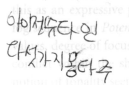this as an expressive pictorial quality that pervades the shots. For example, the [fog sequence in] *Potemkin* has as its dominant the tonal quality of gloom. Light[ing], degree of focus, graphic shapes, and all the other factors that can generate [tone within a] shot now become the source of tonal dominants. Lest the notion of tonality seem vague, Eisenstein is quick to insist that such a quality can be measured; the gloomy shot can be assigned "a mathematical coefficient for a simple degree of illuminatio]n" (1929e:189).

4. All three previous types of montage concern editing on the basis of some dominant feature—shot length, overall content, primary expressive qualities. *Overtonal* montage, by contrast, involves "taking full account of all the stimulants in the shot" (1929e:191). Eisenstein claims to have innovated the visual overtone in *Old and New*, where several sequences replace the dominant with "'democratic' equal rights for all the stimulants, viewed together as a complex" (182). The religious procession of peasants hoping to relieve the drought is edited to bring out secondary expressive qualities: the solemn advance of the icons, the frenzy of the supplicating peasants, the broiling heat of the sun, and parching thirst.

Eisenstein believed that the concept of the visual overtone was one of his most important contributions, and he would return to it in his later writing. In "The Fourth Dimension in Cinema" the overtone is considered a sensuous quality subordinate to the overall expressive cast of the shot. Later, as he began to conceive of montage as a "polyphonic" structure, he began to subsume the notion of overtones into a larger category, that of the "motif" or "voice," which included recurrent framings, objects, or gestures (1940h:330–331).

5. As in the earlier typology, *intellectual* montage constitutes the highest stage of montage form. This involves "resonances of overtones of an intellectual order" (1929e:193). Interestingly, Eisenstein does not allow the possibility that intellectual relations can serve as a dominant. Even *October*'s "Gods" sequence starts from a

"universally human" *emotional* tonality associated with the images of deities and only then moves toward "class-intellectual . . . resonances."[4]

According to Eisenstein, each of these formal possibilities produces a specific effect on the spectator. Metric montage arouses the most primitive kinesthetic effect, such as tapping the foot or rocking the body. Rhythmic montage triggers a "primitive emotional" effect, while tonal montage yields something of a higher physiological order, a "melodic-emotional" response (1929e:190). Overtonal montage, Eisenstein says, repeats at a higher level the motor effect of metric montage, since in music a thoroughgoing organization of timbres will create emergent beats. And intellectual montage triggers the spectator's concept-forming processes, although these too must be seen as no less physiological than the other types. The common denominator of all these visual phenomena, and of all acoustic phenomena too, is cross-modal physiological sensation: no longer "I see" or "I hear" but rather "I feel."

This scheme is challenging enough, but we have not yet plumbed its audacity. Eisenstein brings back dialectics. He insists that all the juxtapositions he has itemized should be conceived as conflictual. The overtone is potentially in opposition to the dominant, intellectual overtones clash with other sorts, and so on. A sequence may even set two local dominants in conflict. The dialectic thus leaps up the ladder, to be resolved, at best provisionally, in the spectator's experience.

Once more, Eisenstein construes the concept of dialectic so broadly as to make it vacuous or unchallengeable, and he posits an implausibly elaborate spectatorial activity. Still, if one drops the commitment to the absolute notion of conflict and grants that there can be relative degrees of dynamic contrast between shots, what remains is a useful heuristic tool for filmmaking and film analysis. By noting that there is a hierarchy of elements and qualities in the image, and by suggesting that a filmmaker can organize a sequence so as to create contrasting or harmonizing patterns out of them, Eisenstein moves us close to moment-by-moment fluctuations of cinematic texture.

In addition, Eisenstein's overarching musical analogy (dominant, meter, rhythm, tone, overtone) may be an attempt to extend and systematize 1927 Formalist insights. Although Eikhenbaum used the language metaphor ("cine-phrase"), he emphasized that montage most resembles musical phrasing, grouping shots around an "accentual nucleus" (1927b:22). Tynyanov's account also stresses meter and rhythm in the jumps from shot to shot. Eisenstein, in offering a comprehensive parallelism with musical construction, moves toward a conception of formal "laws" operating across media. Not surprisingly, his later writing builds

---

4. This typology is not quite as clear-cut as my list might suggest. In principle, when one factor is made the dominant, any secondary factor ought to become a candidate for being an overtone. For example, when metrical cutting is the dominant, the subsidiary rhythmic factors ought to become overtones of that. In practice, Eisenstein usually takes "tonal" montage as the prototypical case of cutting on the dominant. He then applies the term *overtones* only to subsidiary aspects of the image. Other subordinate structural factors, such as metrics or rhythm, are labeled, casually and confusingly, "secondary dominants" (1929e: 189).

upon this second typology in considering how visual montage works with musical structure.

In both of the 1929 essays, Eisenstein fails to square his commitment to a hardheaded reductionist reflexology with a belief that "higher-level" qualities somehow emerge from dialectical interaction. He is, in effect, trying to graft the Dialecticians' position onto his original Mechanism. Such conceptual problems may be partly a result of the circumstances surrounding the composition of the manuscripts.[5] The disheveled state of Eisenstein's dialectical ruminations may also owe something to rapid changes on the academic front. In 1929 the rout of the Mechanists began in earnest. In April a nationwide conference of scientists passed a resolution condemning Mechanism as a departure from Marxist-Leninist doctrine. Shortly thereafter the Party Central Committee ordered that the Dialectical standpoint be established in the natural sciences. But later in 1929, a revisionist group of "New Philosophers" accused Deborin of founding a philosophical sect.

Gradually this attack gained adherents. In December 1930 Stalin labeled Deborin the leader of a Trotskyite deviation. The "reactologist" Kornilov suffered a similar fall. Although his theory was endorsed by a major 1930 conference on human behavior, by the end of the year he found himself one of the "Menshevizing idealists" denounced by Stalin. It would probably have been incautious for Eisenstein to polish and publish strongly "dialectical" essays in such an unstable period.

Whatever their shortcomings as a general account of "film language," Eisenstein's articles from the late 1920s contribute a great deal to our understanding of cinematic form. In their attention to the detailed choices facing the filmmaker, they surpass nearly all the theoretical initiatives of his Soviet contemporaries. He echoes a premise of the *technē*-based tendency when he claims that in Japanese lyric poetry the meaning "is embellished and developed on the basis of the material" (1929b:140), but he might as well be talking about the way in which his own dissection of shot composition and editing springs from close attention to the stuff of his medium. In order to shape the spectator's response, the artist must work the finest grain of the material. Eisenstein's reflections on the compositional relations within and between shots and on the dominant and its overtones yield a more nuanced discussion of film style than anyone had previously produced.

The Eclectic Modernist

Eisenstein's 1920s writings bequeath us a unique conception of cinematic form and effect. The film will be assembled—"mounted," like an engine—out of stimulants. Within and between shots, the stimulants involve everything from meter

---

5. "The Dramaturgy of Film Form" and "The Fourth Dimension in Cinema" were written concurrently and piecemeal in the spring, summer, and fall of 1929. The first essay was not published in Russian, and only a portion of the second article was. The obscurities and scrappiness of the arguments betray considerable haste, as would be expected in a year in which the author had to finish *Old and New* before going abroad in August.

and rhythm to dominant and overtone, all harboring some possibility of conflict. These formal possibilities will in turn be shaped by the response they can evoke in the spectator—a response involving perception, emotion, and a degree of cognitive awareness. Conceiving the stimulants as "attractions" stresses the perceptual and emotional dimensions; conceiving them as "signs" plays up their intellectual aspects. In either case, the film leads the spectator to an experience that evokes ideological conclusions: a piece of agitation, propaganda, or, at the limit, abstract demonstration such as the *Capital* project. Yet Eisenstein insists that perceptual and emotional impact ought to be present in even the most intellectual forms of cinematic discourse.

To a great extent, this theory grew out of concrete problems in Eisenstein's filmmaking. Admittedly, the technical issues are comparatively narrow. He focuses primarily on composition and editing, and these at a fairly local level. For a "formalist" he is notably uninterested in overall organizational principles. Probably several factors in his milieu account for this: debates about the "plotless film," theorists' interest in the peculiar capacities of the film medium, and the Constructivist emphasis on *faktura* (the surface working of materials). Not until later will he develop a theory of larger-scale patterning.

Much of this theory reinforces the image of Eisenstein as a doyen of Constructivism in the cinema. His revisions of biomechanics, his machine-based conception of materials and montage, his call for a rational-engineering approach to art, and his constant assumption that art must serve a social purpose are indebted to that broad trend of Constructivist thought that swept through the arts after the Bolshevik Revolution. Yet his theory remains far less pure an instance of doctrinal Constructivism than, say, Vertov's. Eisenstein was a very eclectic artist, eager to assimilate disparate, even contradictory, intellectual sources.

In the way he conceived his own role, for example, he took a definite stand against extreme Constructivist tendencies. He declared himself an artist. Against those who hoped that art would be replaced by mass production, Eisenstein insisted that art was a distinct activity with a "materialist essence" (1925d:62). When Vertov and others charged *Strike* with appropriating Kino-Eye techniques for "artistic" ends, Eisenstein rejoined that despite Vertov's Productivist disclaimers, he too produced art—but art that refused to organize its material fully and thus relinquished many possibilities of stirring the audience.

Eisenstein's commitment to art led him toward a view not typically stressed in Constructivist programs: the power of art to organize emotional responses. Proletkult's principal theorist, Alexander Bogdanov, insisted that art organized "living images, not only in the sphere of knowledge but also in that of feeling and aspirations" (1974). Echoes of this conception reverberate through Eisenstein's early writings, especially in "The Montage of Attractions." In 1928 Eisenstein signed the manifesto of the short-lived "October" group, which echoed Bogdanov in demanding that artists organize mass psychology.

Mayakovsky's and Brik's Lef group, with its mixture of Futurism and Productivism, also affected Eisenstein's aesthetic. Here Sergei Tretyakov's influence was decisive. According to Tretyakov's recasting of Bogdanov, by mastering art's scientific basis the artist could calculate a work's emotional effects. Tretyakov's first manifesto in *Lef*, published several months before "The Montage of Attractions," called for the artist to apply dialectical materialism "to the problem of organizing the human psyche *through the emotions*" (1923:216). Thus Tretyakov envisioned the artist as a kind of industrial engineer. Along similar lines, Eisenstein's most markedly Productivist essay, "The Problem of the Materialist Approach to Form" (1925), urged artists to adapt the methods of heavy industry to problems of aesthetic form. Despite his affinity with Tretyakov, however, Eisenstein remained a marginal member of Lef, and he eventually underwent criticism during the group's "factographic" phase.

Eisenstein's ideas on the filmic sign and on montage were shaped by Russian Formalist literary theory, particularly the work of Victor Shklovsky and Yury Tynyanov. Unlike Kuleshov and the FEX directors, however, Eisenstein never collaborated with the Formalists on film projects, and his writings pointedly omit mention of them. Moreover, he diverges sharply from certain Formalist tenets. He avoids discussion of "defamiliarization" *(ostranenie)* and leaves no room for the gesture of "baring the device"—that is, flaunting material or formal qualities of the artwork. Against the Formalists he insists that form is inherently political, since it cannot be divorced from a social and ideological context (1929d:155–158).

Although Eisenstein's appeals to behavioral science could also be considered a Constructivist impulse, his enthusiasms are far from doctrinally rigid. Starting with a version of strict reflexological materialism, he flirts with the Deborinist dialectical position. Off the page, he pursues inquiries into psychoanalysis, hypnosis, Gestalt psychology, Vygotsky's semiotic psychology, and Kurt Lewin's field theory.

Eisenstein's aesthetic tastes lie far from any orthodoxy. While seeing himself as a modern Leonardo and revering the art of the Renaissance, he discovers the "montage of attractions" in the work of Grosz and Rodchenko. He finds analogies with film in Japanese art, Daumier, Balzac, Toulouse-Lautrec, Debussy, and Scriabin. Amid debates on industrial art, he embarks on a study of the *Mona Lisa* and Myron's discus-thrower. In 1928, asked what writers' works are most suitable for filming, he claims interest in Serafimovich, Babel, and other Soviet contemporaries but confesses that his greatest attachments are to Joyce and Zola—an odd pair for any "pure" Constructivist to admire.

One issue enables us to gauge the mixture of eclecticism and individuality in Eisenstein's thinking. Soviet artists and cultural bureaucrats constantly debated the proper attitude toward prerevolutionary art. The Futurists rejected the past absolutely, calling for the destruction of museums and libraries. Wrote Mayakovsky: "We call anyone who treats old art with hatred a Lefist" (Thomson 1978:65). Lenin, Lunacharsky, and Bogdanov believed that such draconian views were irresponsible; the proletariat had to learn from the past and select what should be preserved. Though distancing himself from what he regarded as regressive tastes,

Eisenstein also argued that the modern artist should assimilate all available traditions. "The Montage of Attractions" announces that the means of affecting the audience lie as much in Shakespearean soliloquy as in a drumroll or firecrackers in the auditorium (1923b:34). In 1926 he declares that "art admits *all* methods except those that fail to achieve their ends" (1926b:69). And a year later he asserts: "If in our day the most powerful response in the auditorium calls for symbols and analogies with the machine—then we shoot a "heart attack" in the machine-room of the battleship; if on the other hand tomorrow it's all false noses and theatrical rouge, we'll switch to false noses and theatrical rouge" (1927a:78). Eisenstein's view is pragmatic—whatever works is admissible—but it also assumes that the artist will creatively rework whatever is taken from the past. The borrowed material is subordinated to the immanent demands of form and intended effect.

From this perspective, the variety of sources in Eisenstein's work represents an urge to subject an enormous diversity of artistic traditions, both recent and distant, to his idiosyncratic eye. The *technē*-centered tradition of his day trained him to find principles of style, structure, and effect manifested in all manner of artworks and intellectual doctrines. If his borrowings from philosophy, philology, art history, and psychology seem intellectually promiscuous, it is because, like many creators who also speculate on their craft, he reads his sources "opportunistically," seizing on elements that confirm his hunches or prod his imagination. But unlike most artists, he seeks to systematize those reactions, drawing them together into an articulable method.

The chief test of his method is practice. The past furnishes models of stirring, engaging art. The Soviet artist must master those methods that have proved successful. We touch here upon what I earlier called Eisenstein's "Leninist formalism." Just as Lenin argued that the Soviet system would enable workers to use the techniques of Taylorism to free themselves from exploitation, so the self-conscious Marxist artist can extract formal methods from classic works and use them for progressive purposes. Traditional theatre furnishes successful attractions; bourgeois science yields knowledge of physiology; later Eisenstein will claim that religious and spiritual traditions provide models of "ecstasy." At the limit, this tendency to absorb techniques into an ever-grander synthesis reveals Eisenstein's affinity for Hegelian conceptions of artistic and philosophical progress.

This widening spiral of assimilation becomes yet another justification for Eisenstein's reluctance to build his theory upon cinematic specificity. He asserts film's kinship to other arts and searches for constructive principles that transcend media. As a historical phenomenon, cinema poses problems of form, expression, and response that are central to all arts. These problems can be illuminated by findings in other domains of research. This is the Eisenstein who is interested in "everything . . . besides the cinema."

Alongside him, however, stands the practicing director burning to disclose those "particularities of method" that will yield detailed, systematic knowledge of his craft. Of all theorists of the silent era, Eisenstein most actively brings film study close to the techniques of literary and art-historical analysis. By fastening on fine points of cinematic texture and reflecting on what larger functions individual devices might serve, Eisenstein increases the options available to the director and at the same time forges a more sophisticated conception of film style than any other theorist had developed. In his hands film theory becomes not a quest for an essence of the medium but a reflection on concrete problems, a critical study of artistic achievements, a scanning of other arts for instructive parallels, and a scrutiny of "how a film is *made*"—in short, an empirical poetics of cinema.

4.

Practical Aesthetics:

Pedagogy

In May 1928 Eisenstein was appointed to head the direction course at the State Cinema Technical College (GTK), the Soviet film academy. He taught a workshop there through the following year while filming and editing *The General Line*. In 1932, after his return from North America, he launched a full-scale program of courses at the school. Through early 1935, when he took leave to work on *Bezhin Meadow*, he led the direction faculty of what had become the All-Union State Cinema Institute (VGIK). During his evacuation to Alma-Ata, he continued to conduct courses while filming *Ivan the Terrible*. He returned to his VGIK duties for a few months in 1945–46 before illness forced him to cease.

Eisenstein never managed to collect his lectures into his planned volume on direction. Some talks found their way into the unfinished treatise on montage, and stenographic transcripts of several class sessions have been published in his selected works and in the 1958 volume, *Lessons with Eisenstein*, assembled by his pupil Vladimir Nizhny.

These documents show us a somewhat different Eisenstein from the polemicist and thinker we encounter in the published writings. Although he did occasionally lecture on broad theoretical questions, most of the pedagogical material consists of detailed probings of specific problems. This work can be most fruitfully understood as a fresh attempt to build a poetics of film.

Suppose that we take poetics to be a kind of middle-level theorizing—an attempt to describe or explain particular craft practices while tying them to broader issues of form, response, and social function. Within this framework,

Eisenstein's theoretical writings tend to argue "from the top down." Even though his filmmaking propelled him toward specific problems, his essays typically appeal to general doctrines of mental function and social structure in order to arrive at the principles informing film practice.

By contrast, Eisenstein's teaching approaches poetics from the bottom up. He confronts us with a specific technical problem and demands that we justify making one concrete choice rather than another. To answer, we must move up to that middle level of principled craft knowledge that guides the artist's activity. Only then might Eisenstein invoke comparisons with other arts or broader philosophical doctrines. The result is "film theory" rather in the sense in which musicians speak of "music theory": a systematizing of the principles behind specific creative decisions.

Pragmatic necessities led him to the bottom-up approach. In his teaching Eisenstein continued to insist on cinema's connection with the other arts. The aspiring film director would have to study literature, theatre, painting, and music, as well as psychology and related sciences. In 1933 and 1934 Eisenstein drafted a curriculum for the director's course that situated cinema within an enormously broad cultural framework. The program included physical training (gymnastics, boxing, voice training); the study of biographies of "outstanding creative personalities" (Lenin, Gogol, Henry Ford); the examination of the laws of expression revealed in the writings of some twenty thinkers, from Plato to Pavlov; and the study of images in language, theatre, and the visual arts (Nizhny 1958:143–164).

Yet straightforwardly mapping these ideas onto directorial practice would not have been effective in the classroom. Eisenstein realized that most of his pupils, admitted under the Cultural Revolution's policy of advancing the children of workers and peasants, had little practice in handling abstract ideas. He therefore structured the class around exercises and puzzle-solving, tying abstract issues to practical problems. The sessions were liberally salted with advice—the sort of pen to use on storyboards, the possibilities of different lenses—and brief orienting lectures. A Zola passage could trigger an excursus into French literature; designing a set could segue into a disquisition on inverted perspective in Japanese art.

It would have been fruitless, however, to bring vast cultural traditions to bear on practical matters willy-nilly. Eisenstein, trained as an engineer and versed in the *technē* tradition of the NEP, sought to turn out "film engineers, specialist masters in the class-based formation of the consciousness of the mass audience" (1928e:125). The VGIK had to go beyond mere technical training. It had to teach a *method*, revealing the systematic principles governing film direction. The school would thereby continue the characteristically Soviet effort to strip the creative process of its mystique. The course should offer a "practical aesthetics" (1934d:68). It would move from the bottom up, from specific problems to a broadly applicable method congruent with the creative process in the other arts.

In the search for "a synthetic constructive methodology" (1934d:69), Eisenstein's pedagogical ambitions recall those of his own teacher Meyerhold. And certainly some of his ideas can be seen as developed out of Meyerhold's practices.

But Eisenstein's pedagogy can also be related to that of another theatre director who had created his own aesthetic "system." In 1930 Eisenstein had declared the Moscow Art Theatre to be "the exact antithesis of all I am trying to do" (Seton 1952:115). Yet by the mid-1930s Stalinist culture had made Konstantin Stanislavsky the paragon of theatrical artistry, and Eisenstein discovered new possibilities in Stanislavsky's method. He suggested, for example, that the famous "System" could help the actor synthesize a series of details into a general emotional quality. This process constitutes a sort of montage within the actor's performance (1937a:138–145).

Eisenstein's absorption of Stanislavsky into his own "system" is part of a broader shift in his thinking—about the nature of the mind, the construction of the film, the nature of montage, the functions of image and sound. The next chapter will examine the most general and abstract aspects of this shift. For now we can examine Eisenstein's pedagogy as a cogent, stimulating marriage of theory and practice. His classroom exercises introduce several of the assumptions governing his more speculative theorizing. Moreover, Eisenstein's pedagogy foreshadows many of the most striking directorial strategies he would himself pursue. *Alexander Nevsky* and *Ivan the Terrible* are not fully comprehensible outside of the "method" he devised in his pedagogical work.

This chapter thus forms a hinge between Eisenstein's early and later writings. His empirical poetics becomes a microscope, exposing the details of film structure and style. We watch his students—he called them the "twenty-headed director"—confront basic questions. Why pivot the actor this way? Why put the camera there? What is the point of the scene? In wrestling with such questions, his teaching works out a practical poetics of direction, a systematic investigation of his craft. In the process he gives us a wealth of insights into the process of filmmaking.

Structure and Style: The Episode

Eisenstein's most vivid teaching centered on assigned exercises. Students would tackle a concrete artistic task and then discuss their diverging solutions to it. For example, he spent an entire term in 1933 on how to play a simple situation: a soldier, returned from the front, finds that his wife has borne a child who is not his.

Most exercises were not so skeletal. A separate section of the VGIK supervised the writing of scenarios, so Eisenstein's lessons presupposed that the director started from a preexisting text. This assumption was quite congenial to an artist with theatrical training. Yet in the classroom this text was not a script in the normal sense. Eisenstein's allegiance to the "literary scenario" continued through the 1930s, and in his course he made it one of students' assignments to turn a prose text into a shooting script. Most often he started with a novel, a historical account, or a passage from a play. He asked the students to plan the staging of

an incident from Dessalines's Haitian revolt or to adapt a scene from *Père Goriot,*
Crime and Punishment, or Shostakovich's opera *Lady Macbeth of Mtsensk.*

The plot action of the hypothetical film or sequence is thus given in advance;
directorial method consists in presenting that action most forcefully. Suppose that
we want to show a figure fallen from a great height. Eisenstein urges the director
to do everything necessary to make the event perceptually striking and emotionally
arousing. He suggests that the director incline the surface that the figure falls
upon, use diagonal architecture "to nail the attention of the viewer to the figure,"
have a woman tumble crosswise upon the figure, and employ starkly opposed
costume colors to emphasize the design (1946g:711–712).

Even this rudimentary instance exemplifies what Eisenstein calls *imagicity (ob-*
raznost')—the expressive unfolding of an essential emotional quality. He casts
scorn upon flat, "affidavit" renderings of dramatic action; they give essential
narrative information "but without any author's relation to it" (Nizhny 1958:98).
If art is to move the audience, the artist must interpret the material.

From the perspective of Eisenstein's theoretical development, imagicity was a
new version of the expressivity that he earlier located in the performer's movements, in the montage of attractions, and in tonal and overtonal montage. Later
he discussed the psychological side of imagicity, considering what processes of
association might govern the ability to saturate concepts with feeling. In his VGIK
courses, however, he treated imagicity with a minimum of flourishes. Instead he
concentrated on detailed exploration of directorial choices that would generate
in the spectator an emotion-laden "image" of the material.

According to Eisenstein, the director must not simply recreate the pre-text but
must also interpret it and disclose a central emotional point, a *donnée* or "theme."
In Rogozhin's attack on Prince Myshkin in *The Idiot,* for example, the essence is
found to be the conflict between Rogozhin's irrational hatred and Myshkin's
impossibly virtuous response to the attack.

Eisenstein's constant claim is that the chosen theme guides formal choices.
This idea can be seen as updating his earlier claim that the filmmaker's task was
to "cinefy" the political slogans of the moment. The precept also tallied with
emerging Socialist Realist doctrine, which placed thematic concerns at the center
of artistic practice. The choice of theme, according to *Iskusstvo* in 1934, is "one
of the first steps in the formulation of one's ideas" (Golomstock 1990b:218). Yet
Eisenstein also claims that his method avoids "routine, stereotypes and clichés"
(1946i:183). For him the theme must be expressed vigorously, even stunningly,
so as to evoke fresh, sharpened responses from the spectator.

Eisenstein assumes that the theme will be found as much in expressive and
metaphorical dimensions of the text as in the literal narrative situation. He therefore probes his pre-text for complex associations and evocative emotional qualities. His reading of the original text often fastens on figurative images that challenge the director to find filmic equivalents. In *Goriot,* for instance, the characters
are linked to motifs of animality, prison, sewage, and masks, and all these metaphors supply inspiration for directorial handling. Similarly, Raskolnikov's murder

of the pawnbroker occurs in a stifling room, so the director must somehow convey the sense of suffocation; Eisenstein suggests doing this by a tight, high-angled framing of the figures. By the time he is finished with an exercise, the "theme" has been transposed from an item of textual material into a welter of motifs that embody imagicity. His teaching of 1933–1935 thus starts to articulate the motif-based constructive principle that was manifested in his filmmaking practice from *Strike* onward.

Once the *donnée* is found, all the expressive means of spectacle can be deployed in order to manifest it in a forceful way. He tells his class: "One and the same characteristic can be developed in different spheres of expressive portrayal. In one instance it can be portrayed by a graphic delineation of the *mise en scène*, in another—by gesticulation, in a third—by stammering speech . . . If you wish, you can give it several of these embodiments simultaneously" (Nizhny 1958:116). Herbert Marshall recalled that Eisenstein assigned his class to stage and restage the assassination of Caesar in Shakespeare's play: first as a stage performance, then as a silent film montage, then as a sound film sequence, and finally as a color sequence (Marshall 1945:16, 25). Eisenstein's typology includes three expressive techniques: theatrical staging *(mise en scène),* editing (montage), and cinematography *(mise en cadre).*

The determining realm of directorial control is *mise en scène,* conceived in a traditional theatrical way: the staging of the entire action in a specified locale.[1] How, Eisenstein asks his class, shall we express a character's entrapment: by the movement of other characters, by the design of the set, by the placement of furnishings, or by some combination? How shall we arrange the seating at Mme. Vauquier's dinner table when Vautrin is arrested? How shall we divide a room into distinct zones, appropriate for this or that turn of the plot? How shall we plan the transitions from one action to another within the space? Can we even find plastic "rhymes" in the setting—as when a man pulling up a tablecloth as a shield makes an arc that repeats the diagonal line of his attackers? *Mise en scène* takes into account all theatrical techniques—acting, set design, costume, lighting, and performance tempo.

What assures a proper directorial solution is fidelity to the original *donnée* of the work. The *mise en scène* diagrams the text's expressive essence. Eisenstein explicates this process in several illustrative exercises. In planning the scene from *Père Goriot,* he suggests that Mme. Vauquier's rooming house reflects, at the lower end of the social scale, the class stratification and divisions of society as a whole. Thus a long table in the dining room could be used to rank the characters. This would reiterate the ranking suggested by Balzac in assigning the characters to various floors of the house, thus faithfully embodying the novel's central theme of class antagonism. Here as elsewhere the overall *mise en scène* must seem natural while still providing "a graphic scheme of what in its metaphorical reading defines

---

1. Jacques Aumont points out that Eisenstein uses both the traditional Russian word *postanovka* ("staging") and his own coinage from the French, *mizanstsen* (Eisenstein 1989: 277).

the psychological content of the scene and the interaction of the characters" (1937c:20).

More complex is the episode showing the French colonialists' attempted arrest of Jean-Jacques Dessalines. The episode's main image, Eisenstein suggests, is that of encirclement. The kinetic manifestation of the theme is initiated when the priest embraces Dessalines. Then he is gradually surrounded by his hosts. At the point of maximum intensity, Dessalines discovers his enemies' purposes and breaks the circle. He leaps to the banquet table, hurls a candelabrum at the officers, and dives through a window. His escape ignites a rebellion that will swallow up the colonialists. "The sensation of doom and trap—the situation in which Dessalines at first finds himself—passes over to the handful of colonialists as they hear all round them the cries and cheers calling to revolt . . . If we want an epic finale, we can end the episode with a sense of the encirclement of the French group by the island's population in revolt" (Nizhny 1958:25).

In such exercises, the *mise en scène* becomes "a graphic projection of the character of the action," a "spatial calligraphy" (1937c:15). It must clarify and dynamize the essential dramatic movement while at the same time presenting an expressive image of the scene. *Mise en scène* thus provides the primary patterning of the episode. It yields an "interlacing of self-contained lines of action, each having its own laws for the tone of its rhythmic design and its spatial displacements, all braiding into a unique and harmonious whole" (1989:54–55). At the same time, in unfolding the essential theme, *mise en scène* seeks to sharpen oppositions: contrasts among characters, among scenes and moods, between characters and stage space as a whole. *Mise en scène* thus selects from a panoply of materials and procedures to create a thematically unified, forceful production.

At certain points in the unfolding *mise en scène,* the essential theme will crystallize in moments of the actors' performance. As Nizhny recalls, "We first established in terms of the *mise en scène* where and how the action happens, how and on what spaces it is played, why the critical moments and transitions arise, and then at each stage we marked the playing by the highest level of expressive manifestation—gestures, mime, and speech" (1958:70). Eisenstein cites Stanislavsky on the importance of the psychological subtext in the actor's performance, but he emphasizes that the subtext is nothing more than the emotional formula at the root of the whole production.

The director whose earliest theoretical sallies involved expressive movement returned to the issue throughout the 1930s and 1940s. Quite late in his life he proposed that the performance dimension within *mise en scène* could usefully be considered under the rubrics of *mise en jeu* and *mise en geste.*

Mise en jeu ("putting into performance") determines the actor's overall representation of the character. At this phase, the director settles on matters of comportment, voice, facial expression, and so on. *Mise en jeu* makes manifest both the character's conscious motives and the impulses that the character seeks to control. Eisenstein advises his students to examine Bely's *Craftsmanship of Gogol* to see how Gogol manifests his themes through characters' habitual demeanors: how, for instance, the circuitous personality of Chichikov in *Dead Souls* is expressed in his sidewise shiftings and his refusal to sit straight (1933c:59).

For Eisenstein, the actor's performance is not fully realized until the characters engage in scenically contextualized physical action. This is the phase of *mise en geste* ("putting into gesture"). The borderline between this and *mise en jeu* is somewhat fluid, but a distinction can still be made. Whereas *mise en jeu* supplies a thematically unified repertoire of characteristic behaviors, *mise en geste* embodies the essential theme in a suite of specific acts at a definite moment of the action: "leaning forward or backward, a movement of the hands up or down, a movement which splits a sentence, or an exclamation that comes in the middle of a movement" (1948b:722).

Eisenstein's most detailed example is a suggested staging of Rogozhin's attempt to stab Prince Myshkin (1948b:722–736). Since Dostoevsky's text specifies that Rogozhin encounters Myshkin in a furtive manner, the *mise en geste* must reveal this quality. Eisenstein proposes that the actor draw his knife with his right hand but stretch the arm diagonally leftward across his chest. This action will also block off the lower half of his face and call attention to his eyes, which are the only features described by Dostoevsky in the passage.

Myshkin's movements require a more complex *mise en geste*. The novel characterizes him as innocently contrary in his reactions; he never responds as others do. Eisenstein cites a passage in which Myshkin complains, "I always have the *opposite* gesture," and this trait of the performer's basic *mise en jeu* must determine the play of gesture here. When Rogozhin attacks him, Myshkin does not try to stop him; he is instead shocked by the unsuspected depths of human hatred.

Eisenstein interprets Myshkin's gestures as passing from innocent fascination to horrified realization. First, the childlike Myshkin approaches his assassin; this unlikely reaction expresses his contrariness. He squints and stretches out one hand to touch the knife. The contact with the blade drives home to him the moral instability of the world, of which Rogozhin's hatred is only an indication. Myshkin's attitude changes. He exclaims: "I don't believe it!" Now he moves slowly backward. Eisenstein decomposes Myshkin's response into separate gestures: the head is fixed, still fascinated; the feet retreat; the eyes widen; and the protesting shake of the head we might expect gets transferred to a zigzag movement of the arms. Myshkin's horror is embodied in his bulging eyes, his widespread arms, and his extended fingers—all forming what Eisenstein calls "concentric circles of terror," which would in a full production expand still further outward into decor, lighting, perspective, and other aspects.

Thus the characters' basic demeanor—their *mise en jeu*—can become a dynamic, intensified, and organically shaped *mise en geste*. As an aspect of *mise en scène*, *mise en geste* functions to heighten the basic theme. Eisenstein's *mise en geste* lectures bring to light constructional principles evident in his silent films, as in the interweaving of individuals' gestures in the prelude to the Odessa Steps. The lectures also constitute a more naturalistic revision of the concepts of "expressive movement" and Meyerhold's biomechanics.

For Eisenstein, cinema is not opposed to theatre in some exclusive specificity. Cinema includes theatre, since both are founded on *mise en scène;* but the new medium represents a "leap" beyond the old. Historically, cinema synthesizes the expressive possibilities of theatre, literature, and painting while advancing its own distinct means. Aesthetically, film techniques do not simply record or adapt theatrical *mise en scène;* they transform it. In Eisenstein's teaching, the theatrical model serves only as a point of departure. A three-dimensional staging of the action is not an end in itself but rather the material for another phase of formal processing. Once one has conceived the action in space and time, one can then "cheat" the positions of actors and decor from shot to shot; one can change the framing for the sake of compositional development; one can elide phases of a movement by a judicious cut. The filmmaker will transform theatrical *mise en scène* by means of editing (montage) and shot composition *(mise en cadre).*

Montage is the ongoing process that articulates the text's emotional essence within a specific domain of materials. After determining the *mise en scène* of a sequence, the director can plan montage. Editing, Eisenstein asserts, is "predetermined by the *mise en scène*"; *mise en scène* functions as "the embryo shot-script" (Nizhny 1958:20, 63). But whereas theatrical *mise en scène* takes place in stage space, in cinema *mise en scène* "flows *around* the camera, that is, around the spectator" (Nizhny 1958:63). The edited sequence will be thoroughly "filmic" in its freedom of vantage point.

The key to planning montage, Eisenstein claims, is the breakdown of the staged action into editing units. To some extent, an editing unit is simply a heuristic device to assist the filmmaker in planning the total shot breakdown. The editing unit presents a specific phase of the action from a predominant spatial orientation (that is, roughly comparable camera setups). For the next articulation of the *mise en scène,* the filmmaker devises a different editing unit—marked by a distinct shift in visual orientation. As a result, the editing unit assures an intermediate level of unity between the *mise en scène* episodes and the individual shot-to-shot relations. It thus permits the filmmaker to judge the most precise way to break down the action into actual shots.

> During the dismemberment that forms the editing units, without yet [any] break-up into shots, a whole series of acting passages is given roughly and without yet maximum expressiveness. But if you try to start at once with division into shots, then at any time before each new shot might arise the question: where should this shot be taken from? From which setup should it be taken— below or above? What criterion should be used in the choice?   (Nizhny 1958:78)

In effect, the editing unit creates a rough indication of how the action will be displayed, supplying an orientation not yet specified as a particular shot's view but one nevertheless more defined than in theatrical *mise en scène.*

For example, at one phase of the Haitian rebellion sequence, Dessalines has leaped to the banquet table and is confronting the officers below him. Eisenstein suggests using at least five shots to show Dessalines stepping forward, breaking a

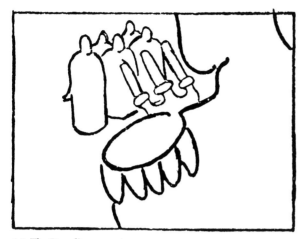

4.1 The Dessalines exercise.

4.2 The Dessalines exercise.

china plate, and lunging with the candelabrum (Nizhny 1958:86). All the shots are from approximately the same angle, but some provide distant framings, some present close-ups, and all reorder the compositional elements within the frame (4.1–4.3). As this exercise suggests, the editing unit emerges in the finished film as more than simply an aid to planning the breakdown of the action. It becomes a distinct stylistic segment and provides a momentary clustering of motifs, an implication connoted by Eisenstein's idiosyncratic term for the unit, *uzel* ("knot" or "node").

In the finished film, the editing unit is revealed as a series of shots that demarcates a piece of action already articulated in the *mise en scène*. These shots will gain coherence by sharing a predominant spatial orientation. One of these shots, called the "thesis shot" or "theme shot," might be said to christen the entire series, since it displays most adequately the expressive elements of *mise en scène* that the series will elaborate. Usually the thesis shot comes first in the unit. At

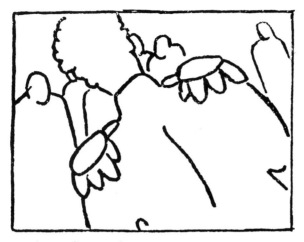

4.3 The Dessalines exercise.

the next twist in the *mise en scène,* the filmmaker presents another editing unit, possibly by means of a linking shot that creates "the feeling of the transition to a new level of action" (Nizhny 1958:76).

What, apparently, could be more alien to the director who dreamed of filming *Capital* than this patient mapping of a theatrically unified action into shots? The concept of the editing unit marks an important change in the practice of a filmmaker whose silent style was famous for farfetched shot juxtapositions and disjunctive cutting patterns. The new method is perhaps best seen as Eisenstein's attempt to find a rigorous style within the emerging conditions of Socialist Realist cinema: based on coherent theatrical scenes, centered upon individual protagonists, unified in dramatic time and space, bereft of the "intellectual" and "monumental" dimensions of "plotless" filmmaking.

In another sense, however, the editing-unit strategy is only a shift of emphasis, for each of Eisenstein's silent films draws upon the technique occasionally. For example, the opening of *Old and New* provides a simple montage unit. A medium long-shot of the *izba* (4.4) is followed by a shot taken only slightly farther back, with the brothers standing in the foreground (4.5). Two "concentration" cuts move in on the brothers (4.6, 4.7). Throughout the series, the compositional emphasis modulates from the building to the figures, while the constancy of camera orientation enhances the abruptness of the cuts.

Still, promoting this tactic to a dominant role may appear to mark Eisenstein's acceptance of Hollywood's axis-of-action or "180-degree" principle of filming. If one examines Eisenstein's concrete examples (such as the Dessalines episode), one might take the editing unit as the series of shots that creates an axis of action; the thesis shot then might become what dominant filmmaking considers the establishing shot.

Yet Eisenstein's method diverges from the orthodox approach in important ways. For one thing, the thesis shot does not have to be an establishing shot.

4.4 *Old and New.*

4.5 *Old and New.*

4.6 *Old and New.*

4.7 *Old and New.*

Some of Eisenstein's examples are fragmentary, close views. More important, in passing from one editing unit to another the filmmaker may change the spatial orientation drastically, even by shifting point of view 180 degrees. "The camera," as Nizhny puts it, "can not only dissect out a view from inside the circular *mise en scène,* but can also as though flank it from the outside" (1958:63). Even a single violation of the axis of action—a cut to an opposite angle within an editing unit— can be used to accentuate the action without destroying the viewer's sense of the dominant orientation of the unit. From unit to unit, Eisenstein encourages the filmmaker to choose orientations that break the previously established axis of action.

Once the editing unit is determined, the filmmaker proceeds to plan montage. The editing unit guides the director in deciding on the number and pattern of shots. In the Dessalines exercise, one editing unit represents some officers drawing their swords. The thesis shot gives the most forceful representation of the action: three hands clasping swords fly up at an angle. To build up to this, however, more shots are needed. Eisenstein proposes an initial shot of the men's hands grasping the swords and a second, frontal shot of the swords being drawn. Then the thesis shot will have a summative emotional effect (Nizhny 1958:89).

There is thus a tendency in Eisenstein's late montage theory to avoid the ABA alternation characteristic of editing in classical narrative cinema. As our frames from *Old and New* indicate, his editing units create shot clusters that present the same person or action from slightly different views (A1, A2, A3); the film will then pass on to another unit (B1, B2, B3). Portions of space are plumbed successively, each module expanded to heighten perceptual nuances and intensify expressive qualities. As we shall see in Chapter 6, this strategy shapes many scenes of *Alexander Nevsky* and *Ivan the Terrible*.

Although the *mise en scène* controls the montage pattern, editing does not simply transmit a unified profilmic event. Editing transforms the staged action, fragmenting it in "impossible" ways that are nonetheless the most forceful manifestation of the scene's emotional essence. Eisenstein thus leaves the director the option of mismatching images, and even body parts. He was fascinated by Daumier's and El Greco's ability to represent a figure whose limbs executed different phases of a movement at the same instant—a technique exploited in the silent films and revived in *Ivan the Terrible* (1937a:111).

After the *mise en scène* has been broken into editing units, and as they have begun to take shape as a suite of shots, the filmmaker confronts the task of *mise en cadre*. Eisenstein points out that in theatre the stage space constitutes an "invariable datum," a constant with respect to the audience. But the film frame creates a box for every shot. Thus staging an action for cinema involves calculating the relation between the actors' *mise en geste* and the edges of the frame.

As earlier in his career, Eisenstein stresses that the margins of the frame make the screen a vertical plane. Thus the three-dimensional, horizontal *mise en scène* of the stage will not necessarily be effective on film. Techniques of painting will therefore supply useful models of *mise en cadre*. For example, Eisenstein takes Serov's portrait of the actress M. N. Yermolova as a demonstration of how cropping the depicted event by different framelines produces not only varying compositions but also different viewing angles on the object (1937g:87–91). Seen within the widest framing, she seems to be at eye level; but if the framing captures only her and the mirror reflection, she seems to be looking down at us (4.8, 4.9). Eisenstein here returns to a topic that always interested him—the spatial incompatibilities that are common in perspectival depiction.

The verticality of the screen also requires the director to examine how depth can be compellingly represented in the frame. Since the viewer's orientation given by Serov's portrait shifts according to what is in the foreground and what is in the distance, the painting also illustrates the importance of depth relations within the shot. The murder of the moneylender in the *Crime and Punishment* étude exemplifies Eisenstein's willingness to intensify foreground/background relationships in a way that recalls compositions in *Old and New* (4.10, 4.11) and anticipates not only *Bezhin Meadow* (4.12) but also the work of Orson Welles and William Wyler (4.13, 4.14). Such tendencies toward deep-space staging and composition encouraged use of the wide-angle 28mm lens, but he insists that such choices be dictated by the essential theme: if contrast of scale should be heightened, use the 28mm lens; if scale contrast should be less noticeable, use longer lenses (Nizhny 1958:98).

Eisenstein's most striking example of *mise en cadre* principles is his proposed

4.8 V. Serov's portrait of the actress M. N.
      Yermolova.

staging of an episode from *Crime and Punishment*. The task is to play the entire
scene of Raskolnikov's murder of the pawnbroker in a single shot, with no camera
movement. The emotional *donnée,* according to Eisenstein's interpretation, is the
suffocating pressure that triggers the murder and Raskolnikov's metaphoric "fall."
When "the hatchet crashes down on the old woman's head, it is his will that
crashes, and with it his entire philosophy of the 'superman'" (Nizhny 1958:127).

Here is a problem in imagicity. The suffocation will be conveyed through
camera position (a downward, compressive angle), and the student's rise and fall
will be shown in the *mise en scène* (the actor gradually getting larger, then suddenly
smaller). The old pawnbroker advances in zigzag to the foreground, followed
along a parallel line by Raskolnikov (4.15). Graphic composition and *mise en geste*
foreshadow the climax: when, in close-up, the moneylender examines Raskolnikov's pledge, the compositional diagonal anticipates the splitting of her head. As
Raskolnikov brings the hatchet down, the moneylender drops out of the foreground, but her hands, hugely enlarged, instantly fly back into frame from the
bottom. (This is equivalent, Eisenstein says, to making sparks sputter up.)

4.9 The Yermolova portrait reframed by Eisenstein.

4.10 *Old and New.*

4.11 *Old and New.*

4.12 *Bezhin Meadow.*

4.13 *The Magnificent Ambersons* (Orson Welles, 1942).

4.14 *The Little Foxes* (William Wyler, 1941).

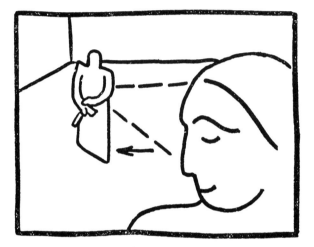

4.15 The *Crime and Punishment* exercise.

As the murderer strikes a second time, his face comes into huge close-up. "The enlargement lets one show Raskolnikov's feverishly blazing eyes and the tortured despair that begins to master him" (Nizhny 1958:127). Immediately he shrinks back into depth as the woman's body falls into the shot; after robbing her, he races out in the far distance. Confinement to a single camera position enables the director to give the action many dynamic relations to the frame edges, and the exaggeration supplied by the 28mm lens renders Raskolnikov's rise to spatial prominence and the immediate collapse of his will.

In Eisenstein's VGIK class, the *Crime and Punishment* exercise served as an extreme instance of what could be accomplished in the realm of *mise en cadre*. Most commonly, *mise en cadre* was conceived as being coordinated with the act of montage: breaking up the editing unit into significantly composed shots. After all, Eisenstein insists, "*Mise en scène* contains in itself all the elements concerned with the editing break-up into shots" (Nizhny 1958:139). The unitary shot is a "montage complex" harboring a potential breakup into shots. In this sense, he can speak of the Raskolnikov scene as involving "hidden editing," anticipating by more than a decade André Bazin's contention that filmmakers such as Welles used the deep-space shot in order to create a "virtual editing" (Bazin 1982:115).

Eisenstein here harks back to his 1920s idea that elements juxtaposed within the shot create "potential montage." But now he does not speak of dialectical tensions and a frame that bursts into conflicting shots; instead he posits a "leap" at the moment when the dramatic intensity requires several shots (conflicting or not). Instead of looking to Engels, he now finds the ancestors of montage in medieval miniatures depicting several successive actions, or in the works of Tintoretto, Daumier, and Serov (1937a:110–115). In 1934 he assigned each of his students to bring out the montage latent in Leonardo's *Last Supper* (Pipisnashvili 1967:52).

Mise en cadre therefore interacts with montage. Eisenstein insists that the Soviet film acquired its aesthetic rigor through a careful coordination of composition and shot-by-shot progressions. "At a certain stage our cinema displayed the same strict responsibility for each shot admitted into a montage sequence as poetry did for each line of verse or music for the regular movement of a fugue" (1934a:290). Examining a series of shots in *Potemkin,* he points out that from the standpoint of plot they could be arranged in any combination, but the images' internal design and the microscopic patterning of the editing create a rigorous guiding of the spectator's attention.

Montage is a "micro-dramaturgy" (1941a:10), and so is *mise en cadre.* "The object must be *selected, oriented,* and *arranged* within the frame in a way which will engender not only a representation but also a complex of associations which redouble the emotional-semantic charge of the shot. Thus is created the *dramaturgy* of the frame. Thus *the drama* itself finds its roots in the very tissue of the work" (1989:59). As in his 1929 essay, Eisenstein sets out a "dramaturgy of film form," a conception of cinematic style that makes every parameter capable of expressing the underlying premise of the scene. Again, the editing unit proves a handy guide. In the Dessalines episode, Eisenstein plots diagonal compositions and balances groupings within the shots so as to develop the emotional theme as already articulated within the thesis shot, now creating moment-to-moment compositional development. *Mise en cadre,* by cooperating with montage, achieves cinema's equivalent of what Bely calls "the inscription of the plot [*syuzhet*] in the details" (Eisenstein 1989:60).

In his lectures on film direction, Eisenstein offers an artisanal poetics of cinema. Taken as a whole, his teachings furnish a systematic, practice-based model of film style and a principled guide to the director's craft. By moving from the emotion-laden, imagistic "theme" to the composition of the single shot, he carries the process of cinematic composition into the finest grain of the material, assuring the artist control over every aspect of the medium. The process can be summarized in the accompanying diagram.

Most of Eisenstein's course assignments concentrated on single scenes. This strategy, though suited to VGIK's educational demands, might seem to confirm

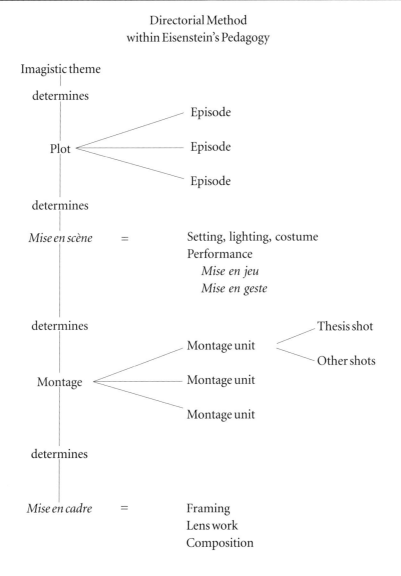

Directorial Method
within Eisenstein's Pedagogy

Imagistic theme
| determines

Plot
Episode
Episode
Episode

determines

Mise en scène   =   Setting, lighting, costume
Performance
Mise en jeu
Mise en geste

determines

Montage
Montage unit — Thesis shot
Other shots
Montage unit
Montage unit

determines

Mise en cadre   =   Framing
Lens work
Composition

Eisenstein's reputation as the "director of the episode," devoted to wringing the maximum emotional intensity out of one dramatic climax before proceeding to another. Yet Eisenstein's lessons did not sacrifice attention to the work as a formal whole. We have already seen that the 1920s films balanced episodic construction with a concern for overall unity, involving both abstract plot architecture and motivic repetition and variation. This concern for the whole work would become more explicit in his theoretical writings of the late 1930s. For now it is worth looking briefly at how Eisenstein's sense of the director's construction of an entire work emerges from the pedagogy of the period—how, as he put it, the director becomes the "composer of the audio-visual complex of a film" (1934d:69).

Structure and Style: From Episode to Work

In planning the overall structure of the film, Eisenstein, with his habit of motivic construction and his proclivity for making a text's metaphors and images the basis of a directorial solution, naturally inclined toward analogues in the verbal arts. He was already sensitized to the power of motif-based systems by Bely's research into Pushkin and Gogol, as well as by his study of *Ulysses* and critics' commentaries on it. His script for *An American Tragedy* made explicit use of light/dark antinomies and parallels of posture and gesture. At this time he also encountered Caroline Spurgeon's work on Shakespeare, which revealed that a field of metaphors dominates each of the plays (light and dark in *Romeo and Juliet,* the dismembered body in *Lear*). "The structure of images," he noted, "connects very closely with the fundamental theme of such and such a work, and runs a whole verbal course" (Christensen 1990:128). As for the theatre, he claimed *mise en scène* to be the point of departure for the work as a whole. *Mise en scène* creates "interlacings and intersections among the different characters, or rather among the characters' traits and motifs" (1989:55). In his teaching, Eisenstein took a controversial opera as an example of such a dynamic structure.

Shostakovich's *Lady Macbeth of Mtsensk* premiered in January 1934 to great acclaim. An adaptation of a classic short story by Nikolai Leskov, the opera traced the story of the passionate Katerina Izmailova, married to a boorish provincial merchant. When her father-in-law learns that she is having an affair with Sergei, a strutting servant on the estate, she poisons the old man. Later, after a frenzied copulation, Katerina and Sergei murder her husband. As Katerina and Sergei are about to be married, the merchant's corpse is discovered and the couple are arrested. The opera ends with a scene of a convicts' march through Siberia. Katerina drowns herself and the young convict woman who has become the new object of Sergei's lust. "A quiet Russian family who beat and poison one another," Shostakovich is said to have remarked. ". . . Just a modest picture drawn from nature" (Volkov 1979:268).

At first *Lady Macbeth of Mtsensk* (soon to be known simply as *Katerina Izmailova*) was praised as a fulfillment of the Party policy on art. Its sensational sexuality and aggressive score helped it to attain success in Moscow and Leningrad, as well as in Europe and the United States. In 1936, however, a *Pravda* article rumored to have been written by Stalin himself accused *Lady Macbeth* of rampant "formalism." The opera was withdrawn, and Shostakovich was vilified by his fellow composers. The attack on *Lady Macbeth* marked the intensification of the "cultural terror" that would soon engulf Meyerhold, Babel, Mandelstam, and Tretyakov.

When Eisenstein offered *Lady Macbeth* as a classroom exercise, however, the opera was still held in esteem. Dissatisfied with the Moscow production, Eisenstein took the opportunity to show his students how to build an entire production's *mise en scène.*

What is the piece's theme? Shostakovich called *Lady Macbeth* a "tragic-satiric opera" (Volkov 1979:107), but Eisenstein finds its emotional essence to be a grotesque mixture of comedy and tragedy, or more extremely, buffoonery and horror. He therefore encourages his students to go beyond the rather static staging of the Moscow production and bring out the grotesque qualities of the piece.

Moreover, Eisenstein reads the text as centering on two forces: Katerina's justifiable struggle against her economic environment, and Sergei's corrupt careerist intrigues. Eisenstein fuses these thematic lines by taking the bed as the central image of the production. Katerina's sexual longings make it her natural field of battle, and both men want a "place in bed" with her. Their sexual rivalry is also a socioeconomic one, since Sergei wants to possess what the merchant owns. Eisenstein therefore presents the bed as the arena of the characters' conflict. It will haunt the staging of every scene.

His next step is to delineate the expressive development of the entire action. In a sense, any production's expressive structure is that of an episode writ large. If staging a single scene requires the director to determine the "nodal" points of its action, the director must locate the emotional and thematic "summit" of the whole play (1934e:542). In *Lady Macbeth*, Eisenstein claims, the murder of the husband constitutes the crisis. He therefore recommends starting to plan the production from this episode. Its tension, he claims, will "radiate" to other scenes.

The husband returns. Sergei and Katerina overpower him, strangle him, and carry his corpse to the cellar. How to play the scene? By taking the bed as the central motif and making it a stage within a stage, a distinct acting area, Eisenstein develops the murder scene in four phases. In sequence, they logically exhaust the possibilities of the relationship of space to action.

Phase 1. Dynamic space/calm action:
>After their coupling, Sergei and Katerina lounge on the bed. It is close to the footlights and thrust at an angle to the audience. The bed is unrealistically large, stressing the men's struggle over Katerina as a fight for "a place in bed." The bed is also tilted, and the floor is inclined, thus foreshortening the bed and creating a high-angle viewpoint. But in this perspectively distorted set, the characters at first hardly move: Sergei is asleep, Katerina sits across from him.

Phase 2. Conflicting action/calm space:
>When the couple hear Katerina's husband return, they hurry to put the room in order. The stage revolves, giving the bed a more placid orientation while Katerina hides Sergei. The husband enters; he and Katerina struggle.

Phase 3. Explosion: dynamic space/conflicting action:
>Sergei breaks into the fight, knocking the bed at a cocked angle and reinstating the dynamic diagonal of phase 1. The characters' scuffle and the angled bed create "a chaos of imbalance" (1934e:545). Sergei kills the husband, leaving him sprawled on his bed as if snoozing. This action embodies the comic side of the grotesque *donnée*, rendering violent murder as peaceful death. Eisenstein also suggests some Grand Guignol touches, such as letting the twisted hands of the corpse crawl up over the bedstead.

Phase 4. Dynamic space/calm action

Sergei and Katerina carry the body out of the bedroom. A dropped curtain signifies the boundary of another room through which they move. They lug the body down to the cellar through a trap door very close to the audience. After returning from the cellar, Katerina and Sergei crouch on the bed, sitting at the highest point in the set. This is, emblematically, the high point of the romantic triangle. The rest of the play traces their descent. As a prophetic fillip, Eisenstein considers having the bedpost cast a shadow pointing to the trap door. The comic-grotesque has become the tragic-grotesque.

Eisenstein goes on to build the entire production around this culminating scene. Elements must be repeated and varied, coming forward at decisive points and creating contrasts and parallels with aspects of the murder scene. The director must interweave dramatic motifs and then cluster or "knot" them at key moments.

Working backward to episodes immediately before the murder, Eisenstein recommends making the staging calm and restrained, representing the struggle between Katerina and her husband solely by means of acting. Thus the murder will be an intensification of this conflict, using all the means of spectacle to convey the grotesque situation. Certain elements in the murder scene will also be "planted." In the earlier bedroom scenes, for instance, Eisenstein seeks a kind of permutational exhaustiveness in the various anglings of the bed and the positionings of the curtain that will be used in the murder scene. At one point a curtain veils the bed, all the better to intensify the naked revelation of the bed before the murder. Similarly, the blocking of Sergei's first visit to Katerina can prefigure his movements during the murder, "the first tracing of that fateful line over which Izmailov's corpse will be dragged" (1934e:580).

For the scenes that do not take place in the bedroom, Eisenstein suggests using graphic configurations to anticipate or recall the murder scene. In the courtyard where Sergei first meets Katerina, the lines of the set create an "exterior cube" that compositionally foreshadows the huge four-poster bed. At the wedding banquet, the bed becomes the huge table over which Sergei now presides in the place of the husband. In the police station, after the couple's arrest, the setting becomes the inverse of the bedroom, with the walls outlining the absent bed. The final scene of the convicts' march develops the loss of sexual union. Now no contours trace the outline of the bed, positively or negatively. Eisenstein suggests that an empty space in the center will remind us of the bed. The final murder-suicide will be played as a contrast to the killing of Izmailov: not close to the audience but far away, high on a bare platform that echoes the bed's geometry. At the climax Sergei and his mistress mock Katerina in the "bed zone" and Katerina attacks her. Additionally, in all these scenes Eisenstein stages important business over the spot that marks the trapdoor to the cellar in the murder episode.

This summary cannot do justice to the hair-raising ingenuity of Eisenstein's lengthy *étude*, but at least four of its implications deserve notice. First, the exercise shows that the artistic image must be constructed out of concrete and minimally plausible scenic elements. Katerina's bed is a realistic datum of the locale, even though the *mise en scène* saturates it with emotional expressivity and "generalizes" it diagrammatically. With this as a guide, the director will not be tempted to leave the confines of Socialist Realism. Moreover, by the early 1930s Eisenstein believed that pure abstraction impoverished the work. Just as his drawings balance abstraction of contour and texture against concrete portrayal, his scenic design for *Lady Macbeth* builds its patterns out of realistically motivated material.

Second, Eisenstein constructs the entire production as a mesh of emotionally charged motifs. He thus brings out for scrutiny the principle of motivic development at work in his silent films. *Strike* makes circular shapes manifest themselves as flywheels or barrels; Smirnov's pince-nez is a node for all the hanging objects and eyeglasses and eye imagery in *Potemkin;* the opposition of God and country, made explicit in the statue of Alexander III at the opening, works its way through *October.* Now Katerina's bed, at once a graphic design and a thematically saturated representation, becomes a master motif from which the staging strategies of all scenes will radiate. In this exercise, Eisenstein articulates a conception of motivic braiding and knotting that will emerge in his more abstract theoretical work as a conception of organic unity and "polyphonic" form.

Third, each facet of theatrical spectacle—lighting, props, performance, setting, and so on—can pick up an expressive quality initially attached to another parameter. For instance, Eisenstein suggests that the corpse's black boots against the orange bedcover will create a colored contrast that reiterates the way in which the bed thrusts out volumetrically. Eisenstein's fascination with the "naked transfer" of qualities in Kabuki, the way in which an expressive meaning could leap from setting to performance to music, resurfaces. ("One and the same characteristic can be developed in different spheres of expressive portrayal.") In his later theoretical writings, he will systematically explore the process under the rubric of synesthesia, and color and music will be his primary objects of attention.

Finally, Eisenstein displays a tendency toward what we might call an exhaustive variation of parameters. Everything in the polyphonic weave must be prepared for, by subtle gradations and careful balancings of forces. An opposing or alternative solution is the strongest lead-up to the preferred effect. Some exercises reveal this tactic at work within the single episode, as when Dessalines at the banquet learns of his danger first through pantomime, then through broken phrases, and finally through direct statement. Similarly, across the entirety of *Lady Macbeth* the professor is not content until each variant of the bed's position, of the curtain's placement and hue, of the lines of the setting (echoing the bed positively or inversely or through absence) is absorbed into the production somewhere, as a contrasting or preparatory moment. It is as if a humdrum acting exercise—do everything you can with a single prop, or play every variant of a line of dialogue—furnished the principle of formal organization for an entire production. This permutational exhaustiveness will become important not only in the late theoretical essays but also in the films.

Such intricate pattern-making is not simply formalism. ("Believe me, as an old

formalist myself, I'm not bad at smelling it out!" [Nizhny 1958:14].) The variations in the directorial solution fix and nuance the spectator's associations, alter
the emotional tonalities, and deepen the spectator's engagement with the theme.
As ever, the expressive form of the object serves primarily to excite the specator
perceptually, emotionally, and intellectually.

Assaulting the Eye

Two eyes stare out in huge close-up, and a title urges: "Proletarians, remember!"
Faces swing toward us in challenge or threat. A ferocious cossack slashes his sword
at the camera. A battleship's cannons swivel deliberately, muzzles aiming directly
at us. The same battleship victoriously steams ahead; we see it from below, its
prow ripping upward across the frame. In such images, *Strike* and *Potemkin* turn
agitation toward assault and battery. The Kino-Fist is pugilistic. Eisenstein admires
Arsenal because "Dovzhenko can shoot you *in the face*" (1929a:137).

Such aggressive arousal, appropriate to a theory of "artistic shocks" and "plotless" cinema, could not be straightforwardly sustained within the program of
Socialist Realism. Yet Eisenstein continues to build his aesthetic around the spectator's dynamic relation to the spectacle. His pedagogy laid the groundwork for
the conception of spectatorial effect that dominates the later writings and films.

For him, aesthetic form was always, in Kenneth Burke's words, "the psychology
of the audience" (Burke 1957). The artwork's design elicits the audience's response. Eisenstein's emphasis on motivic construction and repetition across different sensory channels suggests that he still presumes that the spectator's associations must be created, fixed, and developed. The "polyphonic" organization of
the work will shape those associations according to the work's expressive purpose.

The curve of gradual excitement will also be complicated by accents, reversals,
and sudden breaks. Eisenstein chides the student who wants to show Dessalines
entering on the side opposite his enemies because "the director will have given it
all away in advance" (Nizhny 1958:37). The full conspiracy must be revealed only
at the end, "when we want to give the spectator the final blow, as an 'emotional
kick'" (ibid.). Eisenstein speaks of giving the spectator a "double blow" by repeating
an action with greater intensity (ibid.:33). The formal devices all aim at a maximum excitation of the spectator, a process echoing the perceptual-emotional-
intellectual arousal that he identified in the 1920s and would later recast as
"ecstasy."

Eisenstein's emotional hyperbole conjures up spatial constructions that directly
address the viewer. In the *Lady Macbeth* murder scene, it is a short step from a
space built for the perceiver (high-angle, distorted view) to a space that aggressively returns the spectator's look. In justifying the angular placement of the bed,
Eisenstein compares it to a gun or missile aimed at the audience. The same scene
provides the dialectical formula of Eisenstein's scenography. On one hand, he
creates a diagonal view in order to draw the viewer deep into the scene's space.
On the other, he creates an inverted perspective *à la chinoise*, which places the

vanishing point out in front of the picture plane—that is, where the audience already is. Thus the action "flows around" the spectators in two senses: they enter into it, and it comes out to meet them.

Depth and projection, with the spectator as the constant and explicit reference point, become the poles of Eisenstein's later scenography. Eisenstein seldom conceives of figures moving laterally; he thinks of them as moving to and from the camera (Nizhny 1958:97). The advantage of the 28mm lens lies not only in its enhancement of depth but also in its distortion of the object as it approaches the viewer: the lens "allows characters stepping two or three paces away from the camera to come into close-up" (ibid.:98–99). Movement becomes confrontational, played "to camera" with a vengeance.

Most evident is a frontality of figure behavior that does not allow the spectator to escape being addressed directly. The Dessalines exercise devolves into an orgy of such effects: Dessalines jabs a candelabrum at the audience (a shot not motivated as the officers' point of view); the soldiers unsheath their swords, row by row, with the foreground row last so that the swords slice across the frame in close-up; and when Dessalines runs into close-up and roars with rage, the camera recoils (Nizhny 1958:90). In Eisenstein's proposed adaptation of *Thérèse Raquin,* to be performed on a revolving stage, the paralyzed Mme. Raquin, witness to murder, haunts the lovers with her inflexible stare. The two concentric rotating circles on the stage supply ever-changing compositions in depth. But at the end of the play, when the lovers commit suicide, Mme. Raquin breaks from the circular tableau. Her chair (under its own power) rolls out straight toward the footlights as she glares malevolently at the audience (1934h).

Similarly, in the Raskolnikov étude, the fixed frame is motivated as a window in the moneylender's shop. "Then every approach into close-up will play as an approach to the window" (Nizhny 1958:106). The movement of the actors to the camera is strictly correlated with a heightening of intensity. But this movement is no less confrontational. In holding Raskolnikov's pledge up to the light, the pawnbroker pivots it toward the camera. And when Raskolnikov strikes, the hatchet swings out toward the viewer, the woman's hands fly up, and the play of depth becomes at the same moment a gruesome assault on the spectator. Such instances recall those eye-smiting moments from the silent films—the slashing cossack, the *Potemkin*'s cannons, close-ups of eyes, and so forth. For Eisenstein, an emotional climax usually summons up a movement to the foreground and an address to, if not an attack on, the viewer.

In later life Eisenstein was fond of claiming that the creative process does not necessarily follow the demands of logic. The artist was not always an engineer; the creative moment was more comparable to a whirlwind or a volcanic eruption (1946g:709). Yet he also believed that much of artistic activity could be explained in great detail, as long as the explanation remained alert to the open-ended qualities of that skilled practice known as *masterstvo.* "The 'regularity' within the creative process can be detected and revealed. There is method. But the whole evil consists in the fact that not even a fig will grow from preconceived methodological positions. In just the same way, a tempestuous flow of creative potential that is not regulated by method will yield even less" (1932a:223). Guided by "method" rather than by "methodology," his pedagogical efforts of the 1930s and 1940s record an indefatigable, "bottom-up" search for the principles of cinematic *technē*. Eisenstein's discoveries bring to light principles of form and style that, taken together, constitute a rich practice-based aesthetics of cinema.

As in the 1920s, Eisenstein's later teaching and writing explore the medium from a strictly instrumental stance: given a certain effect to be produced, how can one intensify it? Assume that a fiction film is composed through and through, from the moment that an action is staged for the camera; and then draw upon Western (and Eastern) traditions of theatre, painting, literature, and music for analogous solutions to formal problems. The poetics of cinema could be understood only with knowledge drawn from other artistic traditions. In a climate where concern for such issues was quickly branded "formalism," Eisenstein's teaching kept alive the *technē*-centered impulse of Meyerhold, the Formalist critics, and others in the 1920s avant-garde.

5.

Cinema as Synthesis:

Film Theory, 1930–1948

Eisenstein produced comparatively few theoretical essays during his travels through Europe and North America. After he returned to the Soviet Union, however, his teaching and his slowed filmmaking pace gave him ample opportunity to write. In the last fifteen years of his life, he published more than 150 articles, both occasional and of broader import. He finished one book, *The Film Sense* (1942), and he saw *Film Form*, a collection of articles, through the editing stage. He also worked on several unfinished treatises, including *Direction, Montage, Non-Indifferent Nature, Cinematism*, and *Color*. The great amount of material that remains in manuscript prevents any exhaustive explication of Eisenstein's later theorizing here. We can nevertheless chart the ideas that have proved most significant, as well as many that seem today most original and promising.

Eisenstein's theoretical explorations remain thoroughly prescriptive; he seeks the principles underlying valuable filmmaking. At the most detailed level of analysis, he still scrutinizes cinematic texture. The later writings undertake an unprecedentedly exact study of cutting, staging, color, and sound/image relations. At another level, he continues to study cinema by appeal to broader doctrines, ideas circulating in aesthetics, anthropology, and philosophy.

Despite these continuities, the 1930s and 1940s can be seen as a new phase in Eisenstein's theorizing. Most superficially, he changes his writing style: though still digressive, it is more prolix, more oblique, and more reliant on extensive quotations. In the unfinished manuscripts especially, his jottings tie far-ranging speculation to technical problems in a manner reminiscent of the notebook entries of his idol Leonardo da Vinci. More deeply, in this second phase Eisenstein articulates new conceptions of psychological activity, of film form and style, of films' effects on spectators, and of the relations between cinema and other arts.

Such changes are not surprising. During the Cultural Revolution (1928–1932), many Left artists repudiated their previous positions. Even though Eisenstein was out of the country at the height of the proletarian attacks, his writings were vulnerable to charges of petit-bourgeois formalism. For example, an unsigned attack in *Proletarskoe kino* of December 1931 noted: "It is essential to subject to criticism the vulgar materialist, mechanical theory of Eisenstein's montage of attractions, and his other ideas that are alien to Marxism" (Kenez 1988:424). With the waning of reductivist Mechanism, his physiological-materialist theory of cinema became untenable. Eisenstein's later writings accordingly adjust to the new Soviet philosophical climate. He draws considerably from ideas about art, language, and mind circulating in the Stalinist academy during the 1930s.

On the whole, however, Eisenstein does not adopt these ideas defensively. He borrows, revises, and elaborates Socialist Realist precepts. Combining them with his wide-ranging insights into other arts and the "practical aesthetics" that emerged from his pedagogy, he constructs a rich and detailed poetics of film. The very breadth of his interests made him flexible; his approach to Socialist Realism was no less pluralistic than his modernism had been.

From Agitprop Formalism to Socialist Realism

Socialist Realism came to prominence after the dissolution of the Russian Association of Proletarian Writers (RAPP) and other proletarian artistic organizations. Following discussions that began in 1932, it was established as official artistic policy at the Soviet Writers' Congress of August 1934.

The premises of Socialist Realism were deliberately vague: depiction of reality "in its revolutionary development"; faithfulness to "typical" characters and situations; a treatment of social milieus in their totality; an idealizing optimism, expressed in "heroic realism" or "revolutionary romanticism"; adherence to "Party spirit" and "national spirit." As a compromise among various artistic traditions of the 1920s, Socialist Realism immediately won many adherents. Artists welcomed a chance to escape the dictatorship of the proletarian organizations. Many cultural bureaucrats promised that Socialist Realism was not a style but rather a broad position that could accommodate many tendencies. At the Writers' Congress, assembled beneath portraits of Shakespeare, Balzac, and Cervantes, writers were urged to study the classics. Gorky challenged writers to learn technique from their predecessors, while even Zhdanov, who announced that bourgeois art had passed its apogee, insisted that artists must "critically assimilate" the best world literature (1935:22). In execution, Socialist Realism would soon become a narrow, dogmatic policy, but initially many artists saw it as offering reasonable artistic latitude.

Eisenstein undoubtedly welcomed the overturning of the proletarian groups' authority. His 1929 essay "Perspectives" had denounced RAPP's doctrine of the "living man" (1929h:158–160). At the same time, however, he seems to have realized that there could be no going back to Left cinema, in theory or practice. In key essays of 1934 Eisenstein indicated his agreement with Gorky's delineation of Socialist Realism, seizing the opportunity to stress cinema's parallels with literature and to put his intellectual, "de-anecdotalized" cinema firmly in the past. The following year, in his keynote address at the 1935 film workers' conference, he called for the general recognition of "the single style: Socialist Realism" (1935a:148).

Many of his subsequent essays endorse Socialist Realism explicitly. He invokes its criteria in judging other works, as when he attacks American cinema for losing typicality in exaggerating the role of individuals (1947h:104). He criticizes his beloved Joyce for adhering to superficial impressions of consciousness and ignoring broader social phenomena. When Stalinist art historians revive the nineteenth-century realist painter Surikov as a prototype of Socialist Realism, Eisenstein works an analysis of a Surikov work into an essay (1939f:23–26). He also rereads his earlier films in the light of current canons. *Strike* can be defended as presenting the typical methods of the labor underground and the equally typical operations of police repression (Seton 1952:68). *Potemkin* is now revealed as portraying typical events, while "the demolishing of houses in *The General Line* was typical for the particular district at that time" (1934c:490). He further claims that the theory of typage is congruent with Socialist Realist demands.

But Eisenstein is not simply accommodating himself to a new policy. His theoretical work of the 1930s and 1940s constitutes a sustained attempt to lift certain premises of Socialist Realism to the realm of serious aesthetic reflection.

One strategy in this effort is to exploit the new doctrine's public rationales. Faithful to the impulses he displayed in the 1920s, Eisenstein takes quite seriously Socialist Realism's avowed pluralism. His 1935 address seeks to enroll others in service to a new "classicism" that absorbs methods from many prior traditions, "the huge endowment left us" (1935a:149). Later he cites Lenin—"The heritage of all mankind is ours to master and apply"—to support his demand that Socialist Realism assimilate a broad range of artistic traditions (1939c:77).

Most contemporary historians agree that in practice Socialist Realist art made no genuine attempt to canvass the discoveries of the past. The policy's vaunted "pluralism" consisted largely in finding progressive subjects and themes in earlier art. Eisenstein goes beyond this opportunistic tactic by undertaking a search for advanced "methods." Throughout the 1930s and 1940s he ransacks widely different traditions for techniques, forms, and styles. Soviet cinema needs to learn about characterization; therefore let Balzac be the tutor. In the realm of montage organization, Zola, Gogol, and Pushkin provide instructive "shot lists." To understand plots the director can study Dumas, O. Henry, detective stories, and Shakespeare. Of course, Eisenstein admits, these classics require critique and correction, but the very one-sidedness of many of these traditions makes them vivid instances of particular aesthetic strategies. And Eisenstein's estimate of the absorptive powers of the new realism is generous:

> Now every style had its own feature. From the Art Theatre we take those elements which help us to reflect. From the Symbolists we take sensations. From the Romantics the elements of emotion and throw away all the unimportant features . . .
>
> Our realism, the realism of the future, must embody all the old arts. But the old arts by themselves were not enough. This is not only socialism but it is the complete method of artistic creation.
>
> In the creative work you do, you must use the entire experience of mankind through the ages.   (1934c:492–493).

This passage from a 1934 lecture might seem to embody an optimism that was soon proved false by the regimentation of Soviet artistic policy. In the second half of the 1930s, Socialist Realism sharply narrowed the range of acceptable subjects and styles. Yet in 1940 Eisenstein continues to hold that "what once took shape in art on the springboard of a change of style now becomes the means for variations and nuances within our single style of socialist realism . . ." (1940e:203). As late as 1946 he continues to insist that Soviet cinema will unify not only different stages of society but all the figurative and abstract movements in the history of art (1946d:519–520).

For Eisenstein, the "classicism" of Socialist Realism is achieved in its synthesis of various techniques. What he calls "success in a single sector" cripples each "ism" of bourgeois art, but truly realistic works can absorb diverse tendencies (1940c:99–100). In theatre Socialist Realism offers a middle way between the abstract schematism of Expressionism and the disorganized detail found in Surrealism. Realistic painting blends naturalistic inclinations with stylization. Serov's portrait of Yermolova (4.8) is superior to the Expressionism of Munch and the Cubism of Delaunay because it is aesthetically richer: it offers expressivity, a fracturing of point of view, and a realistic portrayal, all organically integrated (1980b:244–248). If Socialist Realism is to be an academicism, Eisenstein wants this academicism to absorb Daumier and Disney, El Greco and Ellery Queen, Scriabin and Saul Steinberg. Socialist Realism can thrive only if its historical task of integrating traditions is informed by a vital and generous pluralism of styles.

This pluralism yields one rationale for bringing Eisenstein's analytical skills to bear on specific issues. If Socialist Realism must draw upon the "one-sided" experiments of the past, the theorist must concentrate on the specific formal contribution each tradition makes. Supplied with this tenet Eisenstein can conduct research that is not only form-centered but also downright Formalist. He can point to ways in which Dickens bares the device of literary crosscutting: a digression in *Oliver Twist* is nothing less than "Dickens' own 'treatise' on the principles of this montage construction of the story [*syuzhet*] which he carries out so fascinatingly" (1944:223). He can recall Shklovsky's slogan that art breaks the "glass armor" of ordinary perception by suggesting that, like Snow White in her glass coffin, the true resources of color film can be liberated only by smashing the "everyday relations" of phenomena (1946b:184).

The pluralist rationale also allows Eisenstein to name paradigmatic workers on problems of "method." For each artist, one must examine "that quality that makes him a master" (1939c:83). Now less interested in anchoring his theories in empirical scientific research, he draws his theoretical inspiration from artistic practice. His models are creators as various as Diderot, Wagner, Poe, Scriabin, Orozco, and El Greco. The true Socialist Realism will absorb the accomplishments of these and other giants.

Pluralism takes him only so far, however. Eisenstein's boldest strategy is to recast categories and concepts already canonized by Socialist Realism. He will build a rich, flexible poetics out of the loose philosophical dogmas of the new order.

Stated baldly, those assumptions seem fairly unpromising. According to Socialist Realist aesthetics, ordinary human perception grasps the objective world's material properties, but only reflective thought allows one to grasp the essence of phenomena. Like science, art can reproduce these essential properties of reality. Art should not simply copy surface phenomena; that is sterile naturalism. Rather, the valuable artwork embodies reality's ceaseless movement. Art thus has a cognitive function. But whereas science knows reality by means of abstract concepts and laws, art supplies concrete "images," typical aspects of reality's inner dynamic. In aesthetic terms, Socialist Realism is an eclectic, superficial mix of Romantic and Realist aesthetic traditions.

This view, decried by Soviet aestheticians of the post-Stalin era as "vulgar gnoseologism," was felt to be in accord with Lenin's "copy" theory of perception and Engels' conception of reality as ceaseless movement. The theory also relied heavily upon German idealism, a powerful influence on Soviet philosophy of this period. Socialist Realism's use of such dualities as form and content, ideality and reality, the universal and the particular, as well as its penchant for a loosely dialectical explanation of all phenomena, owed a good deal to the idealist tradition. From the Hegelian literary critic Vissarion Belinsky came several ideas, notably that of "the artistic image" and the emphasis on the artwork's pathos and organic unity.

Eisenstein's theoretical work of the 1930s and 1940s enriches such rudimentary notions. Apart from his theory's intrinsic interest, its historical significance lies in its attempt to raise official banalities to the level of significant aesthetic consideration. The rest of this chapter considers the three principal areas of Eisenstein's investigation.

Most basic, though least developed, is his conception of psychological activity. By the early 1930s he starts to abandon his reductive materialism and to treat the mind as a repository of ideas, associations, and images. In this period he develops three informal theories of mental process: a version of associationism based largely on Joyce's *Ulysses;* an idea of "inner speech" that is strongly influenced by contemporary linguistic and anthropological research; and an empiricist sketch of concept formation, which assimilates older Russian traditions involving "thinking in images." The last two tendencies attempt to ground Socialist Realist aesthetics in broader accounts of mental activity.

Questions of film form also remain at the center of Eisenstein's concerns. In his 1935 address he boldly asserts that in order to achieve a "new classicism," he seeks "a general method and mode for the problem of form, equally essential and fit for any genre of construction within our embracing style of *socialist realism*" (1935a:147). Naive as this hope may have been on this occasion (his contemporaries found his program hyperintellectual), Eisenstein's address not only acknowledges his form-based pedagogy but also points toward the researches that will consume the rest of his life. Within the ambit of Socialist Realist assumptions, Eisenstein creates a theory of the film as an organic whole, with new notions of montage playing a key part.

As ever, questions of form are finally inseparable from matters of effect. Just as Eisenstein had cast montage in reflexological terms, he now seeks to explain how organic form can move the spectator. He abandons hopes of "restoring to science its sensuality" (1929h:158); instead of inculcating slogans or dialectical reasoning, art aims for the spectator's passionate absorption. Eisenstein nonetheless endows this pallid doctrine with new vitality. He tries, for example, to give genuine content to contemporary clichés about "pathos" in art. And his idea of an ecstatic "leap" into a new quality creatively exploits current conceptions of dialectical transformation.

Conceptions of mind, theory of film form, conceptions of montage, and finally notions of effect: these topics form the core of Eisenstein's later theory. Insofar as it seeks to refine and enrich key precepts of Socialist Realist doctrine, it risks seeming apologetic or opportunistic. But it can also be understood as a historically significant enterprise, parallel to, and in many ways surpassing, Brecht's and Lukács' theories of realism during the same decades. Moreover, Eisenstein's reflections yield broad aesthetic insights. His vision of cinema's cultural role makes film the laboratory for experiments that reveal fundamental laws of art. Most important, Eisenstein's reflections yield an elaborate, provocative poetics of cinema. Like his 1920s essays and his pedagogical explorations, his later writings present an account of "how films are made" that reflects directorial practice, the minutiae of film form and style, and the range of spectators' responses.

Conceptions of Psychological Activity

As in the 1920s, Eisenstein believes that a theory of aesthetic form and response must be based on a conception of the way the mind works. "Only that which proceeds in accordance with laws of nature can affect" (1947c:17). His earlier essays had sought such laws of nature in reflex-based theories. In the 1930s, he increasingly turns to accounts that emphasize mental representations—ideas, feelings, images. Throughout the decade he retreats from physiological and psychophysical explanations and moves toward more anthropological and psychological ones.

The goal, as ever, is to instill in the spectator emotion-laden ideas. Now, however, he reconsiders the very notion of "idea." For his "intellectual montage," the idea was a slogan or proposition. For instance, the point of *October*'s "Gods" sequence might be formulated as "The idea of God is culturally relative and socially regressive." After Eisenstein's return to the Soviet Union and under a barrage of criticism, he repudiated this notion of intellectual cinema. Now the artwork is said to convey concepts that are much less tendentious. We are again in the realm of imagicity, the creation of an "expressive abstraction": the meaningful emotional qualities of an action or situation, for instance.

Eisenstein's writings of the 1930s work with three sketchy notions of human concept formation, all of which recur later. The earliest conception is that of *inner monologue;* the second is that of *sensuous thought;* and the third is that of *representation and image.*

The inner monologue has its source in *Ulysses.* When Eisenstein read Joyce's novel in 1928, he saw it as an example of how a text could generate abstract conclusions with "physiological" methods. He saw its "de-anecdotalization" as parallel to his *Capital* project. But in the early 1930s, probably under the influence of Edmund Wilson's *Axel's Castle* (1931) and Stuart Gilbert's *James Joyce's "Ulysses"* (1932), he came to see the novel as significant for its use of stream of consciousness.

In a lecture he explained that Joyce had portrayed the concrete process of thought. "When you think to yourself you don't use words, you have another system. Some words you have, some you think in images, and from that is formed the arrangement of speech which, if you were to say it out loud, would be incoherent" (1934b:141). Here is a typical passage from *Ulysses,* when Bloom is riding in a funeral carriage.

> He passed an arm through the armstrap and looked seriously from the open carriage window at the lowered blinds of the avenue. One dragged aside: an old woman peeping. Nose whiteflattened against the pane. Thanking her stars she was passed over. Extraordinary the interest they take in a corpse. Glad to see us go we give them such trouble coming. Job seems to suit them. Huggermugger in corners. Slop about in slipper-slappers for fear he'd wake. Then getting it ready. Laying it out. Molly and Mrs. Fleming making the bed. Pull it more to your side. Wash and shampoo. Never know who will touch you dead . . .   (Joyce 1961:87)

According to Eisenstein, such a collage of impressions, associations, and memories exemplifies the "alogical system" of thought. But Joyce is limited purely to language, and Eisenstein believes that the cinema can go further. "Only the sound film is capable of reconstructing all the phases and all the specifics of a train of thought" (1932b:235).

Eisenstein sketches the inner-monologue method in describing his plans for

filming *An American Tragedy* at Paramount. Clyde Griffiths must fight down
urges to murder his pregnant lover, Roberta. In order to express his inner struggle,
Eisenstein seeks to take us into Clyde's mind.

> Like thought itself [the montage lists] sometimes proceeded through visual
> images, with sound, synchronized or non-synchronized . . .
>
> sometimes like sounds, formless or formed as representational sound
> images . . .
>
> now suddenly in the coinage of intellectually formed words, as "intellectual"
> and dispassionate as words that are spoken, with a blank screen, a rushing
> imageless visuality . . .
>
> now in passionate disjointed speech, nothing but nouns or nothing but verbs;
> then through interjections, with the zigzags of aimless figures, hurrying along
> in synchronization with them.
>
> Now visual images racing past in complete silence,
>
> now joined by a polyphony of sounds,
>
> now by a polyphony of images.
>
> Then both together.
>
> Then interpolated into the external course of action, then interpolating ele-
> ments of the external action into themselves.   (1932a:235–236)[1]

Eisenstein also planned to use the inner-monologue technique in his aborted
MMM project.

The Joycean model of mind quickly proved untenable. As early as 1933 Eisenstein was edgily defending it against charges of idealism (1933a:246–247). He had
advanced it at an inopportune moment, for in the years 1932–1934 Socialist
Realism was moving to center stage. At the Soviet Writers' Congress of 1934, Karl
Radek denounced Joyce as decadent and began a process of official condemnation
of his works; after 1937 Joyce was virtually ignored. Eisenstein defended *Ulysses*
against Radek's attacks and praised its attempt to reconstruct "the reflection and
refraction of reality in consciousness" (1940a:184); but the Joycean inner monologue moves to the periphery of his concerns. He briefly revives the idea in some
sketches for *Boris Godunov,* but here it is treated as a local technical device. His
comments near the end of his life on the "pathological introspection" of *Lady in
the Lake* and *Rebecca* suggest that he finds that the capitalist cinema has led the
inner monologue to a dead end (1986a:151). Eisenstein employs the idea of the
inner monologue chiefly in order to step away from the "ascetic abstraction" of
purely intellectual montage (1935a:129). Two broader conceptions of mind will
be more significant for his later theory.

In his speech at the 1935 All-Union Conference of Soviet Cinematography
Workers, Eisenstein proposed that the psychology of art could best be understood
in the light of "sensuous thought." This concept derives principally from the ideas
of the anthropologist Lucien Lévy-Brühl, who was held in high esteem by the

---

1. In two versions of the script, the scene employs a more traditional, predominantly verbal, psychological monologue. See *FS*: 236–242, and Montagu 1969:294–295.

Soviet academic establishment. Introducing a 1930 Russian collection of his works, the editors stressed that the "collective representations" of primitive society are not abstract concepts but rather "images fused with emotional and motor elements" (Editors of "Atheist" Publishers 1930:8). Primitive thought, according to Lévy-Brühl, does not differentiate among concepts, feelings, and actions; nor does it distinguish between subject and object. Lévy-Brühl's famous "law of participation" holds that it is possible for primitive thought to violate the logical principle of noncontradiction. For primitive logic, the "I" may be at once itself and something else. The Bororo Indians believe that they are both human and a form of red parakeet.

Lévy-Brühl's speculations were not of solely ethnographic interest. He claims in his introduction to the 1930 Russian edition: "There are not two forms of thinking for mankind, one logical, the other prelogical, separated from each other by an impenetrable wall. They are different thought structures that exist in the same society and often, perhaps always, in one and the same mind" (Tul'viste 1987:14).

Eisenstein read Lévy-Brühl during his visit to the West. In his address to the 1935 conference, published as "Film Form: New Problems," he draws upon Lévy-Brühl's concept of prelogical thought. He proposes that besides rational, logical thinking there also exists "sensuous thought." This is "the flow and sequence of thinking unformulated into the logical constructions in which uttered, formulated thoughts are expressed" (1935a:130). Logic requires that concepts and categories be differentiated, but sensuous thought springs from a more holistic sort of perception. (Here he echoes a point made in the 1920s, when he claimed that the "monistic ensemble" of Kabuki reflected a precapitalist lack of differentiation in Japanese culture.)

Eisenstein goes further than Lévy-Brühl in proposing "laws" of sensuous thought, all based on the lack of differentiation. What is significant is that each "law" can be seen as emerging both in primitive culture and in artistic form. For example, the hunter wears a bear's tooth as a talisman to give him strength. Eisenstein sees this as an instance of *pars pro toto,* taking the part for the whole. He finds that it reemerges in the use of synecdoche in art, as in Smirnov's dangling pince-nez in *Potemkin.* Similarly, the Bororo tribe's refusal to distinguish humans from parakeets reveals a fusion of self with other. This tendency reemerges in more "developed" artistic practices, such as acting. "At the basis of the creation of form lie sensual and imagist thought processes" (1935a:130).

Art thus combines logical organization (the choice of a theme, the selection of means of conveying it, and so on) with sensuous thinking. The artist must fuse the appeals of "primitive thought" with fully self-conscious artistic method.

Eisenstein calls sensuous thought "inner speech" *(vnutrennaya rech')* a term that had already acquired specific connotations in Soviet culture. Discussing cinema, Boris Eikhenbaum posited inner speech as something the spectator must construct in order to understand a silent film; here the term seems little more than a metaphor for inference making (1927b:11–12). V. N. Voloshinov, in *Marx-*

ism and the Philosophy of Language (1929), conceived of inner speech as the internal "words and intonations" through which the individual maintains consciousness; it is an internalized dialogue, derived from the social context of verbal exchange. By contrast, Lev Vygotsky's *Thought and Language* (1934) treated inner speech as the "ingrowth" of the child's egocentric speech. But for both Voloshinov and Vygotsky, inner speech remained an internalized, abbreviated version of vocalized social speech.

Eisenstein's usage is identical with none of these. He adheres to an empiricist-associationist model inimical to Voloshinov's position and explicitly opposed by Vygotsky (1934:212–214). According to Eisenstein, inner speech does not derive from linguistic activities, either dialogue or monologue. Indeed, inner speech in his sense would seem to be a prerequisite for language acquisition. It is, moreover, a mixture of concepts and purely sensory qualities. The phenomenon is thus probably better labeled by Eisenstein's alternative term, *sensuous thought*. This is roughly parallel to Vygotsky's *preverbal thought*, which ontogenetically precedes the development of what Vygotsky considered inner speech (Vygotsky 1934:84–94).

Despite Eisenstein's use of the term *inner speech*, his ideas probably owe more to quite different trends in linguistic speculation. By the early 1930s Nikolay Marr had become the most influential Soviet linguist. Eisenstein was susceptible to Marrism: Marr's "stadial" theory of language change, whereby vocal language develops on the basis of manual or gestural sign systems, would have struck a sympathetic chord in the theatre director who thought of expressive movement as more basic than language. Marr's theory further posited a link between the origin of speech and the development of work processes. Marr praised Lévy-Brühl's work for offering proof that "thought and language were brother and sister, children of the same parents, industry and social structure" (Marr 1930:19).

Eisenstein's 1935 talk, delivered only a year after Marr's death, announces that Marr's theories have a methodological value beyond the field of linguistics. Marr had asserted that "Mankind created its speech in the process of labor in circumscribed social circumstances and has recreated it with the recrudescence of new forms of living in accordance with new forms of thinking" (Phillips 1986:83). Eisenstein's address obliquely revises this formulation by suggesting that some activities do not change in tempo with the historical development of labor. Everyday customs and beliefs remain tied to "earlier forms of thinking" that are "sensual-imagistic" in nature (1935a:131).

Eisenstein calls upon the model of sensuous thought throughout his later theorizing. Sometimes he seeks to show the power of nonlogical formal choices. More often he stresses that concrete representational qualities of art tap prelogical processes, so that the most advanced and effective works combine knowledge of the conceptual implications of a phenomenon with a strongly sensuous formal appeal. For instance, he finds that the *Valkyrie* displays Wagner's intuitive understanding of the power that images have over primitive thought (1940j:15–16). In addition, as we shall see later in this chapter, Lévy-Brühl's notion of "participation" contributed a good deal to Eisenstein's concept of "ecstasy."

Like the Joycean inner monologue, Eisenstein's notion of sensuous thought came under fire. In the 1937 pamphlet denouncing *Bezhin Meadow*, Ilya Vaisfeld attacked the ideas the director had propounded at the 1935 conference. Vaisfeld charged that seeking the sources of artistic effect in "primitive thought" ignored the changes that tribal thinking had undergone within social development, and particularly within contemporary life. *Bezhin Meadow* had been condemned for presenting the peasantry by means of fancifully primal, "mythic" symbols of good and evil; Vaisfeld implied that the film's failure confirmed the inadequacy of the director's theory. He suggested that the mistakes of *Bezhin Meadow* should teach Eisenstein the importance of the artistic "image [*obraz*]," particularly insofar as it affected actors' performances and the graphic and figurative dimensions of the shot.

As if in reply to Vaisfeld, Eisenstein proposes a third model of thought. He initiates it in the unpublished treatise "Montage" (begun in 1937 after the banning of *Bezhin Meadow*) and develops it most fully in the 1939 essay "Montage 1938." Now Eisenstein tells a story of concept formation that is broadly empiricist. Again, the psychological account is meant to provide a natural ground for a process-based theory of artistic form.

According to Eisenstein, we ordinarily build concepts out of repeated exposure to sensory data. We form these concepts by association, or what Hume called "constant conjunction." For example, when we think of "five o'clock" we summon up not simply the configuration of clock hands but a host of associations: shops closing, traffic thickening, a certain slant of light. We have acquired this concept, Eisenstein claims, through repeated experience of the world's regularities. At five o'clock, certain things tend to happen, and we have registered those regularities in our memory. When we see a clock face, we summon up not a dry abstraction, five P.M. as simply distinct from four or six P.M., but a synthetic idea rich in associations. Eisenstein calls this an "image" *(obraz)* and the formal, plastic element that triggers it—say, a configuration of the clock hands—a "representation" or "depiction" *(izobrazhenie)*.

Eisenstein's example concerns only image formation in ordinary life. What of art? According to Eisenstein, art uses images that are more saturated with emotion than is usual in daily experience. The artistic image will be an expressive one. For example, in Maupassant's *Bel ami*, while a man waits for his lover several city clocks strike midnight, then one o'clock: "When Maupassant needed to impress on his readers' minds the *emotional significance* of midnight, he did not limit himself to simply letting the clocks strike twelve and then one o'clock. He made us experience this perception of midnight by having twelve o'clock struck in various places by several clocks. Combined together in our minds, these distinct sets of twelve strokes have merged into a general impression of midnight. *The separate depictions have fused into an image*" (1939d:303–304). Instead of "cinefying" Party policy and slogans, the filmmaker is charged with presenting a more diffuse, evocative concept.

Eisenstein stresses the partial quality of the atomistic representations. Each one makes sense, he claims, by virtue of the principle of *pars pro toto,* the figure that exemplifies "primitive thought." Only our synthesizing consciousness, a characteristic of higher evolutionary development, can combine the depictions into a comprehensive whole. He also indicates that science works in the same way, deriving wholes from partial representations; but in science the generalization is a conceptual law, while in art it is a feelingful image (1937a:97).

The Maupassant example illustrates another feature of image formation in art. Eisenstein claims that in ordinary life we try to save effort, so we tend to forget the chain of particular experiences which produced the image. But art, which aims at creating a new and impressive image, dwells on the intervening steps. In *Bel ami* the repetitions of "midnight" in conjunction with the hero's ebbing hopes evoke the expressive concept, "midnight, the hour of decision." The artwork lingers over its representations, multiplies them, varies them in scale, register, and emphasis. Through modulated repetition, artistic form coaxes the perceiver to create a synthetic image. Whereas ordinary life is concerned only with the product of concept formation, "a work of art directs all the subtlety of its methods towards the *process*" (1939d:302). Eisenstein's classroom exercises, which oblige the director to display an expressive quality across a gamut of techniques and reiterate it through stages of an activity, now find their justification in a conception of art as a means of dwelling upon the process of synthesizing an image out of data.

The depiction/image conception of mind is the only one to give Eisenstein a strong analogy with the overall shape of aesthetic experience. Joycean stream of consciousness specifies no beginning or end; significantly, Eisenstein seeks to apply it only on the small scale, as in the scene from *An American Tragedy.* The laws of "sensuous thought" govern only local aesthetic devices, such as synecdoche or decorum. But the depiction/image formula offers a model of large-scale process. The overall unfolding of the artistic work can be correlated with the process of forming an emotionally expressive image. In this respect, the developing *obraz* serves a function parallel to the materialist dialectic in Eisenstein's earlier thinking.

Formalistic art dwells on the depiction as an end in itself, while abstract, didactic works present only pre-formed images lacking fresh emotional impact. True art mobilizes images for maximum effect. Furthermore, throughout the 1930s and 1940s Eisenstein maintains that the artist must feel the theme that he or she wishes to impart. Once this image is traced to its sources in concrete experience, the artist will devise and arrange objective representations that will induce the spectator to form such an image. The spectator is drawn into a creative act that is guided by the author but that also offers a degree of participation and discovery.

More than the other two models, the depiction/image account opens a path to ideologically pointed art. Eisenstein insists that a realistic work of art must contain "in an indissoluble whole *both* the representation of a phenomenon *and* its image; by 'image' is meant a generalized statement about the essence of the particular phenomenon" (1937c:4). His example is a picture of a barricade during the Paris Commune. A representation that did not present the barricade as clashing with the forces of the bourgeoisie would have failed to bring out the quality of struggle that the very concept of the barricade possesses. Therefore, he demands that the barricade trace a jagged, disruptive outline; he even suggests a framing that shows the barricade as pushing down (literally "over-throwing") the sign hanging outside a shop (ibid.:24–27). In Socialist Realist art the concept-laden image will imbue expressive form with political meaning.

The depiction/image conception of mind revises many concerns of Eisenstein's earlier work. In assigning a place to repetition of information and the spectator's act of association, the idea recalls the reflexological premises of Eisenstein's 1920s writings.[2] Now, however, there is no assumption that psychic activity can be reduced to purely physiological excitation. Art is still both emotional and conceptual, aiming to transmit both meanings and feelings; but now the artist's meanings are no longer doctrinal slogans, and the feelings are no longer conceived as responses to calculated stimulation. This third conception of psychological activity fits Eisenstein's evolving practice and poetics: its picture of a spectator who gathers items into a meaningful expressive whole correlates with the motif-based strategies of the silent films and the weaving-and-knotting precepts he urged upon his VGIK students.

This conception of mental life also explicitly reworks several commonplaces of Socialist Realism. Eisenstein's terminology faintly echoes Lenin's "reflection-" or "copy-" theory of perception, according to which percepts are "images" of the external world. But Eisenstein differs from Lenin in claiming that the image has the power to synthesize isolated sensations. He thereby carries on a long tradition of Russian speculation about the "imagistic" nature of thought and artistic creation.

Under the influence of Hegel, Vissarion Belinsky (1811–1848) introduced the idea of the image *(obraz)* into Russian aesthetics. According to Belinsky, the image objectively fuses idea and material form in the art work. The artist is one who "thinks in images." Alexander Potebnya (1835–1891) recast the concept by distinguishing between external form (the sensory surface that the perceiver grasps) and "internal form," or the work's true image. For Potebnya, the image triggers a generative process in the minds of the creator and the perceiver. "Thinking in images" here means finding an expressive image that can, once manifested in external form, induce the perceiver to grasp a significance broader than the external form alone can represent. Belinsky's and Potebnya's views left their mark on Soviet art theory and became a central source of Socialist Realist aesthetics.

In particular, the concept of the "artistic image" *(khudozhestvennyi obraz)* was keenly debated during the 1920s. Whereas RAPP adherents treated the image

---

2. "One of the aims of art is to blaze new trails in our awareness of reality, to create *new chains of association* on the basis of utilizing those which already exist. (In phases of greater 'rigour' in my thinking about the mechanism of such phenomena, I formulated this as 'the aim of creating new conditioned reflexes on the basis of existing unconditioned reflexes'; that was in 1923–4.)" (Eisenstein 1937d: 260).

purely as reflecting the writer's ideology, shapers of Socialist Realist theory took the image as having a tie to reality. Valery Kirpotin, for example, called the image "the essential content of the real world" (quoted in Ermolaev 1963:187). Such views opened the way to conceiving the artistic image as a dynamic transformation of the world. This position was advanced at the 1934 Writers' Congress. Gorky claimed that the artist's task is "to extract from the sum of a given reality its cardinal idea and embody it in imagery—that is how we got realism" (1935:44).

Eisenstein's third conception of psychological activity implicitly justifies such an aesthetic. By describing the mind as naturally moving from atomistic representations to an imagistic whole, he lays the groundwork for treating art as a dynamic, synthesizing process derived from reality but transformed by the artist's sensibility. His formulations thus offer a way of addressing contemporary debates. He suggests, for instance, that an artistically adequate "typicality" of character and situation, so prized by Engels and Socialist Realism, depends upon the mind's movement from representation to artistic image: "the typical, fully realized so as to embrace both objective representation and generalized image" (1937g:101).

Eisenstein's emphasis on the emotional expressivity of the artistic image is also in keeping with current discussions. Belinsky had claimed that the artwork does not simply embody an idea, as science could, but also possesses a quality of emotion, or "pathos" (pafos). Contemporary readings of Potebnya's work often treated the work's "inner form" as feeling-laden. At the Writers' Congress, for instance, Bukharin cited Potebnya to support the idea that art reflects objective reality through symbols imbued with emotion (Bukharin 1935:192). In addition, an emphasis on art's affective power had been a commonplace of Russian aesthetic theory for a century. This view had particular appeal for those 1920s critics who called for rousing, socially committed art. We shall see that pathos plays a major part in Eisenstein's conception of spectatorial response.

Still other sources swirl through Eisenstein's speculations on mind in this period. His new interest in "primitive thinking" and diffuse emotional states probably owes a good deal to his stay in Mexico. His discussion of prelogical thought reflects his continuing affiliation with Vygotsky and Luria, who studied children, preliterate cultures, and brain-damaged patients in search of cognitive processes at variance with deductive reasoning. Eisenstein also quietly continues to assimilate elements of Formalist literary theory. By contrasting ordinary life's automatic perception with art's tendency to linger over the sensory act, he echoes Shklovsky's dictum that art aims "to increase the difficulty and length of perception because the process of perception is an aesthetic end in itself and must be prolonged" (Shklovsky 1917:12). At the same time, certain aspects of Socialist Realist aesthetics, such as the emphasis on concreteness, expressivity, and "imagicity," are congenial with his own predispositions.

It would thus be too schematic to see watertight divisions among Eisenstein's three conceptions of mental life. The inner monologue, generalized and "deverbalized," becomes inner speech. Inner speech has important links with the depiction/image account of perception. He acknowledges that it was necessary to make "creative 'cruises' through the 'inner monologue' of Joyce, through the 'inner monologue' as understood in film, and through so-called 'intellectual cinema'" before arriving at the identification of inner speech with sensuous thinking (1944:250). Eisenstein takes the generalization from representation to image as a development of "primitive" sensuous thought, brought under artistic control and made universally accessible (1986b:82–83).

This continuity lends a certain consistency to Eisenstein's writings throughout his career. He remains convinced that both emotional and cognitive processes are central to experience, and he continues to treat repetition and association as central to the acquisition of concepts. On the matter of the relation of mind to language, he continues to treat linguistic form largely as the articulation of social and sensuous experience. Artworks may draw upon verbal figures, as when in the VGIK *Crime and Punishment* exercise the crash of Raskolnikov's hatchet enacts the "fall" of his egoistic theory (Nizhny 1958:127). Nonetheless, both picture and word spring from the same prelinguistic source—sensuous thought. Eisenstein cites Potebnya as showing that the origins of language are themselves figurative. When *Strike* depicts the massacre as "a bloody slaughter-house," it shows that Soviet silent film sought a kind of "film-speech" based on metaphors. But now directors have learned that all language has an imagist basis, and montage has become "an organic embodiment of a single idea conception [*sic*], embracing all elements, parts, details of the film work" (1944:254).

Eisenstein's 1930s speculations about psychological processes do not ground a theory of knowledge. His version of associationism, for instance, is vulnerable to the objection that associations alone cannot yield reliable knowledge of causation. Screeching tires may typically accompany a car chase, but they do not cause it. Eisenstein's discussions of mental activity are perhaps best seen as loose assumptions that enable him to mount a film practice and a film poetics. Although associationism may be a shaky basis for an epistemology, it probably plays a central role in our experience of artworks. In art the perceiver wants not guarantees of knowledge but cues for an engaging experience. In a film, screeching tires can vividly evoke a car chase.

Throughout all this Eisenstein remains eclectic, drawing from intellectual doctrines that permit him to treat art as a process involving both rational and nonrational capacities. What notions such as the conditioned reflex yielded in the 1920s, concepts such as "sensuous thought" and the synthesizing "image" yield now: a non-conscious level of experience that art can exploit and express. Eisenstein's reflections on mind accordingly serve to ground his continuing explorations of art and of the poetics of cinema.

Film Form: Organic Unity

In his later theoretical writings, Eisenstein continues to assert that artistic form is congruent with properties of the world and of human consciousness. Marxism has disclosed the regularities governing social life, and if art is to be effective, it must reflect those regularities not only in the work's subject and theme but also in its internal organization. For example, the struggle of opposites is a basic feature of objective reality; it thus properly forms the basis of conflict in a drama or musical piece (1947f:681). Similarly, an artwork will vitally engage the spectator only if it reflects processes of perception, emotion, and thought. "The most accomplished type of composition is that which takes as its basis man's structure of behavior or the course of the emotional and mental processes which go on in him" (1980b:234–235). A work becomes shallow and "formalistic" when the artist chooses an arbitrary form that flouts the laws governing human expressivity.

All three of Eisenstein's models of mind emphasize the psychological bases of form. The inner monologue in art is homologous with the stream of consciousness in ordinary life. Prelogical thought is embodied in a range of formal devices, such as synecdoche and decorum; and it is present as a sensuous element in every authentically appealing work. Most elaborately of all, the process whereby concrete representations coalesce into images, or felt concepts, is the basis of the dynamic unfolding of the work.

In all these models, especially the last, Eisenstein sees the principle of a strict unity. Following Engels, he postulates that organic unity in nature presents a "higher unity" than that of mechanical assemblage. A phenomenon is unified when "one and the same principle will nourish every part, appearing in each of them with their own special qualitative distinctions" (1939f:10).

Sometimes this unifying principle is conceived as a quasi-geometrical schema. In the 1939 essay "On the Structure of Things," Eisenstein attributes *Potemkin*'s organic unity to two factors. The film's major parts compose a five-act tragedy, with each act being structurally identical. Each act is divided into two parts by a caesura marking a transition to an opposite treatment of the theme. Moreover, the architecture of the plot reflects the same abstract principle: the film's five parts break into two groups of two each, with the third segment, "An Appeal from the Dead," constituting the large-scale caesura. So much reveals a rather rigid symmetry. But Eisenstein goes on to claim that the film's proportions also reveal a 2:3 ratio (1939f:6–22). Each part divides not in the middle but about two-fifths of the way through, and the caesura at the film's "center" comes at the beginning of the third reel. In addition, the appearance of the red flag on the *Potemkin*, which might have formed the exact midpoint of the film, actually comes at the 3:2 point. Eisenstein claims that this asymmetrical principle also yields a compositional stability. Ultimately he traces it to natural proportions, such as the spiral of a seashell, and to the Golden Section ratio in classical painting and architecture.

This somewhat geometrical sense of unity represents only one side of Eisenstein's thinking. More common is a notion of organic unity that owes a good deal to Belinsky's aesthetics, which inherited from German idealism the concept of the artwork as a significant whole. The idea was taken up by Socialist Realist aestheticians, who called for "organic unity" as a cure for Left art's machine worship and the reductive materialism of the philosophical Mechanists.

The most effective artwork, according to Eisenstein, is controlled by a single expressive theme. He enriches this cliché in two particular ways. First, organicism allows him to pursue an indefatigably "formalistic" search for all the elements of cinema that can serve the unifying idea. The expressive image must be embodied in a plot, in particular episodes, in specific turns of action, and finally in the staging, framing, and cutting of shots and the selection and arrangement of sound. We have seen in the previous chapter how investigation of this process governs his laboratory exercises in method.

Apart from inventorying technical resources, Eisenstein uses the concept of organicism to treat art as a dynamic, time-bound phenomenon. A quasi-mathematical schema may govern *Potemkin*'s overall architecture, but at the level of scene and shot there is said to be a "leap" into expressive qualities, a constant "transition from one intensity to another" (1939f:30). In this moment-by-moment process the film's theme of expanding revolutionary activity is manifested. The idea of ongoing formal development in the service of an expressive theme is central to Eisenstein's conception of organic unity. And here his third notion of mental activity, that of depiction and image, serves as a guide. The shots and their components furnish depictions, while montage creates the relevant artistic "image."

The individual shot, or "montage piece," exists as what Eisenstein calls "a *partial depiction* of the single overall theme which in equal degree pervades all the sequences" (1939d:299). His pedagogical exercises in *mise en scène,* montage, and *mise en cadre* offer techniques for giving each shot maximum significance and force, but now he considers the artist's task from a more general perspective.

Eisenstein assumes that in treating the expressive theme the artist will not leave the bounds of more literal denotation. His 1937 manuscript "Montage" argues that narrative processes should be ordered so as to yield a continuous imagistic accompaniment. He posits that narrative montage, such as analytical editing or crosscutting, yields a depictive or merely "semantic" level of effect, while imagistic montage is kinetic and expressive (1937e:227–228). Imagistic processes, such as the picture of the barricade, tend to "generalize" the narrative phenomenon. Once more, he maps the depiction/image model of mind onto the moment-by-moment development of the film's stylistic texture.

How is imagicity to be harmonized with the depictive function of the film shot? For Eisenstein the basic task of visual composition is to lay out a path for the spectator's eye in accordance with the theme. Thus the perceptual qualities of the shot afford a range of emotional possibilities. Above all, contours have the "generalizing" power to express emotions or create metaphors. In the *Black Majesty* exercise, when Dessalines pulls up a tablecloth as a shield, its arc repeats the curve of the officers' grouping; in the *Crime and Punishment* étude, the splitting of the moneylender's skull is foreshadowed by the watch chain that "splits" her face (Nizhny 1958:85, 111–112). The beauty of Disney's work lies partly in "animating" the line, as when waves become boxing gloves punching a ship's hull (1986b:23). Given what can be done with the line, Eisenstein criticizes purely abstract art as unnecessarily impoverished; the expressive contour can depict a plot situation while also yielding an emotion-laden concept.

The linear composition of the shot can articulate depth as well. Again techniques must guide literal perception while developing the artistic theme of the work. Orthodox perspective systems draw the spectator's eye into imaginary recesses, but Eisenstein is more interested in systems that exaggerate the process expressively. Piranesi designs his phantasmagoric prisons so that one line leads us into depth, only to be broken by another; and when we pick up the first orthogonal, it is often unexpectedly reduced or expanded in scale, yielding an overwhelming sense of vast vaults.

Another sort of exaggeration can be found in certain cinematic techniques of portraying depth, such as that afforded by the 28mm wide-angle lens (2.130–131). Eisenstein finds that a composition with a very close foreground and a distant background is thus well suited for creating tension between themes. In the *Glass House* project, steep angles would have juxtaposed dissonant elements seen through transparent floors and ceilings. Rugs and doors would have loomed up in the foreground. "Don't forget the compositional power of carpets thrown on the glass floors," he notes (Leyda and Voynow 1982:45). Wide-angle lenses can also suggest a pervasive unity between planes, as in the famous shot of Ivan's profile above the procession at the end of *Ivan the Terrible* Part I. Here several of the concerns of the 1929 "Dramaturgy of Film Form" essay have been recast, with the insistence upon dialectical conflict now balanced by a concern for an overriding synthesis.

Line, depth, and other compositional features make each shot a depictive unit. In combining and repeating such units, the filmmaker creates a controlled context for associations. By dwelling on the process of forming those associations, the artist obeys the process whereby images are formed in life. After building up emotional intensity, the artist presents the most effective representations. Now the spectator feels the theme at its highest pitch.

An example may clarify the process. In the reconstructed version of *Bezhin Meadow*, one sequence depicts the peasants turning a church into a workers' club.[3] Most abstractly, the informing idea is the triumph of the people's vital energy over lifeless deities. The first shot of the sequence alludes to the theme: the church stands in inverted reflection in a pool of water (5.1). The sequence thus starts with the church turned upside down. As workers dismantle and haul out the icons, the shots depict the artifacts as merely lumps of matter, empty of divine significance. The camera now frames workers as if they were icons themselves (5.2, 5.3). Biblical imagery is parodied and recontextualized: Christ's descent from the cross is rendered as manual labor (5.4), in Mary's place stands a smiling mother (5.5), and a peasant Samson heaves down the pillars before the altar. The sequence culminates in a shot of a boy lifted above the crowd and wearing a tipsy

---

3. This reconstruction may differ from what Eisenstein would have done with the sequence on the editing table, but in its present form it is useful for illustrative purposes.

5.1 *Bezhin Meadow.*

5.2

5.3

5.4

5.5

5.6

crown; the image blasphemously revises that of Christianity's crowned child (5.6). The "overturning" of religion and the sanctification of the peasant—the moment when the meek inherit the earth—is expressed in various materials and to differing degrees until all factors cooperate in presenting the theme with maximal vividness. The point could have been presented more directly in a title or line of dialogue, but then it would not have become an image built up out of emotional associations.[4]

If formal development is a gradually intensifying process, there must be ways

4. Interestingly, this sequence reenacts, in more narratively concrete form, the overthrow of abstract sign systems that occurs in *October.*

of hinting, lingering, accumulating pressure. Eisenstein accordingly emphasizes what he calls "calculated transitions." He notes that a description in *Oliver Twist* moves from purely visual elements to aural elements, and then from a rumble to a roar (1944:216). As the example indicates, Eisenstein often conceives of such transitions as systematically varying a technical parameter, such as line, light, or color. In the Katerina Izmailova exercise, the bed's outlines recur in scene after scene, while the permutational differences in the treatment (with the bed half-seen, not seen, seen completely) yield varying expressive effects. By working backward from the strongest effect, the artist assigns to subordinate moments lesser formal options that prepare the way for the "fullest" possible representation.

The *Bezhin Meadow* sequence shows how various film techniques can be parceled out for maximum effect. The scene begins with only a bare diagram of the theme, the church upside down, rendered as spatially static and with tiny human figures. In the course of the sequence the thematic burden is taken up by the human figures and the props around them. The sequence ends on a crescendo based upon contrasting the fall of the pillars and the upward thrust of the child's exaltation: the strongest representation in a sequence that steadily increases in dynamism and emotional appeal.

By conceiving each aspect of the shot as a manipulable factor, Eisenstein recalls the "monism" of his earlier theorizing. "One and the same characteristic," he tells his students, "can be developed in different spheres of expressive portrayal. In one instance, it can be portrayed by a graphic delineation of *mise en scène,* in another—by gesticulation, in a third—by stammering speech" (Nizhny 1958:116). But instead of positing a collision among these different channels, he now calls for them to accompany one another. A film's form achieves organic unity by building representations toward an emotion-laden "image" of the theme. He therefore proposes to treat film form as a series of ongoing "lines" so coordinated as to achieve an expressive effect.

Eisenstein's most common analogy for this process is musical composition. Each element in the film—a character or setting, an object or a color, an angle or curve, a gesture or framing or musical phrase, an emotional quality; in short, anything that can function as a recurring motif—can be plotted on a line, like a melody or a fugal voice. Here the motif-based construction of the silent films and of the *Lady Macbeth of Mtsensk* exercise finds theoretical articulation. Eisenstein compares the process to Asian scroll painting, such as the Japanese *makimono.* Each "line," such as clouds or mountains or trees or human figures, winds its way across the surface, alternately receding from notice or coming to prominence, reinforcing other lines or standing on its own. This analogy echoes Eisenstein's 1928 reflections on the "monistic ensemble" in Kabuki, in which each sensory channel operates independently; but now he emphasizes the overall cooperation of lines, not their potential for disjunction.

Still, cooperation does not mean uniformity. Eisenstein suggests that contrast, sometimes called "counterpoint," should govern the overall integration of lines. This will make moments of "unison," usually associated with climactic passages

5.7 *Battleship Potemkin.*   5.8

of a scene, all the more powerful when they come. Contrast can be achieved by interruption or the "breaking of inertia" (1941a:16–17). Alternatively, enjambment, the non-coincidence of beginnings and end points in simultaneous lines, can create binding continuities, as when, just before a shot ends, a new figure appears that dominates the next shot.

Above all, the lines must genuinely intertwine. One line may simply alternate in importance with another, as in this series of three shots:

	Shot 1	Shot 2	Shot 3
	x	y	x
	y	x	y

Eisenstein shows this sort of organization at work in the graphic motifs that knit together fourteen shots in *Potemkin.* The dramatic action of the sequence crosscuts two dramatic lines: the yawls speeding toward the ship and the people of Odessa watching. But the organization of the sequence is based on developing verticals, horizontals, and arch shapes. "The subjects dominate alternately, advancing to the foreground and pushing one another into the background" (1934a:290). Shot 1 emphasizes the horizontal vector (the movement of the skiffs across the sea) and plays down the verticals (the yawls' masts) (5.7). In shot 2 the vertical columns in the foreground dominate the horizontal axis, while the arch motif makes its appearance as a minor element (5.8). In shot 3 the arch becomes the pictorial dominant, subordinating both horizontal and vertical motifs (5.9). The next shot restates the vertical motif in the figures while picking up the arch in the curve of a parasol (5.10). This intertwining of "lines" recalls the concept of the visual "overtone," enabling Eisenstein to treat all the shot's subsidiary elements as contributing to the stream of sensory appeal.[5]

The *Potemkin* case exemplifies fairly simple "wickerwork" construction. In dissecting sequences from *Ivan the Terrible,* however, Eisenstein concocts a notational scheme and complex tables in order to chart the play of lines. As we shall

5. The sequence given in Eisenstein's text does not correspond exactly to any print of the film I have examined. In versions available in the West, the first five shots are followed by those labeled by Eisenstein as shots VIII–XII, then by shot VII. The other shots appear much later in the sequence.

5.9   5.10

see below, music and dialogue not only bring in new lines but also introduce patterns of rhythm that must be synchronized with the visual motifs.

A film's texture must therefore be through-composed; every stylistic choice is governed by the evolving expressive context. By interlacing motivic "voices," the artwork achieves a dynamic organic unity and involves the viewer in creating the emotional image of the theme.

Montage: The Musical Analogy Revisited

Eisenstein's conception of organic unity assigns a central role to montage, the process that controls the braiding of the work's lines. Construed narrowly, montage still constitutes the technique of film editing. But editing is only the most evident case of the principle by which depictions coalesce into an artistic image. Cinema has "micro-montage" at the level of frames, "montage proper" in editing and framing, and "macro-montage" in joining scenes and parts into an entire film (1937a:109). Most broadly, montage is a formal principle ruling all arts. Pushkin "edits" details in *Poltava;* Flaubert "intercuts" conversations in *Madame Bovary;* Leonardo coordinates lines of movement in his notes for drawings of the Deluge; in El Greco's works, it is as if separate "photos" were assembled in violation of the laws of linear perspective (1980a:18–21). "Montage" no longer carries Constructivist echoes of machine assembly. It is now the process whereby various lines, without losing their individuality, dynamically interact to create an organic unity.

Eisenstein accordingly extends his musical analogy. *Polyphonic,* or "contrapuntal," montage governs the interlacing of the "voices" on the film's unrolling visual track. Shots are linked through the *"simultaneous movement* of a number of motifs" (1940h:330). Each line builds and continues a thematic movement, and each shot contains one or more lines. Factors in shot composition can supply such lines. Thanks to montage, contours can be repeated through a series of shots or can develop into various graphic patterns (1937c:56–58). From shot to shot, a foreground element can alternate with a background element, or the montage can isolate one or the other in a single shot for maximum intensity (1986a:108n).

Potemkin's yawls passage, analyzed above, illustrates how graphic motifs can function as lines on a shot-to-shot basis.

Despite the implications of smoothness evoked by its name, polyphonic montage may violate what conventional cinema would regard as continuity. In an example drawn from *Ivan the Terrible* Part I, Eisenstein singles out one portion of the scene at Anastasia's bier. Three principal "voices" here are Ivan's posture, his facial expression, and the crucifix dangling from around his neck. By cutting to different shots of Ivan clinging to the coffin, Eisenstein emphasizes Ivan's posture in one shot, his face in another, the crucifix in another, all the while maintaining the other "lines" as subsidiary elements. But in doing this Eisenstein can freely violate continuity editing by altering Ivan's position from shot to shot (1945a:302). The "acting without transitions" saluted in the 1928 Kabuki essay now becomes a by-product of polyphonic montage.

In their 1928 "Statement" on sound film, Eisenstein, Alexandrov, and Pudovkin had declared that the soundtrack should be "contrapuntal"—that is, offering "a sharp discord with the visual image" (1928d:114). Although the musicological naiveté of this formulation was pointed out at the time (see Messman 1928), Eisenstein continued throughout the 1920s to think of image/sound "counterpoint" as involving conflict. In the 1930s, however, he starts to use the term in the more organic sense we have already considered, and his conception of the formal role of sound alters accordingly.

The case for audiovisual montage rests upon the belief that the spectator is predisposed to grasp correlations of sound, color, and graphic design. Throughout his life Eisenstein was fascinated by synesthesia, the process of mixing sense modes in experience. To call a shirt loud or to hear a melody as swaggering is, according to Eisenstein, to hark back to a stage of undifferentiated human expressivity. In the 1920s he had discovered synesthesia in the Kabuki theatre's monistic ensemble. ("The notes I can't reach with my voice I'll point to with my hands" [1928f:119].) Now all three models of mind allow him to pursue the theme. In Joycean inner monologue, images and sounds mix indiscriminately. Lévy-Brühl's concept of sensuous thought invites the researcher to consider how various "laws" are manifested equally in different sensory modes. And the depiction/image process is especially pertinent to synesthesia. The "five o'clock" example illustrates how a concept can be built out of a mixture of visual and auditory stimuli. Eisenstein delightedly reports that one of Luria's patients, the fabulous mnemonist Mr. S., had retained the chain of associations that normally gives way to the generalized image. In addition, Mr. S.'s mind worked synesthetically: he saw sounds as colors, colors as sounds (1940i:368).

The relations of image to sound become part of the overall weave of the work, and Eisenstein calls these relations *vertical montage*. The name derives from a famous diagram in which the juxtaposition of shot to shot is paralleled by a "vertical" coordination with the soundtrack.

For Eisenstein, the problem of integrating sound into the organic work comes down to "synchronization." He rejects as theoretically uninteresting a simple "factual" synchronization of picture and sound, as when a croaking frog is filmed and we hear a croak on the track. In practice, of course, the ordinary filmmaker can hardly repudiate this sort of synchronization, but in an organically constructed work, such "affadavit" treatment will be accompanied by more expressive possibilities.

To discover these, Eisenstein returns to an old theme. He posits that the unity of sight and sound has its source in human expressivity. All the time, every day, our feelings are revealed in a natural synchronization between our gestures and our tone of voice. There must be a coordinating principle that permits the two sense modes to run in parallel. Eisenstein finds that principle to be movement. Movement, in a range of manifestations, will thus be the basis of vertical montage.

In tracing out the range of audiovisual possibilities, Eisenstein revamps his 1929 typology of "methods of montage" along organic lines. First, he posits a *metric* version of vertical montage. Here the lengths of the shots and the stretches of the soundtrack become the deciding factor. There is also the possibility of vertical montage according to *rhythm*. Here the filmmaker coordinates the rhythm of the soundtrack—typically, music—with the rhythm of the shots' internal contents and their lengths. There is also *melodic* vertical montage, in which the shot's visual design carries the melodic line of the music (1947e:278). These last two categories require some closer scrutiny.

In discussing rhythmic audiovisual montage, Eisenstein posits that each track possesses stronger and weaker moments. That is, each shot has an *accent:* a shift in light, figure movement, gesture—anything that breaks the inertia of the picture. Likewise, the accompanying music will possess a pattern of accents. The filmmaker's task is to locate a basic rhythmic pattern on one track and interweave it with the pattern on the other track. The simplest "wickerwork" option sets a strong visual accent against a weak sonic one, and vice versa. As usual in Eisenstein's organic model, the simultaneous sounding of strong accents on both tracks is to be reserved for moments of maximum intensity.

Eisenstein complicates his model by pushing rhythmic non-coincidence to the threshold of perceptibility. He assumes that the subtlest expressive possibilities involve enjambment, or the non-coincidence of shot and musical measure. Inventorying the variables involved (shot, cut, measure, accent in either sound or image), he generates a typology permitting very complex vertical-montage relations. The cut may coincide with a strong or weak accent in the picture or with a strong or weak accent in the music. At the limit, he confesses, the subtlety of accent may yield more or less random, "in-between" instances (1945a:351–353). In search of movement at the finest grain of audiovisual texture, Eisenstein echoes Bely and the Russian Formalists, who spoke of verse rhythm as arising from the disparity between speech schemas (for example, intonational stress superimposed upon a fixed meter). In cinema, as in music and poetry, dynamic form is born from the interaction of accentual patterns.

Vertical montage controls not only rhythmic relations but also *melodic* ones. Eisenstein is concerned to find movement not only in a musical melody, phrase,

5.11 *Alexander Nevsky.*   5.12

5.13

or motif but also in the shot's graphic design. For example, the play of light or volume in a shot can be synchronized with music. In one of his homages to Disney he praises a Silly Symphony in which the shimmering of a peacock's tail matches the wavering melody of Offenbach's "Barcarole" (1941b:373). Even a static shot, Eisenstein maintains, contains pictorial movement. A visual line is always the trace of a movement—of the hand that limned it, of the figure that it depicts, or at least of the eye that pursues it. Eisenstein accepted the widespread contemporary belief that we scan a shot along the main contours of the composition. For expressive purposes, the filmmaker can synchronize this time-bound scanning of the shot with the continuing melody of the soundtrack.

The implications of melodic montage as a formal resource can be seen in Eisenstein's most notorious piece of formal analysis: his study of image/sound interactions during the opening of the Battle on the Ice in *Alexander Nevsky.* This discussion rests on assumptions similar to those underpinning his account of the yawls-and-onlookers passage in *Potemkin.*

As in the *Potemkin* instance, Eisenstein groups the shots into "phrases" (for example, a series of long shots, a group of close-ups) and finds that the visual dominants shift between foreground and background. He claims that here the eye scans the compositions from left to right, tracing an overall trajectory of slow, arching rises and sudden drops to a horizontal base. Transitional shots modulate from one emphatic composition to another; the cut from 5.11 to 5.13 would be too jarring, so 5.12 is inserted between them. Such a shot, breaking the rightward "melodic" flow of the compositions, creates an accent that heightens the overall sense of direction.

Prokofiev's music is said to synchronize with the scanning of the shots in several ways. There are "metric" correspondences, as when a "shot phrase" coincides exactly with matching bars of music. Rhythmically, a particular note or chord may be perceived at the same moment that a flag or a figure is. Melodically, quite different shots may match the same musical phrase: the music may synchronize with the contours, with the eye's movement from foreground to background, with the tonal shift from darkness to light, or even with the actor's performance, as when a soldier's puff of breath coincides with single notes.

Eisenstein carries the concept of melodic montage further by asserting that an abstract rising and falling movement unites sound and picture. As we might expect, bodily expressivity provides the link. Eisenstein claims that if you try to portray the movement in the sequence with your hand, you will spontaneously sketch a horizontal line, then a rising arc, and then an abrupt fall. This schema unfolds in the musical progression and the compositional flow across shots. According to Eisenstein, the very pattern is deeply kinesthetic. The "artistic image" evoked by the sequence is that of "uneasy anticipation": a calm (the horizontal flow) followed by tension (the arc) and then a fall, like a sigh (1941b:397). In its audiovisual organization, the sequence enacts the movement of holding one's breath.

Most commentators have considered the *Nevsky* analysis forced. All viewers probably do not scan every shot at the same rate, so the music is unlikely to synchronize with the tempo of each one's eye movements. Moreover, whereas onscreen movement and the eye's tracking of the shot's composition are genuine physical displacements, the concept of "musical movement" is already quite metaphorical, and Eisenstein works the metaphor very hard.

Still, we cannot easily dismiss the premises that we do attribute "movement" to music, and that this movement can synchronize with our visual perception. For instance, Western listeners do hear music as rising or falling, and such perceptions are often successfully correlated with corresponding pictures or words. (See Kivy 1984:53–57.) It is likely that the perceiver has some inborn capacity to match auditory and visual streams of information in quite precise ways; it would be difficult for the newborn infant to *learn* to synchronize the mother's lip movements with the phonic stream. It also seems likely that this capacity has been refined through training, background information, and conventional association. In this light, minute audiovisual correlations are a likely resource for filmmakers to tap. In coming to understand this phenomenon, no one has improved on Eisenstein's account, particularly in his sensitivity to enjambment, accent, and localized synchronization. The concepts of rhythmic and melodic montage enabled him to launch the most detailed inquiry into sound/image interaction that film theory has yet produced.

Eisenstein's taxonomy of vertical montage includes one more possibility, which he calls *tonal* montage. Like the tonal montage of his 1929 taxonomy, it involves light values. In keeping with his new emphasis upon movement as a common denominator for sound and picture, tonal montage is seen as "an *oscillatory* movement, whose various characteristics we perceive as sounds of different pitch and key" (1940h:335). We have already seen this quality at work in the *Nevsky* sequence, where the opening fade-in coincides with an initial "lightening" of the music. The fullest exploration of tonal montage, however, occurs in Eisenstein's growing preoccupation with color.

Like sound, color might be thought to tie the cinema to "factual" reproduction. Instead, Eisenstein insists that color's aesthetic importance lies in its capacity to trigger associations. Red, for instance, can evoke a sense of heat, danger, passion, or anger. There is no universal psychological correspondence between a specific color and a certain feeling, but the artist can either call upon one already established in the culture or, preferably, create a context that gives the color a new emotional significance. Thus the clichéd opposition between white and black is reversed in *Alexander Nevsky,* in which the Teutonic villains wear white (the color of cold and death) and the heroic Russians wear gray and black (which links them to the dark soil). Because color associations are culturally conventional, the artist is at liberty to alter them as the work at hand requires.

Moreover, color is, like graphic contour, detachable from specific objects. Pure color can evoke emotion and suggest concepts: the red and green circles on a painted toy horse strive to become metaphorically "objectified" as apples. Color can also "generalize" the object by linking it to other objects. Children's crayon work and the popular *lubok* (broadside) prints spill color beyond the figures' boundaries, displaying the dynamism of "tonal" qualities and creating new connections among compositional elements (1947i:513–517).

Across the film, the color tonalities of a shot can become "depictions" or "representations" that coalesce into a color "image." The color scheme may reflect developments in the drama, as in the progression from black tonalities to white ones in Pudovkin's *Mother.* Eisenstein compares this strategy to Beethoven's dramatic transformations of a theme (1937d:264–265). Alternatively, the filmmaker can start by exposing the film's palette, associating certain colors with particular narrative elements, and then building each episode around a dominant color or color combination. This option is Eisenstein's preferred solution because it maximizes the interaction of color motifs within the film's polyphony. He compares this strategy to Bach's counterpoint, but Wagnerian implications are no less evident: "The theme expressed in color leitmotifs can, through its color score and with its own means, unfold an inner drama, weaving its own pattern in the contrapuntal whole, crossing and recrossing the course of the action, which formerly music alone could do with full completeness by supplementing what could not be expressed by acting or gesture" (1948a:128). When color is granted this much freedom, it reinforces the inner unity of picture and sound.

Although Eisenstein discusses color in Disney and in literature, his most detailed analysis of its contributions to tonal montage is, naturally enough, the banquet scene in *Ivan the Terrible* Part II. We will consider this scene again in the next chapter, but it is worth mentioning here that the sequence has the air of a theoretical experiment. It restricts itself to a narrow palette, and it refuses to link each color with a particular character. Eisenstein sought to build the sequence out of the progression of four "color themes": red and black (both associated with death), gold (the tsar's majesty), and blue (an ideal realm). These are all announced in the frenzied dance that opens the scene. Thereafter the black gradually blots out the other colors and yields a transition back to black-and-white footage (1947e:288–289). Presumably, if *Ivan* had been in color throughout, some episodes would have been dominated by red or gold or blue, and the associations in this sequence would have been correspondingly enriched. In such ways color helps make each shot a representation that will contribute to the expressive image of the whole, and montage takes up the task of regulating the play of color lines that weave through the film.

In redefining montage as polyphonic and vertical, Eisenstein takes cinema out of the realm of avant-garde experimentation. Montage is no longer to be a technique of provocation or a stimulus triggering a response. It will now be a method by which a film achieves an organic unity parallel to that found in the greatest works of literature, drama, music, and the older visual arts. Principles of montage enable artistic form, unfolding in time, to "reproduce the process through which new images are built up in the mind of a person in *real life*" (1939d:302).

Eisenstein's organic conception of the artwork and his specific elaboration of this along the lines of musical analogies must be reckoned as one of the major accomplishments in the history of film theory. No writer before him had proposed an account of the overall stylistic organization of a film; theorists such as Arnheim, Kuleshov, and Pudovkin concentrated on understanding how isolated technical choices might have local narrative or expressive value. Like them, Eisenstein takes for granted that the film has a plot that style will articulate. He thus does not pose basic questions of narrative as, say, André Bazin will in his essays on accident and ellipsis in Neorealist cinema. Nonetheless Eisenstein's essays and his pedagogical work offer a structural stylistics, a dramaturgy of *film* form, that provides an account of how techniques may cooperate to create a unified context and an expressive effect.

Pathos and Ecstasy

Eisenstein's theorizing of the 1920s began from ideas of expression and response. How can the artwork manifest emotional qualities? How can it guide spectators' reactions? His later aesthetic reiterates these concerns, albeit in somewhat different form.

When Eisenstein recasts expressivity as "imagicity," the ability to synthesize data into a feelingful whole, he significantly alters his conception of the artist's activity. His new-found fascination with the creative process suggests a return to a Romantic conception of the artist as pouring powerful feelings into his work. Even Prokofiev's ability to memorize phone numbers as an intonational crescendo manifests the artist's power to infuse representations with emotion (1946h:153– 154).

The earlier writings had sought to develop a conception of expression without committing the artist to feeling the expressive qualities before or during the making of the work. Whereas the mainstream Constructivists had been loath to ascribe feeling to their purified artworks, Eisenstein had freely designed emotional appeal into his; but even then, the work's expressivity was "objectified," quite distinct from the calculating rationality of the maker. In his later work, Eisenstein accepts the more traditional view that art's expressivity is bound up with the experiences of the artist. Sometimes he acknowledges that the film embodies his passions about the subject, as with *Qué viva México!* or the representation of sons and fathers in *Ivan the Terrible*. More often, he claims that the creative act involves a more impersonal discovery of the artistic image through the same process of empiricist generalization that occurs in ordinary perception.

> A certain image hovers in front of the author's inward eye, an image which for him is an emotional embodiment of the theme of this work. He is then faced with the task of turning that image into two or three *partial depictions,* which in combination and juxtaposition will evoke in the mind and emotions of their perceiver precisely that initial generalized image which the author saw with his mind's eye.   (1939d:308)

Eisenstein taught his VGIK pupils that the capacity to form such intuitive thematic images of the material was the first step of directorial method. He accordingly explains that his researches into directorial method are meant not as formulas for creation but rather as an exploration of creative laws and principles that the artist often follows unawares. He now quotes Wagner: "When you act, you do not explain" (1941b:399).

Taking the artist's task as the expression of an image obliges Eisenstein to reconsider the work's effect on the spectator. Art no longer communicates slogans or theses; it presents an emotion-drenched experience of the theme. It absorbs the perceiver. Eisenstein grows steadily more interested in ways in which artworks have sought to draw the spectator into them, as in the inverse perspective of Asian painting or in theatrical staging in the round. At the highest level, this absorptive tendency affords a glimpse of the future unity of the individual and the collective; but in its deepest appeals it also reflects a regression to an undifferentiated primal state. In either case, the artwork is more than a simple object. It becomes the site of an emotional communion between artist and perceiver.

Eisenstein's effort to delineate this process leads him to two key concepts. The idea of *pathos* functions as a way of indicating how the formal processes of organic unity and polyphonic and vertical montage produce expressive qualities. The second concept, that of *ecstasy*, can be considered Eisenstein's attempt to define the most exalted experience that art can offer its spectators. Both ideas require him to recast some commonplaces of his time.

Most straightforwardly, *pathos* denotes an emotional quality attached to an artwork, but in the history of Russian and Soviet criticism it took on a more complex set of meanings. For Belinsky, what distinguished art from science or philosophy was the way in which the idea is suffused with emotion *(pafos)*, particularly a commitment to social justice. During the 1920s, as we have seen in relation to *Potemkin*, "pathos" was recruited to the cause of "heroic realism." In Socialist Realist aesthetics, an emotionally powerful work might be described as achieving "heroic pathos" *(geroicheskii pafos)*, an idealistic commitment to socialism. By the time Eisenstein develops the concept, pathos has come to connote exaltation and grandeur. Heroic pathos can be somber as well, as long as the artwork acknowledges the certainty of socialism's ultimate victory.

Although Eisenstein is not always consistent on the matter, he usually treats pathos as a feature of the work itself, rather than as an effect on the perceiver. The work achieves pathos in its subject, its theme, or its form. Not surprisingly, Eisenstein concentrates on pathos as a quality that emerges from the work's organization. But how can a quality emerge from formal properties, which are after all no more than physical patterns (lines, sounds, colors, and the like)?

Eisenstein finds the answer in the redefinition of Engels' dialectical process announced by Stalin and the "philosophical front." After the philosophical controversies between the Mechanists and the Dialecticians in 1929–1931, an orthodoxy emerged that promoted a more organic, gradualist version of Engels' "dialectic of nature." Stalin described the dialectic as "the struggle between the old and the new, between that which is dying away and that which is being born" (1938:11). Accompanying this redefinition was an emphasis on Engels' law of the transformation of quantity into quality, as when by increasing the velocity of water molecules a liquid becomes a gas; this occurs via a "leap" *(skachok)* into a new quality. This is one of many swerves toward the Hegelian dialectic found in Soviet "materialism" of the period.

Since 1929, Eisenstein had found that techniques of editing obeyed such laws, and in his VGIK exercises he had restated that there was a "dialectical leap" from the shot to editing (Nizhny 1958:124). The later Stalinist version of the dialectic allows Eisenstein to postulate pathos as a quality that emerges from the structural unfolding of the artwork.[6] Pathos arises when the artwork is constructed according to principles of unity characteristic of the dialectic. He discusses two of these principles in detail.

---

6. Eisenstein refers to pathos intermittently in various lectures and essays (most of them unpublished) of the early and mid-1930s. But it may be significant that after Stalin's definitive recasting of the doctrine of dialectic in his 1938 essay, "On Dialectical and Historical Materialism," Eisenstein launched a flurry of essays on pathos: the essays "On the Structure of Things" (published in 1939) and "Once Again on the Structure of Things" (published in 1940), the essays in *The Film Sense* (published from 1939 through 1941), and the unpublished pieces in *Nonindifferent Nature* (written from 1940 through 1947).

First, an artwork's pathos is based on the dialectical unity of conflicting factors. For instance, Eisenstein suggests that an actor can achieve pathos by fusing antithetical traits within a performance (1947g:102). He likewise emphasizes the "dynamic of opposites" in the Odessa Steps sequence, in which the downward rush of the crowd contrasts with the upward thrust of the mother carrying her child.

Second, the artwork achieves pathos by obeying the law of the transformation of quantity into quality. In the Odessa Steps massacre, the downward movement is initiated by the soldiers, spreads to the crowd, and culminates in the bouncing descent of the baby carriage. The impulse jumps from a few men to a mass to a condensed symbol of the mass, from walking to running to rolling. Eisenstein sees these as ever greater leaps—in tempo, in symbolic force, in emotional expressivity. The "aroused" stone lion himself incarnates the final dialectical movement from literal to purely figurative imagery: "Visual rhythmic prose seems to jump over into visual poetic speech" (1939f:31).

The pathos structure need not involve this sort of crescendo. Eisenstein allows for the tactic of "reverse contrast," whereby an exalted moment passes over into something more mundane and imbues the latter with a new intensity. He gives as an example *Chapayev,* in which hymnlike language is spoken in a conversational way (1940e:211).

In manifesting the unity of opposites and the transformation of quantity into quality, the artwork achieves pathos. It can thereby move the spectator emotionally. "A structure of pathos is that which compels us, in repeating its course, *to experience the moments of culmination and becoming* of the norms of dialectic processes" (1939f:35). As usual, Eisenstein "psychologizes" form, immediately translating structural features into cues for the spectator's active involvement. We are not far from the language of "attractions" here: "Pathos is what forces the viewer to jump out of his seat. It is what forces him to flee from his place. It is what forces him to clap, to cry out" (ibid.:27). And this experience exemplifies aspects of the dialectic. "To be beside oneself is unavoidably also a transition to something else, to something different in quality, to something opposite to what preceded it (no motion–to motion, no sound–to sound, etc.)" (ibid.).

Pathos does not exhaust the expressive possibilities of the artwork. A work may exhibit aspects of the grotesque, which Eisenstein attributes to a deliberate lack of synthesis among the work's lines (1946i:90; see also 1934e:538–541). Comedy, humor, and irony create a similar disparity. Eisenstein describes Kerensky's climb up the stairs in *October* as a parody of pathos, in which there is only repetition without a leap into a new quality (1947g:145–146). Still, Eisenstein believes that pathos-based composition is the most important for his era.

Closely tied to the concept of pathos is that of ecstasy. This is one of Eisenstein's most elusive ideas. Most simply, "the effect of the pathos of a work consists in bringing the viewer to the point of ecstasy" (1939f:27). Ecstasy results from the overwhelming organic-dialectical unity of the artwork; the formal "leaps" take the spectator along. One of Eisenstein's chief examples is the Gothic cathedral, which pulls the spectator into its leaps from painting to architecture, from columns to vaults, from fabric to stained glass (1947g:159–166).

Eisenstein reiterates that *ecstasy* means "out of stasis." This is a state of transport, getting carried away. It seems likely that the idea derives from Longinus' conception of the sublime in rhetoric and poetry: "Genius does not merely persuade an audience but lifts it to ecstasy. The astonishing is always of greater force than the persuasive or the pleasing . . . That is truly effective which comes with such mighty and irresistible force as to overpower the hearer" (1962:147).

In being transported, the perceiver loses any sense of boundary between subject and object. Ecstasy fuses the self and the other, creating "a feeling of general unison" (1947g:178). We recall that for Eisenstein, sensuous thought is undifferentiated. Ecstasy becomes a psychologized version of Eisenstein's early, physiological version of empathy. Ecstasy is similar to what Lévy-Brühl called primitive "participation," a process whereby the concreteness of prelogical thought obliterates distinctions between part and whole, self and other.

The term *ecstasy* might suggest egoistic pleasure, but Eisenstein explicitly rejects such connotations. He claims that eroticism and drugs supply surrogates for ecstasy, and he explains (to Wilhelm Reich!) that sex is only a "transition" to genuine ecstasy (1934g:85). As he indicates in his discussion of the cream separator in *Old and New*, religious ecstasy more closely approximates what he is aiming at. From a Marxist viewpoint, religious ecstasy is ideologically misguided, but as a "formal method" it creates successful participation. The mystic's trance, the saint's rapture, and the celebrants' Mass blend the self with a transcendent Other. This is "agitation" at its highest pitch. For the Marxist, barred from religious ecstasy, only art can tap undifferentiated thinking and carry the spectator completely outside himself, into a sensuous communion with the work.

And perhaps with the artist. In revising his conception of expressivity, Eisenstein sees the artwork's form as the "embodiment" of the creative transport of the director. He suggests that the agitated human being is both source and model for the expressivity of the work: the individual's gesture is paralleled by the work's *mise en scène,* his unfolding emotion by the montage, his synchronization of verbal intonation with feeling by the audiovisual counterpoint (1937f:293–294). If pathos is a way for the artist to objectify the creative process, the spectator's ecstasy in perceiving the work parallels the artist's in making it. In experiencing the artistic image, "the spectator does not only see the depicted elements of the work; he also experiences the dynamic process of the emergence and formation of the image in the same way that the author experienced it" (1939d:309). Eisenstein here echoes Potebnya: "We can comprehend the poetic work to the extent we can participate in its creation" (Fizer 1987:88).

Although ecstasy may be a universal experience, Eisenstein pauses to speculate that its forms may vary culturally. In Asia he finds a "quietistic" version, in which contraries are united by being dissolved into one another. Here ecstasy is felt as rapt contemplation. In the West, ecstasy is experienced as a sharpening of opposites before they interpenetrate and burst into a new quality. Western ecstasy is explosive, as seen in Piranesi's delirious perspectives, in the hysterical torsion of El Greco's bodies, and in the protoplasmic writings of Disney's characters. Eisenstein celebrates such hyperactive ecstasy, delighting in the 28mm lens because of its distorting capacities: it is "the ecstatic lens par excellence" (1980a:83).

At its furthest reaches, Eisensteinian ecstasy yields a direct insight into what philosophy and science can portray only by abstraction. In ecstasy, the perceiver grasps the sheer dialectical movement of things: "Ecstasy is a sensing and experiencing of the primal 'omnipotence'—the element of 'coming into being'—the 'plasmaticness' of existence, from which *everything* can arise" (1986b:46). In abolishing subject/object difference, ecstasy also blurs the distinction between perception and thought, yielding an unmediated apprehension of the essential dynamic of reality. Ecstasy-through-pathos yields the sense of "participation in the laws governing the course of natural phenomena" (1947g:168–169).

Nothing might seem more inimical to the flinty severity of Soviet ideology than Eisenstein's lyrical version of pathos and his near-mystical idea of ecstasy. Yet Socialist Realism contained a strong dose of Romantic aesthetics. Eisenstein's ideas seem not wildly out of keeping with irrationalist trends that were reacting against the scientism of 1920s Left art. The revival of Russian nationalism under Stalin also led to an intellectual inquiry into the nature of Christianity. Moreover, Eisenstein's treatment of the creative process was in step with Socialist Realism's celebration of the artist as a demiurge driven by spontaneous creation. This emphasis on the inspired individual was consistent with Stalin's "psychologizing" of historical materialism by means of the cult of personality and the announcement that moral qualities such as courage and determination could override matters of economics. Here as elsewhere Eisenstein's theory echoes ideological tendencies within his immediate circumstances.

A Mature Poetics

When compared with his 1920s writings, Eisenstein's later theorizing presents several dramatic shifts of interest and emphasis. The reductive materialism of his earlier conception of mind is replaced by a series of psychological models, all of them relying on such *qualia* as ideas and emotions, inner monologue and sensuous thought. Against the artwork as a machine construction, "mounted" for maximum efficiency, his later work posits a more organic conception of an internally unified system that concretizes an expressive theme. In place of a sloganistic intellectual cinema of conventional signs, we have a cinema of the "artistic image," that "felt concept" that cannot be reduced to "filmic reasoning." A materialist dialectic yields to a more idealist one. The conflicts of montage are absorbed into a harmonic unity that oversees both polyphonic and vertical relations within the work. Instead of stimulus and response, Eisenstein offers pathos and ecstasy. Despite many continuities with his earlier thinking, such changes warrant our considering the period 1930–1948 a distinct phase in his theorizing.

As in his earlier writings, cinema is assigned to carry on explorations initiated in other media. But now, in a sweeping movement, cinema is seen as fulfilling those media's greatest accomplishments. It presents "a synthesis of painting and drama, music and sculpture, architecture and dancing, landscape and man, visual image and uttered word" (1947a:205). Eisenstein's fascination with Scriabin, Diderot, and Wagner issues partly from his belief that film had become the century's *Gesamtkunstwerk,* the "total artwork" that would unify all those arts that had become separated "after the peak of Greek culture" (1940a:181).

By taking cinema as the consummate blending of other arts Eisenstein once more refuses arguments for cinematic specificity. This is one reason that his theoretical writings become so wide-ranging in the last two decades of his life. To know cinema, one must know the various media and traditions it brings to fruition. Eisenstein's "Leninist formalism" analyzes classic works and extracts their methods, making them available for contemporary application. At the same time, concrete problems of cinematic method drive the inquirer into the intricacies of each art. The problem of film color leads to solutions achieved in painting and poetry; the problem of visual design carries the researcher to the history of perspective and the fantasies of Piranesi. The study of cinema reveals the centrality of expressive movement, montage, sensuous thought, and the synthesizing image in every art. In mastering cinema one masters the laws of art as a whole.

Eisenstein's quest for synthesis can be seen as part of that "Promethean" tradition of Russian thought that took as its prototype the sensuous fascination of the liturgy and was pursued through Scriabin's color symphonies and the writings of Kandinsky and Malevich (Billington 1966:478–504). More proximately, Eisenstein's affinities with Hegelian idealism may have been strengthened by a deep Soviet interest in the thinker during the 1930s. At the same time, a trend toward "synthetic spectacle" was emerging in other arts, notably in the movement toward vast "brigade paintings" and the cathedral-like Palace of the Soviets and the Moscow Agricultural Exhibition.

Eisenstein's drawing upon the range of Eastern and Western culture demonstrates his continuing tendency to appropriate all of art for his "system." Having learned *poiēsis* from the moderns, he projects its principles back into the art of all ages and places; in classical and realist art he seeks the basic laws of material, form, and function brought to light by the avant-garde.

There are therefore two ways of regarding his accomplishment. His public rationale is that he provides Socialist Realism with perhaps its most valid and coherent theory: a loose psychology of art, a respectable theory of form, and a reconciliation of the Russian aesthetic tradition (Belinsky, Potebnya, the radicals) with precepts drawn from the *technē*-centered tendencies of the NEP. Perhaps if Eisenstein had not been such a comparatively conservative avant-gardist, he could not have produced his own version of Socialist Realism.

Many moments in these writings appear to proceed from genuine attempts to create a rich, flexible theory out of a cynical and oppressive state policy. This is nowhere more evident than in Eisenstein's arguments about film as master art. Cinema's synthesizing potential makes it the ideal avatar of Socialist Realism. For

Eisenstein, a comprehensive Soviet aesthetic does not confine itself to ransacking the works of antiquity or the Renaissance for fleeting moments of "revolutionary optimism," "joy of life," or "love for the people." A Socialist Realist aesthetic is committed to a *technical* pluralism too. As a synthetic spectacle, cinema naturally incorporates formal strategies to be found in earlier traditions. By adapting the technical accomplishments of its predecessors, Socialist Realism in cinema can fulfill its historical mission as a true synthesis of the arts.

From the standpoint of a cinepoetics, things look slightly different. Here one can take the Eisenstein System as the master impulse, with Socialist Realism just one more source to be assimilated and adapted. The director has not lost his passion for sorting and scrutinizing the "particularities of method" that occupy the film craftsman.

It is too early in our understanding of Stalinist culture to draw firm conclusions, but there is evidence that until at least the mid-1930s, brilliant scholars in many disciplines continued to produce a rich body of research into artistic practice. Shklovsky and Eikhenbaum, Bely and Mikhail Bakhtin, Boris Asafyev and Sergei Protopopov pursued inquiries that continued the *technē*-centered impulses of the 1920s. Their ideas in many respects ran parallel to Eisenstein's. The foldout chart in *The Film Sense* displaying *Nevsky*'s vertical montage has a kinship with the visual aids by which Bely displays the "dialectical" interaction of theme and rhythm in Pushkin's *Bronze Horseman* (1929). Eisenstein's interest in the image and the intonational qualities of sound have counterparts in the work of the musicologists Asafyev and Protopopov. Bakhtin's notion of polyphony may have influenced Eisenstein's conception as well.

After the mid-1930s Eisenstein was almost alone among filmmakers in continuing to take an unabashedly "formalist" approach to studying artistic technique. Pudovkin, Vertov, and Kuleshov virtually stopped writing, and most film publications featured hollow celebrations of each season's official triumphs. But Eisenstein kept going; if anything, he wrote faster, thought more imaginatively, dug deeper. His writings after 1930, along with his pedagogical work, yield a poetics of cinema of unprecedented scope and depth.

Its virtues come into relief when we compare Eisenstein's accomplishments with those of two contemporaries, both also working within the canons of Soviet Marxism. Like Georg Lukács and Bertolt Brecht, Eisenstein balances a concern for psychological factors (in the creative process, in the spectator's response) with acknowledgment of social and ideological forces (political consciousness as historically conditioned, artistic options as constrained by social circumstances). He shares with Lukács an appreciation of the power of nineteenth-century critical realism, but Eisenstein's theory has a place for Zola as well as for Balzac, Dostoevsky as well as Tolstoy. Like Brecht, Eisenstein acknowledges the discoveries of Symbolism, Cubism, and other modernist trends. But Eisenstein will have nothing of Brechtian "distancing"; his conception of sensuous spectacle calls for the spectator to be carried away.

Described this way, Eisenstein seems a golden mean, or as he might put it, a "golden mediocre" (Nizhny 1958:103). Yet he more fully absorbed certain lessons of modernism than did his two contemporaries. Modernism's stringent insistence on details of form and material emerges with greater subtlety in his work. Brecht constantly invokes the concept of montage without clarifying or exploring it; Eisenstein's typologies of montage display a much greater sensitivity to nuances of stylistic rigor and variation. Similarly, Eisenstein's analyses display a finesse not evident in most of Lukács' criticism. For instance, Eisenstein's discussion of "audiovisual counterpoint" in the racetrack scene in *Anna Karenina* (1937f:283–285) discloses a "modernist," permutational side of Tolstoy's narration that goes unremarked in Lukács' famous "Narrate or Describe?" (1936).[7] By opting for a poetics rather than an aesthetics Eisenstein brought out subtleties of structure and technique that escaped aestheticians in the orthodox Marxist tradition.

Like Brecht and Lukács, Eisenstein also faced compromises and moments of bad faith. Often enough, his justification of a theoretical point smacks of official rhetorical extravagance. How else could he proclaim that his version of pathos was visible only now, thanks to his society's progress in realizing the promise of history? "We and only we of all the inhabitants of the earthly sphere have been given the greatest thing of all—actually to experience step by step each moment of the steady process in which the greatest achievements in social development are taking place . . . This experience of a moment of history is imbued with the greatest sense of unity with this process" (1939f:36). In the midst of the Great Terror, he proclaims that to live in Stalin's Russia is to know ecstasy.

Yet alongside official cant his late writings display an undiminished delight in tracing out the slightest options afforded by the film material. Up to the moment of his death, when he was composing an essay on color to be sent to Kuleshov, he was thinking boldly and looking closely. He raised central questions about film form, style, and effect, and he made fair progress toward answering some of them. Whatever the defects of his general theory, his intellectual energy, wide learning, and immense curiosity bequeathed us a wealth of concrete suggestions about how films work.

7. Since Lukács' essay was published during his stay in Moscow, Eisenstein's analysis might be a reply.

6.

History and Tragedy:

The Late Films

Since the early 1970s, Eisenstein scholars have become increasingly convinced of the significance of his 1930s and 1940s work—not just his theory but also *Ivan the Terrible* (1944–1946), which many now consider his finest film. Yet that work and its predecessor, *Alexander Nevsky* (1938), are likely to bewilder a viewer coming to Eisenstein's late films for the first time. What made them so different from their predecessors? Are they a betrayal of the principles of montage? Do they represent Eisenstein's final capitulation to Socialist Realism?

The late films are comprehensible within the contexts we have been considering in this book. Eisenstein's practical pedagogy and his later theoretical reflections supply some points of entry, but another important context is furnished by contemporary filmmaking practice.

The term *Socialist Realism* came abruptly into being around 1932 and was taken up two years later as a general term for contemporary Soviet art. Initially it did not designate a rigid doctrine. Its advocates declared that it fostered pluralism, "an open competition between the various creative tendencies" (Bassekhes 1935:28). The new policy purported to offer not a style but a "method" that would transcend bourgeois art's war among stylistic "isms." Moreover, the very vagueness of the slogan hampered the establishment of fixed principles of form or technique. Certainly nonrepresentational and apolitical art fell out of bounds, but those options had already been foreclosed by the mid-1920s. For a few years, artists who considered themselves loyal to the Communist regime believed that they could create within the ambit of the new policy.

The prototypes of Socialist Realist literature *(Mother, Chapayev, Cement)* had all been produced several years before, and no contemporary work had yet achieved the status of model. Thus the early 1930s saw some diversity of approach. Artists struck compromises between affirmative realism and their own interests. Similarly, despite Shumyatsky's efforts to create a cinema "intelligible to the millions," remarkably experimental films continued to be made: *Road to Life* (1931), *Alone* (1931), *The Golden Mountains* (1931), *Men and Jobs* (1932), *Ivan* (1932), *A Simple Case* (1932), *Twenty-Six Commissars* (1933), *Outskirts* (1933), *Deserter* (1933), *The Great Consoler* (1933), *Lieutenant Kizhe* (1934), and *Boule de Suif* (1934).

Soon, however, a narrow version of Socialist Realism came to dominate the arts. A few years of pluralism had yielded models: in literature, Nikolai Ostrovsky's *How the Steel Was Tempered* (1932–1934), Yakov Ilin's *The Big Conveyor Belt* (1934), and Mikhail Sholokhov's *Quiet Don* (1934); in opera, Ivan Dzerzhinsky's *Quiet Don* (1936); in painting the works of Mikhail Nesterov and Sergey Gerasimov. Comparatively established artists such as Shostakovich and Meyerhold fell under savage attack. In the cinema, the *Bezhin Meadow* affair, along with Alexander Dovzhenko's problems with *Shchors* (1939), warned directors against going outside bounds. Canons were forming. *Counterplan* (1932) brought "production novel" conventions into film. *The Youth of Maxim* (1935) idealized the ordinary person's contribution to a revolutionary epoch. The supreme exemplar was *Chapayev* (1934), which showed a rough, spontaneous popular hero accomplishing great deeds under the guidance of the Party. These films' affirmative, "romantic realism" was believed to counter both the "formalist" and "naturalist" tendencies of earlier Soviet cinema and of foreign filmmaking.

The prestigious films moved close to standard literary policy. The "positive hero," a nineteenth-century concept revived in the 1920s, was recast for the epoch of the Five-Year Plan. Great men, Stalin remarked in 1931, "correctly understand [contemporary] conditions and know how to alter them . . . Marxism never denied the role of heroes" (Yaresh 1956:88). According to Zhdanov, the positive protagonist would represent political virtues and optimistically look forward to socialism. In the course of the decade, hero and deed became ever more grandiose, propelled by the Stalin cult, the Russian chauvinism that he cultivated, the Stakhanovite movement, and a "gigantomania" in the public sphere.

The new Soviet film, then, would emphasize heroic characters, dramatic action, and the vision of a socialist future. Criticizing Eisenstein's *October,* a writer demanded that cinema provide "real human images of heroes whom one can love or hate" (Messer 1938:255). Even a man without vices, Shumyatsky insisted, can be flesh and blood (1935:364).

To ensure accessibility, this cinema drew upon already-proven means. Actors from accomplished theatre troupes lent dignity to approved projects. Stirring iconography of crowds and leaders might be borrowed from the silent revolutionary classics. Although the films of the early 1930s often displayed a roughness of technique, by the mid-1930s picturesque and well-scrubbed sets, gleaming high-key lighting, musical accompaniment, and continuity editing showed the influence of Hollywood studio filmmaking. The major releases of the middle 1930s—*We from Kronstadt* (1936), *The Baltic Deputy* (1937), *The Return of Maxim* (1937), *Lenin in October* (1937), *A Lone White Sail* (1937)—confirmed the dominance of a well-crafted, ponderous academicism.

Certainly not all Soviet films constituted a pure embodiment of Socialist Realism. Just as there was a "middlebrow" literature that mixed Party-mindedness with romance, adventure, or historical intrigue, so there was a light entertainment cinema as well, epitomized in Alexandrov's slapstick comedy *Happy Guys* (1934) and his romantic musical *Volga Volga* (1938). Although Eisenstein seems to have considered doing something along these lines in *MMM,* he soon committed his energies to a cinema that would parallel the contemporary literary works of Gorky, Alexei Tolstoy, Sholokhov, Alexander Fadeev, and others. As the most famous of Soviet directors, he accepted his historical role to lead the cinema into the "classical" phase announced in his 1935 speech.

That cinema revolved around two principal genres. One, pioneered by *Counterplan,* was the topical film displaying the contemporary construction of socialism. Eisenstein's principal effort in this sphere was *Bezhin Meadow,* his fictional version of the Pavlik Morozov story.

In many respects, *Bezhin Meadow* attempted to follow the emerging norms. The story's present, in good Socialist Realist fashion, stands poised between a mythical past and a utopian future. Instead of taming the countryside with machines brought from the city, the film offers a pure pastoral, centering on the struggle among men in that "model provincial microcosm" familiar from literature of the period (Clark 1981:109). But, as Shumyatsky noted, Eisenstein invested the received pattern with a degree of stylization that evoked abstract, elemental forces.

Seeking the "artistic image" that would unify his tale, he amplified the story's mythical dimension through a variety of techniques: parallels with Turgenev and the Bible, iconographic citations (6.1), experiments in auditory monologue and back-projection, and, most strikingly in portions that survive, use of the 28mm wide-angle lens (6.2). He may have hoped thereby to endow the events with some of the monumentality of his Mexican project (6.3, 6.4). Perhaps Eisenstein believed that portentous parallels in the manner of *Ulysses* might coincide with Stalinist culture's attempt to glorify daily life. When his efforts failed, he confessed to using "mythologically stylized figures and associations" that shattered any consistent realism (1937b:375). *Bezhin Meadow,* he noted in "Montage, 1937," upset the balance between depiction and the artistic "image" by losing touch with "concrete reality and generalization in its social . . . form" (1937c:47).

Besides the topical film of contemporary life, there was another major genre, the historical film. Eisenstein seems to have believed that in this prestigious genre he could realize his long-standing dream of a film that would survey different epochs in a series of episodes, rather like Carl Dreyer's *Leaves from Satan's Book*

6.1 *Bezhin Meadow.*

6.2 *Bezhin Meadow.*

6.3 *Qué viva Mexico!*

6.4

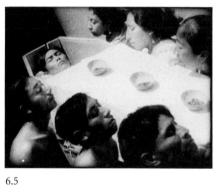

6.5

6.6

(1921) or Fritz Lang's *Der müde Tod* (1921). The impulse runs back to the 1924 project *Toward Dictatorship*, but the *Qué viva México!* undertaking offers the most concrete model.

The project was to trace Mexican history through "chapters" set at different periods. Although the nature and order of the stories was constantly changing, the film was to contain at least a Prologue (6.5); Sandunga, a portrayal of the paradisaical life in Tehauntepec (6.6); Fiesta, a bullfight story (6.7); Maguey, a drama of the exploitation of peons in the pulque industry (6.8); Soldadera, a tale of a female fighter in the revolution; and an Epilogue, Death Day, showing a popular festival (6.9). The overall film would trace the history of Mexico from

6.7

6.8

6.9

6.10 The foreman's spurs in the Maguey episode.

precolonial times through Spanish conquest to contemporary times. Eisenstein compared *Qué viva México!*'s patterning to that of a serape and a symphony of several movements, but it is also a cinematic equivalent of the Mexican murals he admired.

The structure was to be given a sweeping motivic unity. Each episode was to be filmed in a different style (Alexandrov 1976:146) and dedicated to a different Mexican artist (Siqueros, Rivera, Posada, and so on). Each would also base itself on some primal element (stone, water, iron, fire, air). The film's encyclopedic stacking of motifs betrays Eisenstein's debt to *Ulysses*, every chapter of which has its distinct time of day, mythological parallel, bodily organ, and so on. Each central episode of *Qué viva México!* would concentrate on a romantic couple: the carefree boy and girl of the tropics, the couple victimized by the Spanish land-owner, and the couple as comrades in arms in the revolution. Concrete items of costume or setting would recur across episodes (6.10, 6.11). Threading through all parts was the theme of life and death, culminating in the mockery of death in the carnival (6.9).

In the Soviet Union, under the auspices of Socialist Realism Eisenstein occa-sionally revived his hope of creating an all-incorporating form of the sort he found in Joyce's novel: "a 'world system' *vu à travers tempérament*" (Michelson 1989:73). During 1932–33, when Stalin was planning to rebuild Moscow, Eisen-

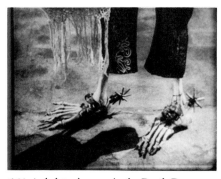

6.11 A skeleton's spurs in the Death Day
    sequence.

stein conceived *Moscow through the Ages,* which was to follow generations of a
worker's family from ancient Moscow through the eras of Ivan and Peter to the
Revolution and contemporary times. Each of the film's four epochs would center
upon one area of the city and build its motifs around water, earth, fire, or air
(1933b:62–67). *Ferghana Canal,* a 1939 project, was to be another four-part
chronicle framed by prologue and epilogue, using the recurring motifs of water,
sand, and labor (Levaco 1973:8–9). After the banning of *Ivan* Part II, Eisenstein
sketched plans for *Moscow 800,* a colossus of seven episodes. In the prologue, a
rainbow is overcome by blackness; each episode thereafter is assigned a color of
the spectrum; the epilogue concludes with the the rainbow fully revealed. The
entire film was built on elaborate correspondences between colors and concepts,
with the Chinese five elements an integral part of the structure.

   These vast designs reveal Eisenstein's continuing belief in the artwork as a
master discourse capable of synthesizing a culture's systems of knowledge, as
Ulysses did and as Wagner's *Ring* and Zola's Rougon-Macquart novels had. This
belief combined with a Hegelian conception that art encapsulates phases of historical development. Such plans for a new Soviet epic might also have seemed
congenial to the era. The "monumentalism" of high Stalinist culture, with its
multipart novels and plays, its immense architecture and statuary, its huge parades, and its insistence on the size of mighty Russia, may have encouraged
Eisenstein to think that such epochal surveys had a chance of being realized.

   The films that he did complete belong to the cycle of mainstream historical
spectacles that emerged in the late 1930s, largely in response to Stalin's message
to the 1935 film workers' conference: "Soviet power expects from you new suc-
cesses, new films which, like *Chapayev,* will glorify the grandeur of the historical
exploits of the workers and peasants of the Soviet Union in their struggle for
power" (Stalin 1936). The historical films showed heroes of distant epochs as
popular, energetic leaders whose progressive views prefigured the victory of socialism. In accord with the increasing demand for patriotic sentiment, these
spectacles were also imbued with a vigorous Russian chauvinism, as if confirming
that "socialism in one country" had been historically inevitable.

Many projects of this sort were undertaken, including Pudovkin's *Minin and Pozharsky* (1939) and *Suvorov* (1941). The prototype was Ivan Petrov's adapation of Alexei Tolstoy's novel *Peter the First,* which had won the first Stalin prize for literature. For decades Petrov's film (released in two parts, 1937 and 1939) was considered "the image of Soviet patriotism, forging a link between the present and the finest pages of the heroic past of the Russian people" (Yurenev 1974:67).

The search for "progressive" Russian monarchs stemmed partly from Stalin's own self-image and partly from a trend in Soviet historiography. Eisenstein may have been converted to the new ideas fairly easily. Certainly after *Old and New* he was far more willing to center films on exemplary individuals. John Sutter, Clyde Griffiths, Dessalines, Stepok in *Bezhin Meadow,* and Maxim in *MMM* all typify social forces of their epoch. Eisenstein also seems to have been inclined toward the progressive-ruler conception; years before he had asserted that a film about Ivan the Terrible should reveal him as "the Czar who enriched and strengthened Russia's economic position" (1930b:26–27).

So it is not surprising that his first Soviet release since 1929 was *Alexander Nevsky* (1938), a patriotic tribute to a medieval prince who repulsed foreign invaders. Adhering to Gorky's advice to turn to native oral traditions for inspiration, and perhaps impelled by his own conception of "primitive thought," Eisenstein offered a film modeled on the folk epic in both structure and style. It rehabilitated his career and won him the Order of Lenin in 1939.

After considering other projects and ceasing work on *Ferghana Canal,* Eisenstein went on to make *Ivan the Terrible,* another film based on a forward-looking Russian hero. According to a 1944 historian, "the power of the wisdom of the people . . . evaluated and firmly held in its consciousness the truly progressive features of [Ivan] the Terrible" (quoted in Yanov 1981:219). Again Eisenstein was rewarded, this time with a Stalin Prize, First Class.

By the early 1940s, the role accorded to the hero had expanded beyond even the early years of Socialist Realism. "In the personality of the new Demiurge, the *conscious creator of history,*" wrote one critic, "our art finds its true pathos and deep dramatism" (quoted in Reavey 1947:163). Both *Nevsky* and *Ivan* accordingly celebrate the leader who shapes the people's destiny. But both projects also presented a dramaturgical problem. How was one to make a drama about an "objectively progressive" protagonist with whom Stalin identified his regime? To give the hero flaws of character or errors of judgment would invite criticism, but to portray the protagonist as infallible would risk making the film simply a procession of triumphs, devoid of suspense or surprise. In *Nevsky* the problem is solved through two means. Alexander is flawless, but he is confronted with external threats and traitors in his camp. In addition, Eisenstein surrounds his hero with lesser mortals who play out a romantic rivalry.

The problem of the progressive leader becomes far more acute in *Ivan the Terrible.* True, one can still wring drama out of invasion and treachery. But now Ivan must combat enemies quite close to him—-the powerful feudal lords, or boyars, some of whom are his kin. Moreover, this tsar was known as insanely cruel. Eisenstein seeks to deal with the problem by presenting, in most of Part I, an infallible leader who is simply ignorant of many of the conspiracies hatched against him. Part II, however, must deal with the problem of Ivan's madness, and Eisenstein tries to solve it in a striking way. He turns the infallible protagonist of Socialist Realist historical spectacle into one who possesses the grandeur of the tragic hero. Eisenstein's protagonist becomes "fearful and entrancing, attractive and terrible, utterly tragic in the inward struggle with self waged by Ivan Grozny concurrently with his struggle against the enemies of his country" (1942:62). The question of how a progressive ruler can harbor tragic qualities produces a complex, even contradictory, narrative.

The fact that the late films were commissioned should not lead us to consider them impersonal projects. Eisenstein became deeply absorbed in *Ivan* particularly, which invites elaborate psychobiographical interpretations that Eisenstein anticipated. His memories of his father as a "domestic tyrant" informed his "artistic image" of political power. Is not the coronation of the young tsar, he asks, "the coming to maturity of an heir, freeing himself from the shadow of the prototype father?" (1964:28). He points out Vladimir's homosexuality, defined by an excessive attachment to his mother (Seton 1952:436–437). What Eisenstein does not acknowledge, at least in writings available to us, is the larger homosexual drama that *Ivan* plays out. The murdered wife/mother gets replaced by a cadre of loyal men, all of whom will betray Ivan except the one who has bent most completely to his will.

Eisenstein also seems to have welcomed these commissioned projects as opportunities for stylistic experimentation. Most official Socialist Realist spectacles adapted Hollywood techniques in straightforward fashion. Eisenstein's late films are "readable" in the light of mainstream narrative filmmaking, but his return to production enabled him to put into practice many of his pedagogical ideas on direction. And just as his writings attempt to build a subtle aesthetic out of Socialist Realist premises, so the films can be seen as efforts to work through the official style toward something more authentic, powerful, and idiosyncratic— even "ecstatic."

Central to this strategy is the use of historical distance to motivate a systematic sylization. For instance, both films put into practice conceptions of expressive movement—*mise en jeu* and *mise en geste*—worked out in Eisenstein's VGIK courses. Acting becomes hyperbolic and hieratic, yielding statuesque staging in *Nevsky* and baroque contortions in *Ivan*.

Both films likewise explore and expand the montage-unit method elaborated in his pedagogy. The action is blocked in distinct phases, each filmed from a fairly restricted range of camera positions. Figures are typically positioned frontally and move through the scenic space in depth. Very often, the cuts are *axial:* they bring the subject closer or make it retreat by juxtaposing shots taken on the axis running from the camera to the subject. While the technique falls within the boundaries of "permissible" continuity editing, most directors would vary the angle far more. In Mark Donskoy's *Among People* (1939), for example, a scene begins with a

6.12 *Among People* (Mark Donskoy, 1939).

6.13 *Among People.*

6.14 *Among People.*

6.15 *Alexander Nevsky.*

6.16 *Alexander Nevsky.*

6.17 *Alexander Nevsky.*

medium shot of a mother and her little girl (6.12). A change of angle occurs with the cut to a long shot of the parlor as young Gorky comes in (6.13). A cut-in, again changing angle, takes us to the rear area as the woman greets him (6.14).

By contrast, consider the scene in *Nevsky* in which a survivor tells the Novgorod citizens of the Teutonic Knights' takeover of Pskov. Four shots, all joined by axial cuts toward him, create a simple montage unit (6.15–6.18). The silent films had sporadically explored this technique, as we have seen (4.4–4.7). In *Nevsky*, however, this technique comes into its own. Eisenstein uses it in conjunction with flattened shot design and static figure placement in order to create a stylized series of tableaux.

6.18 *Alexander Nevsky.*

6.19 *A Lone White Sail* (Vladimir Legoshin, 1937).

Ivan the Terrible builds virtually all its scenes around the montage-unit method, but now depth and figure movement are far more salient. During the late 1930s and early 1940s, Soviet directors (like their Hollywood and European counterparts) cultivated a mild "deep-space" scenography (as in 6.19). In *Ivan,* however, and especially in Part II, Eisenstein develops his own form of depth staging that relies on several techniques stressed in his VGIK classes. He puts foreground figures quite close to the camera, exaggerated by the wide-angle lens. He develops the scene by propelling the characters to the camera, making them bear down on the viewer. Then he cuts back to a more distant view and starts the process over, developing the action so that the characters gradually or abruptly move forward to fill the shot. This technique recurs throughout Eisenstein's pedagogical work, as we saw in Chapter 4, and he acknowledges its centrality to his later films. "In my work set designs are inevitably accompanied by the unlimited surface of the floor *in front* of it, allowing the bringing forward of unlimited separate foreground details . . . The last point in this method is the close-up of the actor carried beyond all thinkable limits" (1947g:152). We can call this the technique of the "unfolding foreground."[1]

Many nineteenth-century Russian social realist paintings, such as Repin's *Haulers on the Volga* (1873), include characters fiercely challenging the spectator to witness their social situation. Another example is Klaudii Lebedev's *The Fall of Novgorod* (6.20). A similar address to the audience was a feature of 1920s "heroic realist" painting and theatre. Thus it is not surprising to find Peter hailing the audience in a climactic moment of Petrov's film (6.21). Eisenstein makes straightforward use of this convention, not only in *Ivan*'s battle scene ("Now I am truly the tsar!"; 6.22) but also at the end of *Ivan* and *Nevsky* (6.23, 6.24).

Such mild direct address was never enough for the director who believed that every shot was a "stimulant" and whose films repeatedly assaulted the audience. After *Nevsky*'s completion, he writes admiringly of how the last shot in *Potemkin,* with the ship's prow moving up the screen, "cut" the very surface of the image

1. A rudimentary effort toward this technique can be found in the scene in *Old and New* in which the peasants try to steal the cooperative's money (4.10, 4.11).

6.20 *The Fall of Novgorod* (Klaudii Lebedev, 1891).

6.21 *Peter the First* (Vladimir Petrov, 1937).

6.22 *Ivan the Terrible.*

6.23 *Ivan the Terrible.*

6.24 *Alexander Nevsky.*

and burst into the auditorium (1939f:34). Accordingly, Eisenstein's new staging practices allow him to give to-camera address a violent force. Especially in *Ivan* Part II, he uses his "unfolding foreground" to hurl characters out at the viewer and to let their gazes confront ours.

In both late films as well, Eisenstein is concerned to implement his theories of synthetic spectacle. Music plays a central role in creating a unified work. Most of *Nevsky*'s leitmotifs are spacious melodies that carry strong associations. Although the film is sometimes compared to an oratorio or cantata, its musical structure is closer to that of 1930s Soviet "song symphonies." *Ivan*'s denser score uses a welter of brief motifs as well as a few ensemble pieces, the whole acquiring an operatic tinge reminiscent of Mussorgsky. Both films seek to create the complex interplay of visual and auditory lines that Eisenstein considered necessary for the completely organic work.

Throughout the silent films, Eisenstein increased organic unity by means of visual and dramatic motifs. In *Nevsky* he works with comparatively simple motivic clusters, partly in order to shift emphasis to the sound track in his first experiment with montage of musical motifs. Once this is mastered, Eisenstein pushes organic construction to new extremes in *Ivan*. Although some motifs line up on one side of the conflict or the other, he also employs "floating" motifs that echo widely diverse situations and create a complex associational network.

Hieratic performances; abstract or expressionist settings; audiovisual montage; framing and cutting that make *mise en scène* "flow *around* the camera, that is, around the spectator" (Nizhny 1958:63); rich motivic construction—all can be seen as creating a far more intense absorption of the viewer than that conceived in ordinary Socialist Realist cinema. The "pathos" of the structure is designed to generate an emotional transport that fuses spectator and spectacle. This process is not necessarily "pleasant" in the bland sense—witness the abrasiveness and shocks of direct address; rather, it aims at something higher than pleasure. Whereas films such as *Peter the First* aim to create emotional attitudes toward the characters, *Nevksy* and *Ivan* seek more: the enfolding of the viewer into the ongoing formal-expressive process of the artwork as a whole.

Thus the late films, like the early ones, manifest a distinct poetics of cinema. It is not just that they embody and test Eisenstein's theoretical ideas, although they do this often enough. As with the silent films, they also extend the written work in confronting concrete problems of narrative and style, pattern and effect.

Alexander Nevsky (1938)

After apologizing for *Bezhin Meadow*, Eisenstein declared ringingly: "The subject of my new work can only be of one type: heroic in spirit, militant in content, and popular in its style" (1937b:377). Recent historiography had singled out as a national hero Prince Alexander Yaroslavich of Novgorod, called "Nevsky" because of his defeat of the Swedes at the Neva in 1240. Later he led a campaign against the invading Teutonic and Livonian knights. His exploits were known principally through brief poems from the late thirteenth or early fourteenth century. Alexander was canonized by Ivan the Terrible in the sixteenth century.

The film's script, originally called *Rus*, made Alexander's struggle against the Teutonic invaders the basis of an appeal for patriotic loyalty. The knights became "the ancestors of the contemporary fascists" (1939e:92). In repelling the invaders,

Nevsky unified the masses—a clear message for Russians fearing German invasion. As for the film's style, most observers then and since have seen *Alexander Nevsky* as altogether Eisenstein's most accessible work. Worldwide, it became his most popular film since *Potemkin.*

Yet even this commissioned project furnished an occasion for experimentation. Urged to make a simple film, Eisenstein characteristically went to an extreme. Avoiding the idealized Hollywood-style legibility of Petrov's *Peter the First,* he created an exaggerated simplicity. Pudovkin understood immediately: "The spirit of the folk narrative was perceptible in the scenario. The figures of the Novgorod heroes Vaska Buslay and Gavrilo Oleksich came from folk tales, as did their quick wits and the joyous and confident spirit with which they fought countless enemies" (1939:94). In both narrative and style *Nevsky* strives for the bare, grand outlines of pageantry or legend.

At the time, other Soviet artists were adapting the folk epic, or *bylina,* to the needs of Socialist Realist literature. Vigorous, decisive heroes, accompanied by crude, good-natured followers, were sent to battle the enemies of the regime. The move toward pseudofolk forms coincided with a shift in Stalinist ideology pointed out by Katerina Clark (1977). After the mid-1930s, allegiance to the state was sought by means of two analogies: the family (Stakhanovite workers as the leader's loyal sons and daughters) and the tribe (Russian unity based upon long-established bonds). If *Bezhin Meadow* failed to prove the superiority of the collective family to blood ties, *Nevsky* establishes Alexander as a father figure and a tribal chieftain.

The film's plot is more schematic than that of any earlier Eisenstein film. Already paying tribute to the Mongols, Russia is attacked by Teutonic Knights, who capture the town of Pskov, near Novgorod. The Novogorod citizens debate how to deal with the threat. Officials, merchants, and churchmen urge capitulation, but warriors convince the people to summon Alexander to lead a defense. He gathers an army of peasants and after a brief skirmish confronts the Knights on Lake Chudskoe, where by a pincer tactic he defeats them. Alexander enters Pskov to acclaim. He honors his fallen soldiers, metes out justice to invaders and traitors, and warns that Russia will always repel its foes.

Alexander is flawless. He is identified with a pure masculinity, ruling a utopian community of young and old men. He stands up to the Mongol occupiers, who invite him to join the hordes. Although he would rather fight than weave fishing nets, he will not oppose the Teutonic invaders unless the Novgorodians accept his leadership. In an echo of *October's* identification of aggressive masculinity with the Bolshevik seizure of the Winter Palace, Alexander derives his pincer tactic from a folk story about a hare who rapes a vixen while she is stuck in a cleft tree. The robed, long-haired Germans are in effect ravished by the vigorous Russian troops.

Since Nevsky cannot fail, conflicts and uncertainties must be built up by other means. The script creates a secondary plot line around romantic relationships. The warriors Vasily and Gavrilo compete for Olga, who declares that she will marry the man who proves bravest in battle. The friendly rivalry, as well as uncertainty about whether both will survive, provides fresh plot momentum. Vasilisa, the daughter of the army commander murdered in Pskov, also takes up arms, and her courage attracts Vasily, who gives up claims on Olga in order to marry Vasilisa. Thus the final scene in Pskov concludes with the couples pairing off under the benign auspices of Prince Alexander. The romantic subplot (more reminiscent of Hollywood than of folk epic) also helps "humanize" the military drama, supplying an emotional warmth that the majestic, severe Alexander largely lacks.

Whereas *Peter the First* decks out its "typical" characters with bits of individuality and psychological motivation, *Nevsky*'s figures are deliberately two-dimensional. Flanking Alexander are "types" representative of factions who recognize his natural leadership. This very schematism seems to have encouraged Eisenstein to treat characterization, in Formalist fashion, as governed by the necessities of plot and theme. Alexander unites the boldness of Vasily with the wisdom of Gavrilo (1939a:41). According to Eisenstein, Ignat the armorer also answers to a plot need. The people inspire Alexander to decide upon the pincer tactic, so the proverb-loving Ignat tells the folktale of the hare trapping a vixen. Once Ignat is given this essential plot function, he can be developed as a representative of the patriotism of the artisanal class. He is also given a humorous "refrain" in his complaint that his armor is too short, but this motif then plays a decisive role: his defective armor makes him vulnerable to Tverdilo's knife. This turn of events arouses hatred of the invader and makes the humble craftsman noble in death (1946k:44–51).

Patriotism is the general theme, but the film severs Russian nationalism from any religious roots. Eisenstein eliminates virtually all reference to Orthodox Christianity in order to play up the Knights' Catholicism, caricatured in the craven bishop and the harmonium-playing monk. The Russian church is represented chiefly by the treacherous monk Ananias. As Alexander enters Pskov in triumph, the church elders are shown briefly and distantly but are quickly forgotten. It is Alexander who addresses the people from the steps of the cathedral. The church has relinquished its place to the secular leader.

Nor is patriotism treated as merely a matter of defense against aggression. Most historical spectacles of the period balance concern for external foes with a pervasive anxiety about enemies within the gates. In *Nevsky* the invaders are a serious threat, but traitors are even more to be despised. Ananias argues against patriotism ("Where you lay your head, there is your homeland") and carries information to the enemy camp. Pskov's mayor, Tverdilo, collaborates with the invaders and treacherously stabs Ignat. Captured, Tverdilo pulls a wagon into Pskov. Reduced to bestiality in harness and horse collar, he receives the harshest punishment: the enraged citizenry beat him to death. The Stalinist climate of suspicion, the denunciation of spies and saboteurs, leaves its traces on the film. Such qualities will be intensified in *Ivan the Terrible*.

The stark simplicity of the plot leads Eisensein to break it down into a series

6.25

6.26

6.27

of big scenes and linking passages. Most of the former are grandiose public tableaux: Alexander facing down the Mongols, the debates and rally in Novgorod, the Germans' pillage of Pskov, the Battle on the Ice, and the recapture of Pskov. The linking passages are brief scenes showing Alexander's recruitment of the peasants, quick skirmishes and battle plans, and so on.[2] As in *Potemkin,* the big scenes stand in parallel relations, as when the Mongols' visit to Alexander contrasts with the Novgorodians' delegation to beg his help. And as in *October,* the narration often creates comparisons by alternating scenes showing opposing sides. Ceremonies in the Knights' camp, with its church-dominated hierarchy (6.25), contrast with the egalitarian campfire of the Russian forces.

The last scene presents a vast tableau that condenses several of the others. Set in Pskov, it recalls the German occupation; compositions are repeated to contrasting effect (6.26, 6.27). As a gathering of the Russian people, the last scene recalls the two sequences in Novgorod, especially in its use of a public tribunal and the churchbells on the soundtrack. The merchants' earlier concerns about commodity trading are echoed in Alexander's decision to swap the German prisoners for soap. The final scene also combines several musical melodies heard

2. According to Leyda, Eisenstein planned every shot and sequence in advance (1960:349). Nonetheless, Eisenstein was obliged to work with the codirector Dmitri Vasiliev, and many of the linking scenes are filmed and cut in an undistinguished way. We might therefore speculate that Eisenstein divided the labor so that he could concentrate on the large-scale scenes, which tend to be "nodal" points in the narrative.

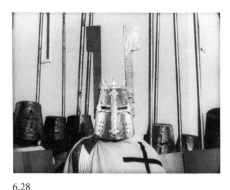

6.28   6.29

earlier. The romantic plot is resolved, and Vasily's choice of Vasilisa recalls the earlier brawl on the Novgorod bridge,[3] when his attraction to her is established. And Alexander's final warning to invaders recalls Gavrilo's medium-shot address to the Novgorodians ("Call Alexander!").

Visually, the film's simplicity emerges as a picturesquely folkish stylization. Bleached town buildings, scrubbed peasants and warriors, diagrammatic compositions—all radiate what Eisenstein confessed was a certain "staginess" (R. Taylor 1979a:129). "In this film," writes Dušan Makavejev, "you sense the stage wings and the pasteboard, you perceive painted horizon lines in the background, and a snow of plaster and chalk falls on heroes with trimmed mustaches and beards" (1975:10). At the time, however, Vishnevsky praised the film's clean exaltation, so much purer than the dingy chiaroscuro that bathed old Rus in most films (1939:25).

Overall, the effect of "epic" expansion is achieved by prolonging scenes, broadening acting, stiffening postures. The staging often suggests a cinematic equivalent of icon painting or heraldic design (6.28). Writing of El Greco and the Mexican muralists, Eisenstein identified "ecstasy" with frontality, a "burning look," and "hysterical" bodily convolutions (1980a:70–77). *Nevsky*'s frontality and to-camera address owe less to this tradition than to the stolidity of Socialist Realist sculpture. One of the few moments of "expressive movement" comes when Vasili, ogling Olga, excitedly flourishes his battle ax before daintily combing his mustache with its enormous blade.

The visual motifs are sharply opposed. The Russians' costumes are identified with earth tones and the Knights' with sepulchral whiteness (1940i:370). The pseudo-medieval harmonies of the Germans' pilgrim hymn contrast with the simpler but more melodic Russian tunes. Calling on elemental symbolism, Eisenstein also links the invaders with fire and ice. The Russians, bound to the motherland, are associated with more fecund natural elements. Alexander fishes on Lake Pleshchenko; water eventually swallows up the invaders. In a striking passage, Alexander's troops summon peasants out of the ground (6.29), an affirmative

3. This scene occurs in the missing reel. (See page 27.)

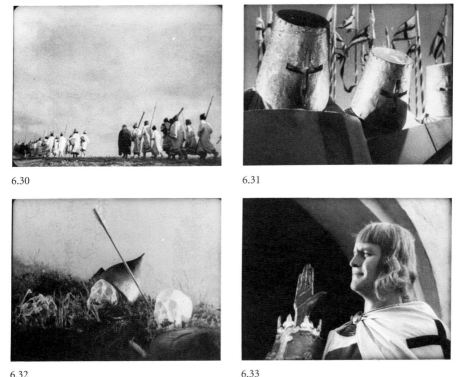

6.30

6.31

6.32

6.33

version of the recruiting of the lumpenproletariat in *Strike* (2.22). A later shot shows the peasants, sprung from the earth, now freed from gravity as they seem to march across the sky (6.30)—a literalization of the song's exhortation to the Russian people to "arise."

Likewise, the open-visored, tapering headgear of the Russians (resembling the onion domes on their churches) stands against the Germans' bucketlike helmets. The enemy, encased in shells, become faceless and inhuman, peering out through tank slits (6.31). During the battle, Eisenstein delights in showing these helmets bashed in like tin cans. In the course of the film the helmet motif develops significantly. In the prologue, helmets adorn skulls (6.32), denoting the Russians' defeat by the Mongols but also prefiguring the invaders' fate. Our introduction to the Knights emphasizes that the Grand Master wears a helmet of bull's horns, while his princes' helmets bear a bird's talon or a hand. Eisenstein frames the latter in a way that evokes the Nazi salute (6.33). The Germans freeze gestures into blazons. The drowning knight sinks beneath the icy water without a struggle, his emblematic hand merely the effigy of a spontaneous gesture (6.34). Only in defeat does the Grand Master, one horn lopped off, raise his arm in pitiful resignation (6.35).

In *Nevsky*, Eisenstein's editing strategies are also simplified. While the cutting is somewhat freer than what one would find in Hollywood, it generally creates a coherent and consistent space. By and large the editing follows the dialogue. At

6.34

6.35

6.36

6.37

6.38

6.39

times Eisenstein experiments with graphic interplay of the sort analyzed in his 1934 essay on *Potemkin*. A cut-in to Olga makes her two suitors vanish (6.36, 6.37). A cutback from the bishop's tent makes the black monks seem to spring up from nowhere (6.38, 6.39). When the Grand Master points, the cut to his trumpeters picks up the diagonal thrust of his gesture (6.40, 6.41). Eisenstein then cuts to a shot that continues the diagonal but drastically shifts the angle (6.42), then to a shot that reorients the players but adds to their number (6.43).

As we might expect from Eisenstein's pedagogical exercises, some of these examples make use of the axial cut. *Nevsky* introduces the montage-unit method to Socialist Realist scenography. It is relatively rough and sketchy: witness the

6.40

6.41

6.42

6.43

6.44

6.45

mild frontality and the simple diagonal staging of the delegates' visit to Alexander's home. By reducing figure movement, Eisenstein achieves rather pure instances of the strategy, as in the survivor's address to the people (6.15–6.18). Most typically, the axial cut-in and cutback introduce a scene or a subscene. An instance is the film's first extended sequence, which uses the axial cut-in and cutback to establish Alexander's estate (6.44–6.49). *Ivan* will go further, building entire scenes out of a rigorous application of the method.

The montage-unit approach probably reaches its expressive high point in the portrayal of the Germans' destruction of Pskov. The sequence starts by gradually introducing the situation. From an archway, successive cutbacks on a line show

6.46

6.47

6.48

6.49

6.50

6.51

the city laid waste, the knights hovering implacably over the rubble (6.50–6.52). A cut-in, apparently redundant, allows Eisenstein to match the slight turning of the Knight on the left with that of a monk in the same position in the following shot (6.53, 6.54). A cutback expands the field of reference to the whole city, blackened by smoke (6.55). Later shots take us into the central square (6.56), toward knights in another arch (6.57; compare 6.50), along the lines of soldiers (6.58), and up to the Grand Master (6.59). Working with almost completely static figures, the sequence creates a series of slightly varying shots that share subject matter and overall orientation.

6.52

6.53

6.54

6.55

6.56

6.57

6.58

6.59

At the same time, the Pskov sequence illustrates how an "artistic image" or "felt concept" can be communicated by visual and auditory means. The expressive image of the scene seems to be "annihilating domination." The editing takes us from a few knights and an area near Pskov's gates, through a wider and more central area, to the troops massed in the heart of the city. Visually, the scale of the Knights' assault grows more shocking. On the music track, hammering chords coincide with the first shots, then enjambment takes over until some stinging higher notes synchronize "tonally" with our vision of the smoke curling over the wasted city. Only when the image of absolute domination has been built up through audiovisual means does Eisenstein provide a verbal formulation: the toadying Tverdilo kneels beside his master and declares: "Pskov lies at your feet!"

Like the film's "staginess" and stasis, the music is governed by a direct, uncomplicated emotional arousal. Sometimes music conveys background information, as when the opening song recalls Alexander's victory over the Swedes on the Neva. Sometimes it creates illustrative effects, as when a flurry of arrows provokes a hectic treatment in the strings. In traditional fashion, music creates motifs aligned with the two forces: the folkish tunes of the Russians versus the German invaders' Catholic hymn ("Peregrinus exspectavi pedes meos in cymbalis"). Other motifs are associated with the Russian land and the Teutonic invaders' trumpet call (restated as the waters envelop them). But in keeping with his theory of "vertical montage," Eisenstein seeks a tighter unity of image and sound than orthodox film scoring allows.

Prokofiev's cooperation proved critical here. After moving to the Soviet Union, the composer had begun to simplify his style in such works as *Peter and the Wolf* (1936) and several choral pieces, notably *Songs of Our Days* (1936) and a cantata to the twentieth anniversary of the October revolution. These can be regarded as continuations of the genre of "song-symphony" that flourished in the early 1930s. As in the song symphonies, Prokofiev's choral works combined complex orchestral part-writing with folkish, often strophic vocal parts.

A similar strategy governs *Nevsky*, which relies on large blocks of four-bar melody and often attaches choral songs to a tableau-episode. When a tune reappears, it triggers recollection of both action and lyrics. Thus in the final scene, the procession bearing the Russian dead is accompanied by a march based upon the "Field of the Dead" melody, which was originally sung by a soprano lamenting the loss of her lover. The tune returns when the women of Pskov, whose husbands and children were murdered by the Germans, confront the captured collaborator Tverdilo. The recurrence of the melody thus "generalizes" the people's outrage. In addition, the long-lined melodies permit Eisenstein to prolong and intensify such moments through visual development. "Eisenstein's respect for music was so great," Prokofiev claimed, "that at times he was prepared to cut or add to his sequences so as not to upset the balance of a musical episode" (Schwarz 1972:136).

Nevsky also displays instances of audiovisual montage. In the Pskov scene already discussed, enjambment of cuts and musical bar lines allows the coincidence of musical, pictorial, and editing accents to stress certain moments: the curling plume of smoke, the raising of the bishop's head, the recoil of the women, and the defiant posture of Vasilisa's father as he faces the Knights.

Another vivid sequence is the scene of Alexander's arrival in Novgorod. As he offers to take up arms, a bell tolls steadily, punctuating his speech, then Ignat's, then a merchant's, before the tolling merges with the crowd's cries. Now a song is launched ("Arise, People of Russia!"). This builds toward a climax of patriotic fervor by mixing metric and rhythmic montage. As bells toll and torches wave, each shot becomes one or two bars in length; sometimes the cut coincides with the start of a new phrase, and sometimes it comes on the second, stronger accent of the measure. This passage underscores the complete unity of the crowd with Alexander.

As members of the crowd prepare for battle, the music fades to the background, but characters' actions and dialogue still coincide with major accents and melodic phrases. Soon the choral forces are divided to create "tonal" associations. Women's voices accompany Vasilisa's fitting up in armor ("Stand up, our own mother Russia!"); men's accompany Gavrilo and Vasily's wooing of Olga ("For our fathers' home . . ."). A final montage juncture emerges on the soundtrack at the end of the episode. The "Arise" song has barely ended when the Germans' snarling hymn starts wheezing out of a harmonium.

Eisenstein regarded the Battle on the Ice as the film's furthest reach of experimentation. (It was the first sequence shot, in the summer of 1938.) Thematically, it is the culmination of the celebration of Alexander's prowess and the people's patriotism. Stylistically, it offers a remarkable antithesis to the heroics of *Peter the First*, whose smooth, mechanically rousing battle scene resembles those in Michael Curtiz' *Charge of the Light Brigade* (1936). Eisenstein employs stylized, even awkward and "unrealistic" means of evoking the heroic power of the folk epic. Although this is one of the few sequences that does not employ the montage-unit method, Eisenstein finds other formulas to create an extravagant simplicity.

Eisenstein seeks to convey the battle's "physiognomy," its clearly marked phases (1940g:13). Tissé explained that the initial appearance of the Knights in the distance was filmed in slow motion, their arrival in the middle ground at normal speed, and their foreground attacks at rates as little as 14 frames per second (1956:108). The battle's stages are articulated by abrupt breaks in the soundtrack as well. In the first phase, for instance, Prokofiev's galloping ostinato accelerates as the Germans charge across the ice, but as they crash into Vasily's central forces, the music simply halts and naturalistic battle sounds emerge. Similarly, Alexander's cry "For Rus!" launches his and Gavrilo's pincer attack, which the score accompanies with a sprightly melody. At this point the swarming of the Russian hordes over the Germans is conveyed by playing the same phrase six times over.

In the pitch of battle, the score suddenly cuts off, and diegetic sound prevails until Vasily whacks a German's helmet. Then an abrupt cut to the Russians' band creates a "leap" into a new mood: players pipe out a victory tune. Another clashing

6.60

cut takes us to the Germans' trumpeters blowing the signal to form an impregnable circle. Music accompanies this tactic, which presents a new obstacle for the Russians.

Diegetic sound resumes and accompanies the Russians' successful efforts to hack through the German lines. In shielding Alexander, Gavrilo is speared. Music reenters as Alexander rides into the German lines and challenges the Grand Master to a duel. The scene is emptied of diegetic noise, and new musical themes rhythmically imitate their clashing swords. The Master, defeated, is hauled off. Alexander shouts in triumph, and natural sound takes over to render the frantic retreat.

The audiovisual montage is not yet finished. As the ecclesiastical tent is overrun and the monk at the harmonium is dragged away, he gets off a few last drooping notes. Ignat's chopping down the tent pole triggers a new passage of music—the joyous Russian allegro heard at Alexander's charge, now accompanying the Germans' retreat. Finally, as the invaders scramble across the lake, tympani, snare drum, and cymbals accompany the cracking of the ice and the drowning of the invaders. (The percussion ironically recalls the hymn title: "A foreigner, I expected my feet to be shod in cymbals.") The last victim sinks (6.34), and the German hymn is heard in a descending trombone gurgle that would have done Disney proud.

The entire sequence merits close study. Musically, it incorporates many earlier motifs, including some associated with Lake Pleshchenko and the Russian land. The Germans' first charge, filmed in a strikingly distant landscape shot, is followed by a series of compositions that foreshadow, diagrammatically, the attackers' eventual encirclement by the Russian forces. The battle gains kinetic impact from fast-motion, reverse-action, and handheld images (which seem to have influenced Orson Welles's battle in *Chimes at Midnight,* 1966). Eisenstein's high angles show the Russians swarming over the Germans, a wave of black figures blotting out a mass of white. Again and again, Eisenstein's stately warriors, like Homer's or Milton's, occupy an almost monadic space. Sandwiched between back projections of lances and foreground close-ups of clashing swords (6.60), these fighters stand rooted to the spot, talking calmly to one another and striking out rhythmically at unseen opponents.[4] The visual stylization of the sequence, jolting switches between music and diegetic sound, and infectious "leaps into new qualities" distinguish the battle from Petrov's more polished but comparatively inexpressive combat scenes in *Peter the First*.

Eisenstein's script of *Nevsky* concluded with Alexander's attempt to deceive the Mongols into believing that he would join them (as he is invited to do in the film's second scene). Poisoned, he dies and is celebrated by the peasants. But Stalin eliminated this ending. "Such a good prince must not die!" (Heller and Nekrich 1986:297). The implications were not lost on the director. Eisenstein compared his protagonist to "the greatest strategist in world history—STALIN!" (H. Robinson 1987:350). More generally, the film played a major role in the revival of interest in Alexander, whose name graced an order of distinguished soldiers. Khrushchev, perhaps influenced by hours of enforced late-night Kremlin screenings, recalled the close of the war in cinematic terms: "We were overjoyed at the destruction of our enemy . . . The words of Alexander Nevsky rang in our ears: 'He who comes to us with a sword shall perish by the sword!'" (1971:230).

Alexander Nevsky can also be seen as Eisenstein's attempt to propose a direction for contemporary filmmaking. As the first picture in a new "historical" series approved by the Party, it could point the way toward a fresh style (Pudovkin 1939:96). Just as Eisenstein's silent films explore alternatives within the mode of "heroic realist" cinema, so *Nevsky*'s self-conscious stylization offers one option for the emerging genre of historical spectacle. If Socialist Realism was not to become an ossified academicism, Eisenstein believed, it had to assimilate a wide range of impulses—here, iconostasis, pseudofolk narrative, montage-unit scenography, and a bold, almost cartoonish use of music. *Ivan the Terrible* was to experiment with a riskier and more complex model for Soviet historical drama.

Ivan the Terrible (1944/1946)

Like *Nevsky*, the *Ivan* project emerged from reawakened interest in a historical figure. As early as the mid-1930s Stalin displayed his admiration for Tsar Ivan IV. In the early 1940s historical studies began presenting Ivan and his military guard, the *oprichnina*, as progressive forces. The principal source was Robert Wipper's *Ivan Grozny*, originally published in 1922 and revised and republished in 1942. Wipper portrayed Ivan as the unifier of Russia, struggling against both the Livonian threat and internal enemies. The new edition quoted Stalin on the tsar's accomplishment in creating an "aristocratic military bureaucracy" (1947:105). Ivan's failing, according to Wipper, was that he underestimated the threat presented by the boyars and the traitors in his ranks. Writers hastily turned out

---

4. The shots may aim to recall such passages as this from the twelfth-century Old Russian epic, *The Song of Igor's Campaign*: "Fierce Bull Vsevolod! / You stand your ground, / you spurt arrows at warriors, / you clang on helmets / with swords of steel" (Anonymous 1960:40).

novels and plays that rehabilitated Ivan. Most of these portrayed Ivan as forging economic pacts with the West, expanding Russia's domain through the conquest of Livonia, and unifying the Russian state by dominating the feudal landowners. Eisenstein followed the general outlines of this formula, but, as with *Nevsky,* he confronted a problem. How was he to present a historical prefiguration of Stalin? Drama thrives on imperfections in character and gaps in knowledge; how could these qualities be ascribed to a progressive hero? True, there would be the opportunity for Ivan to confront external enemies, such as the Livonians, and internal ones, such as the boyars. There would even be traitors, such as Ivan's friend Prince Kurbsky. Moreover, drama could be created through keeping Ivan ignorant of stratagems until a moment of discovery.

Nevertheless, the tsar had a psychological dimension that Alexander lacked. Any historical treatment would have to offer a rationale for Ivan's reputation as a mad, torturing murderer. In an early statement of the film's purpose, Eisenstein echoes Wipper's urge to revise the image of the "insensate maniac Ivan" (1942:61). But how to justify Ivan's depredations as the acts of a progressive ally of the people?

Eisenstein could simply have presented Ivan's decisions as cold-bloodedly calculating. Stalin would evidently have preferred this treatment. "Ivan the Terrible executed someone and then he felt sorry and prayed for a long time. God hindered him in this matter. Tsar Ivan should have been even more resolute" (quoted in Eisenstein 1947d:8). Instead, Eisenstein sought to "humanize" Ivan. His strategy was to present the tsar as one who suffers for his total dedication to the cause of making Russia strong and whole.

Surrounded by enemies and traitors, increasingly isolated from family and friends, Ivan ruthlessly pursues his goal. Yet the closer he comes to achieving it, the more empty of human contact his life becomes. In a letter to Tynyanov, Eisenstein calls this "the tragic inevitability of the coincidence of autocracy and solitude" (Lary 1986:241). Having offered the pseudo-folk epic as one model of Socialist Realist historical spectacle, Eisenstein now proposes another—a revision of the tragic tradition whereby a figure's "objectively progressive" historical role obliges him to suffer nobly.

Eisenstein's desire to present Ivan as tormented could be seen as an extension of the approved tendencies in portraying the Bolshevik hero. One critic's description of the literary Chapayev applies perfectly to Ivan. He is "the sorely tried leader, hemmed in by the demands of public policy, by personal privation, and set off by the solitude of leadership, summoning the resources in himself and in others to accomplish the task he believes history has set for him" (Mathewson 1975:190). By intensifying the demands, the privation, and the solitude, Eisenstein seeks to endow his hero with tragic grandeur. Moreover, he strives to humanize the historical spectacle as epitomized in Petrov's *Peter the First.* Several parallels with Petrov's film suggest that Eisenstein wished to give current clichés of the progressive hero a new emotional force through somber shading.

In the same gesture, *Ivan the Terrible* would "Sovietize" the tradition of tragedy in nineteenth-century Russian literature and drama. Here the principal analogy would seem to be Pushkin's *Boris Godunov*. In 1940 Eisenstein advocated that directors take the play as a model for the new historical film (1940g:7). *Ivan* recalls many elements in *Godunov:* a scene of the populace appealing to the leader to take the throne, a coronation, characters named Basmanov and Kurbsky, boyar plots and foreign wars, a comparison of the tsar to a wicked biblical king. Just before starting work on *Ivan*, Eisenstein sketched a color treatment for Boris' hallucination scene, which itself may have been a prototype for the cathedral scene in Part III.

While working on *Ivan*, Eisenstein also became intrigued by the "tragic duality" of Dostoevsky's protagonists (Lary 1986:89). He began planning an adaptation of *The Brothers Karamazov* and sketched out a plan for staging Myshkin's stabbing in *The Idiot*. He also became interested in Shakespeare's historical dramas, in Elizabethan revenge tragedy, and in Jonson's drama of humors. In all, it is as if Eisenstein sought to give the Soviet historical film tragic depth while updating literary traditions through a properly Bolshevik recognition of the "historical necessity" of suffering.

This suffering necessarily gives the film a psychological dimension, which Eisenstein refers to as Ivan's "inner contradictions" (1947g:105). But Ivan cannot possess a tragic flaw or make an error of judgment, as in the Western tragic tradition. Eisenstein instead shows Ivan torn by the clear recognition of a cause and a growing awareness of its cost in human terms. Ivan displays trust, love for his wife, loyalty to his family, a need for intimates. But his wife, Anastasia, is murdered because he has enraged the boyars. The murderer, his aunt Efrosinia, must be punished, and her punishment includes the murder of her son Vladimir. Ivan's commitment to Russian unity thus costs him his family ties. In addition, his two closest friends, Prince Kurbsky and Philip Kolychev, come to oppose him. Each must be eliminated. Personal affection is replaced by the institution-based loyalty of the *oprichnina*. Yet two of the most loyal of these, Basmanov and his son Fyodor, also betray Ivan.

Thus the tsar's apparent cruelty is only one of "those traits, unexpected, at times harsh, and often terrible, which were indispensable in a statesman of an epoch so fraught with passion and blood" (quoted in Seton 1952:427). In the end, Ivan achieves his goal. His domain stretches to the ocean. But his one unwavering lieutenant, the executioner Malyuta, dies upon sight of the sea, leaving Ivan in solitary triumph.

In the course of the action, the threats to Ivan's project oblige him to sacrifice his emotional impulses, to harden himself in the name of the cause. This in itself might be considered a tragic loss of the ruler's humanity. Eisenstein, eager to intensify each developing moment of the drama, presents certain decisions as triggering regret, even anguish. But he seeks to absorb such moments of weakness into a larger movement of pathos. Ivan always overcomes pain and strengthens his commitment to imperial power. For the sake of ideology, the struggle must be brief, and his will must be reasserted vigorously.

Ivan's "struggle with self" becomes that of a good man who is obliged to become ruthless and who briefly succumbs to doubts about whether the struggle is worth the pain. Dramaturgically, moments of reflection are necessary if he is to achieve tragic stature of any sort. Yet these moments of introspection risk making Ivan seem weak and indecisive.

Part I avoids the trap fairly skilfully. One critic quickly accepted the film's premise: Ivan's rule exemplifies "the tragedy of a state that stands in need of unification for its further development . . . His tragedy lies in the fact that he himself is the first to fall victim to his chosen course" (Bachelis 1945:8–9). But Part II, with its greater stress on Ivan's sudden about-faces from uncertainty to renewed effort, was attacked. Stalin's remarks suggested that Ivan should have been portrayed as an all but flawless protagonist. His momentary irresolutions were denounced as "Hamlet-like"—a long-standing term of abuse among the politicized Russian intelligentsia. Eisenstein's attempt at Socialist Realist tragedy, based upon his view that the artwork should incorporate and transcend "contra-dictory" emotional elements, proved untenable in Zhdanov's cultural terror dur-ing the postwar era.

Eisenstein's urge to innovate within the approved Socialist Realist canon also finds expression in the realm of style. On the one hand, the films' use of music is "legible" within the norms of Soviet prestige cinema. *Ivan*'s affinities with Wagnerian music drama echo Eisenstein's recent staging of the *Valkyrie;* he had declared Wagner "quite a natural step in my creative path" (1940d:85). *Ivan*'s score owed something as well to an outburst of Russian musical nationalism. Under Stalin, Borodin and Tchaikovsky were declared authentic Russian geniuses. After the 1939 Mussorgsky anniversary celebrations, *Boris Godunov* became an official masterwork. Prokofiev, who had written incidental music for Pushkin's *Boris Godunov* play, manifested the influence of Mussorgsky in the score for *Nevsky,* and he pursued it in the darker, more declamatory and motif-based score for *Ivan.* Within these conventions, Eisenstein could continue to pursue his fascination with vertical montage and audiovisual synchronization.

His complementary concern with polyphonic montage, a weaving of "voices" that engenders an ever-changing visual and auditory elaboration of an emotional theme, reaches a culmination in the two films. Like his earlier works, *Ivan the Terrible* builds connotations around its action by means of objects. But now the objects proliferate as never before, creating wide-ranging linkages among char-acters, situations, and moods. Likewise, motifs of music, graphic design, and framing gather an unprecedented richness of association and cross-reference.

Alexander Nevsky had proved that a simplified version of the montage-unit method was acceptable within the staging and editing norms of Socialist Realist cinema. The *Ivan* films push the new technique further. Eisenstein uses it to create a more systematic rigor; he establishes spatial and narrative parallels between situations; and he develops an "unfolding foreground" technique that allows scenes to be staged dynamically, thrusting characters to the front and seeking a more direct engagement of the audience. Working with a new complexity in the interweaving of motifs, Eisenstein's handling of space gives *Ivan* a visual density sharply different from *Nevsky*'s self-conscious archaism.

All these issues will be considered more closely in the analysis that follows. I examine the two completed parts of *Ivan* as a single tale, occasionally referring to the script of Part III to help fill out the overall design of the trilogy.

Tragedy and Affirmation

Part I's action unfolds over nine major sequences. After a brief prologue with voice-over narration, Ivan is crowned tsar (scene 1). He announces his plan to unify Russia, to tax the boyars and the church, and to pursue an aggressive foreign policy. His proclamations arouse resentment, and Efrosinia Staritsky, his aunt, nearly faints with fury. The resistance of the boyars is elaborated in scene 2, a wedding banquet for Ivan and Anastasia. Here Ivan permits his friend Philip Kolychev to go to a monastery; but he is unaware that his other friend, Andrey Kurbsky, is jealous of him and desires his fiancée Anastasia. The Moscow populace bursts in, whipped up by a religious fanatic. Ivan wins their support by promising that he will ruthlessly execute enemies of Russia. The external threat to his reign emerges when an ambassador from Kazan strides in to announce that his empire will subdue Russia. Ivan vows to take Kazan.

The battle with Kazan (3) not only shows Ivan's victory but also maintains the theme of internal enmity when Kurbsky heatedly raises his hand to strike the tsar. In the battle, the commoner Malyuta Skuratov is revealed to be doggedly loyal to Ivan. Here too Ivan meets the cannoneer Alexey Basmanov, who warns him against the boyars. Such warnings are timely, for when we see Ivan in scene 4, he is gravely ill, and the boyars refuse to pledge their allegiance to his heir, Dmitry. Efrosinia urges them to support her halfwit son, Vladimir. Kurbsky, thinking to woo Ivan's widow, is prepared to throw in his lot with the boyars, but when Anastasia hints that Ivan will survive, Kurbsky swears his loyalty to his master, in time for the recovered Ivan to reward him with a post on the Livonian front.

Efrosinia's thwarted desires lead her to plot Anastasia's death (5). Anastasia's illness (6) gives Efrosinia an opportunity; she leaves a poisoned cup of wine on the ledge for Ivan to give his wife. Scene 7 shows Ivan mourning Anastasia at her bier in the cathedral. He then learns that Kurbsky has gone over to the Livonians. Overcome with grief, he begins to doubt his cause. But when Archbishop Pimen attempts to break his will, Ivan's spirit resists. He decides to create a military guard who will be loyal to him. Ivan also decides to withdraw temporarily from public life; if the people call him back, he will know that God supports his reign. Basmanov gives his son Fyodor to his master before Ivan feverishly embraces his dead wife a final time.

After a public announcement of Ivan's withdrawal (8), the first part concludes with Ivan summoned back to Moscow by a huge procession of common people (9).

Part II, more introverted and Jacobean, concentrates upon intrigue within Ivan's ranks. In Livonia, Kurbsky pays court to the Livonians and then learns that

Ivan is returning to Moscow (10). Upon Ivan's return, he confronts recalcitrant boyars while striving to keep Philip Kolychev—returned from the monastery as a metropolitan—as a friend and ally (11). A pair of flashbacks presents scenes from Ivan's childhood, when his mother was murdered and the boyars made him a puppet ruler.

Malyuta tempts Ivan to overrule his alliance with Philip and with Ivan's permission executes leading boyars. In the meantime Ivan seizes on Fyodor Basmanov's hint that Anastasia was murdered (12). The boyars meet with Philip and agree that Ivan must be brought to heel: Philip will be the "avenging angel" for their cause (13).

In the cathedral Ivan and his retinue interrupt a pantomime enacting Nebuchadnezzar's casting of the innocents into the Fiery Furnace (14). In confronting Philip, Ivan suddenly realizes that his aunt Efrosinia poisoned Anastasia. Ivan thereupon decides to become "Terrible" (that is, "awe-inspiring"). He executes Philip, which impels Efrosinia to plot Ivan's assassination (15). Ivan invites Vladimir to a banquet, which provides the ideal opportunity; Efrosinia and Pimen dispatch the youth Pyotr to murder Ivan.

At the banquet, during a frenzied dance of the *oprichnina*, Ivan gets Vladimir drunk and invites him to play tsar in a mock ceremony (16). This exchange of identities makes Vladimir Pyotr's victim, and Efrosinia, stunned with grief, is taken to be executed. In an epilogue (17) Ivan warns that a tsar must be on guard against treachery and announces his intention to turn his wrath against foreign enemies.

In the scenario, Part III opens with a scene showing Kurbsky plotting in Livonia (18). Pyotr confesses to Ivan that Pimen has forged an alliance between Pskov, Novgorod, and Livonia (19). In a bloody march Ivan seizes Novgorod (20). In the cathedral he suffers remorse until he learns that his confessor, given him by Philip, has been a spy (21). Meanwhile leaders of foreign countries intrigue against Russia (22).

At a feast of the *oprichnina*, Ivan announces that he knows he has a traitor in his midst (23). Basmanov rises, and Ivan orders Fyodor to murder his father. He obeys his master, but only after being tempted by his father to enrich the family line by accepting wealth that Basmanov has stolen from the tsar. Ivan sees through this ruse, and Fyodor is executed.

There follows a massive battle in Livonia, during which the loyal Malyuta is fatally wounded (24). Kurbsky sinks in a bog, and Ivan's forces carry the day. The film concludes with his march to the sea: Malyuta dies within sight of it, and Ivan strides along the shore, the waves seeming to bow down to him (25).

In many respects *Ivan the Terrible* draws upon Petrov's *Peter the First* (1937/ 1939), the model of the treatment of progressive Russian leaders. Petrov's film contains scenes that serve as rough sketches for the seige of Kazan, the deathbed scene, the leader's announcement of his new policies, and the murder of treacherous kinfolk. But whereas the earlier work has a stolid literality, Eisenstein seeks a majestic stylization. And in place of Petrov's rather episodic chronicle, *Ivan the*

Terrible offers Eisenstein's most intricate plot, demonstrating a mastery of momentum and organic parallelism.

The coronation scene (1) introduces all of Ivan's major antagonists, both external (the ambassador from Livonia) and internal (church, boyars, Efrosinia, Kurbsky, Philip). The next two scenes concentrate on external threats while keeping internal ones rumbling in the background. Once Ivan defeats the Kazanians, the internal struggle becomes paramount. But other lines of action have already emerged. Kurbsky's treachery builds up as a secondary problem in scenes 1–3, becoming a major pivot when his master's illness fully reveals his venality (4). After Kurbsky is sent to command the troops on the front, the emphasis shifts to the boyars' camp, where Efrosinia plans and executes the poisoning (5–6). But she has already been actively menacing in scene 4, when she urges the boyars to support her son if Ivan should die.

After Anastasia's death, Eisenstein begins to explore his hero's "inner contradictions." Until this point Ivan has been the wise and prudent leader. He announces that he will cut off heads ruthlessly (2), but during the siege of Kazan he assails Kurbsky for his cruelty in sacrificing prisoners. He has also already begun to become isolated. At the wedding, Philip declares that he will go to a monastery, and Kurbsky announces that his friendship is at risk. With both men away, Ivan tells Anastasia: "I only have you" (6).[5] Consequently, at her bier (7), with Kurbsky now a defector, he begins to doubt. "Am I right in my heavy struggle?" he asks Anastasia's corpse. As Pimen recites a psalm of lament, Malyuta reads the list of those who have turned traitor and fled. But when Pimen says that Ivan has no "comforters," Ivan bursts out: "You lie!" The rest of the film will be devoted to showing that he enjoys popular support—from his iron guard, who suddenly swarm out of the darkness to rally around him; and from the mass of people who will make a pilgrimage to his retreat.

This despondency-and-recovery pattern will sharpen in Part II. Eisenstein acknowledges that the bier scene could be considered the beginning of the second part of the film (1945a:322). At this point, however, it seems only a moment of pathos. Ivan's doubt is fleeting, and his commitment is intensified. He orders Philip to return to Moscow, and he accepts Basmanov's suggestion that he form the *oprichnina*, men who have renounced all family and pledge loyalty only to him. He also takes Fyodor as his protégé. In addition, Ivan will resolve his doubts by receiving a sign that he is on the right path: "The call of the people will express God's will." Taken alone, Part I does not press the tragic implications very far, since Ivan's brief wavering is quickly canceled by a burst of popular sentiment.

In Part II the support of the people can be taken for granted, and Eisenstein concentrates upon Ivan's tragic dimension. The oscillation between self-laceration and decisive action will become Ivan's predominant psychological pattern. The approved Socialist Realist tendencies were two: either the hero lacks full mastery

---

5. All dialogue quoted is based on the translation of the shot transcript published in 1970. Translations in film and video versions vary.

and resolution and acquires it in the course of the film (as when proletarians learn to follow the Party's guidance), or the hero is masterful and resolute from the start and simply exercises his gifts in several domains (like Petrov's Peter and Eisenstein's Alexander Nevsky). Instead, Eisenstein seeks to give his hero ideologically correct qualities and then to create drama from his momentary relinquishing of them. Eisenstein thus runs the risk of making his hero seem Hamlet-like—a charge that was raised in the 1946 banning of the film. Yet he claimed to be following Belinsky, who saw "an organic unity" in Ivan's transition from "the meek" to "the terrible" (Eisenstein 1947g:105).

In Part II the process is initiated in Ivan's attempt to regain Philip's friendship (scene 11). He confesses his loneliness, using his childhood experiences to show how long and solitary his struggle has been. Philip plays upon Ivan's weakness in order to extract promises that he will not persecute the boyars. Immediately, however, Ivan gives in to Malyuta, who willingly accepts responsibility for executing the boyar leaders (12). The tug-of-war is dramatized in two kisses, the first a pledge of friendship between Ivan and Philip, the second Ivan's reward to his servant Malyuta.

This oscillation is followed by another. As soon as Malyuta has departed, Ivan rises in agony, asking himself: "By what right do you wield the sword of justice?" His question is tacitly answered by Fyodor, who plants the suspicion that Anastasia was poisoned. This strengthens Ivan's resolve. The tsar's inner dynamic is expressed in an ecstatic gestural "leap" at the end of the scene: confronted with the boyar corpses, he begins to cross himself piously but then raises his head and completes the gesture by extending his arm imperiously and declaring: "Too few!"

As we shall see, Ivan's hesitation is motivated partly by his ignorance of the truth. Once he learns that Efrosinia has poisoned his wife, the way is clear for him to seek vengeance. He seems to have left behind all hesitation; now he will become "Terrible." But a new problem confronts him. Malyuta can take on the burden of killing boyars and Philip (who is slain after he challenges Ivan in the cathedral); but it would be a suicidal precedent to give inferiors permission to kill members of the tsar's family. Ivan must therefore turn Efrosinia's plot against her.

The banquet (16) cynically parodies Ivan's confession to Philip: he confides to Vladimir that he has no friends ("I am alone, a poor orphan"), solely with the purpose of eliciting information. Once Vladimir hints that an assassination is in the offing, Ivan proposes the mock ceremony that will lead to Pyotr's mistaken stabbing of Vladimir.

The murder scene concludes with a muted reaffirmation of Ivan's remorse. After Vladimir's death Ivan prays, covering his face with his hand and murmuring a line from the *oprichnina* chant that accompanied the procession: "For the sake of the great land of Russia." In the epilogue (17), however, Ivan sits brooding on his throne. He tells the viewer that the tsar must reward the good and punish the wicked. "A tsar who hesitates in this will never make a tsar!" Asserting that from this moment he will strike those who oppose Russia, Ivan closes the film on a fierce rejection of his agonized soul-searching.

The film treats Ivan's psychological dynamic as an overcoming of doubts and a strengthening of resolve. In the framework of Eisenstein's poetics, such "braking" of the drama should intensify the final outburst of the principal emotion. Later, after the criticisms of Ivan's irresolution, the director acknowledged that the protagonist's inner conflicts "prevented an adequate exposition in my film of those objective political results in which was expressed the overcoming of these inner contradictions" (1947g:105). This is tantamount to an admission that Eisenstein's conception of film form as a process of creating unity through tensions among parts had to give way to a more static delivery of a preformed "point."

Ivan's inner conflicts manifest themselves most vividly in the climactic moment of Part III, in what Eisenstein claimed was the *donnée* of the entire script: Ivan's confession in Novgorod Cathedral (21). The script portrays the tsar lying prostrate underneath a fresco of Judgment Day while his confessor and his lieutenants read off lists of his victims. Remorse "burns, tortures and devours" Ivan's spirit as he "ponders his responsibility" (1943:236). He ferociously genuflects to God, banging his head on the floor until blood runs down his face. Groaning, he begs to confess his sins. This episode immediately reintroduces psychological oscillation: his attempt to confess to God is interrupted by his sudden realization that his confessor is a spy and traitor. Now he is all force once more: "Ivan advances on Eustace as one about to crush the head of a hedgehog" (1943:241).

But this is still not the end of Ivan's suffering. He must learn that the Basmanovs, father and son, plan to betray him. In Part III's banquet scene, after Fyodor has killed his father, Ivan watches Fyodor die:

A single tear rolls down the grey beard of Tsar Ivan.
It remains suspended on the point of his beard like a raindrop on a funeral wreath.
Ivan: Have pity on me, O Lord, have pity . . .   (1943:252)

Thereafter the battlefield heroics make the film extroverted in the manner of other Stalinist historical epics. Upon Malyuta's wounding, Ivan kisses him once more: "You are the last, the only one who remains to me . . ." (24). Malyuta's death leaves Ivan by the sea, the culminating image of "the tragic inevitability of the coincidence of autocracy and solitude" (Lary 1986:241). The theme has been carried to its limit: Ivan's power is at its zenith, and he is utterly alone.

Stalin's permission to remake Part II as a revised version of Parts II and III would have forced Eisenstein to forfeit the "inner contradictions" in Ivan's character. Eisenstein's 1946 apology acknowledges his error in emphasizing "the private, unimportant and non-characteristic" matter of Ivan's doubts (1946j:462). In the two-part revision, Eisenstein noted, "the theme of Ivan's loneliness and the love-affair—Ivan and the People—are barred" (quoted in Leyda 1962:48). As it stands *Ivan the Terrible* offers virtually the only attempt in the period to create tragedy within Soviet Socialist Realist cinema.

Although the tragic crux centers on Ivan's suffering for the sake of Russian unity, the film's narrational mechanism requires that he be kept in a state of ignorance that helps motivate his hesitation. As in *Alexander Nevsky,* we know long before the protagonist does that traitors are plotting against him. But whereas *Nevsky* extracts no extended drama from disclosing the collaboration of Ananias or Tverdilo, Ivan's discovery of Kurbsky's treachery intensifies his sense of solitude. And at the end of Part I, Ivan still does not know that the cup he gave Anastasia was poisoned, so that this momentous disclosure can cause him more doubt and anguish in Part II. There he discovers that not only ties of friendship but also those of blood must be severed in the name of Russian unity. Similarly, in Part III Ivan learns that his new allies, the Basmanovs, are no less treacherous than Kurbsky and Efrosinia.

The way in which Ivan discovers certain intrigues is one of the most fascinating problems generated in the film. He never has any concrete evidence that Efrosinia killed his wife. When Fyodor hints at poison (12), Ivan immediately concludes that Anastasia must have been poisoned, and he declares that Efrosinia gave him the cup. During the Fiery Furnace scene (14), a little boy points to Ivan and cries: "Mother, is that the terrible and godless tsar?" Vladimir smiles guilelessly, and Efrosinia shrinks from Ivan's gaze. Suddenly Ivan gasps to Fyodor that he knows Efrosinia is guilty.

The recognition is prepared more at the motivic level than at the causal one. The Fiery Furnace scene's plethora of children (singing boys, innocent child) recalls Ivan as a boy witnessing his mother's poisoning at the boyars' hands— itself a prefiguration of Anastasia's death. Upon entering the cathedral, Ivan tells the Basmanovs that harm will come to Efrosinia only if she seeks to become the mother of a boyar tsar. This admonition reasserts a parallel between Ivan and Vladimir that runs through the film. Vladimir's smile and Efrosinia's guiltily averted eyes seem to convince Ivan of her designs on the throne, which in turn makes her the likely murderer of Anastasia. At the end of scene 15 Ivan will have Malyuta deliver to her an empty cup, signaling his knowledge of her guilt.

Part II in effect grants Ivan the power to divine conspiracies at the proper moment. This ability will be exercised again in Part III, when he inexplicably knows that Fyodor has secretly agreed to preserve the fortune that the elder Basmanov has witheld from the tsar (23). Dramaturgically, such intuitions give the protagonist flashes of omniscience that balance his moments of ignorance. But Ivan's divinations also confirm that enemies lurk everywhere, their designs discernible only by those preternaturally attuned to them.

The narration occasionally invites the spectator to enter into this paranoid frame of reference. When Ivan says that Efrosinia gave him the poisoned cup, the spectator will probably be surprised, since it was not evident that Ivan saw Efrosinia leave the cup on the ledge and duck away (scene 6). Yet Ivan's remark obliges the viewer to correct the earlier impression and endow Ivan with greater knowledge. Similarly, the scenario of Part III includes Pyotr's confession (19), during which he declares that not only Efrosinia and Pimen but also Philip and Kurbsky incited him to murder. Such was certainly not evident in the relevant scenes of Part II, but again the spectator may be inclined simply to recast memory and let the conspiracy swell. In such moments the film creates a shadowy realm of usurpers, intriguers, and wreckers in which no legal proof is required, or even available, and the leader's hunch becomes truth by fiat.

From the standpoint of what we might call the film's "sympathetic paranoia" one narrational tactic becomes highly significant. The original script recounted Ivan's life in chronological order, beginning with his childhood. The finished film, however, moves the childhood material into a flashback at the start of Part II, when Ivan is pleading with Philip to be his friend and explaining his reasons for fervently opposing the boyars. The murder of Ivan's mother ("That's how I came to be an orphan, alone and abandoned"), the boy's manful attempts to govern, and his eventual arrest of the boyars (triggered by their sullying of his mother's name) prefigure Ivan's decisive actions in Part II while also justifying his vengefulness. By inserting the childhood episodes at this point, the plot vividly confirms Ivan's anxieties about boyar treachery and presents his aims in a favorable light. It becomes yet another narrational device for intensifying his tragic stature.

Textual Volume

Part I's organization into a prologue, seven majestic scenes, a brief linking segment (scene 8), and a grandiose finale allows Eisenstein to return to *Potemkin*'s mode of constructing parallels between large-scale episodes. Parts II and III multiply the possibilities, creating a vast architecture in which virtually every moment of the action cross-references some other scene in the trilogy.

From the start, the parallels develop certain dramatic tensions to higher levels of intensity. For example, in both the opening coronation and the ensuing wedding feast Ivan announces his program. But whereas the coronation creates a closed aristocratic milieu, the wedding feast is invaded by the populace. In scene 1 Ivan formally addresses the nobles on behalf of the country, but in the next scene he speaks plainly to the people and wins their loyalty. The crowd's incursion into the wedding banquet is repeated at increasing levels of intensity, first when the *oprichnina* burst into the bier scene, then at the end when the people summon Ivan to return to Moscow.

Throughout succeeeding parts, such parallels continue to intensify the dramatic conflict. The coronation parallels the scene of Ivan's illness (at which foreign emissaries gather once more), the scene at Anastasia's bier, and the Fiery Furnace sequence, in which Ivan must again struggle for supremacy against the forces he confronted at the film's beginning. The three scenes of boyars plotting in secret (5, 13, and 15) trace steadily growing threats to Ivan's reign. Similarly, the three banquets (wedding in Part I, *oprichnina* feast in Part II, victory celebration in Part III) mark stages in the gradual elimination of those around Ivan: first Philip, then Efrosinia and Vladimir, and finally the Basmanovs. Part II acquires closure by a specific echo of Part I; both assert Ivan's indomitable willingness to sacrifice all "for the sake of Russia's greatness."

Other parallels create equivalences among the characters, so that the drama is informed by a series of substitutions and exchanges. In Part I Kurbsky is the tool of the boyars; in Part II this role is assumed by Philip. The similarity between scene 10 at the Livonian court and the opening coronation scene makes it clear that Kurbsky is taking King Sigismund as a master in place of Ivan. Parallel replacements are at the center of the film's internal intrigue: as Efrosinia kills Anastasia through Ivan, Ivan kills Vladimir by means of Efrosinia. The poisoning of Anastasia (6) is shown before that of Ivan's mother (11), but in retrospect both women blend into an emblem of the "good mother" to which Efrosinia will be contrasted. Correspondingly, at the *oprichnina* banquet in Part II, Vladimir becomes not only a grotesque parody of the crowned Ivan of the first scene but also a pathetic evocation of young Ivan orphaned by his mother's death. Similarly, Kurbsky and Philip Kolychev are replaced by the elder Basmanov and particularly by the peasant Malyuta. Malyuta, the "tsar's eye," is at once a representative of the people and an aspirant who can forget his ties to what he calls the "rabble" and who, Eisenstein noted, can let his jealousy of Philip launch a mischievous "revelry of destruction" (*IP* 6:495).

The dynamics of exchange imply tensions within sexual and kin-based relations. At Ivan's wedding feast, his two closest friends cool toward him: Philip sets out for a monastery, while Kurbsky plots to take Anastasia away. The murder of Anastasia leads Basmanov to offer his son, Fyodor, as what Eisenstein calls "an *ersatz* Anastasia" (*IP* 6:512). Upon accepting the offer, Ivan surmounts Anastasia's corpse and feverishly embraces her for the last time. Thereafter Fyodor becomes Ivan's closest confidant, hugged close on the couple's bridal bed and mourned with a single tear after his execution in Part III.

In offering Fyodor to Ivan, Basmanov also executes a gesture characteristic of the film, whereby a child is pushed into the bloody arena of political intrigue. The mother-son relation, which runs back to the endangered children of *Strike* and the Odessa Steps, becomes central: Anastasia's Dmitry is in competition with Efrosinia's Vladimir; the boy Ivan is left alone by his mother's murder. Efrosinia's pressure on Vladimir to take the throne leads to the climactic mock-crowning of Vladimir and the masquerade that triggers his murder.

These parallels and substitutions are reinforced by an unprecedently intricate network of motifs. Eisenstein contrasts *Nevsky*, which develops its motifs in a horizontal or "linear" fashion like a Chinese picture scroll, to *Ivan*, which he compares to a film strip coiled back on itself, acquiring a textual "volume" through the sheer number of motifs and the complexity of their superposition (1945a:340). As Kristin Thompson has pointed out, the film uses many more motifs than a mainstream film would; it does not always attach them to a single character or setting; and they are often not used causally in the narrative (1981:158–163). Objects such as coins, candles, fur, and cups; patterns of lighting; gestures

6.61 *Ivan the Terrible.*

6.62

6.63

6.64

6.65

6.66

such as a kiss or an upraised arm—all acquire a penumbra of implications through being interlaced with each other and with fluctuations in the dramatic situation.

Up to a point, the interplay of motifs corresponds to Eisenstein's theoretical formula: "depictions" coalesce through repetition into the felt "image" of a general theme. A straightforward example is the graphic motif of the ray, which dominates the Kazan sequence in the form of a wheel, an emblem of the sun, a configuration of clouds, a convergence of fuses, and an explosion (6.61–6.65). Across the film, the ray motif becomes the basis of Ivan's "power gesture" (6.66), reinforced by icons that intensify the sunburst effect (6.67). The theme of Ivan's authority is embodied in the "artistic image" of the bursting ray, which is in turn decomposable into single manifestations in different channels of expression.

Similarly, in the banquet scene color motifs are treated as an image-building resource—not, as Eisenstein insisted, simply by the assignment of a color to each character but rather by the detachment of colors from objects and the association of each color with a theme. Thus he claims that the blue of the sets represents the theme of the "firmament," while in the costumes red represents intrigue and vengeance, black stands for death, and gold symbolizes debauchery (1946a:237–238). But even these develop and interpenetrate. Thus the dance, in exposing all the colors to be developed, becomes a display of "fireworks," while a series of shots may present a more muted "glissando" of color from, say, red to blue (ibid.:238–239).

Still, to see the film's motivic construction as a direct mapping of themes onto image complexes is probably too simple. Although many of the motifs start with a certain semantic weighting, the density of the film's stylistic development quickly gives them a chameleonic fluidity. Vladimir's blue blush, notoriously hard to understand while we are viewing the film, is a case in point. In his writings, Eisenstein does not connect the sudden blueing of the youth's face with the "firmament" theme. He offers instead a range of context-bound justifications that recall the open-ended semantic fields associated with *Potemkin*'s leaping lions. He tells us that the shift to a monochromatic shade prepares for the upcoming return to black and white; the blueing is the tragic equivalent of a Disney character's turning bright red; and it expresses Vladimir's horror by suggesting the draining of blood from his face (1946f:230–231). At this point, blue becomes metaphorical in an elusive, open-ended way.

Thus instead of the stark motivic contrasts found in most of the silent films and *Nevsky*, we have in *Ivan the Terrible* something closer to the ever-expanding valences of *Potemkin*. Almost no item can be considered in isolation. At first, for instance, the cup seems to form a fairly distinct motivic "depiction." The wedding celebration, with its clanking goblets, seems directly echoed in the scene of Anastasia's illness, which ends with the fatal cup tipping to obliterate her face. Later, at the *oprichnina* banquet Vladimir will drink from a cup, suggesting that he, like Fyodor, has taken Anastasia's place. But this reprise of the cup motif is accompanied by a return of the swans we have seen in the wedding (6.68), and they are black rather than white (6.69). This echo is paralleled in the banquet's treatment of Fyodor, whose mask recalls Anastasia (6.70) and suggests that he plays Ivan's "true" bride to Vladimir's false one. The cup motif is thus caught up in a network of associations.

Similarly, the parallels among the murders of Anastasia, Ivan's mother, and Vladimir are reinforced by an expanding motivic cluster. As Ivan's mother is hauled away in agony, Eisenstein gives us a shot of her dangling hands dragging on the floor (6.71). When Ivan begins to suspect that Anastasia was poisoned, his

6.67

6.68

6.69

6.70

6.71

6.72

hands creep out of his sleeves to grip the bedclothes (6.72); to the mother's inert posture is opposed an active grasping that gives the hands virtually a life of their own. The motif is transformed again after Vladimir's death; his corpse is dragged away, as Ivan's mother's was, and the oversized crown slips off his head (6.73). The shot is a passive version of Ivan's power gesture, while the echo of Macbeth's ill-fitting garments links Vladimir to the boy Ivan, awkward on a throne too big for him (6.74).

As in *Potemkin,* the motif of the eye affords a more pervasive example of the process of enriched connotation. Characters' gazes, glances, and stares are em-

6.73

6.74

6.75

6.76

6.77

6.78

phasized throughout the film by means of highly stylized eye movements. Ivan has the burning look that Eisenstein found in El Greco, and his adversaries—notably Efrosinia in the Fiery Furnace scene—often give themselves away by refusing to face it. With this norm established, Eisenstein harks back to *Potemkin* and creates a motif of the single eye. This becomes associated, in turn, with joy (6.75), suspicion (6.76), surveillance (6.77), and quasi-godlike omniscience (6.78). The single eye is what Thompson (1981) calls a "floating motif"—in itself strictly meaningless, but a repeated element that can, according to context, acquire a range of expressive implications.

Such floating motifs, modeled upon the Wagnerian leitmotif, display Eisen-

6.79 6.80

6.81

stein's determination to wring a wide range of emotional effects out of every element, no matter how small. In his theory, an expressive image coalesces from the conjunction of individual representations; in his practice, however, the simple "additive" implications of such an idea are overtaken by the sheer swelling of associations. It is as if he wished to demonstrate that any concrete particular, once situated within the thickly intertwining "lines" of the film's *mise en scène,* could accrete expressive implications indefinitely.

Image and Montage

Eisenstein's urge to create an all-encompassing network of motifs often controls his scenography. Thus when Ivan is asserting his power, as in the coronation scene or during the wedding banquet, composition and characters' flanking eye-lines often place him at the center of the space (6.79, 6.80). The ray motif and the power gesture are diagrammatic expressions of Ivan's centrality. By contrast, spaces associated with the boyars are not clearly organized around a center or around the act of looking; in conversation, characters tend not to face eace other (6.81), and the locale does not define a "power zone" for anyone to occupy.

Eisenstein can vary his *mise en scène* still further. Although the coronation scene and the wedding banquet are structurally parallel, the first is staged according to a principle of flanking spatial arrangements, with the coronation at the center, while the second displays a much deeper (but also still static) "tunnel" configuration. The deathbed scene initiates a new approach, that of suggesting the space behind the camera, which will come to prominence in Part II. Eisenstein exploits the absence of establishing shots (a tactic from the heyday of Soviet montage cinema) to organize virtually every episode around a different spatial principle.

The fact that *mise en scène* carries so much significance pulls the film close to German Expressionism. The actor blends into an expressively distorted compositional design. Cherkasov was forced to hold contorted postures for uncomfortably long periods; Serafina Birman, who played Efrosinia, had to walk in flowing robes while fixing her eyes and head at odd angles. The result is a larger-than-life world: intriguers dart in and out of doorways resembling mouseholes, Ivan's territorial ambitions are conveyed through gigantic silhouettes (6.82), and his triumph at the end of Part I is presented within an architecture whose aperture echoes his and Fyodor's contour (6.83).

Eisenstein uses such stylization to evoke many pictorial traditions. The coronation echoes the frontality and verticality of icons (6.84). More baroque religious imagery is suggested by the prisoners lashed to the ramparts during the siege of Kazan (6.85). At other moments the pictorial inspiration seems close to El Greco (6.86), an evident source for Eisenstein's working sketches.

The film's "expressionism" extends to physical action as well. In several instances the actor's *mise en jeu* becomes a compromise between central and peripheral bodily processes in the manner of Eisenstein's early strictures on expressive movement. Ivan and Philip duel in a swirl of cloaks, creating exaggerated arcs and explosive, Piranesi-like diagonals (6.87, 6.88). *Ivan* makes particular use of the technique of "retracted motion," which sets the primary movement off against an opposing gesture that precedes it (1947c:105n). Often, when Ivan glares he stretches his neck forward like a heron before suddenly recoiling.

The editing assists such abrupt contrasts, as in the scene at Anastasia's bier when Ivan learns of Kurbsky's treachery. The transformations of gesture exploited in the silent films, and articulated in the pedagogical method of treating montage as a transformation of *mise en scène,* are now presented in Ivan's sudden twists and torsions. From an uptilted profile (6.89) he swivels to the right, head down (6.90); cut to him now with head lifted again (6.91), already turning sharply left (6.92). Eisenstein had admired a Chinese screen that depicted a bird's turning flight by rotating the body in three sharply demarcated stages (6.93) (1980a:46–47). Here, editing creates comparably measured contrasts and continuities across Ivan's gesture.

More generally, editing is used to create a constant ebb and flow of information and expression. The montage-unit method becomes far more flexible than in *Nevsky.* The coronation scene, for instance, uses flanking eyelines to create a "hole" into which Ivan steps as he takes the crown. In the same scene, axial cutting stresses the crown, Anastasia, and the singer who acclaims Ivan. The Kazan siege (3) shows that now one montage unit can nest within another. In long shot, Malyuta comes up from mining the Kazanian hillside; an axial cut takes us backward to an extreme long shot in which he crawls up the hillside to Ivan and

6.82

6.83

6.84 "Like an icon in its frame the Tsar is encased in golden garments" (1943:48).

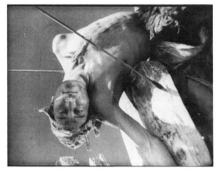

6.85

6.86

6.87

6.88

6.89

6.90

6.91

6.92

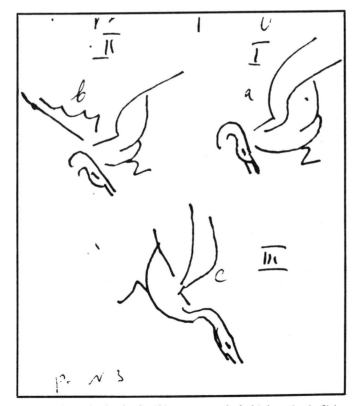

6.93 An Eisenstein sketch of a Chinese portrayal of a bird turning in flight.

6.94 *Ivan the Terrible.*   6.95

6.96   6.97

Kurbsky. An axial cut-in presents the three men in long shot as they discuss strategy. A new unit now presents three low-angle shots of the men, varying as to scale and the presence of Malyuta. The episode is rounded off by returning to variants of the first and second compositions.

This virtually invisible cutting does not achieve one purpose of the montage-unit method: the bridging of the gap between spectator and spectacle. Interestingly, Eisenstein makes little appeal to direct address in *Ivan* Part I. True, Ivan does gaze at the audience during the coronation and in his triumph at Kazan (6.66). On the whole, though, characters seldom look at the viewer. (Efrosinia has a perfect opportunity during the poisoning scene, but her eyes flit over the camera without settling on it.) Instead, Part I seeks the absorption of the spectator through a gradual development away from the fairly static staging and cutting of scenes 1–3.

At Ivan's sickbed (4) the montage-unit method begins to incorporate movement, particularly through creating the "unfolding foreground." For instance, while mourners gather at the bed, the découpage enacts a movement into and out of the room. First, cutting carries us forward through axial shot changes (such as 6.94, 6.95). When Ivan rises to beg the boyars to kiss the cross for his son, however, the actor's *mise en geste* motivates camera movement and cutting that "back out" of the depths (such as 6.96, 6.97). At the scene's climax, both editing

6.98

6.99

6.100   6.101

and the actor's movement carry us forward again as Ivan returns to his bed and seems to expire (6.98–6.99).

A more extended use of the strategy involves Kurbsky, whose performance in the areas outside the sickroom requires him constantly to rush diagonally forward (such as 6.100, 6.101). In the manner of Raskolnikov's thrust to the camera in the VGIK *Crime and Punishment* exercise, Kurbsky's zigzag movements create new zones of offscreen space in the left or right foreground. The action also compels the editing to carry the spectator further "backward." The unfolding foreground of the deathbed scene reaches its climax when Ivan advances to the altar and dispatches Kurbsky to Livonia. Both men gaze rapturously off "at" that country—another region lying diagonally in the foreground (6.102)!

Part II, by contrast, builds steadily toward bold, even conspiratorial direct address. The opening scene with Kurbsky and Sigismund, centered and static, recalls the opening of part I (6.103), but in a lifeless fashion suitable for the decadent Polish court (6.104). Ivan's return to Moscow initiates a more flamboyant unfolding of space. The film becomes baroque: the wheeling draperies and somber chiaroscuro are accompanied by zigzag staging, aggressive pivots and thrusts of the performers, and dynamic axial cutting. Now characters hurl themselves into close-ups "beyond all thinkable limits." Cherkasov describes performing in Ivan's first confrontation with Philip: "I had to run up to the camera for a close-up within twenty inches of the lens, taking good care to have my chin,

6.102

6.103

6.104

6.105

6.106

6.107

nose and forehead well within the camera's eye, then look wrathfully and speak lines that were supposed to terrify not only the metropolitan but the spectators too" (1953:106). The principal antagonists, Philip and Ivan, vie for the viewer's attention, casting commanding stares at the camera (6.105, 6.106). Static frontality reappears only in the staging of the Fiery Furnace pantomime (6.107).

The most striking instance of Part II's thrusting *mise en scène* is sequence 15, in which Efrosinia and Pimen arrange for the murder of Ivan. The previous episode has ended with Ivan's eyebrow-waggling address to the viewer (6.106). This scene begins with Efrosinia running desperately in to tell the boyars that Philip has been arrested. Her initial thrust to the camera (6.108) becomes the

6.108

6.109

6.110

6.111

6.112

6.113

basis of several more such impulsive movements, as Pimen (6.109), Vladimir (6.110), and Efrosinia press the camera into various corners of the room. But at the scene's climax Efrosinia must recoil in the face of another thrusting movement. As an intruder enters, she and Vladimir shrink back (6.111, 6.112). They pull away from the foreground (6.113) to allow Malyuta to stride solemnly forward (6.114, 6.115) and proffer a cup (6.116). Alone at the end, Efrosinia frankly acknowledges the audience (6.117) before discovering that the goblet is empty. The scene, like its predecessor, ends with a glance toward the lens, but now the look is puzzled and slightly foreboding (6.118). This finds its calmer counterpart in the film's finale, when Ivan addresses the viewer in the spirit of Alexander Nevsky, warning against external aggressors (6.23, 6.24).

6.114   6.115

6.116   6.117

6.118

Throughout *Ivan*, the montage-unit editing, the staging of action so as continually to rush the camera, the wide-angle distortions, and the to-camera address can be seen as Eisenstein's efforts to bridge the gap between spectator and artwork. In the essay "Stereoscopic Cinema" (1986a) he implies that such techniques also constitute a stage in cinema's historical mission. He asserts that throughout the history of the theatre, producers have striven to reconnect the audience with the spectacle. Efforts were made to bring the spectators into the theatrical space (as in the Renaissance custom of letting some viewers sit onstage) or to fling a bridge from the spectacle to the audience (as in the Japanese *hanamichi*). In his essay, Eisenstein insists that the modern cinema transcends these rather artificial solutions and moves closer to forging a unity between the perceiver and the spectacle.

Eisenstein associated the unity achieved through such visual effects with the idea of ecstasy. Insofar as this concept involves the dissolution of the spectator's awareness of subject/object relations, some techniques may lend themselves to this function. The grotesque 28mm lens is "the ecstatic lens par excellence" (1980a:83). In deforming objects, Eisenstein says, it carries them out of their normal relationships. Since this lens also exaggerates the speed of movement into and out of depth, it is not surprising that Eisenstein also considers his tactic of moving the figures into foreground close-up to be an "'ecstatic' method of construction" (1947g:152). In addition, the spatial devices serve either to "pull" the spectator into the represented space or to thrust the action "out" to the spectator. By figuratively breaking the barrier between spectator and spectacle, these scenographic tactics help the filmmaker create a rich, organically unified work that, Eisenstein believed, could provoke ecstasy.

Sound and Image

To the expressivity of motivic networks, performance, imagery, and editing Eisenstein of course adds that of sound. The traditional use of musical motifs is heightened and expanded. Ivan is given several motifs, most notably a strong fanfare emphasizing his power and a more serene, hymnlike melody linking his bearing to the destiny of Russia. In addition, recurrent motifs create parallels by signaling conflict, confrontation, and death. During the scene of Anastasia's poisoning, her wavering theme alternates with the grim, pulsating one associated with Efrosinia.

Although *Nevsky*'s score is more widely known (chiefly because of the cantata Prokofiev derived from it), *Ivan* makes music more structurally prominent. Eisenstein asked Prokofiev to compose a Wagnerian score that would incorporate ongoing motivic development. Some scenes, such as the coronation, the wedding, the Fiery Furnace play, and the *oprichnina* dance, form integral musical set pieces. One of the most important is Efrosinia's lullaby (scene 15). Singing to calm Vladimir's fears of their assassination plot, she tells of huntsmen killing a beaver to make a cloak for "Tsar Vladimir." As Eisenstein indicates, the song frightens Vladimir instead of soothing him: he watches Efrosinia's passion take her to the edge of madness (1947e:272–273). The song's narrative motifs, such as the regal cloak, anticipate the impersonation and murder of the banquet scene; it is about stalking and killing Ivan, but Vladimir will become the prey. The lullaby's musical material also recalls earlier scenes. Eisenstein even expects the spectator to find a parallel with the coronation scene in Efrosinia's quavering rendition of the word *black*. The lullaby becomes the auditory equivalent of the "knotting" of visual motifs.

Other scenes are marked by a fairly continuous accompaniment, as when the Polish court is characterized by a lumbering mazurka punctuated by pompous fanfares. Most operatic of all is the steadily intensifying musical climaxes that accompany Ivan's sickbed collapse (4), Malyuta's arrival in Efrosinia's quarters (15), and the finales of each part.

Music may burst in at any moment. Certain musical phrases, notably a slow, striding figure in brass and woodwinds, repeatedly punctuate the action at full blast, creating sharp-edged sonic cuts akin to those marking stages of the battle in *Nevsky*. In scene 2, the florid accompaniment to the shots of burning Moscow breaks off as Efrosinia returns to the wedding feast, and the music of that event wells up.

Governing most uses of music is Eisenstein's principle of vertical montage, the ongoing, deep-rooted synchronization of image and sound. A detailed plan survives for the scene of Ivan's mourning at Anastasia's bier (1945a:310–327). The imagistic theme, the growth of despair into doubt, is the first instance of the tragic oscillation we have already charted. Sonically, the scene is staged as an antiphony, with Pimen reciting a psalm while Malyuta reads a dispatch announcing all of Ivan's supporters who have deserted. Ivan's uncertainty is thereby externalized as a passive "voice" (Pimen, pleading for resignation and repentance) and an active one (Malyuta, trying to stir the tsar to anger). In addition, a choir sings the dirgelike and accusatory "Eternal Memory." Eisenstein diagrams these sonic lines in a hatch-marked grid that displays their interaction with dramatic factors (ibid.:320). The polyphonic process culminates when Ivan roars "You lie!" at Pimen and sends two enormous candelabra crashing down. At the same instant the offscreen choir bursts into a fierce "Peace be unto you." "The basic conflict in the tsar's soul—'right or wrong'—whether to continue the cause or reject it—seems to grow out of the interaction of all the elements of the scene, which act as separate phases of this inner struggle and blend into one at the culmination of overcoming his doubts . . ." (ibid.:323).

As in *Nevsky*, sound affects the rhythm of the editing. The *oprichnina* banquet in Part II was staged to Prokofiev's prerecorded music, and the dance was cut to the rhythm of the score (1947e:288). In "wickerwork" fashion, Fyodor's neck-snapping gestures coincide with the musical accents while the cut falls on the weaker beat. By means of axial editing and other montage-unit principles, the cuts fragment dancers' movements and bring color themes to greater or lesser "tonal" prominence in the course of the dance. In all, Eisenstein creates an equalization among movement, music, color, and shot changes (see Thompson 1981:234–247).

Virtually any sequence illustrates the dynamic interpenetration of narrative, motivic play, and sound structures, but the murder of Vladimir offers a particularly rich instance. The action is the culmination of scene 16, the *oprichnina* banquet. In the first major part of the scene the song and dance of the *oprichnina* are intercut with dialogue among Ivan, Vladimir, and Basmanov. In the second segment, Ivan forces the drunken Vladimir to play tsar in the mock-coronation. As he realizes that his cousin would gladly take the throne, he intuits that the quiet Pyotr in the corner is a source of danger. Abruptly Ivan declares the farce over and invites the *oprichnina* to end their revels and turn to God. He awakens Vladimir, asleep on the throne, and orders him to lead them to the cathedral. On the threshold Vladimir's face turns abruptly blue, stressed by a moaning choral

6.119   6.120

6.121   6.122

murmur, before he nervously moves out toward the cathedral and into black-and-white film again.

As the black-robed *oprichnina* had earlier filed into the banquet hall, blotting out the other colors in the frame, they now advance ominously on Vladimir (6.119), recalling Efrosinia's quaver on the word *black* in her lullaby. Vladimir ventures into the corridor, the choir's largo murmur of the *oprichnina* loyalty song alternating with the same theme expanding in the orchestra. At the scene's climax, a wailing choir and orchestra join with a throbbing baritone voice to accompany Vladimir's pause before a fresco of the Last Judgment. A cymbal crashes, recalling the accompaniment to Efrosinia's sight of the empty cup in the previous scene. As Pyotr rushes up, the music softly restates a fragment of the *oprichnina* dance, but this is abruptly cut off. Eisenstein provides a leap into a new quality: Vladimir is stabbed in silence.

He cries out. A swirling, descending string theme repeats the motif heard when he recoiled from his mother's lullaby (15). As Vladimir falls, he sketches Ivan's power gesture (6.120). He drops his candle (6.121) in a shot that calculatedly recalls Ivan's taking the scepter in his coronation (6.122) and Ivan's accepting a candle during his illness (6.123). The motivic interplay insists on Vladimir as the pale, clownish substitute for the tsar.

Pyotr is seized, to a repetition of the turbulent string passage. The music halts. Efrosinia rushes forward in a reprise of all her hurtling movements in previous

6.123

6.124

6.125

6.126

scenes. Rejoicing that "The beast is dead!" she surmounts the corpse like a hunter and proudly strikes the power attitude (6.124). But then she turns, as if antici-pating the grim pulse that wells up in the orchestra. The *oprichnina* ranks part, and Ivan stalks slowly to the foreground (6.125). The next shot recenters him in the action, establishing him as the locus of power he has been in the coronation scene and the wedding feast (6.126).

Another silence follows as Efrosinia turns over the corpse and sees her son, at last crowned. Like a wounded animal she rears back and emits a tearing shriek; both her movement and her cry are continued by Pyotr, thrashing in the arms of his captors (6.127, 6.128). The "matching" of the gestures recalls cuts among victims on the Odessa Steps (2.82, 2.83). Ivan comes to pardon Pyotr, the two making a studied contrast: black cross on white skin, white cross on black robe (6.129)—an image recalling Efrosinia's earlier judgment on Pimen ("His cowl is white but his soul is black").

Vladimir's body is hauled off. The stunned Efrosinia keens her lullaby. As her son's body slides out of the tsar's crown, she sings of skinning the beaver and making a cloak for Tsar Vladimir. She continues to croon her lullaby, but an offscreen male choir overwhelms it in a reassertion of the *oprichnina* vow. With a jerk of his thumb Ivan orders Efrosinia removed. Pensive, he strides to the altar to pray, displaying a characteristic moment of regret as he speaks the anthem's final line under the choir's dark murmur: "For the sake of the great Russian land

6.127

6.128

6.129

. . ." The film's tragic rhythm has isolated Ivan once more. But his prayer is immediately canceled by the epilogue, in which he reasserts the need for severity and prudence and the music surges up with the motif associated with his power.

The suppression of *Ivan* Part II and of other films by major directors formed part of a general movement to reassert Party control of the cultural sphere. The 1946 edict singled out Eisenstein's portrayal of the *oprichnina* ("a degenerate band rather like the Ku Klux Klan") and of Ivan ("weak and indecisive, somewhat like Hamlet"). Eisenstein quickly acknowledged his errors. After the 1947 meeting with Stalin, he and Cherkasov agreed to eliminate Ivan's "psychological contradictions" (Molotov's phrase, quoted in Eisenstein 1947d:8). The salvageable portions of Part II were to be incorporated with Part III, most of which remained to be shot. Yet it was unlikely that Eisenstein, now in very weak condition, would complete the project.

We cannot settle the dispute about the film's real political purpose, if it indeed can be said to have had a single one. Alexander Solzhenitsyn's prison-camp inmates in *One Day in the Life of Ivan Denisovich* spoke for many in reading the film as an homage to a tyrant. Yet Mikhail Romm recalled that when a group of prominent directors saw the nearly finished film, they were stunned by its audaciously obvious parallels: Ivan as Stalin, Beria as Malyuta, the *oprichnina* as Stalin's acolytes. While the directors sat in fearful silence, Eisenstein stood before them smiling: "Well, what's the matter? What's wrong? What's troubling you? Tell me frankly" (Romm 1965:17).

In the wake of Romm's assertion, some historians have claimed that Eisenstein intended Part II as a critique of Stalin's regime. One suggestion is that Part II uses Stalin's admiration for Ivan as a pretext for an allegorical attack on Party purges (Uhlenbruch 1990:278–282). Another writer interprets the film's portrayal of the solitude of the autocrat as a warning to Stalin (Kozlov 1990). Whatever Eisenstein's private political intentions, however, the complexity of his portrayal of Ivan owes at least as much to his attempt to enrich the tradition of the progressive hero.

From our perspective, the two-thirds of Eisenstein's trilogy represent his last effort to merge theory and practice. *Ivan the Terrible* embodies his attempt to combine idiosyncratic experimentation with an equally wide-ranging ransacking of artistic traditions—all within the ambit of his recasting of Socialist Realism. Noting in 1934 that Joyce carried the methods of "bourgeois" art as far as they could go, Eisenstein remarked: "And what must we do? We must study that experience of going to the limit and go further . . ." (1934b:138–139). Eisenstein's last project carries to astonishing extremes his experiments in narrative architecture, *mise en scène*, audiovisual synthesis, and the interweaving of motifs. The career of the tempestuous young man of 1923 concluded with a work so rich in formal and stylistic invention, so strong in emotional appeal, and so evocative in significance that cinema indeed seems the natural heir of Joyce, Shakespeare, Balzac, Zola, Scriabin, Wagner, Piranesi, and El Greco. Majestic and outlandish, *Ivan the Terrible* marks the triumph of film as both the synthesis and the equal of the other arts.

7.

The Making and
Remaking of
Sergei Eisenstein

When President Ronald Reagan arrived at the Moscow summit in 1988, he greeted his hosts with a quotation from *Film Form:* "The most important thing is to have the vision. The next is grasp and hold it . . ." Three years later, Soviet citizens pulled down monuments to Lenin with the vigor of the crowds swarming over the tsar's statue in *October.* Eisenstein's words and images continue to live in our present, and they seem likely to do so for a long time to come. We can usefully end our survey of Eisenstein's cinema with a brief history of how his life, his films, and his ideas were interpreted in several historical contexts.

Legend in Life

Eisenstein, supremely sensitive to the ways in which images were made, fashioned many of himself. Few directors so adeptly created a "biographical legend," the standard story that shapes the way spectators regard their work. Through publications, interviews, and correspondence he presented himself as the bourgeois boy from Riga, the youth carried away by the Revolution, the speculative artist following the tradition of Leonardo, and the Goethean polymath who could draw freely on the entirety of Western and Eastern culture.

Still, no artist has the final word in how the work and the life are used. What we call an artist's influence is often less a matter of direct transmission than one of selective transformation. An artist's work and life get drawn into other agendas, reshaped according to various premises and purposes. Eisenstein made films, theories, and versions of "Eisenstein," but they were all remade, several times, by others.

A good deal of Eisenstein's authority derived from his striking physical presence. A short, stocky body running to tubbiness in later years; fine curly hair flaring away from a long face; mischievous gray eyes and a clown's smile; a formidable brow that loomed ever larger as he balded—all became familiar sights in the 1930s art world. In Katharine Anne Porter's "Hacienda," a short story based on the *Qué viva México!* filming, he was the director Uspensky, a man with a face "like a superhumanly enlightened monkey's" (1940:255). His trips abroad made converts to the cause of Soviet film and culture.

His films exercised an influence on the scale of Griffith's and Chaplin's. John Grierson and the rest of the British documentary school, many of the Italian Neorealists, and most left-wing filmmakers around the world found his work a source of inspiration. Hollywood got its own version of Eisenstein in the émigré Slavko Vorkapich, who tamed his theories and muted his practice (Kevles 1965:41–42).

Eisenstein's influence began to be felt in the West in 1926, when he visited Europe to arrange for the music for *Potemkin.* The international release of *October* and *Old and New* coincided with his travels abroad, making him the most visible representative of Soviet cinema. He was interviewed constantly, and Western journalists covered his comings and goings. His films were enthusiastically supported by the avant-garde activists Kenneth MacPherson and Winifred Bryher in the journal *Close Up.*

At the same period Eisenstein's Western theoretical profile was established. In the early 1930s some of his writings began to be translated, most prominently in *Close Up.* These came from the period after the making of *October* and quickly identified him with the idea of "dialectical montage." ("The Dramaturgy of Film Form" was published in the West long before it appeared in Russian.) "The Montage of Film Attractions" (1924), "The Problem of the Materialist Approach to Form" (1925), "Béla Forgets the Scissors" (1926), and other pieces could have nuanced the Western conception of Eisenstein's theory, but they lay largely unknown for decades.

During the late 1920s and early 1930s he had keen partisans among Western leftists. Workers' organizations throughout Europe screened and distributed his films. Léon Moussinac, Harry Alan Potamkin, and other journalists used Eisenstein to publicize Soviet film and to propagandize for the U.S.S.R. Around the American magazine *Experimental Cinema,* a group of left-wing film enthusiasts gathered to celebrate the accomplishments of montage cinema. According to Lewis Jacobs, his work "expresses cinematically the social forces released by the proletarian revolution. Impelled by this upheaval, he has evolved autonomous laws of cinematic form sharply related to the needs of the Russian masses" (1931).

Eisenstein's Western reputation was strengthened by the *Qué viva México!* production. It was to be a revolutionary epic free of Hollywood exoticism and shot under the very nose of Mexico's reactionary regime. *Experimental Cinema* publicized the project, aided by a special Eisenstein issue subsidized in part by Upton Sinclair. When Sinclair closed down the shooting, Eisenstein became a martyr. The release of *Thunder over Mexico* led *Experimental Cinema* to launch a campaign to save the negative footage. Seymour Stern wrote that Eisenstein had made a "fatal mistake" in trusting Sinclair, "a self-styled friend of the Soviet Union" (1934:3). As the American Left began breaking into doctrinal factions, the *Qué viva México!* controversy pitted *Experimental Cinema* against the *Daily Worker* and the *New Masses.*

To his admirers outside the Soviet Union Eisenstein remained largely untarnished, and the worldwide success of *Alexander Nevsky* confirmed his stature. By the end of the 1930s his place in film history seemed secure. His works were celebrated in Paul Rotha's *The Film Till Now* (1930), Rudolf Arnheim's *Film* (1933), and Maurice Bardèche and Robert Brasillach's *Histoire du cinéma* (1935, Eng. trans. 1938). Lewis Jacobs' *Rise of the American Film* (1939) devoted half a dozen closely printed pages to Eisenstein on the grounds that he and his colleagues had provided Hollywood with a new standard of excellence. Throughout the 1930s and 1940s the British Film Institute's journal *Sight and Sound* published articles on his work and essays from his hand.

In the Soviet Union Eisenstein was a far more controversial figure. Since *Strike,* he had been attacked by Proletkult, *New Lef,* Proletarian groups, Boris Shumyatsky, and other directors at the 1935 congress. The *Bezhin Meadow* incident threatened to end his career and perhaps his life. But the accolades heaped upon *Alexander Nevsky* and *Ivan the Terrible* Part I brought him renewed stature. After the banning of the second part, however, his reputation plummeted once more. Along with the now-standard criticism of the 1920s pioneers for failing to grasp the personal side of the struggle for socialism, critics made more severe objections to Eisenstein's work.

A withering bill of particulars was drawn up in Nikolai Lebedev's massive official history of Soviet silent cinema, published a year after the banning of *Ivan* Part II. Lebedev presented Eisenstein's career as an object lesson in formalism. He recalled Eisenstein's origins in such bourgeois groups as Lef and Proletkult. He criticized Eisenstein's conception of reflex-based montage, his refusal to concentrate on heroes, his search for analogies between cinema and language, his efforts toward intellectual cinema, and his rejection of the "steel scenario." According to Lebedev, *Potemkin* was able to overcome these problems by virtue of its "pathos" (1947:134), but the "formalist foolery" of *October* and *Old and New* made evident the weaknesses of the director's theories (102). Worse, Lebedev charged Eisenstein with hindering the development of Soviet film. Only with the failure of *Bezhin Meadow* did he realize that he had lost contact with reality. Although Lebedev was obviously setting the stage for the triumph of *Nevsky* (to be discussed in the never-published second volume), his attack reminded readers in 1947 that the director's current disgrace was only the most recent episode in a wayward career.

The Assimilation into Orthodoxy

Eisenstein's reputation, already in decline when he died in 1948, remained low in his motherland for several years. Pudovkin portrayed him as an inveterate formalist; even *Potemkin,* he warned, contained traits opposed to Socialist Realism (1949:4–5). Ivan Pyriev judged that the offensiveness of *Old and New* resulted from Eisenstein's "complete lack of understanding . . . of the qualities of his people and from his ignorance of their life" (1951:51). Western leftists dealt gingerly with the controversial films and avoided criticizing the Soviet regime. Discussing the adjustments demanded of *The General Line,* Ivor Montagu recalled that "Eisenstein often told me of the deep impression Stalin's sagacity left with him" (1948:11).

Less partisan observers in the West saw *Ivan* as a grand but lifeless spectacle, and it was widely regarded as signaling the director's decline. He began to be invoked as a case study in Soviet tyranny, a genius destroyed by a dictator. "Since 1929," wrote Dwight MacDonald, "Eisenstein has made every possible effort to adapt his genius to the base and vulgar uses required of it" (1969:284; see also Agee 1964:250). Eisenstein's death brought forth further reflections of this sort (Solski 1949; Ingster 1951).

Yet during the decade following his death his reputation was redeemed. By the early 1960s, in both the Soviet Union and the West he was generally considered one of the finest of all filmmakers, perhaps the very greatest. *Potemkin* became known as the world's greatest film, while Eisenstein's writings were treated as the apogee of film theory. How did this drastic change come about?

In the Soviet Union, Khrushchev's attack on Stalin and the "cult of personality" played the primary role. "De-Stalinization" helped lift the cloud that *Ivan* Part II had cast over Eisenstein. The year 1956 saw an exhibition of his drawings and the first Russian-language collection of articles. Gradually the scripts and montage-lists of his films were published. In 1958, the sixtieth anniversary of his birth, the Soviet filmmaking establishment honored him. He was the subject of a special issue of the principal film magazine, *Iskusstvo kino; Notes of a Film Director* was published simultaneously in several languages; his pupil Vladimir Nizhny compiled *Lessons with Eisenstein;* and a documentary film was made tracing his career.

In the West the growth of his posthumous reputation had rather different causes. Certain institutions had already established him as a major figure. The Museum of Modern Art in New York held Eisenstein collections and screened and circulated several of his films. The British Film Institute did the same, and *Sight and Sound* continued to serve as a forum for discussions of Eisenstein's career.

His associates helped elevate his reputation. The American scholar Jay Leyda had attended his VGIK courses and assisted on *Bezhin Meadow.* Leyda's editions of *The Film Sense* (1942) and *Film Form* (1949) became the basis of collections in other Western languages, and his translations were widely anthologized. He preserved key documents, prepared a study film of the *Qué viva México!* footage, and wrote several articles about Eisenstein's career. Leyda's history of the Soviet cinema, *Kino* (1960), also assigned Eisenstein a central role.

Like Leyda, Marie Seton knew Eisenstein during the 1930s, and her 1952 biography consolidated his reputation as a polymath, a twentieth-century Leonardo da Vinci. Other associates, such as the Englishmen Ivor Montagu and Herbert Marshall, disseminated his writings and promoted his films. Given the dearth of books about film directors in the 1950s, the works of Seton, Montagu, Leyda, and others made his reputation loom very large.

His supremacy in the canon was also trumpeted widely in books aimed at students and the general public. Following the lead of Rotha's *The Film Till Now* and Roger Manvell's *Film* (1944), several historians gave him a leading role in Soviet montage cinema. In France, this treatment was epitomized in Georges Sadoul's survey *Histoire du cinéma mondiale* (1949), which went through many editions. In England, Manvell's third edition of *Film* reprinted Eisenstein's three-page description of the Odessa Steps sequence, "one of the most influential few minutes in cinema history" (1950:54). Ernest Lindgren's *Art of the Film* (1948) made editing the primary film technique and devoted an entire chapter to Griffith and Eisenstein. In the United States, Arthur Knight's *The Liveliest Art* (1957), perhaps the most widely read popular history of cinema, also stressed Eisenstein as a central figure.

In postwar France, *La revue du cinéma* showed an interest in Eisenstein's films, and during the 1950s *Cahiers du cinéma* and other journals published translations of Eisenstein's work, as well as essays by Seton, Sadoul, and others. His films, screened at Centro Sperimentale since the 1930s, had strongly influenced the Italian Neorealist movement, so it is not surprising that a volume of his essays appeared earlier in Italian than in any other European language. Book-length studies were published in Swedish and Spanish.

Eisenstein's rehabilitation reached its apogee at the 1958 Brussels World's Fair. There *Ivan the Terrible* Part II had its world premiere, and an international critics' poll voted *Potemkin* the best film ever made.

This acclaim accelerated the rise of Eisenstein's reputation at home. Soon there appeared a new collection of drawings (1961), a commemorative anthology on *Potemkin* (1962), and the first volume of the *Selected Works* (1964). Monographs appeared in Polish, Czech, and Romanian. The Eisenstein museum was established in 1965; the next year marked the first official Soviet retrospective of his films. The young researcher Naum Kleiman devoted himself to preserving Eisenstein's memory and disseminating his works. In 1967 Kleiman arranged for the remains of *Bezhin Meadow* to be pieced into a study film and assisted with the anniversary reissue of *October*.

In the West interest in Eisenstein and his work continued unabated through the 1960s. Jean Mitry and Léon Moussinac published biographical studies (1961,

1964). Several volumes of his writings appeared in German. English readers gained access to the *Ivan* screenplay, the treatments for *Sutter's Gold* and *An American Tragedy,* and Nizhny's *Lessons with Eisenstein* (1962). As film studies entered university curricula, *Potemkin* and *Nevsky* became required viewing.

Western discussion of Eisenstein's theory and practice centered principally on montage, usually conceived as editing techniques aiming to arouse shock or cerebration. In conjunction with this emphasis, critics elevated *Potemkin,* portions of *October,* and *Nevsky* while playing down the other films. *Strike* was all but unknown, *Old and New* was considered a whimsical minor work, and the two *Ivan* films remained anomalies, apparent repudiations of montage theory. Writers did not examine the early films' artistic and cultural context, largely because the West knew little of Constructivism, Formalist criticism, and kindred movements of the pre-Stalin era.

As Eisenstein's image was being elevated, dissenting voices were also heard. Some writers declared him a mere propagandist who, like his Communist masters, had sacrificed morality to political expediency. After a 1955 Museum of Modern Art series of Soviet montage films, Robert Warshow expressed outrage at the "triumph of art over humanity": "It is hard to feel the pathos of [the directors'] lives when you see them playing with corpses; if they had got the chance, they would have made a handsome montage of my corpse, too, and given it a mean-ing—their meaning and not mine" (1962:270). A Museum of Modern Art exhi-bition in 1960 on Eisenstein's career prompted William S. Pechter to attack "the closed mind of Sergei Eisenstein."

The view of Eisenstein as *homo sovieticus* chimed with themes in émigré and unofficial literature. A famous passage in Solzhenitsyn's *One Day in the Life of Ivan Denisovich* (1962) sets camp prisoners to debating the merit of *Ivan the Terrible.* One man calls it a work of genius, but the other responds: "Call him an ass-kisser, obeying a vicious dog's order. Geniuses don't adjust their interpreta-tions to fit the taste of tyrants!" (1963:84).

Sometimes the political judgments also addressed Soviet montage as an aes-thetic. Warshow and Pechter, for instance, saw Eisenstein's didactic narrowness as linked to a mechanical conception of film form. But within film studies the emerging countercurrent had less to do with anticommunism than with a growing resistance to an aesthetic orthodoxy.

Karel Reisz, for instance, asserted that Eisenstein's long-term influence had been virtually nil. Contemporary cinema, he indicated, told stories in smooth continuity and made conceptual points through sound, not through cutting (1951). André Bazin formulated the most influential "anti-montage" position. Bazin valued the power of cinema to record and transmit the tangible reality before the camera. His position, though hedged about with subtle qualifications, led him to criticize Soviet editing: "Montage as used by Kuleshov, Eisenstein, or Gance did not give us the event; it alluded to it" (1967:25).

Critics influenced by Bazin began treating montage and *mise en scène* as alter-native stylistic options. *Mise en scène* directors respected the action in front of the camera, creating effects by means of performance, staging in depth, and camera movement. "Montage" directors relied on editing in order to force a meaning on the audience; *mise en scène* was freer, more complex, and capable of creating subtler or more ambiguous effects. The growing reputation of Italian Neorealism, Orson Welles, and Jean Renoir, as well as the emergence of widescreen cinema in the early 1950s reinforced this schematic opposition. Typical exponents of the position were Charles Barr, who asserted that montage was suitable for propaganda but was incapable of "gradation of emphasis" (1963:12–13); and Christian Metz, who maintained that montage was "contrary to film's essential vocation" (1974:38).

In retrospect there is little doubt that the mainstream aesthetic exaggerated the importance of editing. But amid the polemic, nuances often got lost. Bazin's theoretical and moral values became the basis of a new set of tastes: Renoir rather than Eisenstein, Preminger rather than Pudovkin. Yet Bazin's claims that certain films were best understood as mixing montage and intra-shot techniques were not taken seriously, with the result that critics tended to miss the Eisensteinian side of Akira Kurosawa's *Seven Samurai*, Welles's *Othello* and *Touch of Evil*, and Samuel Fuller's *Forty Guns*. Moreover, the postwar polemic was limited by translation and by assumptions inherited from the orthdox tradition. The critics, like their opponents, could not explore the subtleties of Eisenstein's conceptions of montage. Nor could they have known that unpublished manuscripts showed him deeply concerned with many aspects of film technique. Eisenstein was systematically exploring *mise en scène*, the long take, and deep focus when Bazin was fourteen. Montage was defined more comprehensively in Eisenstein's writing and pedagogy than the Bazinian tradition allowed, and it remains part of a broad account of film style.

The Exemplary Modernist

By the mid-1960s Eisenstein had become central to reflection about cinema as art and social force. As if in reaction to both aesthetic and political denunciations of the "manipulativeness" of montage, some critics and theorists praised Eisenstein as a pioneer in an avant-garde tradition. He could now be seen as indebted to modern art movements such as Cubism and Soviet Constructivism. Moreover, his work had indisputable relevance to exciting developments in current film-making.

The international art cinema, inheriting and revising modernist trends in other media, offered vivid examples of Eisenstein's contemporary significance. Most notably, the French New Wave abruptly put the issue of discontinuous editing back on the agenda. Alain Resnais opened *Hiroshima mon amour* (1959) by crosscutting sweating lovers with victims of atomic bombardment, and Jean-Luc Godard interrupted *Une femme mariée* (1964) with close-ups of advertisements. Suddenly "montage of attractions" and "intellectual montage" no longer seemed dead ends. *Muriel* (1963) and *Alphaville* (1965) demonstrated that editing could maximize, not eliminate, ambiguity. In a firing-squad scene in *Les carabiniers* Godard dwelt upon an overlapping cut that he considered "proud, moving, Eisensteinian" (1972:198).

Avant-garde cinema had always been more hospitable to Eisensteinian ideas, and it too was attaining greater prominence during the 1960s. Works by Stan Brakhage, Stan Van Der Beek, and Bruce Conner employed many of Eisenstein's montage methods. In 1960 Brakhage defended purely silent cinema by arguing that *Potemkin* and *October* demonstrated mastery of "sound-sense," whereby the images created auditory associations (1963:unpaged).

Eisenstein's contemporaneity seemed evident with respect to both practice and theory. Marie-Claire Ropars-Wuilleumier, writing in 1966, saw *October*'s break with traditional dramaturgy as part of the avant-garde enterprise of affirming the value of purely aesthetic structure. Eisenstein's heirs were Resnais, Chris Marker, and Godard (1970b:198–202). Taking him as a point of departure, Ropars-Wuilleumier developed a theory of cinematic *écriture* predicated on treating montage as breaking with the "transparency" prized by Bazinians (1970a).

During the same years, in a series of articles later gathered in *Praxis du cinéma* (1969), the filmmaker Noël Burch teased contemporary experimental possibilities out of Eisenstein's corpus. Sequences of *Bezhin Meadow* and *Ivan the Terrible* seemed to anticipate Kurosawa, Robert Bresson, and Michelangelo Antonioni (1973:57–74). According to Burch, Eisenstein pioneered a "dialectical," "parametric" conception of filmic structure that had counterparts in Cubism and serial music.

Roland Barthes also found in Eisenstein a "parametric" model of modernist practice. Musing over some frames from *Potemkin* and *Ivan* Part I, he sensed a "third meaning" that outran narrative denotation and symbolic connotation. This "obtuse" expressivity subordinated narrative to the "permutational play" of the image (1970:63). In this respect, Eisenstein's cinema exemplified the new form of reading demanded by contemporary art and literature.

In England, Peter Wollen praised Eisenstein as the filmmaker most aware of the need to reevaluate twentieth-century aesthetics in the light of modernism (1968). The chapter on Eisenstein in Wollen's influential *Signs and Meaning in the Cinema* traced his ideas to various strands in avant-garde thought, stressing the conflict in his thinking between a materialist modernism and a "Symbolist reflux" (1972:60).

Eisenstein's conception of cinematic language was also felt to have anticipated contemporary semiotics. This rereading of his work was strongest in the Soviet Union, where a cybernetic structuralism emerged in the early 1960s. Alexander Zholkovsky based his "generative poetics" upon Eisenstein's teaching method (1969), while V. V. Ivanov saw Eisenstein, Vygotsky, and Bakhtin as creating a distinctly Soviet semiotics (1971). A similar reading was developed in other Eastern Bloc countries (for example, Bystrzycka 1970). In the West, although Metz's early semiological reflections criticized Eisenstein, both Gianfranco Bettetini (1973) and Wollen (1968) found him an important inspiration.

By the late 1960s Eisenstein's work had once again become contested terrain. For some, he remained a great artist; for others, a morally compromised political servant. He embodied a regressive, manipulative aesthetic; or he pioneered a cinematic modernism that was only now coming into its own. For film theorists, his emphasis on the image as a "conventional sign" and on montage as a "film-syntax" opened up the problem of treating filmic communication as a semiotic system.

Most of these assimilations used Eisenstein's work as a point of departure for film practice and further speculation. But once film studies was established as an academic discipline on the Continent and in English-speaking countries, there emerged a body of writing attempting to outline, explicate, and systematize Eisenstein's ideas in their own right. (Examples include B. Henderson 1971; Tudor 1973; Bordwell 1975; and Andrew 1976.) This tendency ran alongside a recasting of the modernist position. Annette Michelson's 1966 essay, "Film and the Radical Aspiration," is perhaps the earliest sign that the debate had taken a new turn.

Michelson maintained that soon after cinema's invention it became integral to the modernist sensibility, and that artists of politically radical or utopian inclinations saw the medium as the very incarnation of the future. Yet she argued that the modernist tradition inherited by contemporary directors such as Godard, Resnais, and Brakhage had been cut loose of political consequence. She looked back to a historical moment in which formal experimentation fused with a commitment to social transformation. "The revolutionary aspiration, both *formal and political,* achieved a moment of consummation in the Russian film of the twenties and early thirties" (1966:38). Michelson took Eisenstein as the emblem of "radical aspiration," visionary and victimized: "The energy, courage and intellectual passion which sustained both theory and work were, of course, among the noblest of our century. Eisenstein is a model of the culture of our era—in his defeat as in his achievement, and down to the very fragmentary quality of his work!" (40) Despite *Nevsky*'s capitulation to Stalinist policy, Michelson believed that Eisenstein's commitment to the double-edged radicality of the modernist project could inspire contemporary artists.

Michelson pursued these themes in a 1973 article in *Artforum* that juxtaposed Eisenstein and Brakhage as two models of the radical potential of the avant-garde. In the same year, tributes to Eisenstein in Moscow and New York reaffirmed his modernist inclinations. By then, however, "radicality" had become identified with particular versions of Marxism. A militant left-wing filmmaking and film theory had emerged.

Revolutionary filmmakers in the Third World were beginning to take Eisenstein as a precursor. Glauber Rocha's *Antonio das Mortes* (1969) pays him homage through an overlapping series of six shots of an assassin stabbing his victim. Fernando Solanas asserted that *La hora de los hornos* (*Hour of the Furnaces*, 1969) was a "documentary" in exactly the same sense that *Strike* and *Potemkin* were (1969:3); the film's first part updates *October*'s intellectual montage. Manuel Octavio Gómez' *Dios del agua* (*Gods of Water*, 1971) concludes with a sequence in which rebels in the Cuban countryside turn their firepower onto their bourgeois oppressors, ranged along a flight of steps. When in 1977 a special issue of *Cine cubano* inquired into the influence of Soviet cinema on Latin American directors, respondents from Bolivia, Argentina, Brazil, and elsewhere attested to Eisenstein's continuing relevance.

In Western cinema, "political modernism" came to be seen as the principal avant-garde development of the late 1960s through the mid-1970s. *Strike,* issued with a musical track in 1967, and *The Man with the Movie Camera,* reissued in 1968, had enormous impact. Along with Brecht and Vertov, Eisenstein became a paragon of politically committed avant-garde art. A writer in *Les temps modernes* greeted *Strike* as "a memory of future fusillades" (Zimmer 1967). The West German Alexander Kluge revived the concept of "dialectical montage," echoing Eisenstein's early theory in remarking: "The film is composed in the head of the spectator . . . Film must work with the associations which, to the extent that they can be estimated, to the extent they can be imagined, the author can arouse in the spectator" (quoted in Liebman 1988:14). The anarchist Kirov(!) in Godard's *La Chinoise* (1967) lists artists who are of use to contemporary political struggles; Brecht, Mayakovsky, and Eisenstein head the list.

After the Paris riots of 1968, French intellectual journals began to reexamine the heritage of 1920s Soviet art. *Cahiers du cinéma,* converted to Marxist-Leninism by the May events, announced: "To us, the only possible line of advance seems to be to use the theoretical writing of the Russian film makers of the twenties (Eisenstein above all) to elaborate and apply a critical theory of the cinema, a specific method of apprehending rigorously defined objects, in direct reference to the method of historical materialism" (Comolli and Narboni 1969:9). *Cahiers* launched a long-running series of translations of Eisenstein essays and in 1971 published a special number devoted to him. For several years, *Cahiers* readers encountered him at every turn. A round table on montage, for instance, led Jacques Rivette to compare Eisenstein's overturning of Griffith's montage with Marx's upending of Hegelian idealism (1969:79).

The Maoist *Cinéthique* objected to the new platform, accusing *Cahiers* of forgetting Eisenstein's debts to bourgeois culture, his "theological" conception of cinema, his Hegelianism, and his actual films (Pleynet 1969:243). (It was at this moment that Godard, deciding that Eisenstein was a bourgeois director, named his filmmaking cadre the Dziga-Vertov Group.) Yet *Cinéthique* was not anti-Eisenstein. A dialogue between Jean Thibaudeau and Marcelin Pleynet contains a remarkable exchange:

> *Pleynet:* It must be recognized that to this day no filmmaker has been led to think his practice theoretically (systematically).
> *Thibaudeau:* Eisenstein . . .
> *Pleynet:* Yes, in a socialist country.   (1969:161)

A new Eisenstein was forged. *Cahiers* articles were translated throughout the West. The disclosure of Eisenstein's notes for a film of *Capital,* published in

Russian in 1973 and swiftly disseminated in other languages, confirmed the sense that here was a filmmaker who sought to fuse leftist commitment and experimental technique. A conference in Italy in the same year devoted considerable space to his Marxism (Mechini and Salvadori 1975), while the left-wing German journal *alternative* devoted an issue to the political implications of his montage theory. As revolutionary politics waned, Eisenstein's work became an ironic reference point. The protagonist of Makavejev's *Sweet Movie* (1974) wears a *Potemkin* sailor's cap; Marker's *Fond de l'air est rouge* (1977), a controversial meditation upon the failures of Left movements, intercuts the Odessa Steps with 1968 news footage.

In the 1970s academic film studies began to establish canonical works and essays, and the Eisenstein debates fed naturally into that process. Eisenstein (like Vertov) became an exemplary "political modernist" of the pre-Godard era. His films were assumed to embody the dialectic of history, interrogate or "deconstruct" mainstream cinema's "impression of reality," and raise revolutionary consciousness through form as well as content. By and large, this view dominates academic discussion of Eisenstein to this day.

Still, during the 1970s a number of writers continued to open up fresh perspectives. After translating several *Cahiers* and *Cinéthique* pieces, the British journal *Screen* undertook its own investigation of 1920s Soviet film culture. Although Eisenstein was invoked occasionally, writers associated with *Screen* were cautious about accepting the political-modernist image. One found the later Eisenstein writings more valuable than was generally granted (Brewster 1975). Another *Screen* contributor suggested that Eisenstein's stress on film as language cut him off from a more fruitful avant-garde tradition that explored the ontology of the medium itself (Wollen 1975).

Critical analysis of the films also sometimes went beyond the political-modernist position. *Ivan the Terrible* was studied from the standpoint of a revised Russian Formalist poetics (Thompson 1981). Other critics subjected the films to "symptomatic readings" that revealed repressed sexual or political content (Oudart 1970; Baudry 1971; Narboni 1976; Britton 1977). Deploying the tools of "textual analysis," three Parisian researchers undertook a two-volume dissection of *October* (Sorlin and Ropars 1976; Lagny, Ropars, and Sorlin 1979; see also Ropars-Weuillemier 1978, 1978–79). Their analysis suggested that the film's stylistic articulations simultaneously reworked and displaced historical issues.

Theoretical discussion also went beyond the political-modernist frame of reference. François Albéra's *Notes sur l'esthétique d'Eisenstein* (1973) mixed Althusserian ideological analysis with *Tel quel* conceptions of modernist writing to produce an account of Eisenstein's "libidinal investment" in theory. A writer working in a Derridean framework explored the philosophical implications of "Beyond the Shot" (Carasco 1979). Aumont's *Montage Eisenstein* (1979) likewise offered a wide-ranging examination of a central concept. Aumont treated the theory of montage as both a project in writing and a struggle between Eisenstein's urge for a master system and his fascination with the unassimilable fragment.

Finally, the semiotic reading of Eisenstein, which had continued through the decade (Ivanov 1976; Eagle 1978; Salvaggio 1979), took a new turn. Marie-Claire Ropars-Weuilleumier revised her conception of cinematic *écriture* along the lines of Derrida's critique of structural theories of signification; she now saw Eisenstein's montage as questioning the sign, engendering a play of abstraction and concreteness modeled upon the ideogram (1981).

Eisenstein Our Contemporary

Along with rapid revisions in Eisenstein's image as Marxist modernist came newly available documents. Throughout the 1970s exhibits of Eisensteiniana were mounted in East Germany, Holland, Japan, Cuba, and France. Shklovsky's book-length memoir was published in 1973, and portions of *Glumov's Diary* were discovered four years later. The six-volume Soviet edition of Eisenstein's writings was completed in 1971, triggering new collections in German (1973–1983), French (1974–1985), and Italian (1981–). Anglophone readers, who had previously enjoyed unparalleled access to Eisenstein's texts, did not benefit much from this largesse. Updated English-language editions were late in appearing. Still, the indefatigable Leyda continued to produce trim collections of essays and lectures, as well as a handsome career survey (Leyda and Voynow 1982).

"All there remains for me to do is to analyze what has been done and from it create a synthesis of knowledge; an understanding of methods which can be applied to the art of cinematography" (Seton 1952:262). By quoting such remarks, Seton had prepared the way for considering her subject a kind of universal genius. As volumes came forth revealing his wide-ranging interests, this Goethean image reappeared in the 1980s; Eisenstein remade yet again.

A theorist of art, culture, language, and psychology; a proto-semiotician; a gifted theatre designer and director; a delightful caricaturist; a friend to Mayakovsky, Meyerhold, Vygotsky, Luria, Babel, Chaplin, Tynyanov, Shklovsky, Rivera, Siqueros—even if he had produced no films, Eisenstein would enjoy a preeminent place in Soviet intellectual history. As in recent revelations about Bakhtin and Shostakovich, newly discovered documents from the Eisenstein files suggested that Stalinism did not still all creative energies.

Few researchers have attempted to survey the colossal range of Eisenstein's thought; the most ambitious attempt in the West is Barthélémy Amengual's mighty *Que viva Eisenstein!* (1980). Instead, scholars have returned to the task of developing Eisenstein's aesthetic reflections into smaller-scale models for analysis of the literary and plastic arts. (See Montani 1991.) As he had envisioned, cinematic processes can reveal, as if in close-up and slow motion, processes at work in other media. So Eisenstein's writings and films are read for the light they can shed on the history of painting (Aumont 1989). An art historian can utilize the notion of "ecstatic leap" to explicate *composto* in a Bernini chapel (Careri 1991). A literary critic examines montage in Babel's *Red Cavalry* stories (Schreurs 1989).

Eisenstein remains of contemporary significance, and not just in academic circles. Directors as disparate as Ritwik Ghatak, Ken Jacobs, Ousmane Sembene, and Peter Greenaway have been crucially influenced by his work. Francis Ford Coppola recalled: "I was about eighteen when I became a disciple of Eisenstein . . . I was dying to make a film. So, following his example, I studied the theatre and worked very hard . . . I wanted to know everything, from every aspect, to have the same breadth of knowledge as Eisenstein did" (Chaillet and Vincent 1985:2).

It is not hard to find specific traces of the films in other works. *Alexander Nevsky* is explicitly cited in Pier Paolo Pasolini's *Gospel according to St. Matthew* (1964) and Welles's *Chimes at Midnight* (1966); Sergio Leone's abrupt editing and florid use of musical punctuation seem indebted to the theory and practice of vertical montage. The claustrophobic stylization of *Ivan the Terrible* has successors in the work of Luchino Visconti, Derek Jarman, and Ken Russell. As we might expect, Eisenstein's shadow stretches over *glasnost* cinema. Valery Ogorodnikov's *Prishvin's Paper Eyes* (1989) features him as a character and intercuts the Odessa Steps sequence with a newsreel, so that Stalin points out victims for the troops. In Alexander Rogozhin's *The Guard* (1989), as a prison train rolls through town, people hurl rocks; dissolves link a starred windowpane to dangling eyeglasses, evoking Smirnov's pince-nez and the old woman's shattered eye.

The Odessa Steps sequence, that staple of film study courses and compilation documentaries, is probably the most cited scene in film history. Woody Allen parodies it in *Bananas* (1971), while Brian DePalma's *The Untouchables* (1987) offers a mannered, slow-motion pastiche. The video artist Zbigniew Rybczynski turns American tourists loose amid the massacre in *Steps* (1987). Juliusz Michulski's gangster comedy *Déja vu*, set in Odessa during the 1920s, includes a chase that repeatedly interrupts Eisenstein's filming on the Steps. In Igor Alimpiev's *Armor* (1991) a pursuit through the Leningrad subway sends a baby carriage bouncing down the gigantic escalator.

Sometimes, however, Eisenstein is given credit for more than he deserves. It is common, for instance, to cite him as the filmmaker who showed that a film's meaning and effect derive from the juxtaposition of shots. Yet this was a premise of Soviet montage cinema generally and was articulated by Kuleshov, Vertov, Pudovkin, and others. Filmmakers and critics have also credited Eisenstein as the source of the Hollywood "montage sequence," television commercials, and music videos. This is quite a drastic "remaking" of his work. Although the rapid editing in such sequences would not have been possible without the Soviet montage cinema, their stylistic strategies lie far from Eisenstein's sophisticated conceptions of montage. At best, the "montage" in such media artifacts is metric and rhythmic, seldom tonal or overtonal, and it makes no attempt to achieve the large-scale motivic density that is central to Eisenstein's practice. An advertisement featuring a roller-skating pizza-delivery boy is not comparable to the Odessa Steps sequence merely because both use "fast cutting." Eisenstein's whole theory insists that techniques may function differently according to context.

Not that Eisensten lacked a genius for vivid moments and technical flourishes.

Every film contains at least one *morceau d'anthologie*—the slaughter of the bull and the workers, the Steps massacre, the rise of Kerensky and his comparison with a peacock, the raising of the St. Petersburg bridges, the triumph of the cream separator, the battle between Russians and Teutonic Knights on Lake Chudskoe, the grieving at Anastasia's bier, the *oprichnina* banquet, and the murder of Vladimir. Eisenstein's overlapping editing, nondiegetic and quasi-diegetic cutting, editing for graphic conflict, deep-focus composition, montage-unit construction, audiovisual synchronization, and "unfolding foreground" technique are permanent enrichments of the filmmaker's repertoire.

Yet the historical significance of his films also stems from his ability to create rich, systematic contexts for such innovations. Partly, of course, the contexts derive from trends in Soviet narrative art of the era. *Strike* and *Battleship Potemkin* utilized the "mass protagonist" formulated in fiction of the early postrevolutionary period. With *October*, individuated Bolsheviks play a more distinctive role, as befits a moment in which drama and literature recognized the importance of Party leadership. In the era of "little men and big deeds," of "heroes who take the initiative," Eisenstein offered Marfa, the spontaneously progressive peasant of *Old and New*. With the intensification of Russian chauvinism under Stalin, Prince Alexander and Tsar Ivan stepped forward as models of the strong, individualized leader who embodies the spirit of the people. The films' technical bravura is also encouraged by the rhetorical cast of the plots, which invite amplification and intensification in the manner of rousing oratory.

But this much is true of, say, Pudovkin as well. In the early films, Eisenstein's version of "plotless" cinema enabled him to situate a narrative action within an overarching compositional structure, each part assigned a distinct purpose and a constantly developing texture. This demand for structural and textural unity guided his use of those technical devices that his contemporaries usually employed to different ends. His stylistic innovations, such as "conflicting" editing and deep-focus imagery, were assigned concrete functions in his ongoing experiments in emotional and intellectual arousal. In his later works, montage-unit construction and audiovisual polyphony yielded a moment-by-moment complexity that nonetheless remained within the norms of Socialist Realist cinema. Armed with his own "systems theory," he devised a "general method and mode for the problem of form" (1935a: 147).

In practice, and later in theory, Eisenstein was arguably the first filmmaker to conceive of the "totally composed" fictional film. The Wagnerian leitmotif led Symbolists to formulate a conception of the self-sufficient artwork, and by the time Eisenstein came to cinema Bely, Eliot, Pound, and Joyce had made motivic unity a salient feature of modernism. We can find this modernist tactic at work in such abstract films as *Ballet mécanique* (1924), but by and large fictional films did not create recurrent patterns at the level of graphic design, camera positions, editing choices, and gestural motifs passed among characters. Most filmmakers were content to achieve motivic unity through dramatically significant props, costumes, or lines of dialogue. The doorway silhouettes in Maurice Tourneur's

Last of the Mohicans (1920), Murnau's locales in *Nosferatu* (1922), Lang's set design in *Siegfried* (1924), and Keaton's theme-and-variations gags (as in *Our Hospitality*, 1923) showed how motifs could gain structural prominence, but these directors did not take the idea to the lengths that Eisenstein did.

He found a way to organize the cinematic text at every stylistic level. *Strike* achieves an unprecedented unity by accreting a variety of visual patterns. Twenty years later, virtually each shot of *Ivan the Terrible* has become the point of intersection of a welter of dramatic, pictorial, verbal, and musical motifs. Giving stylistic texture this degree of intricate patterning remains a rare option even today; the tradition of Hollywood cinema tends to make style subordinate to narrative organization. But filmmakers such as Yasujiro Ozu, Robert Bresson, Carl Dreyer, and Jacques Tati have shown that Eisenstein's insistence on through-composed stylistic organization was not a dead end.

For Eisenstein, what bound all the visual and sonic motifs together was the "theme" of the passage. The Constructivists emphasized material, form, and purpose in the making of a work; Eisenstein adds to this triumvirate the thematic "image." Taken literally, this suggests a rather straightforward mapping of an "idea" onto the artistic "image," which in turn determines specific formal choices. This formulation had some strategic rhetorical value against those who would charge Eisenstein with ignoring "content." In practice, the strategy was not so mechanical as it might seem. A great dynamism is achieved in the development of the circle and water motifs in *Strike*, the dichotomous organization of images in *October*, the transformation of decorative circles into functional ones in *Old and New*, the reaffirmation of Ivan's commitment in the scene at Anastasia's bier.

Throughout this book we have also noticed qualities that are difficult to subsume to a univocal thematic purpose. The stone lions, *October*'s glittering peacock, the momentary blueing of Vladimir, and many other moments arouse a range of associations not easily gathered to a single thematic point. Often Eisenstein follows the material where it leads him, developing a pattern as forceful expression, as a unifying factor, or simply as an occasion for vivid perceptual engagement. In the midgets' tango in *Strike*, Fomka's marriage in *Old and New*, and the arrow-punctured Kazanian hostages in *Ivan*, the momentary, jolting attraction persists. In any given case, the theme-saturated image may be subordinated to other qualities of form and material.

Here practice outruns theory. But theory may also go beyond practice, moving toward basic problems and general "laws" only imperfectly visible in any given work. Eisenstein's general inquiries can be situated within several alternative theoretical traditions.

There is, for instance, the tradition of classical film aesthetics. During Eisenstein's lifetime, theorists were preoccupied with problems of the essential nature of the medium, its difference from other media, and the nature of a specifically cinematic experience. Eisenstein has relatively little interest in such questions. He prefers to ignore issues of cinematic specificity, to emphasize cinema's kinship with other media and arts, and to understand the spectator's experience either in terms of technical strategies or in terms of broad and basic tendencies of human thought. His cinematic poetics, an inquiry close to the contours of craft practice, rejects or recasts central issues of mainstream film theory.

His theoretical writings bear somewhat more upon questions of aesthetics as a philosophical discipline. Like the Formalists, he was little interested in the classic questions of the nature of beauty or the intrinsic qualities of art; but he did state his views on the progressive role of art in society and the power of the creative imagination. Moreover, his reflex-based theory of emotion and his strictures on the artistic image mark significant positions in twentieth-century aesthetics. Yet his views on these matters remain quite undeveloped. They do not constitute full-fledged arguments, let alone persuasive ones. Nor, if I am right, are they meant to: such conjectures are enabling assumptions, governing a more concrete type of inquiry.

Much the same could be said of Eisenstein's theory in relation to semiotics. Historically, his speculations on the cinematic sign have proved prescient, and many semioticians have found them useful points of departure. But his formulations remain fragmentary and probably do not add up to a comprehensive theoretical position.

All of which is not to deny that reading Eisenstein can open up fruitful questions about other arts and sign systems. Nor is it to ignore his many insights into particular works of literature and the pictorial arts. Yet Eisenstein's writings are most coherent and rewarding if we take his desire for a "system" as pointing toward a cinematic poetics—a study of the principles informing effective film practice.

Eisenstein lived before film theory became a scholarly pursuit, so his writing ran the risk of seeming merely a by-product of his trade. He tried to convince his contemporaries that his theorizing and teaching were as important as his filmmaking. His case ought to be easier to mount today. But contemporary film theory has on the whole moved away from Eisenstein's concerns. It has become remarkably rococo in its formulations, recondite in its doctrinal affiliations, and remote from the practice of filmmaking.

Eisenstein's poetics can remind us why we might want to do film theory, and what a useful theory might look like. The *technē*-centered tradition in music, literature, and the visual arts during the NEP period recast "theory" as an enterprise partway between scientific inquiry and a systematization of craft knowledge. Concepts such as *tektonika* (macrostructure), *faktura* (textural working), construction, composition, *fabula* ("story"), and *syuzhet* ("plot") were at once descriptive and explanatory. They picked out discriminable phases within the problem-solving activity of making a work, and they were sufficiently abstract to shed light on broader principles of art-making.

Such middle-level theorizing remains fairly rare in the aesthetics, semiotics, and literary theory of this century. Technique-centered thinking has remained the province of reflective artists, from da Vinci through Coleridge to Schoenberg, Boulez, and Stella. Only a few scholars—E. H. Gombrich, Michael Baxandall,

Leonard Meyer—have found mundane craft practice a fertile source of ideas about art's broader forms and uses. Perhaps the most productive way of reading classical film theory is to search out the passages that operate on this middle level, exhibiting attention to principles of texture and structure informing films.

Seen from this angle, Eisenstein's contribution stands out vividly. It constitutes classical film theory's major poetics of film. Like Aristotle, he asked certain central questions. At bottom, what is this art of cinema? Eisenstein proposed that it is a form of audiovisual spectacle drawing on representational processes akin to those in literature, music, theatre, and the graphic and plastic arts. How are films made? That is, what are the constituent parts of films, and how do those parts form significant wholes? Eisenstein disclosed many suggestive relations of part to part and part to whole: not only various types of editing but also "montage within the shot," dominant/overtone interactions, "vertical" sound/image relations, a polyphonic weave of "voices," and, at the largest scale, motivic "representations" that contributed to the emergence of an emotion-laden "image." And, like Aristotle, Eisenstein asks about the characteristic means and ends of the art in question. He suggests that the formal devices and systems that he discloses aim at the maximal excitation of the spectator—perceptual stimulation, emotional transport, intellectual awareness; at the limit, ecstasy.

Much of the value of this poetics lies in its attempt to lead us to see concrete qualities of texture and pattern. The Aristotelian distinction between form and material was central to Eisenstein's avant-garde contemporaries, and he enriched it in several ways. He analyzed film form as both a geometrical structure (as in the "canon" of five-act tragedy ruling *Potemkin*) and a dynamic, time-bound process (as in overtonal and vertical montage). He developed a conception of film form as a system of technical choices, each serving a distinct purpose under some "dominant" or "artistic image." On the material side, he sought to disclose how the physical qualities of the performer governed the possibilities of kinetic expression. He inventoried parameters of the visual image—composition, line, tonality, movement—and then sought to reduce them to principles that would explain films' effects and give directors more deliberate control. His pedagogy offered at once practical advice on planning a production and analytic concepts for bringing to light the "particularities of method" informing a work's structure.

The result was a poetics of film style unprecedented in its comprehensiveness and detail. Eisenstein used the discoveries of art history and literary and musical theory to bring out common formal problems across media. He was able to show the relevance of Piranesi, El Greco, Poe, and other artists to the problems of cinematic creation. At the same time, his intimate knowledge of filmmaking practice allowed him to start not with abstract doctrines but cinematic qualities that required exposure and explanation. He showed that explicating the principles underlying film craft produces a knowledge that is properly theoretical.

A theoretical knowledge, I am tempted to add, that subordinates political doctrine to the principles and procedures of artistic "making." Much of Eisenstein's work is anchored in Bolshevik thought and Stalinist culture, as I have suggested throughout this book. Yet instead of treating Eisenstein as simply contributing to the tradition of Marxist aesthetics, we can better account for the range and divigations of his theories by seeing notions of class struggle, dialectics, and economic determinism as grist for his idiosyncratic aesthetic system. Böde's gymnastics, Bekhterev's reflexology, Joyce's inner monologue, Lévy-Brühl's anthropology, Marr's linguistics, conceptions of "inner speech" and "imagicity" and "polyphonic voices" and "ecstasy"—along with these, aspects of the Marxist tradition became absorbed into an idiosyncratic conception of artistic practice. Eisenstein was above all a maker of films and theories, and his "Leninist formalism" mined all systems of thought, including Leninism, for their artistic possibilities.

It would be too strong to call Eisenstein the Aristotle of film theory, if only because the strict reasoning of the *Poetics* has little parallel in the polemical rhetoric or associative meanderings of Eisenstein's writing. Furthermore, whereas Aristotle offers what we might call a heavily theoretical poetics, Eisenstein works chiefly in the domain of "descriptive" poetics, delineating the functions of particular devices within the cinematic system. More faithful transmitters of the Aristotelian impulse in his milieu were the Russian Formalists, who articulated a systematic, inductive, and open-ended inquiry into literary art. Nevertheless, in Eisenstein's attempt to show what formal principles yield the most effective artworks, he brings the tradition of Aristotelian poetics into the study of cinema.

The comparison also brings out an important contribution by Eisenstein. Aristotle concentrates on the playwright's making of plots; in his system spectacle (*opsis*) is a secondary factor. Eisenstein almost exactly reverses the proportions. The "attraction" as explained in Eisenstein's 1923 essay is anti-Aristotelian in its refusal to be subordinated to plot structure. Later, when the attraction becomes a unit of spectacle to be integrated into the overall effect, Eisenstein remains less interested in plot, character, and theme than in spectacle. His "dramaturgy of film form" is really a dramaturgy of film style—of lighting, composition, framing, and editing. Later, using such concepts as *mise en scène, mise en jeu,* and *mise en geste,* Eisenstein attempts to explain how a performance is built for the audience. The writings on audiovisual montage also highlight principles of movement common to music and visual spectacle. Apart from his theories of editing, the later Eisenstein offers an analytical description of staging and performance that suggestively supplements the conception of mimetic art offered in the *Poetics.*

Eisenstein often presents his poetics in a dogmatic and incomplete way. Sometimes he simply forces a filmic problem to fit a doctrine imported from another domain—from dialectical materialism, or from Lévy-Brühl's anthropology, or from Marr's linguistics. He ignores some important techniques (such as camera movement) and never comes to grips with narrative construction (perhaps because he believed that the Formalists had satisfactorily covered that area). We may also find his poetics too prescriptive to be broadly applicable.

Nevertheless, as he argued in defending his study of "one-sided" artists such as Zola and Joyce, the issues that Eisenstein raised ought to be faced by any ambitious conception of film form and style. His theoretical writings point toward a conception of cinema sensitive to the fine grain of the medium's representational options. He reminds us that filmmaking is *masterstvo*, skilled activity, and that a theory of film can be powerful and enlightening when it pays systematic attention to the principles governing that skill.

At the end of his life, Eisenstein summed up his recurring concerns:

> The problem of landscape and of cinematic language, the bases of cinematic poetics and the aesthetics of the close-up, the principles and theory of montage, the problem of pathos-based cinema and of audiovisual counterpoint, the symphonic and structural development of color across the entire film, the notion of the musicality of the plastic image, the dramaturgical composition of the film, the principles of epic cine-poetry and of plastic allegory, and the filmic projection of abstract ideas, a state following the conquest of the filmic trope: cinematic metaphor, metonymy, and synecdoche.   (1976:20–21)

That he does not say whether he is talking about his films or his writings only illustrates how completely bound together theory and practice were for him. These problems would be pursued in detail by a film or an essay—the one by experimentation, the other by reflection and analysis.

He died while writing an essayistic letter to Kuleshov. He had just enunciated several principles—color's likeness to music, the possibility of color "lines" weaving their way through the film, color as an element in "vertical montage"—before he turned his attention to particularities:

> I think that from the point of view of method the best thing would be to show such a principle in action on a concrete example.
>   So I shall give a short description of how the color sequence was constructed in *Ivan the Terrible*.   (1948a:123)

The manuscript breaks off at this point.

The Eisenstein portrayed here, the experimentalist and poetician who sought a unity of theory and practice, reflects a still too limited knowledge of his oeuvre and its context. New documents, testimony, and points of view will undoubtedly call this portrait into question. Like other Eisensteins, mine bears the traces of larger purposes and predilections—the belief that filmmakers have a good deal to teach film scholars, the hunch that building a poetics of cinema is a fruitful undertaking, the conviction that these films retain their power to shake and transport us. Eisenstein is one of the very few figures in the history of cinema whose work will be remade, by historians and critics and viewers, for decades to come.

Chronology

1898	10 January (new calendar 22 January): E. born in Riga.
1909	Mother moves to St. Petersburg.
1915	E. enters Institute of Civil Engineering in Petrograd.
1917	Enrolls in city militia and is called up for military service.
	October: Bolshevik revolution.
1918	February: E. volunteers for Red Army work on Petrograd defenses.
	April: Beginning of Civil War.
	September: E. leaves for Northeast Front.
1919–20	Serves as soldier and director of plays for army and local theatre troupe.
1920	September: Demobilized.
	October: Appointed head of design section of Central Workers Theatre of Proletkult.
	November: End of Civil War.
1921	E. continues theatre work with Proletkult.
	March: Adoption of New Economic Policy (NEP).
	September: E. enrolls as student in Meyerhold's directing workshop.
1922	Continues theatre work; studies filmmaking briefly with Kuleshov.
1923	April–May: First performances of *The Wiseman.*
	November: Premiere of *Do You Hear, Moscow?*
1924	January: Lenin dies. Zinoviev, Kamenev, and Stalin emerge as leaders.
	February: Premiere of *Gas Masks.*
	April–November: Production of *Strike.*
	November: E. breaks with Proletkult.
1925	Filming of *The Battleship Potemkin.*
	April: Release of *Strike.*
	December: Premiere of *Battleship Potemkin.*
1926	Stalin begins to consolidate power: Zinoviev, Trotsky, and Kamenev expelled from the Politburo.
	January: Release of *Battleship Potemkin.*

E. begins work on *The General Line.*

November: Begins work on *October.*

1927   Filming of *October.*

November: First screening of early version of *October.* Trotsky and Zinoviev expelled from Party.

1928   January: Stalin orders forcible collection of grain; Trotsky banished.

March: Premiere of revised version of *October.*

May: E. appointed to teach course in direction at state film academy.

June: Resumes filming of *The General Line.*

1929   Beginning of Stalin cult; announcement of first Five-Year Plan, begun in 1928.

Spring: Stalin proposes changes in *The General Line;* filming resumes.

August: E., Alexandrov, and Tissé leave for Europe.

September–November: E. visits Switzerland and England.

October: Release of *Old and New.*

December: Stalin announces "liquidation of kulaks as a class."

1930   January–April: E., Alexandrov, and Tissé visit France, Netherlands, and Germany.

May–October: With Ivor Montagu, E. works on scripts for *Sutter's Gold* and *An American Tragedy* for Paramount; contract dissolved.

December: E., Alexandrov, and Tissé arrive in Mexico to shoot *Qué viva México!*

1931   Filming in Oaxaca, Tehuantepec, Yucatan, Merida, Tetlapayac, and Mexico City.

1932   January: Sinclair halts production of *Qué viva México!*

May: After short stay in United States, E. returns to Moscow; begins work on *MMM* and conducts courses as head of direction faculty at state film academy.

1933–34 Continues teaching, writing, and planning projects.

1934   June: Release of Sol Lesser's *Thunder over Mexico.*

August: First conference of Soviet writers; Socialist Realism adopted as creative policy.

October: E. marries Pera Attasheva.

December: Assassination of Sergei Kirov.

1935   January: All-Union Congress of Soviet Film Workers.

March: E. begins filming *Bezhin Meadow.*

1936   January: Attacks on Shostakovich's *Lady Macbeth of Mtsensk* signal new repressions in cultural sphere.

Spring: After requests for revisions in *Bezhin Meadow* script, E. drafts new version with Isaak Babel.

August: Filming on *Bezhin Meadow* resumes; first Moscow trial leads to death sentences for Zinoviev, Kamenev, and others.

1937   January: Second Moscow trial.

March: Film Committee halts *Bezhin Meadow.*

E. begins work on *Alexander Nevsky.*

1938   Production of *Alexander Nevsky.*

March: Third Moscow trial.

December: Release of *Alexander Nevsky.*

1939   February: E. receives Order of Lenin.

August: Germany and U.S.S.R. sign nonaggression pact; *Nevsky* withdrawn from distribution.

E. plans *The Great Ferghana Canal.*

1940   E. plans *A Poet's Love.*

October: Premiere of E.'s staging of *Die Walküre* at Bolshoi; appointed Artistic Director of Mosfilm.

1941   Begins work on script of *Ivan the Terrible.*

June: Germany invades U.S.S.R.

October: E. evacuated with other Mosfilm staff to Alma-Ata.

1942   Continues work on script of *Ivan.*

August: Publication of *The Film Sense* in New York.

1943–44   Filming of *Ivan the Terrible.*

1944   June: E. returns to Moscow with other Mosfilm staff.

October: First part of *Ivan* submitted to Film Committee.

1945   January: Release of *Ivan* Part I.

E. continues filming Part II.

1946   Renewed attack on "formalism" along with campaign against Western cultural influences.

January: E. receives Stalin Prize (First Class) for *Ivan* Part I.

February: At party celebrating prize, collapses with severe cardiac infarction and taken to Kremlin Hospital; while recovering, writes memoirs.

August: Party committee condemns *Ivan* Part II.

E. resumes writing and planning projects.

1947   February: With Cherkasov, discusses alterations in Part II with Stalin and associates.

E. plans further projects and continues writing.

1948   10/11 February: Dies while writing letter to Kuleshov on color.

13 February: Buried.

1953   5 March: Stalin dies.

1956   February: Khrushchev's "secret speech" on Stalin's crimes.

1958   *Ivan the Terrible* Part II released.

Filmography

Dnevnik Glumova (Glumov's Diary) (1923)

Filmed attraction for the production of *The Wiseman.* 120 meters.

Direction: Sergei Eisenstein. Photography: Boris Frantzisson.

Cast: Grigory Alexandrov, Maxim Shtraukh, Alexander Antonov, Ivan Pyriev, et al.

Stachka (Strike) (1925)

Produced by Goskino, Moscow. Premiere 19 March 1925. Released 28 April 1925. 1,969 meters.

Direction: Sergei Eisenstein. Scenario: Valery Pletnyov, Eisenstein, and the Proletkult collective. Photography: Edward Tissé. Direction assistants: Grigory Alexandrov, J. Kravtchunovsky, Alexander Levshin. Photography assistants: Vasily Levshin, Vladimir Popov. Settings: Vasily Rakhals.

Cast: Alexander Antonov (Organizer), Mikhail Gomarov (Worker), Maxim Shtraukh (Spy), Grigory Alexandrov (Foreman), Judith Glizer, et al.

Bronenosets "Potemkin" (The Battleship Potemkin) (1925)

Produced by Goskino, Moscow. Premiere 21 December 1925. Released 18 January 1926. 1,740 meters.

Direction: Sergei Eisenstein, assisted by Grigory Alexandrov. Scenario: Sergei Eisenstein, from outline by Nina Agazhanova-Shutko. Photography: Edward Tissé. Direction assistants: Alexander Antonov, Mikhail Gomarov, Alexander Levshin, Maxim Shtraukh. Titles: Nikolay Aseev and Sergei Tretyakov.

Cast: Sailors of the Black Sea Fleet of the Red Navy, citizens of Odessa, members of the Proletkult Theatre of Moscow, Alexander Antonov (Vakulinchuk), Grigory Alexandrov (Chief Officer Gilyarovsky), Vladimir Barsky, Alexander Levshin, Konstantin Feldman, Yulia Eisenstein, et al.

Oktyabr (October; also known as *Ten Days That Shook the World*) (1928)

Produced by Sovkino, Moscow. Premiere 20 January 1928. Released 14 March 1928. 2,220 meters.

Scenario and direction: Sergei Eisenstein and Grigory Alexandrov. Photography: Edward Tissé. Direction assistants: Maxim Shtraukh, Mikhail Gomarov, Ilya Trauberg. Camera assistants: Vladimir Nilsen, Vladimir Popov.

Cast: Citizens of Leningrad, V. Nikandrov (Lenin), N. Popov (Kerensky), Boris Livanov, et al.

Staroe i novoe (Old and New); also known as *Generalnaia Liniia (The General Line)* (1929)

Produced by Sovkino, Moscow. Premiere and released 7 October 1929. 2,469 meters.

Direction: Sergei Eisenstein and Grigory Alexandrov. Scenario: Sergei Eisenstein. Photography: Edward Tissé. Direction assistants: Maxim Shtraukh, Mikhail Gomarov, Alexander Antonov, A. Goncharov. Camera assistants: Vladimir Nilsen, Vladimir Popov. Sets: V. Kovrigin, Vasily Rakhals. Architecture: Andrey Burov.

Cast: Marfa Lapkina (Marfa), Vasya Buzenkov (Komsomol leader), Kostya Vasiliev (Tractor driver), Chukmarev (Kulak), Father Matvey (Priest), Khurtin (Peasant), Sukhareva (Witch), et al.

Alexander Nevsky (1938)

Produced by Mosfilm, Moscow. Premiere and released 23 November 1938. 3,044 meters.

Direction: Sergei Eisenstein, with the collaboration of D. I. Vasiliev. Scenario: Sergei Eisenstein and Pyotr Pavlenko. Photography: Edward Tissé. Music: Sergei Prokofiev. Lyrics: Vladimir Lugovsky. Settings and costumes executed from Eisenstein's sketches by Isaac Shpinel, Nikolay Solovyov, K. Yeliseev. Sound: B. Volksy, Vladimir Popov. Consultant on work with actors: Elena Telesheva.

Cast: Nikolay Cherkasov (Prince Alexander Nevsky), Nikolay Okhlopkov (Vasily Buslay), Alexander Abrikosov (Gavrilo Oleksich), Dmitry Orlov (Ignat the armorer), Vasily Novikov (Pavsha, governor of Pskov), Nikolay Arsky (Domach Tverdislavich), Varvara Massalitinova (Amelfa Timofeevna, mother of Buslay), Vera Ivasheva (Olga), Anna Danilova (Vasilisa), Vladimir Yershov (Von Balk, Grand Master of the Livonian Order), Sergei Blinnikov (Tverdilo, mayor of Pskov), Ivan Lagutin (Ananias), Lev Fenin (Bishop), Naum Rogozhin (Black-Robed Monk).

Ivan Grozny (Ivan the Terrible) Part I (1944)

Produced by Mosfilm, Moscow and Alma-Ata. Premiere 30 December 1944. Released January 1945. 2,745 meters.

Ivan Grozny (Ivan the Terrible) Part II (1946)

Produced by Mosfilm, Moscow and Alma-Ata. Banned in 1946. Released September 1958. 2,374 meters.

Direction: Sergei Eisenstein. Scenario and dialogue: Sergei Eisenstein. Associate director: V. Sveshnikov. Photography: Edward Tissé (exteriors), Andrei Moskvin (interiors). Music: Sergei Prokofiev. Lyrics: Vladimir Lugovsky. Conductor: Abram Stasevich. Direction assistants: L. Indenhom, V. Kuznetsova, Y. Bir, B. Bunaev. Cameraman: V. Dombrovsky. Assistant cameraman: F. Soluyanov. Sound recordists: V. Bogdankevich, V. Volsky. Editorial assistants: E. Tobak, L. Indenbom. Sets: Y. Spinel, from sketches by Eisenstein. Costumes: Leonid Naumova, from sketches by Eisenstein. Costume assistant: N. Buzina. Wardrobe: I. Raizman, M. Safonova. Makeup: V. Goryunov, E. Chakon. Props: V. Lomov. Production directors: A. Eidus, I. Soluyanov, I. Zakar. Floor secretary: L. Chedin. Supervisor of set building: Y. Shakhporonov. Religious and historical consultant: Archpriest P. Tsvetkov. Choreographer (Part II): R. Zakharin.

Cast: Nikolay Cherkasov (Tsar Ivan), Ludmila Tselikovskaya (Anastasia Romanovna), Serafima Birman (Efrosinia Staritsky), Pavel Kadochnikov (Vladimir Staritsky), Mikhail

Nazvanov (Andrey Kurbsky), Andrey Abrikosov (Fyodor Kolychev, later Philip, metropolitan of Moscow), Vladimir Balachov (Pyotr Volynetz), Mikhail Zharov (Malyuta Skuratov), Amvrozy Buchma (Alexei Basmanov), Mikhail Kusnetsov (Fyodor Basmanov), S. Timoshenko (Kaspar von Oldenbock, Livonian ambassador), Vsevolod Pudovkin (Nikola, a mad beggar), A. Rumnev (Foreigner), Eric Pyriev (the young Ivan), Pavel Masalsky (King Sigismund), et al.

Further Reading

1. A Life in Cinema

For a summary of Eisenstein's life, see the Chronology.

The biographical sketch in this chapter is drawn from Seton 1952; Sadoul 1960; *IP* 1:572–590; Barna 1973; Swallow 1977; Amengual 1980; Leyda and Voynow 1982; Eisenstein 1989. Eisenstein 1988b is an enlarged edition of the memoirs. Sudendorf 1975 furnishes an indispensable chronology of his career. Yurenev 1985 is a detailed biography. Yurenev 1973 provides recollections, while Shklovsky 1973 is at once a memoir and an appreciation. Fernandez 1975 is a speculative psychobiography.

On the early life, see Eisenstein 1921; Shtraukh 1940; and Yutkevich 1960. Aumont 1987 offers reflections on the memoirs.

The most comprehensive account of Proletkult is Mally 1990. On Proletkult theatre see Russell 1990. Eisenstein's Proletkult work is discussed in Dreyer 1960; Hielscher 1973; Gerould 1974; Gordon 1978; Kolchevska 1985; and Leach 1993. The first volume of the German collection of Eisenstein's writings *(S1)* contains some primary material on his Proletkult period. A rich overview of Eisenstein's relation to the theatre is offered in Lary 1990.

Tretyakov 1982 collects his plays; Tretyakov 1978 is an English translation of *Do You Hear, Moscow?* See also Kleberg 1977 and Kolchevska 1987a. Tretyakov 1977 is a collection of his writings.

On artistic culture of the 1920s, see Gleason, Kenez, and Stites 1985; Brewster 1977; Williams 1977; Willett 1978; Barron and Tuchman 1980; Conio 1987; Lawton 1988; Golomstock 1990b; and B. Taylor 1991. On Constructivism and Productivism see Lodder 1983 and Andel et al. 1990. Soviet theatre of the period is discussed in Segel 1979 and Russell 1988. On Meyerhold and Eisenstein see Worrall 1980; Leach 1989; and Picon-Vallin 1990. *Lef* and *New Lef* are discussed in Stephan 1981 and Kolchevska 1987a.

Overviews of Soviet film history are offered in Babitsky and Rimberg 1955; Leyda 1960; Kenez 1992; and Stites 1992. Taylor and Christie 1988 provides an abundance of documents. Filmmaking of the 1920s is discussed in R. Taylor 1979b; and Youngblood 1985,

1992. Thompson 1992 examines industrial trends of the decade, while Thompson 1993 surveys the reception of Eisenstein's films outside the U.S.S.R.

Albéra 1976 offers a detailed dossier on an important stretch of Eisenstein's travels. The relations between Eisenstein and Joyce are summarized in Werner 1990.

Eisenstein's stay in Hollywood is chronicled in Montagu 1967. This volume also includes the scenarios for *Sutter's Gold* and *An American Tragedy*. On *Sutter's Gold* see also Richardson 1980. On *The Glass House* see Eisenstein 1979.

On the Mexican project see Eisenstein 1937d and 1951; Seton 1953; Leyda 1958; Geduld and Gottesman 1970; Alexandrov 1979; Bixby 1979; Richardson 1989; Karetnikova and Steinmetz 1991.

The era of proletarian cultural organizations is discussed throughout Fitzpatrick 1978. Sokolov 1930 and Anisimov 1931 exemplify attacks on Eisenstein and Left cinema. Shumyatsky's career is analyzed in R. Taylor 1986.

The literature on Socialist Realism is considerable; recent researchers stress the continuity between the 1930s doctrines and the militant aspirations of the 1920s avant-garde. See Ermolaev 1963; Mathewson 1975; Brewster 1976; Clark 1978 and 1981; Robin 1986; Groys 1990 and 1992; Golomstock 1990a; and Bown 1991. Significant speeches from the 1934 Writers' Congress are gathered in Gorky et al. 1935.

On *MMM* see Eisenstein 1980c and 1988a. On *Bezhin Meadow* see *IP* 6:129–152; Amengual 1980:290–306; Heil 1990:367–377; and Simon and Stirk forthcoming. On the 1934–1939 Terror see Conquest 1990; he discusses the fates of cultural figures on pp. 291–307. Eisenstein's *Valkyrie* staging is discussed in Shpiller 1980 and in a dossier in *Sovetskaya muzyka* no. 9 (1979):68–98. Stalin's interest in national heroes is discussed in Yaresh 1956; Struve 1971; and especially Tucker 1990. For background on Stalinist culture, see Fitzpatrick 1976 and Günther 1990. Eisenstein's last days are described in Vaisfeld 1969.

Collections of Eisenstein's drawings include Eisenstein 1961; Karetnikova and Kleiman 1969; Aumont, Eisenschitz, and Narboni 1978; and De Santi 1981. Many also adorn Leyda and Voynow 1982. On Eisenstein's drawings, see Albéra 1978; Elliott 1988; and Kleiman 1988.

Eisenstein's politics are discussed by Dmitri Shostakovich at various points in Volkov 1979. (This volume, purporting to be a transcript of Shostakovich's unguarded reminiscences, has not been firmly established as authentic.) As for Eisenstein's homosexuality, Trauberg refers to it in Van Houten 1989. An article attributed to Shtraukh's widow, Judith Glizer, maintains that Eisenstein had several lovers, including Cherkasov (Petronius 1990). See also Sinko 1977.

On the relation of Bogdanov and Bukharin to systems thinking, see Susiluoto 1982. Bely's "scientific" poetics is explained in Bely 1909 and 1929. Erlich 1981 and Steiner 1984 are in-depth treatments of Russian Formalist literary theory. Shklovsky's "How *Don Quixote* Is Made" is to be found in Shklovsky 1925:72–100. Mayakovsky 1926 remains a fascinating exercise in Constructivist poetics. The standard attack on the conception of art as craft is Collingwood 1938; Howard 1982 fruitfully reconsiders the problem.

Valuable surveys of Soviet history are Schapiro 1971; Fitzpatrick 1982; Hosking 1985; and Heller and Nekrich 1986.

2. Monumental Heroics

Information on Soviet artistic trends of the 1920s can be found in Golomstock 1990b; Günther 1990; Clark 1981; Stephan 1981. On the mass spectacles, see Tolstoy et al. 1990. An excellent examination of Soviet iconoclasm is Stites 1989:65–97. For discussion of

1920s film norms see Bordwell 1985b:234–273; Burch 1991:114–137; Heil 1991; and Tsikounas 1992.

Eisenstein's scripts for *Battleship Potemkin* and *October* have been translated in Eisenstein 1974. The volume also includes useful background on the films' production and the script for *October*'s unproduced second part. Eisenstein 1934f is the literary script of *Old and New.*

A major historical document on the silent films in general is Ivan Anisimov's 1931 attack, "The Films of Eisenstein," published in English in *International Literature* no. 3 (1931) and reprinted in Seton 1952:494–503. Technical aspects are illuminated in Edward Tissé 1956. On the epic tendencies in the films, see Newman 1986:399–447. On Eisenstein's stylistics see Burch 1991:46–69. The films' representation of women is discussed in Mayne 1989. A wide-ranging examination, with specimen analyses of sequences from *October* and *Old and New,* is Albéra 1990b. In addition, see Lawder 1975; Eagle 1984; and Tsikounas 1992.

Strike has received little detailed discussion in the Anglo-American critical literature. Useful pieces include Montagu 1956; Bonitzer 1971; O'Toole 1977; and Reeder 1989. On the film's debts to Constructivism see Lawder 1967. Amiard-Chevrel 1990 offers a detailed analysis. See also Bonitzer 1971. Important contemporary reactions are Kuleshov 1973:137–140; and Shklovsky 1926a:5–6.

On *Potemkin,* Marshall 1978 surveys the film's international impact and includes important memoirs. Mayer 1972, a shot-by-shot transcript of the MoMA print, is indispensable for close study. *Potemkin* is discussed from a Deconstructionist perspective in Selden 1982.

Although there has been surprisingly little analysis of *Potemkin, October* has undergone close critical scrutiny. Three French scholars have collaborated on two volumes of textual analysis: Sorlin and Ropars 1976; and Lagny, Ropars, and Sorlin 1979. The first volume's dissection of the opening has been translated into English (Ropars 1978–79). Sorlin 1980 compares *October* with Pudovkin's *End of St. Petersburg.* Tsivian 1993 traces sources of the film's images. On "For God and Country," apart from Carroll 1973, see Roth-Lindberg 1987. Mayakovsky's poem *Fine!* originally titled *October* and performed as part of the anniversary ceremonies, has interesting resemblances to Eisenstein's film; see Mayakovsky 1986:207–286; and Henderson 1978.

Old and New is discussed in Kuiper 1962; Kepley 1974; and Burns 1981. Responding to an earlier version of Albéra 1977 are Narboni 1976 and Bonitzer 1976. Aumont 1987:73–107 analyzes one sequence, while Sitney 1990:50–52 compares certain passages with the work of Dovzhenko. Valuable background on class differentiations among the peasantry is provided in Lewin 1965. On literary parallels to the film see Clark 1978:191–196.

3. Seizing the Spectator

For introductions to the aesthetics of classical film theory, see Andrew 1976 and Carroll 1988b. Selezneva 1972 surveys Eisenstein's theoretical context.

On theories of Soviet theatre of Eisenstein's period, see Segel 1979; Rudnitsky 1988; Russell and Barrett 1990; Yampolsky 1991. Carter 1924 remains a useful source. Hamon 1978 relates Eisenstein's cinematic montage to his theatre practice.

Lipps's doctrine of empathy and subsequent revisions of it are discussed in Fizer 1981:45–53. For background on the debates around reflexology, see Bauer 1952 and Kozulin 1984. Pavlov's ideas are engagingly summarized in Gray 1980. Bekhterev is discussed at length in Bauer 1952; Rahmani 1973; and Kozulin 1984. See also Bekhterev 1932.

Böde's *Expression-Gymnastics* is available in an English translation (1931). Eisenstein's relation to Freud is discussed in François Albéra's introduction to Eisenstein 1934g.

Constructivist principles of montage are analyzed in several essays in Billeter et al. 1978; see in particular Pastorello 1978. See also Albéra 1990a and Tupitsyn 1992. On montage in Eisenstein's theory, see Aumont 1987.

Versions of Eisenstein's "Dramaturgy of Film Form" are collated and compared in Albéra 1990b:13–109. The rest of the book provides a wide-ranging examination of Constructivist strains in Eisenstein's theories and films.

An early discussion of Eisenstein's conception of the overtone is Aksenov 1940. Thompson 1981 and Bordwell 1988 treat dominant/overtone interplay as dynamics between particular compositional factors rather than as emergent qualities.

The debates between Mechanists and Dialecticians are reviewed in Copleston 1986:313–351. See also the indispensable Wetter 1958. Ahlberg 1962 gives a detailed account of struggle on "the philosophical front." Controversies in the psychological community are surveyed in Bauer 1952 and Kozulin 1984. Joravsky 1978 examines the late 1920s. Eisenstein's interest in Kurt Lewin and Gestalt psychology is treated in Bulgakowa 1989 and van Elterin and Lück 1990.

Soviet views of prerevolutionary culture are surveyed in Thomson 1978. Albéra 1973:42–63 offers a valuable analysis of Eisenstein's Hegelian side.

4. Practical Aesthetics

On Meyerhold's pedagogy, see Leach 1989; on its relation to Eisenstein, see Kozlov 1987. Eisenstein's changing relation to Stanislavsky's doctrines is reviewed in Tereshkovich 1978.

Many stenograms of Eisenstein's course sessions remain unpublished. *Direction* (*IP* 4) and Nizhny 1958, the basic sources for this chapter, remain the most accessible documents of Eisenstein's pedagogy. Some of the direction exercises are available in French translation in *MA*. Romm's preface to volume 4 has been translated into French (Romm 1966). Pipinashvili 1967 offers information about the *Last Supper* exercise. See also Marshall 1949.

Véronneau 1973 is a general discussion. Comolli 1971 interprets Eisenstein's pedagogy as an exercise in materialist aesthetics. The importance of the *Direction* volume in Eisenstein's thought is discussed in Grossi 1984. Lary 1986 has important things to say about the Dostoevsky études. Kepley forthcoming offers a historical discussion of the VGIK course.

5. Cinema as Synthesis

Changes in philosophical doctrine during this period are reviewed in Wetter 1958 and Bochenskí 1963. For the psychological scene, apart from sources mentioned in Chapter 3, see Payne 1968 and Kozulin 1990.

On Socialist Realist aesthetics, particularly useful works are Swiderski 1979; Golomstock 1990b; Günther 1990; Bown 1991; and Groys 1992. A useful document from the period, expressing early hopes for a latitude that was to be denied in practice, is Lunacharsky 1933. Brewster 1976 discusses the academicism of Socialist Realism. The difference between a narrow and broad construal of Socialist Realism in the visual arts is explored in Valkenier 1977:165–177.

An example of the Hegelian influence on Socialist Realist aesthetics of this period is Lifshitz 1938. A good introduction to the work of Belinsky is Terras 1974. On Potebnya, see Fizer 1987. On Lévy-Brühl, see Lévy-Brühl 1985. Marr is treated in L'Hermitte 1987 and Simmons 1951.

Wollen 1972:19–70 traces various strands in Eisenstein's thought. The concept of ecstasy is usefully discussed in Aumont 1987:58–60; Eagle 1987; Lövgren 1987; and Montani 1990.

6. History and Tragedy

On Socialist Realist literature, see Maguire 1968; Mathewson 1975; Clark 1981; Robin 1986 and 1988. Socialist Realism in painting is discussed by Higgens 1971; more revisionist accounts are Bowlt 1972; Guldberg 1986; Golomstock 1990b; and Bown 1991. For discussions of the doctrine's effects on music, see Schwarz 1972 and I. MacDonald 1990. Stalinist historiography is discussed at length in Tucker 1990. A brief survey of Socialist Realist film genres is R. Taylor 1984–85.

Versions of *Qué viva México!* are compared in Bixby 1979. Its principal incarnations are *Thunder over Mexico* (1933), *Death Day* (1933), *Time in the Sun* (1939), and Alexandrov's reconstruction *Qué viva México!* (1979). Jay Leyda created *Eisenstein's Mexican Film: Episodes for Study* (1957) from the project's remaining footage, which Sinclair donated to the Museum of Modern Art in 1953.

Eisenstein's work on the script of *Bezhin Meadow* is discussed in Heil 1990:364–377. See also D. Robinson 1968 and Amengual 1980:290–306. The *Bezhin Meadow* study film circulated in the West was compiled by Sergei Yutkevich and Naum Kleiman. It is a creative reconstruction of the first version of the script, with one sequence from the second version interpolated (Swallow 1977:120–121).

For the script of *Nevsky*, including the original ending, see Eisenstein 1974. Leyda 1965 offers information on the missing reel. Balter 1983 is a psychoanalytic interpretation, Puiseux 1984 an ideological one. Roberts 1977 and Mowitt 1992:187–213 analyze the score.

The published script of *Ivan the Terrible* is translated as Eisenstein 1943. Eisenstein 1970 is a largely accurate shot-by-shot transcript. Birman 1975 is a memoir. Portions of Eisenstein's working notes are translated in Lary 1986. See also Eleonora Tissé 1987.

The most detailed study of *Ivan* in any Western language is Thompson 1981, which examines the film from the standpoint of a revised Russian Formalism. Roberge 1980, another book-length study, is strong on analysis of dramatic progression. Peatman 1975 considers the work from several angles and is especially informative on musical matters. Historical background may be found in Leyda 1959; Yanov 1981; Kozlov 1990; and Uhlenbruch 1990 (especially good on the 1940s Ivan cult). Oudart 1970; Britton 1977; Kinder 1986; Aumont 1987:107–144; and Christie 1987 offer psychosexual interpretations. Kozlov 1987 treats Ivan as a Meyerhold surrogate. Elizabethan influences on Eisenstein's film are discussed in Christensen 1990; and Lary 1990:111–123. On stylistic processes in *Ivan*, besides Thompson and Peatman, see Bordwell 1984.

Eisenstein's work with Prokofiev is discussed in Levaco 1973; Gallez 1978; Stegemann 1978; and H. Robinson 1984. In May 1939 Prokofiev conducted the first performance of his cantata based on the score for *Nevsky* (op. 78). It has been a concert favorite ever since. Since 1987 the film has occasionally been shown accompanied by live orchestra and chorus (see Shear 1987). Prokofiev's music for *Ivan* has had a more varied career. He reused material in the opera *War and Peace* and the ballet *The Stone Flower*. Abram Stasevich arranged an oratorio based on the score and on some fragments not used in the film, publishing the piece in 1962. In 1975 the Bolshoi premiered a ballet based on the

Ivan score; interestingly, its plot does not include the court intrigues of Part II. The ballet was revised and filmed in 1977 by Vadim Derbenev and Yuri Grigorovich. In 1991 Christopher Palmer adapted Prokoviev's score once again, this time as a "concert scenario."

7. The Making and Remaking of Sergei Eisenstein

Christie offers a useful review of Western conceptions of Soviet cinema in Taylor and Christie 1988:1–17. See also Tsikounas 1992. On the changing state of Eisenstein scholarship see Amengual 1975; Goodwin 1981; and Taylor 1988.

An updating of the attack on montage aesthetics can be found in Perkins 1972; its concerns are echoed in Tarkovsky 1989. For a general discussion of developments of the Bazinian tradition, see Bordwell 1985a. An attempt to transcend the terms of this debate can be seen in Mitry 1963–1965, a treatise which critically assimilates both Bazinian and Eisensteinian tendencies.

Eisenstein's importance for Third World film is discussed in Perez 1974 and Gutiérrez Alea 1981. His political modernism forms the subject of Perlmutter 1975; Michelson 1976; Sperber 1977; and Goodwin 1978a and 1978b.

On Eisenstein's relation to Soviet structuralism see Zholkovsky and Shcheglov 1961; Segal 1968; and Levin 1969. The most comprehensive argument for Eisenstein's place in a Soviet semiotic tradition is Ivanov 1976; a brief discussion is Vroon and Vroon 1976. See Zholkovsky 1992 for a reconsideration in the light of recent work on 1930s cultural policy. On Eisenstein's relation to Derrida see Ulmer 1985 and Brunette and Will 1989.

The distinctions among historical, theoretical, and descriptive poetics are made in Hrushovski 1976. Carroll 1988a argues that aesthetics could profit from reorienting itself toward what I have been calling poetics. Bordwell 1989a and 1989b:263–274 discuss prospects for a contemporary poetics of film.

For a thorough discussion of the film's treatment of history, see James Goodwin's *Eisenstein, Cinema, and History* (Urbana: University of Illinois Press, 1993), which was published while this book was in press.

Bibliography

Works by Eisenstein

Because this book is designed primarily for readers of English and French, most of the sources cited below are translations. Original Russian sources are provided for texts unavailable in those languages.

Published works are listed by the year of original publication. Most unpublished works are listed by the year of composition. Works whose date of composition is uncertain or whose composition spanned several years are listed by the date of first (usually posthumous) publication.

Comprehensive bibliographies of Eisenstein's writings can be found in *FE*:188–221 and Aumont 1987:223–235.

1921	"I vot, nakonets, ia zdes" (And now, I'm here). *Iskusstvo kino* no. 1 (1988):67–72.
1922	"The Eighth Art: On Expressionism, America, and of course Chaplin." Written with Sergei Yutkevich. In *W*:29–32.
1923a	"Expressive Movement." Written with Sergei Tretyakov. *Millennium Film Journal* no. 3 (Winter/Spring 1979):30–38.
1923b	"The Montage of Attractions." In *W*:33–38.
1924	"The Montage of Film Attractions." In *W*:39–58.
1925a	"Interview with the Director S. M. Eisenstein." *Kino-nedelya* no. 2 (1925). In *E2*:1–3.
1925b	Letter to the editors. *Kino-nedelya* no. 10 (1925). *E2*:5–8.
1925c	"The Method of Making a Workers' Film." In *W*:65–66.
1925d	"The Problem of the Materialist Approach to Form." In *W*:59–64.
1926a	"Béla Forgets the Scissors." In *W*:77–81.
1926b	"Constanṭa (Whither *The Battleship Potemkin*)." In *W*:67–70.
1926c	"Eisenstein on Eisenstein, the Director of *Potemkin*." In *W*:74–76.

1926d   *Potemkin.* Trans. Gillon R. Aitken. London: Lorrimer, 1968. Ex post facto transcript of the film orig. pub. in Russian.

1927a   "My rabotaem na odny i tu zhe auditoriyu . . ." (We are all working for the same audience). *Iskusstvo kino* no. 1 (1988):73–81.

1927b   "Notes for a Film of *Capital.*" *October* 2 (Summer 1976):3–26.

1928a   "In the Battles for *October.*" In *ADE:*43–50.

1928b   "Literature and Cinema." *W:*95–99.

1928c   "Our *October:* Beyond the Played and the Non-Played." In *W:*101–106.

1928d   "Statement on Sound." Written with Vsevolod Pudovkin and Grigory Alexandrov. In *W:*113–114.

1928e   "The Twelfth Year." Written with Grigory Alexandrov. In *W:*123–126.

1928f   "An Unexpected Juncture." In *W:*115–122.

1928g   "We Are Waiting." Written with Grigory Alexandrov. In Taylor and Christie 1988:218.

1928h   "Zola i kino" (Zola and the cinema). *Voprosy literatury* no. 1 (1968):98–103.

1929a   *"The Arsenal.*" In *W:*136–137.

1929b   "Beyond the Shot." In *W:*138–150.

1929c   "The Dramaturgy of Film Form." In *W:*161–180.

1929d   "An Experiment Intelligible to the Millions." In Taylor and Christie 1988: 254–257.

1929e   "The Fourth Dimension in Cinema." In *W:*181–194.

1929f   "Imitation as Mastery." Lecture at La Sarraz Conference on Independent Film. In Christie and Taylor 1993:66–71.

1929g   "The New Language of Cinematography." In *FE:*32–34.

1929h   "Perspectives." In *W:*151–160.

1930a   "The Principles of the New Russian Cinema." In *W:*195–202.

1930b   "Soviet Cinema." In *FE:*20–31.

1932a   "Help Yourself!" In *W:*219–237.

1932b   "In the Interests of Form." In *W:*238–242.

1933a   "An Attack by Class Allies." In *W:*261–275.

1933b   "Moscou à travers les ages." In *ADE:*61–68.

1933c   "Vozvrashchenie soldata fronta" (Return of the soldier from the front). In *IP* 4:27–535.

1934a   "'Eh!' On the Purity of Film Language." In *W:*285–295.

1934b   "Eisenstein on Joyce: Sergei Eisenstein's Lecture on James Joyce at the State Institute of Cinematography November 1, 1934." *James Joyce Quarterly* 24, no. 2 (Winter 1987):133–142.

1934c   "Excerpts from Eisenstein's Lectures at the Institute of Cinematography, Autumn 1934." In Seton 1952:486–493.

1934d   "GTK-GIK-VGIK; Past-Present-Future." In *FE:*66–76.

1934e   "'Katerina Izmaylova' i 'Dama s kameliyami'" (*Katerina Ismailova* and *The Lady with the Camelias*). In *IP* 4:536–604.

1934f   *"Old and New.*" In Lewis Jacobs, ed., *Film Writing Forms.* New York: Gotham Book Mart, 1934, 24–39, 61.

1934g   "Sergei Eisenstein, Wilhelm Reich. Correspondence." *Screen* 22, no. 4 (1981):79–86.

1934h   "'Tereza Raken'" (*Thérèse Raquin*). In *IP* 4:605–630.

1934i   "Through Theatre to Cinema." In *FF:*3–17.

1935a   "Film Form: New Problems." In *FF:*122–149.

1935b	"The Prometheus of Mexican Painting." In *FE*:222–231.
1937a	"Laocoön." In *TTM*:109–202.
1937b	"The Mistakes of *Bezhin Meadow*." In Seton 1952:372–377.
1937c	"Montage 1937." In *TTM*:11–58.
1937d	"On Color." In *TTM*:254–267.
1937e	"Rhythm." In *TTM*:227–248.
1937f	"Tolstoy's 'Anna Karenina'—The Races." In *TTM*:281–295.
1937g	"Yermolova." In *TTM*:82–105.
1939a	*"Alexander Nevsky."* In *NFD*:32–43.
1939b	"Lenin v nashikh serdtsakh" (Lenin in our hearts). In *IP* 5:253–255.
1939c	"Lessons from Literature." In *FE*:77–84.
1939d	"Montage 1938." In *TTM*:296–326.
1939e	"My Subject Is Patriotism." *International Literature* no. 2:90–93.
1939f	"On the Structure of Things." In *NN*:3–37.
1939g	"Pushkin the Montageur." In *TTM*:203–223.
1940a	"Achievement." In *FF*:179–194.
1940b	"The Birth of an Artist." In *NFD*:140–145.
1940c	"Dvadtsat'" (Twenty). In *IP* 5:98–109.
1940d	"The Embodiment of a Myth." In *FE*:84–91.
1940e	"Once Again on the Structure of Things." In *NN*:200–215.
1940f	"Poor Salieri (Instead of a Dedication)." In *NN*:1–2.
1940g	"Problems of Soviet Historical Films." *Film Criticism* 3, no. 2 (Fall 1978):1–16.
1940h	"Vertical Montage [Part One]." In *TTM*:327–349.
1940i	"Vertical Montage [Part Two]." In *TTM*:349–370.
1940j	"Voploshchenie Mifa" (Embodiment of a myth). Program for *Die Walküre*. Moscow: Bolshoi Theatre, 1940, 13–18.
1941a	*On the Composition of the Short Fiction Scenario.* Trans. Alan Y. Upchurch. Calcutta: Seagull, 1984.
1941b	"Vertical Montage [Part Three]." In *TTM*:370–399.
1942	*"Ivan Grozny."* VOKS Bulletin no. 7/8:60–62.
1943	*Ivan the Terrible: A Screenplay.* Trans. Ivor Montagu and Herbert Marshall. New York: Simon and Schuster, 1962.
1944	"Dickens, Griffith, and the Film Today." In *FF*:195–255.
1945a	"Nonindifferent Nature." In *NN*:216–396.
1945b	"The Twelve Apostles." In *NFD*:9–31.
1946a	"Elaboration des couleurs dans la scène du 'Festin' *(Ivan le Terrible)* (Travail post-analytique)." In *MA*:236–243.
1946b	"First Letter about Color." *Film Reader* no. 2 (1977):181–184.
1946c	"How I Became a Film Director." In *NFD*:9–18.
1946d	"I syuzhet, i tsvet" (Both syuzhet and color). In *IP* 3:512–530.
1946e	Letter to Elizabeth Eagin. Leyda Collection, series B, Museum of Modern Art, New York City.
1946f	"'Le Père Goriot' et la couleur dans *Ivan le Terrible*." In *MA*:207–236.
1946g	"Planirovka" (Planning). In *IP* 4:709–716.
1946h	"P-R-K-V-F." In *NFD*:149–167.
1946i	"Problems of Composition." In *FE*:155–183.
1946j	Reply to criticism of *Ivan*. In Seton 1952:461–463.
1946k	"True Ways of Invention *(Alexander Nevsky)*." In *NFD*:43–52.

1947a   "Always Forward." In *NFD*:203–208.
1947b   Cable to Jay Leyda, 14 March 1947. Leyda collection, series B, Museum of
            Modern Art, New York City.
1947c   "Conspectus of Lectures on the Psychology of Art." In *PC*:16–25.
1947d   "A Conversation with Stalin, Molotov and Zhdanov about Eisenstein's 'Ivan
            the Terrible' (Part Two): Transcript." With Nikolay Cherkasov. *Moscow
            News* no. 32 (14–21 August 1988):8–9.
1947e   "Extrait d'un cours sur la musique et la couleur dans *Ivan le Terrible*." In
            ADE:271–311.
1947f   "Ocherednaya lektsiya" (A routine lecture). In *IP* 4:675–708.
1947g   "Pathos." In *NN*:38–199.
1947h   "Purveyors of Spiritual Poison." *Sight and Sound* 16 (Autumn):103–105.
1947i   "Vyatskaya loshchadka" (The little horse of Viatka). In *IP* 3:500–530.
1948a   "Colour Film." In *NFD*:119–128.
1948b   "K voprosy mizanshcheny: 'Mise en jeu' i 'mise en geste'" (The question of
            mise en scène: *Mise en jeu* and *mise en geste*). In *IP* 4:717–740.
1951   *Que viva Mexico!* London: Vision.
1961   *Drawings.* Moscow: Iskusstvo.
1964   *Immoral Memories: An Autobiography.* Trans. Herbert Marshall. Boston:
            Houghton Mifflin, 1983.
1970   *Ivan the Terrible: A Film by Sergei Eisenstein.* New York: Simon and Schuster.
1974   *Three Films: Battleship Potemkin, October, Alexander Nevsky.* Ed. Jay Leyda.
            Trans. Diana Matias. New York: Harper & Row.
1976   "Dédicace." In *La non-indifférente nature 1.* Trans. Luda Schnitzer and Jean
            Schnitzer. Paris: Union Générale d'Editions: 17–24.
1977–1985   *Mémoires.* Trans. Jacques Aumont, Michèle Bokanowski, and Claude Ibrahi-
            moff. 3 vols. Paris: Julliard. Reprinted in one volume in 1989.
1979   "Stekliannyi Dom" *(The Glass House). Iskusstvo kino* no. 3 (March):94–113.
1980a   "El greco y el cine." In *CIN*:15–104.
1980b   "Ermolova." In *CIN*:221–248.
1980c   "*MMM.*" *Kino* 15 (April):26–36.
1986a   "Du cinéma en relief." In *MA*:97–158.
1986b   *Eisenstein on Disney.* Ed. Jay Leyda. Trans. Alan Upchurch. Calcutta: Seagull.
1988a   "*MMM*: Un scénario inédit de S. M. Eisenstein." *Archives* no. 17/18 (No-
            vember–December):2–27.
1988b   *Yo—Ich Selbst: Memoiren.* 2 vols. Ed. Naum Kleiman and Valentina Korshu-
            nova. Trans. Regine Kühn and Rita Braun. Frankfurt: Fischer. Enlarged edi-
            tion of the *Mémoires,* 1977–1985.

Other Works

Agee, James. 1964. *Agee on Film: Reviews and Comments.* Boston: Beacon Press.
Ahlberg, René. 1962. "The Forgotten Philosopher: Abram Deborin." In Leopold Labedz,
      ed., *Revisionism: Essays on the History of Marxist Ideas.* New York: Praeger, 126–141.
Aksenov, I. 1940. "Polifoniya 'Bronenostsa Potemkina'" (The polyphonic structure of
      Battleship Potemkin). *Iskusstvo kino* no. 12:19–23.
Albéra, François. 1973. *Notes sur l'esthétique d'Eisenstein.* Bron: CERT.
———— 1976. "Eisenstein en Suisse." *Travelling* no. 48 (Winter):89–119.

———— 1977. "Eisenstein est-il stalinien?" *Dialectiques* no. 20:26–39.

———— 1978. "Eisenstein: The Graphic Question." In Christie and Elliott 1988:119–129.

———— 1990a. "Du cinéma des constructivistes au cinéma constructiviste." In Conio 1990:200–211.

———— 1990b. *Eisenstein et le constructivisme russe.* Lausanne: L'Age d'Homme.

Alexandrov, Grigory. 1976. *Le cinéaste et son temps.* Trans. Antoine Garcia. Moscow: Progrès, 1979.

———— 1979. "Na montazhnom stole: fil'm S. M. Eizenšhteina" (On the editing table: The film of S. M. Eisenstein). *Iskusstvo kino* no. 2 (February):93–99.

Amengual, Barthélémy. 1975. "Eisenstein en français." *Cinéma* no. 203 (November):60–78.

———— 1980. *Que viva Eisenstein!* Lausanne: L'Age d'Homme.

Amiard-Chevrel, Claudine. 1990. "Masses en action, action sur les masses: Autour de 'La grève' d'Eisenstein." In Amiard-Chevrel, ed., *Théâtre et cinéma années vingt: Une quête de la modernité.* Vol. 2. Lausanne: L'Age d'Homme, 75–177.

Andel, Jaroslav, et al. 1990. *Art into Life: Russian Constructivism, 1914–1932.* Seattle: Henry Art Gallery.

Andrew, Dudley. 1976. *The Major Film Theories: An Introduction.* New York: Oxford University Press.

Anisimov, Ivan. 1931. "The Films of Eisenstein." In Seton 1952:494–503.

Anonymous. 1929. "*Battleship Potemkin.*" *London Film Society Programmes, 1925–1939.* New York: Arno, 1972, 130–131.

———— 1930. "*The General Line.*" *London Film Society Programmes, 1925–1939.* New York: Arno, 1972, 157–158.

———— 1960. *The Song of Igor's Campaign.* Trans. Vladimir Nabokov. New York: Vintage.

Aumont, Jacques. 1987. *Montage Eisenstein.* Trans. Lee Hildreth, Constance Penley, and Andrew Ross. Bloomington: Indiana University Press.

———— 1989. *L'oeil interminable: Cinéma et peinture.* Paris: Séguier.

Aumont, Jacques, Bernard Eisenschitz, and Jean Narboni. 1978. *S. M. Eisenstein: Esquisses et dessins.* Paris: L'Etoile.

Babitsky, Paul, and John Rimberg. 1955. *The Soviet Film Industry.* New York: Praeger.

Bachelis, Ilya. 1945. "The First Experiment in Producing a Film Tragedy." *Film Chronicle* no. 2 (February):6–13.

Balter, L. 1983. "*Alexander Nevsky.*" *Film Culture* no. 70/71:43–87.

Barna, Yon. 1973. *Eisenstein.* Trans. Lise Hunter. Bloomington: Indiana University Press.

Barr, Charles. 1963. "CinemaScope: Before and After." *Film Quarterly* 16, no. 4 (Summer):4–24.

Barron, Stephanie, and Maurice Tuchman, eds. 1980. *The Avant-Garde in Russia, 1910–1930.* Cambridge, Mass.: MIT Press.

Barthes, Roland. 1970. "The Third Meaning." In *Image Music Text.* Trans. Stephen Heath. New York: Hill and Wang, 1977, 52–68.

Bassekhes, A. 1935. "Painting." In C. G. Holme, ed., *Art in the U.S.S.R.: Architecture, Sculpture, Painting, Graphic Arts, Theatre, Film, Crafts.* London: The Studio, 27–33.

Baudry, Pierre. 1971. "Notes sur 'Alexandre Nevski.'" *Cahiers du cinéma* no. 226–227 (January–February):39–41.

Bauer, Raymond. 1952. *The New Man in Soviet Psychology.* Cambridge, Mass.: Harvard University Press.

Bazin, André. 1967. *What Is Cinema?* Ed. and trans. Hugh Gray. Berkeley: University of California Press.

——— 1982. *The Cinema of Cruelty: From Buñuel to Hitchcock*. Ed. François Truffaut. Trans. Sabine d'Estrée. New York: Seaver.

Bekhterev, V. M. 1932. *General Principles of Human Reflexology: An Introduction to the Objective Study of Personality*. Trans. Emma Murphy and William Murphy. New York: International Publishers.

Bely, Andrey. 1909. "Lyric Poetry and Experiment." In Steven Cassedy, ed. and trans., *Selected Essays of Andrey Bely*. Berkeley: University of California Press, 1985, 222–273.

——— 1929. *Ritm kak dialektika i Mednyi vsadnik* (Rhythm as dialectics and *The Bronze Horseman*). Moscow: Federatsiya.

Bettetini, Gianfranco. 1973. *The Language and Technique of the Film*. Trans. David Osmond-Smith. The Hague: Mouton.

Billeter, E., et al. 1978. *Collage et montage au théâtre et les autres arts*. Lausanne: L'Age d'Homme.

Billington, James H. 1966. *The Icon and the Axe: An Interpretive History of Russian Culture*. New York: Vintage.

Birman, Serafina. 1975. "Life's Gift of Encounters." *Soviet Literature* no. 3:74–119.

Bixby, Barbara Evans. 1979. "The Weave of the Serape: Sergei Eisenstein's *Qué viva México!* as Multitext." Ph.D. diss., University of Florida.

Bochenskí, J. M. 1963. *Soviet Russian Dialectical Materialism*. Dortrecht: Reidel.

Böde, Rudolf. 1931. *Expression-Gymnastics*. Trans. Sonya Forthal and Elizabeth Waterman. New York: Barnes.

Bogdanov, Alexander. 1974. "Le prolétariat et l'art." *Action poétique* no. 59 (September):81.

Bolshakov, I. 1978. "Eisenstein Wanted to Make a Film on Lawrence of Arabia." *Current Digest of the Soviet Press* 30, no. 5 (1 March):11–12.

Bonitzer, Pascal. 1971. "Systeme de 'La grève.'" *Cahiers du cinéma* no. 226–227 (January–February):43–44.

——— 1976. "Les machines e(x)tatiques (Macroscopie et signification)." *Cahiers du cinéma* no. 271 (November):22–25.

Bordwell, David. 1975. "Eisenstein's Epistemological Shift." *Screen* 15, no. 4 (Winter):29–46.

——— 1984. "Narration and Scenography in the Later Eisenstein." *Millennium Film Journal* no. 13 (Fall/Winter):62–80.

——— 1985a. "Mise-en-scène Criticism and Widescreen Aesthetics." *Velvet Light Trap* no. 21:118–125.

——— 1985b. *Narration in the Fiction Film*. Madison: University of Wisconsin Press.

——— 1988. *Ozu and the Poetics of Cinema*. Princeton: Princeton University Press.

——— 1989a. "Historical Poetics of Cinema." In R. Barton Palmer, ed., *The Cinematic Text: Methods and Approaches*. New York: AMS Press, 369–398.

——— 1989b. *Making Meaning: Inference and Rhetoric in the Interpretation of Cinema*. Cambridge, Mass.: Harvard University Press.

Bowlt, John. 1972. "The Virtues of Soviet Realism." *Art in America* 60, no. 6 (November):100–107.

——— 1980. "Russian Art in the Nineteen Twenties." *Soviet Union/Union Soviétique* 7, nos. 1–2:175–194.

Bown, Matthew Cullerne. 1991. *Art under Stalin*. Oxford: Phaidon.

Brakhage, Stan. 1963. *Metaphors on Vision*. Ed. P. Adams Sitney. New York: Film Culture.

Braun, Edward. 1979. *The Theatre of Meyerhold: Revolution on the Modern Stage*. New York: Drama Book Specialists.

Brewster, Ben. 1975. "Editorial Note." *Screen* 15, no. 4:29–32.

——— 1976. "The Soviet State, the Communist Party, and the Arts, 1917–1936." *Red Letters* no. 3 (Autumn):9.

——— 1977. Introduction to "Documents from *Novy Lef.*" In John Ellis, ed., *Screen Reader 1: Cinema/Ideology/Politics*. London: SEFT, 290–297.

Britton, Andrew. 1977. "Sexuality and Power or the Two Others." *Framework* no. 6 (Autumn):7–11, 39.

Brunette, Peter, and David Will. 1989. *Screen/Play: Derrida and Film Theory*. Princeton: Princeton University Press.

Bukharin, Nikolai. 1935. "Poetry, Poetics, and the Problems of Poetry in the USSR." In Gorky et al. 1935:185–258.

Bulgakowa, Oksana. 1989. "Sergej Eisenstein und die deutschen Psychologen." In Bulgakowa, ed., *Herausfordering Eisenstein*. Berlin: Akademie der Künst der Deutschen Demokratischen Republik, 80–91.

Burch, Noël. 1973. *Theory of Film Practice*. Trans. Helen R. Lane. New York: Praeger.

——— 1991. *In and Out of Synch: The Awakening of a Cine-Dreamer*. London: Scolar.

Burke, Kenneth. 1957. *Counter-Statement*. Chicago: University of Chicago Press.

Burns, Paul. 1981. "Cultural Revolution, Collectivization, and Soviet Cinema: Eisenstein's *Old and New* and Dovzhenko's *Earth.*" *Film and History* 11, no. 4 (December):84–96.

Bush, M., and A. Zamoshkin. 1934. "Soviet Pictorial Art." *Painting, Sculpture, and Graphic Art in the USSR*. Special issue, *VOKS Bulletin* no. 9/10:9–30.

Bystrzycka, Maria. 1970. "Eisenstein as a Precursor of Semantics in Film Art." In A. J. Greimas et al., *Sign—Language—Culture*. The Hague: Mouton, 469–484.

Carasco, Raymond. 1979. *Hors-cadre Eisenstein*. Paris: Macula.

Careri, Giovanni. 1991. "Ejzenštejn e Bernini: Montaggio e composto." In Montani 1991:263–274.

Carroll, Noël. 1973. "For God and Country." *Artforum* 11, no. 5 (January):61–65.

——— 1988a. "Art, Practice, and Narrative." *The Monist* 71, no. 2 (April):140–156.

——— 1988b. *Philosophical Problems of Classical Film Theory*. Princeton: Princeton University Press.

Carter, Huntley. 1924. *The New Theatre and Cinema of Soviet Russia*. London: Chapman and Dodd.

Chaillet, Jean-Paul, and Elizabeth Vincent. 1985. *Francis Ford Coppola*. Trans. Denise Raab Jacobs. New York: St. Martin's Press.

Cherkasov, Nikolay. 1953. *Notes of a Soviet Actor*. Moscow: Foreign Languages Publishing House.

Christensen, Peter G. 1990. "Eisenstein's *Ivan the Terrible* and Shakespeare's Historical Plays." *Slavic and East European Arts* 6, no. 2 (Winter):124–138.

Christie, Ian. 1987. "*Ivan Groznii.*" *Monthly Film Bulletin* 54 (December):382–383.

Christie, Ian, and David Elliott, eds. 1988. *Eisenstein at Ninety*. Oxford: Museum of Art.

Christie, Ian, and Richard Taylor, eds. 1993. *Eisenstein Rediscovered*. London: Routledge.

Clark, Katerina. 1977. "Utopian Anthropology as a Context for Stalinist Literature." In Robert C. Tucker, ed., *Stalinism: Essays in Historical Interpretation*. New York: Norton, 180–198.

——— 1978. "Little Heroes and Big Deeds: Literature Responds to the First Five-Year Plan." In Fitzpatrick 1978:189–206.

——— 1981. *The Soviet Novel: History as Ritual*. Chicago: University of Chicago.

———— 1985. "The City versus the Countryside in Soviet Peasant Literature of the 1920s: A Duel of Utopias." In Gleason, Kenez, and Stites 1978:175–189.

Collingwood, R. G. 1938. *The Principles of Art.* Reprint, New York: Oxford University Press, 1958.

Comolli, Jean-Louis. 1971. "Le réalisateur à vingt têtes." *Cahiers du cinéma* no. 228 (March–April):46–49.

Comolli, Jean-Louis, and Jean Narboni. 1969. "Cinema/Ideology/Criticism (1)." In John Ellis, ed., *Screen Reader 1: Cinema/Ideology/Politics.* London: SEFT, 1977:2–12.

Conio, Gérard, ed. 1987. *Le constructivisme russe.* Vol. 1: *Les arts plastiques: Textes théoriques, manifestes, documents.* Lausanne: L'Age d'Homme.

———— 1990. *L'avant-garde russe et la synthèse des arts.* Lausanne: L'Age d'Homme.

Conquest, Robert. 1990. *The Great Terror: A Reassessment.* New York: Oxford University Press.

Copleston, Frederick C. 1986. *Philosophy in Russia: From Herzen to Lenin and Berdyaev.* London: Search Press.

De Santi, Pier Marco. 1981. *I disegni di Eisenstein.* Rome: Laterza.

Dreyer, Regina. 1960. "Eisenstein und das Theater." In Rodenberg 1960:84–107.

Eagle, Herbert. 1978. "Eisenstein as a Semiotician of the Cinema." In R. W. Bailey, L. Matejka, and P. Steiner, eds., *The Sign: Semiotics around the World.* Ann Arbor: Michigan Slavic Publications, 173–193.

———— 1984. "Visual Patterning and Meaning in Eisenstein's Early Films." In Kenneth N. Brostrom, ed., *Russian Literature and American Critics.* Ann Arbor: University of Michigan Slavic Department, 331–346.

———— 1987. "Introduction." In *NN*:vii–xxi.

Editors of "Atheist" Publishers. 1930. "Prefaces to *Pervobytnoe myshlenie* [*Primitive Mentality*]." *Soviet Psychology* 14, no. 3 (Spring 1976):5–16.

Eikhenbaum, Boris. 1926. "The Theory of the 'Formal Method.'" In Lemon and Reis 1965:99–139.

Eikhenbaum, Boris, ed. 1927a. *The Poetics of the Cinema.* Trans. Richard Taylor. Special issue, *Russian Poetics in Translation* 9 (1981).

Eikhenbaum, Boris. 1927b. "Problems of Cine-Stylistics." In Eikhenbaum 1927a:5–31.

Elliott, David. 1988. "Taking a Line for a Dance." In Christie and Elliott 1988:19–40.

Erlich, Victor. 1981. *Russian Formalism: History, Doctrine.* The Hague: Mouton.

Ermolaev, Herman. 1963. *Soviet Literary Theories, 1917–1934: The Genesis of Socialist Realism.* Berkeley: University of California Press.

Fernandez, Dominique. 1975. *Eisenstein: L'arbre jusqu'aux racines II.* Paris: Grasset.

Fitzpatrick, Sheila. 1976. "Culture and Politics under Stalin: A Reappraisal." *Slavic Review* 35, no. 2:211–231.

Fitzpatrick, Sheila, ed. 1978. *Cultural Revolution in Russia, 1928–1931.* Bloomington: Indiana University Press.

Fitzpatrick, Sheila. 1982. *The Russian Revolution, 1917–1932.* Oxford: Oxford University Press.

Fizer, John. 1981. *Psychologism and Psychoaesthetics: A Historical and Critical View of Their Relations.* Amsterdam: John Benjamins.

———— 1987. *Alexander A. Potebnja's Psycholinguistic Theory of Literature: A Metacritical Inquiry.* Cambridge, Mass.: Harvard Ukrainian Research Institute.

Freeman, Joseph. 1930. "The Soviet Cinema." In Freeman et al., *Voices of October: Art and Literature in Soviet Russia.* New York: Vanguard Press, 217–264.

Fueloep-Miller, René. 1927. *The Mind and Face of Bolshevism: An Examination of Cultural Life in Soviet Russia*. New York: Harper & Row, 1965.

Gallez, D. W. 1978. "The Prokofiev-Eisenstein Collaboration: *Nevsky* and *Ivan* Revisited." *Cinema Journal* 17, no. 2 (Spring):13–35.

Geduld, Harry M., and Ronald Gottesman, eds. 1970. *Sergei Eisenstein and Upton Sinclair: The Making and Unmaking of "Qué viva México!"* Bloomington: Indiana University Press.

Gerould, Daniel. 1974. "Eisenstein's *Wiseman*." *Drama Review* 18, no. 1 (March):71–76.

———— 1989. "Historical Simulation and Popular Entertainment: The *Potemkin* Mutiny from Reconstructed Newsreel to Black Sea Stunt Men." *Drama Review* 33, no. 2 (Summer):161–184.

Gleason, Abbott, Peter Kenez, and Richard Stites, eds. 1985. *Bolshevik Culture: Experience and Order in the Russian Revolution*. Bloomington: Indiana University Press.

Godard, Jean-Luc. 1972. "*Les carabiniers* under Fire." In Jean Narboni and Tom Milne, eds., *Godard on Godard*. New York: Viking.

Golomstock, Igor. 1990a. "Problems in the Study of Stalinist Culture." In Günther 1990:110–121.

———— 1990b. *Totalitarian Art in the Soviet Union, the Third Reich, Fascist Italy, and the People's Republic of China*. Trans. Robert Chandler. New York: HarperCollins.

Goodwin, James. 1978a. "Eisenstein: Ideology and Intellectual Cinema." *Quarterly Review of Film Studies* 3, no. 2 (Spring):169–192.

———— 1978b. "The Object(ive)s of Cinema: Vertov (Factography) and Eisenstein (Ideography)." *Praxis* no. 4:223–230.

———— 1981. "Plusieurs Eisensteins: Recent Criticism." *Quarterly Review of Film Studies* 6, no. 4 (Fall):391–412.

Gordon, Mel. 1978. "Eisenstein's Later Work at the Proletcult." *Drama Review* 22, no. 3 (September):107–112.

———— 1991. "Russian Eccentric Theatre: The Rhythm of America on the Early Soviet Stage." In Nancy Van Norman Baer, ed., *Theatre in Revolution: Russian Avant-Garde Stage Design*. New York: Thames and Hudson, 114–127.

Gorky, Maxim. 1935. "Soviet Literature." In Gorky et al. 1935:27–69.

Gorky, Maxim, et al. 1935. *Soviet Writers' Congress 1934: The Debate on Socialist Realism and Modernism in the Soviet Union*. London: Lawrence and Wishart, 1977.

Gray, Jeffrey. 1980. *Pavlov*. New York: Viking.

Grossi, Edoardo G. 1984. "Eisenstein e il progetto di 'Regissura.'" *Studi urbinati* Serie B3: Linguistica, letteratura, arte, 57:219–251.

Groys, Boris. 1990. "The Birth of Socialist Realism from the Spirit of the Russian Avant-Garde." In Günther 1990:122–148.

———— 1992. *The Total Art of Stalinism: Avant-Garde, Aesthetic Dictatorship, and Beyond*. Trans. Charles Rougle. Princeton: Princeton University Press.

Guldberg, Jørn. 1986. "Artists Well Organised." *Slavica Othiniensia* 8:3–23.

Günther, Hans, ed. 1990. *The Culture of the Stalin Period*. New York: St. Martin's Press.

Gutiérrez Alea, T. 1981. "Alienation and De-Alienation in Eisenstein and Brecht." *Cinema Papers*, July/August:248–249, 301, 303.

Hamon, Christine. 1978. "Le montage dans les premières realisations d'Eisenstein au théâtre." In Billeter et al. 1978:145–160.

Heil, Jerry. 1990. "Isaak Babel and His Film Work." *Russian Literature* no. 27–28 (1 April):289–416.

———— 1991. "Theme and Style, and the 'Literary Film' as Avant-Garde." *Avant Garde* no. 5/6:137–162.

Heller, Mikhail, and Aleksander M. Nekrich. 1986. *Utopia in Power: The History of the Soviet Union from 1917 to the Present.* Trans. Phyllis B. Carlos. New York: Summit.

Henderson, Brian. 1971. "Two Types of Film Theory." In *A Critique of Film Theory.* New York: Dutton, 1980, 16–31.

Henderson, Elizabeth. 1978. "Majakovsky and Eisenstein Celebrate the Tenth Anniversary." *Slavic and East European Journal* 22:153–162.

Hielscher, Karla. 1973. "S. M. Eisenstein's Theaterarbeit beim Moskauwer Proletkult (1921–1924)." *Aesthetik und Kommunikation* no. 13:64–75.

Higgens, Andrew. 1971. "The Development of the Theory of Socialist Realism in Russia, 1917 to 1932." *Studio International* 181, no. 932 (April):155–159.

Hill, Steven P. 1978. "The Strange Case of the Vanishing Epigraphs." In Marshall 1978:74–86.

Hosking, Geoffrey. 1985. *The First Socialist Society: A History of the Soviet Union from Within.* Cambridge, Mass.: Harvard University Press.

Howard, V. A. 1982. *Artistry: The Work of Artists.* Indianapolis: Hackett.

Hrushovski, Benjamin. 1976. "Poetics, Criticism, Science: Remarks on the Fields and Responsibilities of the Study of Literature." *Poetics and Theory of Literature* 1:iii–xxxv.

Ingster, Boris. 1951. "Sergei Eisenstein." *Hollywood Quarterly* 5, no. 4 (Summer):380–388.

Ivanov, V. V. 1971. "The Categories and Functions of Film Language." *Film Criticism* 7, no. 3 (Spring):3–19.

———— 1976. *Ocherki po istorii semiotiki v SSSR* (Essays on the history of semiotics in the U.S.S.R.). Moscow: Nauka.

Jacobs, Lewis. 1931. "Eisenstein." *Experimental Cinema* no. 3:4.

———— 1939. *The Rise of the American Film.* New York: Harcourt, Brace.

James, William. 1892. *Psychology: The Shorter Course.* Reprint, Cleveland: Fine Editions Press, 1948.

Joravsky, David. 1978. "The Construction of the Stalinist Psyche." In Fitzpatrick 1978:105–128.

Joyce, James. 1961. *Ulysses.* New York: Modern Library.

Kazansky, B. 1927. "The Nature of Cinema." In Eikhenbaum 1927a:55–86.

Karetnikova, Inga, and Naum Kleiman. 1969. *Les dessins mexicains d'Eisenstein.* Moscow: Sovietski Khoudojnik.

Karetnikova, Inga, and Leon Steinmetz. 1991. *Mexico according to Eisenstein.* Albuquerque: University of New Mexico Press.

Kenez, Peter. 1988. "The Cultural Revolution in Cinema." *Slavic Review* 47, no. 2 (Fall):414–433.

———— 1992. *Cinema and Soviet Society: 1917–1953.* Cambridge: Cambridge University Press.

Kepley, Vance. 1974. "The Evolution of Eisenstein's *Old and New.*" *Cinema Journal* 14, no. 1 (Fall):34–50.

———— Forthcoming. "Eisenstein as Pedagogue." *Quarterly Review of Film and Video.*

Kevles, Barbara. 1965. "Slavko Vorkapich on Film as a Visual Language and as a Form of Art." *Film Culture* no. 38 (Fall):1–46.

Khrushchev, Nikita. 1971. *Khrushchev Remembers.* Trans. and ed. Strobe Talbott. New York: Bantam.

Kinder, Marsha. 1986. "The Image of Patriarchal Power in *Young Mister Lincoln* and *Ivan the Terrible* Part I (1945)." *Film Quarterly* 39, no. 2 (Winter):29–49.

Kivy, Peter. 1984. *Sound and Semblance: Reflections on Musical Representation*. Princeton: Princeton University Press.

Kleberg, Lars. 1977. "Ejenštejn's *Potemkin* and Tret'yakov's *Ryci, Kitaj!* [*Roar, China!*]." *Scando-Slavica* 23:29–37.

Kleberg, Lars, and Haken Lövgren, eds. 1987. *Eisenstein Revisited: A Collection of Essays*. Stockholm: Almqvist and Wiksell.

Kleiman, Naum. 1988. "Eisenstein's Graphic Work." In Christie and Elliott 1988:11–18.

———— 1992. "On the Story of 'Montage 1937.'" In *TTM*:xvii–xx.

Kolchevska, Natasha. 1985. "From Model to Real Object: Four Productions by Mejerxol'd and Ejenstein." *Proceedings of the Kentucky Foreign Language Conference: Slavic Section* 3, no. 1:75–82.

———— 1987a. "The *Faktoviki* at the Movies: *Novji Lef*'s Critique of Ejenštejn and Vertov." *Russian Language Journal* 138–139:139–151.

———— 1987b. "From Agitation to Factography: The Plays of Sergej Tret'jakov." *Slavic and East European Journal* 31:388–403.

Koltsov, M. 1925. Review of *Strike*. In *Stachka* program. Moscow, 6.

Kozintsev, Grigori. 1978. "AB: Parade of the Eccentric." In Ian Christie and John Gillett, eds., *Futurism/Formalism/FEKS: "Eccentrism" and Soviet Cinema, 1918–36*. London: British Film Institute, 11–13.

Kozlov, Leonid. 1987. "A Hypothetical Dedication." In Kleberg and Lövgren 1987:65–92.

———— 1990. "*Ivan the Terrible* and Stalin." Unpublished manuscript.

Kozulin, Alex. 1984. *Psychology in Utopia: Toward a Social History of Soviet Psychology*. Cambridge, Mass.: MIT Press.

———— 1990. *Vygotsky's Psychology: A Biography of Ideas*. Cambridge, Mass.: Harvard University Press.

Kuiper, John. 1962. "Cinematic Expression: A Look at Eisenstein's Silent Montage." *Art Journal* 22 (Fall):34–39.

Kuleshov, Lev. 1917. "The Tasks of the Artist in Cinema." In Taylor and Christie 1988:41–43.

———— 1922. "Chamber Cinema." In Taylor and Christie 1988:74.

———— 1967. "Reminiscences of Eisenstein (1967)." *Film Journal* 1, no. 3/4 (Fall–Winter 1972):28–32.

———— 1973. *Kuleshov on Film: Writings of Lev Kuleshov*. Trans. and ed. Ronald Levaco. Berkeley: University of California Press.

———— 1987. *Selected Works: Fifty Years in Films*. Trans. Dmitri Agrachev and Nina Belenkaya. Moscow: Raduga.

Lagny, Michèle, Marie-Claire Ropars, and Pierre Sorlin. 1979. *La révolution figurée: Film, histoire, politique*. Paris: Albatros.

Lary, N. M. 1986. *Dostoevsky and Soviet Film: Visions of Demonic Realism*. Ithaca: Cornell University Press.

———— 1990. "Eisenstein's (Anti-)Theatrical Art: From Kino-Fist to Kino-Tragedy." *Slavic and East European Arts* 6, no. 2 (Winter):88–123.

Lawder, Standish Dyer. 1967. "Structuralism and Movement in Experimental Film and Modern Art, 1896–1925." Ph.D. diss., Yale University.

———— 1975. "Eisenstein and Constructivism." In P. Adams Sitney, ed., *The Essential Cinema*. Vol. 1: *Essays on the Films in the Collection of Anthology Film Archives*. New York: New York University Press/Anthology Film Archives.

Lawton, Anna, ed. 1988. *Russian Futurism through Its Manifestoes, 1912–1928*. Ithaca: Cornell University Press.

Leach, Robert. 1989. *Vsevelod Meyerhold.* Cambridge: Cambridge University Press.

———— 1993. "Eisenstein's Theatre Work." In Christie and Taylor 1993:110–125.

Lebedev, Nikolai A. 1947. *Ocherki istorii kino sssr* (Essays on the history of the cinema in the U.S.S.R.). Vol. 1: *Nemoe kino* (The silent film). Moscow: Goskinoizdat.

Le Bot, Marc. 1963. "Eisenstein, théoricien de l'art moderne." *Contre-champ* no. 5 (April):53–64.

Lemon, Lee T., and Marion J. Reis, eds. 1965. *Russian Formalist Criticism: Four Essays.* Lincoln: University of Nebraska Press.

Lenin, V. I. 1925. "On the Question of Dialectics." In *Collected Works.* Vol. 38. Moscow: Progress, 1981, 355–361.

———— 1922. "On the Significance of Militant Materialism." In *Collected Works.* Vol. 33. Moscow: Progress, 1965, 227–236.

Levaco, Ronald. 1973. "The Eisenstein-Prokofiev Correspondence." *Cinema Journal* 13, no. 1 (Fall):1–16.

Levin, E. 1969. "S. Èizenshtein i problemy struktural'nogo analiza" (S. Eisenstein and problems of structural analysis). *Voprosy literatury* 13, no. 2:135–143.

Levshin, A. 1966. "Eisenstein and the 'Iron Five.'" In Marshall 1978:63–67.

Lévy-Brühl, Lucien. 1926. *How Natives Think.* Trans. Lilian A. Clare. Reprint, Princeton: Princeton University Press, 1985.

Lewin, Moshe. 1965. "Le problème de la différentiation de la paysannerie vers la fin de la N.E.P.: Les théories du Parti face aux réalités rurales." *Cahiers du monde russe et soviétique* 6, no. 1 (January–March):5–41.

Leyda, Jay. 1958. "Eisenstein's Mexican Tragedy." *Sight and Sound* 27 (Autumn):305–308, 329.

———— 1959. "Two-Thirds of a Trilogy." *Film Quarterly* 12, no. 3 (Spring):16–22.

———— 1960. *Kino: A History of the Russian and Soviet Film.* London: Allen and Unwin.

———— 1962. "Care of the Past." *Sight and Sound* 31 (Winter):47–48.

———— 1965. "The Missing Reel." *Sight and Sound* 34 (Spring):63.

Leyda, Jay, and Zina Voynow. 1982. *Eisenstein at Work.* New York: Pantheon/Museum of Modern Art.

L'Hermitte, René. 1987. *Science et perversion idéologique: Marr, Marrisme, Marristes. Cultures et sociétés de l'Est* no. 8.

Liebman, Stuart. 1988. "Why Kluge?" *October* no. 46 (Fall):5–22.

Lifshitz, Mikhail. 1938. *The Philosophy of Art of Karl Marx.* Trans. Ralph B. Winn. London: Pluto, 1973.

Lindgren, Ernest. 1948. *The Art of the Film: An Introduction to Film Appreciation.* London: Allen and Unwin.

Lodder, Christina. 1983. *Russian Constructivism.* New Haven: Yale University Press.

Longinus. 1962. "On Literary Excellence." In Allan H. Gilbert, ed., *Literary Criticism: Plato to Dryden.* Detroit: Wayne State University Press, 146–198.

Lövgren, Hakan. 1987. "Trauma and Ecstasy." In Kleberg and Lövgren 1987:93–111.

Lukàcs, Georg. 1936. "Narrate or Describe?" In Arthur D. Kahn, ed. and trans., *Writer and Critic and Other Essays.* New York: Grosset and Dunlap, 1971, 110–148.

Lunacharsky, A. V. 1933. "Problems of the Soviet Theatre: On Socialist Realism, Literature and the Theatre." *International Literature* no. 3 (July):88–96.

MacDonald, Dwight. 1969. *On Movies.* Englewood Cliffs, N.J.: Prentice-Hall.

MacDonald, Ian. 1990. *The New Shostakovich.* London: Fourth Estate.

Maguire, Robert A. 1968. *Red Virgin Soil: Soviet Literature in the 1920s.* Princeton: Princeton University Press.

Makavejev, Dušan. 1975. "Eisenstein: Rouge, or, noir." *Positif* no. 176 (December):7–17.

Malevich, Kasimir. 1925. "And Images Triumph on the Screens." In *Essays on Art*. Vol. 1. Trans. Xenia Glowacki-Prus and Arnold McMillan. Copenhagen: Borgen, 1971, 226–232.

Mally, Lynn. 1990. *Culture of the Future: The Proletkult Movement in Revolutionary Russia.* Berkeley: University of California Press.

Manvell, Roger. 1950. *Film*. 3d ed. Harmondsworth: Penguin.

Marr, N. Ya. 1930. "Introduction [to Lévy-Brühl's *Primitive Thought*]." *Soviet Psychology* 14, no. 3 (Spring 1976):17–20.

Marshall, Herbert. 1945. *Soviet Cinema*. London: Russia Today Society.

––––––– 1949. "Studying under Eisenstein." In Rotha et al. 1949:25–28.

Marshall, Herbert, ed. 1978. *The Battleship Potemkin*. New York: Avon.

Mathewson, Rufus W., Jr. 1975. *The Positive Hero in Russian Literature*. 2d ed. Stanford: Stanford University Press.

Mayakovsky, Vladimir. 1926. *How Are Verses Made?* Trans. G. M. Hyde. London: Cape, 1970.

––––––– 1986. *Selected Works in Three Volumes*. Vol. 2: *Longer Poems*. Moscow: Raduga.

Mayer, David. 1972. *Eisenstein's "Potemkin": A Shot-by-Shot Presentation*. New York: Grossman.

Mayne, Judith. 1989. *Kino and the Woman Question: Feminism and Soviet Silent Film.* Columbus: Ohio State University Press.

Mechini, Piero, and Roberto Salvadori, eds. 1975. *Il cinema di S. M. Eisenstein*. Rimini: Guaraldi.

Messer, R. 1938. "Geroi sovetskoi kinematografii" (The hero in Soviet cinema). In I. L. Grinberg, ed., *Obraz bolshevika* (The image of the Bolshevik). Leningrad: Khudozhestvennaia Literatura, 246–291.

Messman, Vladimir. 1928. "Sound Film." In Taylor and Christie 1988:235–236.

Metz, Christian. 1974. *Film Language*. Trans. Michael Taylor. New York: Oxford University Press.

Meyerhold, Vsevolod. 1925. "Intervention à la section théâtrale de l'Académie Russe des Sciences de l'Art (extrait)." In *Ecrits sur le théâtre*. Vol. 2. Trans. Béatrice Picon-Vallin. Lausanne: L'Age d'Homme, 1975, 160–161.

––––––– 1936. "Chaplin and Chaplinism." In Edward Braun, ed., *Meyerhold on Theatre.* New York: Hill and Wang, 1969, 311–324.

Michelson, Annette. 1966. "Film and the Radical Aspiration." *Film Culture* no. 42 (Fall):34–42, 136.

––––––– 1973. "Camera Lucida/Camera Obscura." *Artforum* 11, no. 5 (January):30–37.

––––––– 1976. "Reading Eisenstein Reading *Capital*." *October* no. 2 (Summer):27–38.

––––––– 1989. "Reading Eisenstein Reading *Ulysses*: Montage and the Claims of Subjectivity." *Art & Text* no. 34 (Spring):64–78.

Mitry, Jean. 1961. *S. M. Eisenstein*. Paris: Editions Universitaires.

––––––– 1963–1965. *Esthétique et psychologie du cinéma*. 2 vols. Paris: Editions Universitaires.

Montagu, Ivor. 1948. "Sergei Eisenstein." *Penguin Film Review* 7 (September):10–16.

––––––– 1956. *"Strike." Sight and Sound* 26 (Autumn):105–108.

––––––– 1967. *With Eisenstein in Hollywood: A Chapter of Autobiography*. New York: International Publishers.

Montani, Pietro. 1990. "Le seuil infranchissable de la représentation: Du rapport peinture-cinéma chez Eisenstein." In Raymond Bellour, ed., *Cinéma et peinture: Approches.* Paris: Presses Universitaires de France, 67–81.

Montani, Pietro, ed. 1991. *Sergej Ejzenštejn: Oltre il cinema.* Venice: Biennale/Edisioni Biblioteca dell'Immagine.

Moussinac, Léon. 1964. *Sergei Eisenstein: An Investigation into His Films and Philosophy.* Trans. D. Sandy Petrey. New York: Crown, 1970.

Mowitt, John. 1992. *Text: The Genealogy of an Antidisciplinary Object.* Durham: Duke University Press.

Narboni, Jean. 1976. "Le hors-cadre décide tout," *Cahiers du cinéma* no. 271 (November):14–21.

Newman, John Kevin. 1986. *The Classical Epic Tradition.* Madison: University of Wisconsin Press.

Nilsen, Vladimir. 1936. *The Cinema as a Graphic Art.* New York: Hill and Wang, 1959.

Nizhny, Vladimir. 1958. *Lessons with Eisenstein.* Ed. and trans. Ivor Montagu. New York: Hill and Wang, 1962.

O'Toole, L. M. 1977. "Eisenstein's *Strike* (1924): A Structural Interpretation." *Essays in Poetics* no. 1:30–42.

Oudart, Jean-Pierre. 1970. "Sur *Ivan le Terrible.*" *Cahiers du cinéma* no. 218 (March):15–22.

Party Cinema Conference. 1929. "Resolution: The Results of Cinema Construction in the USSR and the Tasks of Soviet Cinema." In Taylor and Christie 1988:208–215.

Pastorello, Félicie. 1978. "La catégorie du montage chez Tretjakov, Arvatov, Brecht." In Billeter et al. 1978:117–132.

Payne, T. R. 1968. *S. L. Rubinštejn and the Philosophical Foundations of Soviet Psychology.* Dordrecht: Reidel.

Peatman, Mary. 1975. "Sergei Eisenstein's *Ivan the Terrible* as a Cinematic Realization of the Concept of the *Gesamtkunstwerk.*" Ph.D. diss., Indiana University.

Pechter, William S. 1960. "The Closed Mind of Sergei Eisenstein." In *Twenty-Four Times a Second: Films and Film Makers.* New York: Harper & Row, 1971, 111–122.

Perez, F. 1974. "Un tratado cinematográfico." *Cine cubano* 89–90:24–38.

Perkins, V. F. 1972. *Film as Film: Understanding and Judging Movies.* Harmondsworth: Penguin.

Perlmutter, Ruth. 1975. "*Le gai savoir:* Godard and Eisenstein: Notions of Intellectual Cinema." *Jump Cut* no. 7 (May–July):17–19.

Pertsov, V. 1928. "The Lef Arena: *October.*" In John Ellis, ed., *Screen Reader 1: Cinema/Ideology/Politics.* London: SEFT, 1977, 316–319.

Petronius. 1990. "How the Casting Couch Survived under Stalin." *The European,* 26–28 October:13.

Phillips, K. H. 1986. *Language Theories of the Early Soviet Period.* Exeter: University of Exeter.

Picon-Vallin, Béatrice. 1990. "Le cinéma, partenaire ou instrument du théâtre meyerholdien?" In Claudine Amiard-Chevrel, ed., *Théâtre et cinéma années vingt: Une quête de la modernité.* Vol. 1. Lausanne: L'Age d'Homme, 229–262.

Piotrovsky, Adrian. 1927. "Towards a Theory of Film Genres." In Eikhenbaum 1927a:90–106.

Pipinashvili, K. 1967. "'Tainaia vechera' Leonardo da Vinchi v kinomontazhnoi raskadrovke" (*The Last Supper* of Leonardo da Vinci in cinematic montage framing). *Iskusstvo* no. 5:52–55.

Pirog, Gerald. 1982. "Iconicity and Narrative: The Vertov-Eisenstein Controversy." *Semiotica* 39:297–313.

Pletynov, V. 1925. "An Open Letter to the Editors of the Journal *Kino-nedelya*." In *E2*:3–5.

Pleynet, Marceline. 1969. "The 'Left' Front of Art: Eisenstein and the Old 'Young' Hegelians." In John Ellis, ed., *Screen Reader 1: Cinema/Ideology/Politics*. London: SEFT, 1977, 225–243.

Porter, Katherine Anne. 1940. "Hacienda." In *Flowering Judas and Other Stories*. New York: Random House.

Pudovkin, V. I. 1926. *Film Technique*. Trans. Ivor Montagu. London: Vision Press, 1958.

———— 1928. "S. M. Eisenstein (From *Potemkin* to *October*)." In Taylor and Christie 1988:198–200.

———— 1939. "*Alexander Nevsky*." *International Literature* no. 2:94–96.

———— 1949. "Trente ans." *L'écran français* no. 232 (12 December):4–5, 14.

Puiseux, Hélène. 1984. "Le détournement d'Alexandre Nevski au service de Staline." In Marc Ferro, ed., *Film et histoire*. Paris: Ecole des Hautes Etudes en Sciences Sociales, 15–21.

Pyriev, I. 1951. "Our People's Art." In *Soviet Films: Principal Stages of Development*. Bombay: People's Publishing House, 46–58.

Rahmani, Levy. 1973. *Soviet Psychology: Philosophical, Theoretical, and Experimental Issues*. New York: International Universities Press.

Reavey, George. 1947. *Soviet Literature Today*. New Haven: Yale University Press.

Reeder, Roberta. 1989. "Agit-prop Art: Posters, Puppets, Propaganda, and Eisenstein's *Strike*." *Russian Literature Triquarterly* no. 22:255–278.

Reisz, Karel. 1951. "Editing." *Sight and Sound* 19 (February):415.

Richardson, William Harrison. 1980. "Eisenstein and California: The 'Sutter's Gold' Episode." *California History* 59, no. 3 (Fall):194–203.

———— 1989. *Mexico through Russian Eyes, 1806–1940*. Pittsburgh: University of Pittsburgh Press.

Rivette, Jacques. 1969. "Montage." In Jonathan Rosenbaum, ed., *Rivette: Texts and Interviews*. London: British Film Institute, 1977, 69–88.

Roberge, Gaston. 1980. *Eisenstein's "Ivan the Terrible": An Analysis*. Calcutta: Chitrabani.

Roberts, P. D. 1977. "Prokofiev's Score and Cantata of Eisenstein's 'Alexander Nevsky.'" *Semiotica* 21, no. 1/2:151–166.

Robin, Régine. 1986. *Le réalisme socialiste: Une esthétique impossible*. Paris: Payot.

———— 1988. "L'anti avant-garde ou quelques réflexions sur l'influence du réalisme socialiste." *Etudes littéraires* 20, no. 3 (Winter):87–110.

Robinson, David. 1968. "The Two Bezhin Meadows." *Sight and Sound* 37 (Winter):33–37.

Robinson, Harlow. 1984–85. "'The Most Contemporary Art': Sergei Prokofiev and Soviet Film." *Studies in Comparative Communism* 17, no. 3/4 (Fall/Winter):203–218.

———— 1987. *Sergei Prokofiev: A Biography*. New York: Paragon.

Rodchenko, Alexander. 1921. "Conclusions on Construction and Composition." In Andel et al. 1990:66.

Rodenberg, Hans, ed. 1960. *Sergei Eisenstein: Künstler der Revolution*. Berlin: Henschelverlag.

Rokotov, Timofei. 1937. "A Failure and Its Reasons." *International Literature* no. 8:97–99.

Romm, Mikhail. 1965. "The Second Summit." In Eisenstein 1943:16–19.

———— 1966. "Propos liminaires sur le maître." *Cahiers du cinéma* no. 219 (April 1970):17–18.

Ropars-Weuilleumier, Marie-Claire. 1970a. *De la littérature au cinéma.* Paris: Colin.

———— 1970b. *L'écran de la mémoire: Essais de lecture cinématographiques.* Paris: Seuil.

———— 1978. "The Function of Metaphor in Eisenstein's *October.*" *Film Criticism* 2, no. 2/3:10–34.

———— 1978–79. "The Overture of *October.*" *Enclitic* 2, no. 2 (Fall 1978):50–72; 3, no. 1 (Spring 1979):35–47.

———— 1981. *Le texte divisé.* Paris: Presses Universitaires de France.

Rotha, Paul, et al. 1949. *Eisenstein, 1898–1948.* London: Society for Cultural Relations with the U.S.S.R.

Roth-Lindberg, Örjan. 1987. "Transformation as a Device in Eisenstein's Visual Language." In Kleberg and Lövgren 1987:25–38.

Rudnitsky, Konstantin. 1988. *Russian and Soviet Theatre, 1905–1932.* Trans. Roxane Permar. New York: Abrams.

Russell, Robert. 1988. *Russian Drama of the Revolutionary Period.* Basingstoke: Macmillan.

———— 1990. "The First Soviet Plays." In Russell and Barrett 1990:148–171.

Russell, Robert, and Andrew Barrett, eds. 1990. *Russian Theatre in the Age of Modernism.* Basingstoke: Macmillan.

Sadoul, Georges. 1960. "Entretiens sur Serge Eisenstein." *Cinéma 60* no. 46 (May):89–109.

Salvaggio, Jerry. 1979. "Between Formalism and Semiotics: Eisenstein's Film Language." *Dispositio* 4:289–297.

Sampson, Geoffrey. 1985. *Writing Systems.* London: Hutchinson.

Sánchez-Biosca, Vicente. 1992. *Teoría del montaje cinematográfico.* Valencia: Filmoteca.

Schapiro, Leonard. 1971. *The Communist Party of the Soviet Union.* 2d ed. New York: Vintage.

Schreurs, Marc. 1989. *Procedures of Montage in Isaak Babel's "Red Cavalry."* Amsterdam: Rodopi.

Schwarz, Boris. 1972. *Music and Musical Life in Soviet Russia, 1917–1970.* New York: Norton.

Segal, D. M. 1968. "Problema psikhologicheskogo substrata znaka i nekotorye teoreticheksie vozzreniia S. M. Èizenshteina" (The problem of the psychological substrata of the sign and certain theoretical views of S. M. Eisenstein). In L. Matejka et al., eds., *Readings in Soviet Semiotics.* Ann Arbor: Michigan Slavic Materials, 1977, 21–26.

Segel, Harold B. 1979. *Twentieth-Century Russian Drama: From Gorky to the Present.* New York: Columbia University Press.

Selden, D. L. 1982. "Vision and Violence: The Rhetoric of *Potemkin.*" *Quarterly Review of Film Studies* 7, no. 4 (Fall):309–329.

Selezneva, T. F. 1972. *Kinomysl' 1920-kh godov* (Film theory of the 1920s). Leningrad: Iskusstvo.

Selvinsky, A. 1934. "Statement on literature." *Literatures of the Peoples of the USSR.* Special issue, *VOKS Bulletin* no. 7/8:113–114.

Selznick, David. 1972. *Memo from David O. Selznick.* Ed. Rudy Behlmer. New York: Viking.

Seton, Marie. 1952. *Sergei M. Eisenstein: A Biography.* London: John Lane the Bodley Head.

———— 1953. "Eisenstein's Images and Mexican Art." *Sight and Sound* 23 (July–September):8–13.

Shear, Nancy. 1987. "*Alexander Nevsky:* A Masterwork Restored." *Ovation* 8 (November):20–22.

Shentalinsky, Vitaly. 1991. "Babel: Lies, Confessions, and Denials." *Index on Censorship* 20, no. 8 (August/September):32–37.

Shklovsky, Viktor. 1917. "Art as Technique." In Lemon and Reis 1965:3–24.

———— 1925. *Theory of Prose.* Trans. Benjamin Sher. Elmwood Park, Ill.: Dalkey Archive Press, 1990.

———— 1926a. "Eisenstein." In *Bronenosets Potemkin (Battleship Potemkin)*. Moscow: Kinopechat', 5–9.

———— 1926b. "Sergei Eisenstein and 'Non-Played' Film." In Taylor and Christie 1988:161–162.

———— 1930. *Podenshchina* (Day labor). Leningrad: Izdatel'stvo Pisatelei.

———— 1973. *Eizenshtein.* Moscow: Iskusstvo.

Shpiller, N. 1980. "Die Walküre in der Inszenierung Sergej Eisensteins." *Kunst und Literatur: Sowjetwissenschaft* 28, no. 7 (July):773–780.

Shtraukh, Maxim. 1940. "Vstrechy" (Encounters). *Iskusstvo kino* no. 1–2:89–91.

Shumyatsky, Boris. 1935. "A Cinema for the Millions (Extracts)." In Taylor and Christie 1988:358–369.

———— 1937. "The Film *Bezhin Meadow*." In Taylor and Christie 1988:378–381.

Shumyatsky, Boris, et al. 1937. *O Filme "Bezhin Lug" S. Eizenshteina: Protiv Formalizma v Kinoiskusstve* (On the film *Bezhin Meadow:* Against formalism in film art). Moscow: Iskusstvo.

Simmons, Ernest J., ed. 1951. *The Soviet Linguistics Controversy.* Morningside Heights, N.Y.: King's Crown Press.

Simon, Elena Pinto, and David Stirk. Forthcoming. *From the Storehouse of Creation: Eisenstein's "Bezhin Meadow."* Princeton: Princeton University Press.

Sinko, Ervin. 1977. "Eisenstein in the House of Babel." *Australian Journal of Screen Theory* 2 (March):84–87.

Sitney, P. Adams. 1990. *Modernist Montage: The Obscurity of Vision in Cinema and Literature.* New York: Columbia University Press.

Sokolov, Ippolit. 1926. *Kino-stsenarii* (The film scenario). Moscow: Kinopechat'.

———— 1930. "The Legend of 'Left' Cinema." In Taylor and Christie 1988:287–290.

Solanas, Fernando. 1969. "Le tiers cinéma." *Cinéthique* no. 3:1–6.

Solski, Waclaw. 1949. "The End of Sergei Eisenstein: Case History of an Artist under Dictatorship." *Commentary* 7, no. 3 (March):252–260.

Solzhenitsyn, Alexander. 1963. *One Day in the Life of Ivan Denisovich.* Trans. Ralph Parker. New York: Signet.

Sorlin, Pierre. 1980. *The Film in History: Restaging the Past.* Oxford: Blackwell.

Sorlin, Pierre, and Marie-Claire Ropars. 1976. *Octobre: Ecriture et idéologie.* Paris: Albatros.

Sperber, Murray. 1977. "Eisenstein's *October*." *Jump Cut* no. 14:15–22.

Stalin, Joseph. 1936. "Le Camarade Staline salue l'industrie cinématographique." In A. Aroseff, ed., *Le cinéma en URSS.* Moscow, 16.

———— 1938. *Dialectical and Historical Materialism.* New York: International Publishers, 1940.

Stegemann, Michael. 1978. "Sergej Eisenstein und Sergej Prokofieff." *Melos* 4, no. 6:495–501.

Steiner, Peter. 1984. *Russian Formalism: A Metapoetics.* Ithaca: Cornell University Press.

Stephan, Halina. 1981. *"Lef" and the Left Front of the Arts.* Munich: Sagner.

Stern, Seymour. 1934. "Introduction to Synopsis for 'Qué viva México!'" *Experimental Cinema* no. 5:3–4.

Stites, Richard. 1989. *Revolutionary Dreams: Utopian Vision and Experimental Life in the Russian Revolution.* New York: Oxford University Press.

———— 1992. *Russian Popular Culture: Entertainment and Society since 1900.* Cambridge: Cambridge University Press.

Struve, Gleb. *Russian Literature under Lenin and Stalin.* Norman: University of Oklahoma Press.

Sudendorf, Werner. 1975. *Sergej M. Eisenstein: Materialien zu Leben und Werk.* Munich: Hanser.

Susiluoto, Ilmari. 1982. *The Origins and Development of SystemsThinking in the Soviet Union.* Helsinki: Tiedenakatemia.

Swallow, Norman. 1977. *Eisenstein: A Documentary Portrait.* New York: Dutton.

Swiderski, E. M. 1979. *The Philosophical Foundations of Soviet Aesthetics: Theories and Controversies of the Post-War Years.* Dortrecht: Reidel.

Szcsepański, Tadeusz. 1987. "The Wise Man Reconsidered: Some Notes on the Performance." In Kleberg and Lövgren 1987:11–24.

Tarkovsky, Andrei. 1989. *Sculpting in Time: Reflections on the Cinema.* Trans. Kitty Hunter-Blair. London: Faber and Faber.

Taylor, Brandon. 1991. *Art and Literature under the Bolsheviks.* Vol. 1: *The Crisis of Renewal.* London: Pluto Press.

Taylor, Richard. 1979a. *Film Propaganda: Soviet Russia and Nazi Germany.* London: Croom Helm.

———— 1979b. *The Politics of the Soviet Cinema, 1917–1929.* Cambridge: Cambridge University Press.

———— 1984–85. "Soviet Socialist Realism and the Cinema Avant-Garde." *Studies in Comparative Communism* 17, no. 3/4 (Fall/Winter):185–202.

———— 1986. "Boris Shumyatsky and the Soviet Cinema in the 1930s: Ideology as Mass Entertainment." *Historical Journal of Film, Radio and Television* 6, no. 1:43–64.

———— 1988. "Eisenstein 1898-1948-1988." *Historical Journal of Film, Radio and Television* 8, no. 2:189–192.

Taylor, Richard, and Ian Christie, eds. 1988. *The Film Factory: Russian and Soviet Cinema in Documents, 1896–1939.* Cambridge, Mass.: Harvard University Press.

Tereshkovich, V. 1978. "Eizenshtein i Stanislavskii" (Eisenstein and Stanislavsky). *Iskusstvo kino* no. 12 (December):96–105.

Terras, Victor. 1974. *Belinskij and Russian Literary Criticism.* Madison: University of Wisconsin Press.

Thibaudeau, Jean, and Marceline Pleynet. 1969. "Economical, Ideological, Formal." In Sylvia Harvey, *May '68 and Film Culture.* London: British Film Institute, 1978, 149–170.

Thompson, Kristin. 1981. *Eisenstein's "Ivan the Terrible": A Neoformalist Analysis.* Princeton: Princeton University Press.

———— 1992. "Government Policies and Practical Necessities in the Soviet Cinema of the 1920s." In Anna Lawton, ed., *The Red Screen: Politics, Society, Art in Soviet Cinema.* New York: Routledge, 19–41.

———— 1993. "Eisenstein's Early Films Abroad." In Christie and Taylor 1993:53–63.

Thomson, Boris. 1978. *Lot's Wife and the Venus of Milo: Conflicting Attitudes to the Cultural Heritage in Modern Russia.* Cambridge: Cambridge University Press.

Timoshenko, S. 1926. *Iskusstvo kino: Montazh fil'ma* (The art of the cinema: The montage of films). Leningrad: Academia.

———— 1929. *Chto dozhen znat' kino-rezhisser* (What a film director must know). Leningrad: Teakinopechat'.

Tissé, Edward. 1956. "Doklad E. K. Tissé na seminare operatorov kinostudii 'Mosfil'm' 27 Aprelia 1956 goda" (Lecture at the cameramen's seminar of Mosfilm Studio, 27 April 1956). *Iskusstvo kino* no. 2 (February 1979):104–113.

Tissé, Eleonora. 1987. "Some Notes on the Work of the Cameraman in 'Ivan the Terrible': The Visual Construction of the Film Image Form." In Kleberg and Lövgren 1987:133–144.

Tolstoy, Vladimir, et al., eds. 1990. *Street Art of the Revolution: Festivals and Celebrations in Russia, 1918–1933*. Trans. Frances Longman et al. London: Thames and Hudson.

Tretyakov, Sergei. 1923. "From Where to Where? Futurism and Perspectives." In Lawton 1988:204–216.

———— 1928. "'Oktiabr' minus 'Bronenosets Potemkin'" (*October* minus *Battleship Potemkin*). *Iskusstvo kino* no. 11 (1987):102–106.

———— 1977. *Dans le front gauche de l'art*. Paris: Maspéro.

———— 1978. "*Do You Hear, Moscow?*" *The Drama Review* 22, no. 3 (September):113–123.

———— 1982. "*Hurle, Chine!*" *et autres pièces*. Lausanne: L'Age d'Homme.

Tsikounas, Myriam. 1992. *Les origines du cinéma soviétique: Un regard neuf*. Paris: Cerf.

Tsivian, Yuri. 1993. "Eisenstein and Russian Symbolist Culture: An Unknown Script of *October*." In Christie and Taylor 1993:79–109.

Tucker, Robert C. 1990. *Stalin in Power: The Revolution from Above, 1928–1941*. New York: Norton.

Tudor, Andrew. 1973. *Theories of Film*. New York: Viking.

Tul'viste, P. 1987. "L. Lévy-Brühl and Problems of the Historical Development of Thought." *Soviet Psychology* 25, no. 3 (Spring):3–21.

Tupitsyn, Margarita. 1992. "From the Politics of Montage to the Montage of Politics: Soviet Practice, 1919 through 1937." In Matthew Teitelbaum, ed., *Montage and Modern Life, 1919–1942*. Cambridge, Mass.: MIT Press, 83–127.

Tynyanov, Yuri. 1924. *The Problem of Verse Language*. Ed. and trans. Michael Sosa and Brent Harvey. Ann Arbor: Ardis, 1981.

———— 1927. "The Fundamentals of Cinema." In Eikhenbaum 1927a:32–54.

Uhlenbruch, Bernd. 1990. "The Annexation of History: Eisenstein and the Ivan Grozny Cult of the 1940s." In Günther 1990:266–287.

Ulmer, Gregory L. 1985. *Applied Grammatology: Post(e)-Pedagogy from Jacques Derrida to Joseph Beuys*. Baltimore: Johns Hopkins University Press, 265–315.

Vaisfeld, Ilya. 1937. "Teoreticheskie oshibki Eizenshteina" (Eisenstein's theoretical mistakes). In Shumyatsky et al. 1937:21–41.

———— 1969. "Mon dernier entretien avec Eisenstein." *Cahiers du cinéma* no. 208 (January):19–21.

Valkenier, Elizabeth. 1977. *Russian Realist Art: The State and Society: The Peredvizhniki and Their Tradition*. Ann Arbor: Ardis.

van Elterin, Mel, and Helmut E. Lück. 1990. "Kurt Lewin's Films and Their Role in the Development of Field Theory." Unpublished manuscript.

Van Houten, Theodore. 1989. *Leonid Trauberg and His Films: Always the Unexpected*. 's Hertogenbosch: Art & Research.

Vasiliev, S. D. 1929. *Montazh kino-kartiny* (Film montage). Moscow: Teakinopechat'.

Véronneau, Pierre. 1973. "Eisenstein et l'enseignement du cinéma." In *Eisenstein: Pour célébrer le 75ème anniversaire de la naissance de Serguéi Mikhailovitch Eisenstein, 1898– 1948.* Montreal: Cinémathèque Québecoise, 11–17.

Vertov, Dziga. 1984. *Kino-Eye: The Writings of Dziga Vertov.* Ed. Annette Michelson. Trans. Kevin O'Brien. Berkeley: University of California Press.

Vishnevsky, Vsevolod. 1939. *Eizenshtein.* Moscow: Goskinozdat.

Volkov, N. 1926. "From the Critics' First Responses to *The Battleship Potemkin.*" In Marshall 1978:94–95.

Volkov, Solomon, ed. 1979. *Testimony: The Memoirs of Dmitri Shostakovich.* Trans. Antonina W. Bouis. New York: Harper.

Voloshinov, V. N. 1929. *Marxism and the Philosophy of Language.* Trans. Ladislav Matejka and I. R. Titunik. Cambridge, Mass.: Harvard University Press, 1986.

Vroon, R., and G. Vroon. 1976. "V. V. Ivanov's Essays on the History of Semiotics in the USSR." *Dispositio* 1:356–360.

Vygotsky, Lev. 1925. *The Psychology of Art.* Cambridge, Mass.: MIT Press, 1974.

——— 1934. *Thought and Language.* Rev. and ed. Alex Kozulin. Cambridge, Mass.: MIT Press, 1986.

Warshow, Robert. 1962. *The Immediate Experience.* New York: Atheneum.

Weinstein, Marc. "De la théorie et de la pratique (La narration comme poursuite de la poétique par d'autres moyens)." In Conio 1990:35–48.

Weisman, E. 1937. "Mify i zhizn'" (Myths and life). In Shumyatsky et al. 1937:42–51.

Wenden, D. J. 1981. "*Battleship Potemkin:* Film and Reality." In K. R. M. Short, ed., *Feature Films as History.* London: Croom Helm, 37–61.

Werner, Gösta. 1990. "James Joyce and Sergei Eisenstein." *James Joyce Quarterly* 27, no. 3 (Spring):491–503.

Wetter, Gustav. 1958. *Dialectical Materialism: A Historical and Systematic Survey of Philosophy in the Soviet Union.* Trans. Peter Heath. New York: Praeger.

Willett, John. 1978. *The New Sobriety: Art and Politics in the Weimar Period, 1917–1933.* London: Thames and Hudson.

Williams, Robert C. 1977. *Artists in Revolution: Portraits of the Russian Avant-Garde, 1905– 1925.* Bloomington: Indiana University Press.

Wipper, R. 1947. *Ivan Grozny.* Trans. J. Fineberg. Moscow: Foreign Language Publishing House.

Wollen, Peter. 1968. "Eisenstein: Cinema and the Avant-Garde." *Art International* 12, no. 9:23–28.

——— 1972. *Signs and Meaning in the Cinema.* 2d ed. Bloomington: Indiana University Press.

——— 1975. "The Two Avant-Gardes." In *Readings and Writings: Semiotic Counter-Strategies.* London: Verso, 1982, 92–104.

Worrall, Nick. 1980. "Meyerhold and Eisenstein." In David Bradby, Louis James, and Bernard Sharratt, eds., *Performance and Politics in Popular Drama.* Cambridge: Cambridge University Press, 173–187.

Yampolsky, Mikhail. 1991. "Kuleshov's Experiments and the New Anthropology of the Actor." In Richard Taylor and Ian Christie, eds., *Inside the Film Factory: New Approaches to Russian and Soviet Cinema.* New York: Routledge, 31–50.

Yanov, Alexander. 1981. *The Origins of Autocracy: Ivan the Terrible in Russian History.* Trans. Stephen Dunn. Berkeley: University of California Press.

Yaresh, Leo. 1956. "The Role of the Individual in History." In C. E. Black, ed., *Rewriting Russian History: Soviet Interpretations of Russia's Past.* New York: Praeger, 78–106.

Youngblood, Denise. 1985. *Soviet Cinema in the Silent Era, 1918–1935.* Ann Arbor: UMI Research.

———— 1992. *Movies for the Masses: Popular Cinema and Soviet Society in the 1920s.* Cambridge: Cambridge University Press.

Yurenev, Rostislav, ed. 1973. *Eizenshtein v vospominaniiax sovremennikov* (Eisenstein in the reminiscences of his contemporaries). Moscow: Iskusstvo.

Yurenev, Rostislav. 1974. "Art and Ideology: The Soviet Historical Film." *Cultures* 2, no. 1:55–77.

———— 1985. *Sergei Eizenshtein: Zamysly, Filmy, Methoda* (Sergei Eisenstein: Ideas, films, methods). 2 vols. Moscow: Iskusstvo.

Yutkevich, Sergei. 1960. "Sergei Eisenstein in den Jahren 1921–1923." In Rodenberg 1960:107–128.

Zhdanov, A. A. 1935. "Soviet Literature." In Gorky et al. 1935:15–24.

Zholkovsky, Alexander. 1969. "Eisenstein's Generative Poetics." In *Themes and Texts: Toward a Poetics of Expressiveness.* Ithaca: Cornell University Press, 1984, 35–52.

———— 1992. "The Terrible Armor-Clad General Line: A New Profile of Eisenstein's Poetics." *Wiener Slavistisches Almanach* 31:481–501.

Zholkovsky, Alexander, and Yuri Shcheglov. 1961. "From the Prehistory of Soviet Works on Structural Poetics." *Soviet Studies in Literature* 21, no. 3–4 (Summer–Fall 1985):68–90.

Zimmer, Christian. 1967. "Un souvenir des fusillades futures." *Les temps modernes* no. 250 (March):1723–28.

Photo Credits

Most of the illustrations in this book come from the author's private collection. Other sources supplying photographs are:

The Museum of Modern Art Film Stills Library: 1.1, 1.4, 1.7, 1.8, 1.9, 1.13, 1.16, 1.18, 1.19, 1.21.

The British Film Institute Stills Library: 1.11, 1.12, 1.22.

The Jay Leyda Collection, Department of Photography, Tisch School of the Arts, New York University: 1.17.

6.20, *The Fall of Novgorod* (1891) (oil on canvas, 64 × 99 inches, gift of Joseph E. Davies, Ambassador to Russia), by Klaudii Lebedev, is reproduced with permission of the Elvehjem Museum of Art, University of Wisconsin–Madison.

I am grateful to these institutions for their cooperation in supplying photographic material.

Index